Living with Technology

SECOND EDITION

Living with Technology

SECOND EDITION

Michael Hacker
Robert Barden

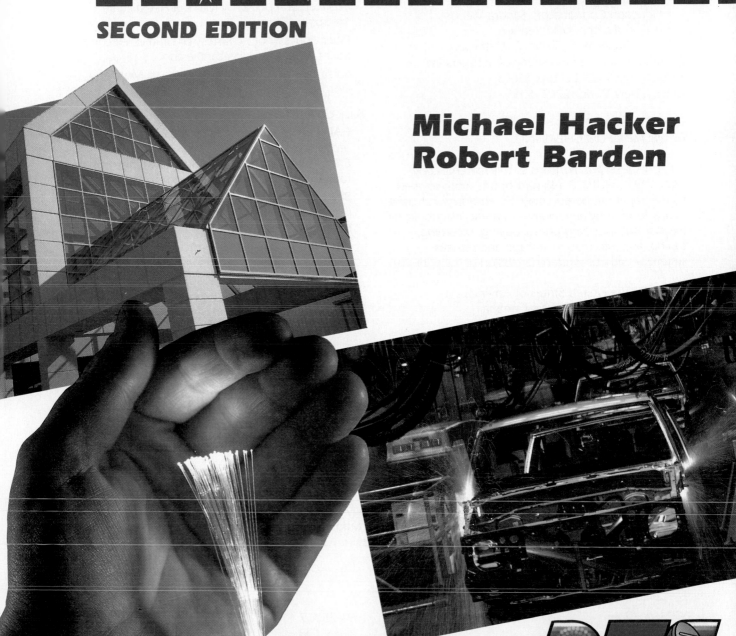

DELMAR PUBLISHERS INC.®

DELMAR TECHNOLOGY SERIES

NOTICE TO THE READER

Delmar Staff
  Associate Editor: Christine E. Worden
  Developmental Editor: Christine E. Worden
  Project Editor: Christopher Chien
  Production Coordinator: Sandra Woods
  Art Coordinator: Mike Nelson
  Design Supervisor: Susan C. Mathews
For information, address Delmar Publishers Inc.
3 Columbia Circle, PO Box 15015
Albany, New York 12212-5015

Printed in the United States of America
Published simultaneously in Canada
by Nelson Canada,
a division of The Thomson Corporation

Cover Photos
  Industrial control photo courtesy of Comstock Inc./ J. Pickerell
  Architectural photo by Michael A. Gallitelli/ Metroland Photo
  Fiber optics photo courtesy of United Telecom/ Sprint; Photo by John Lamberton
  Solar car photo courtesy of General Motors Corporation

Back Cover Photos
  CAD Graphics developed by Engineering Graphics Technology/Oklahoma State University Technical Branch, Okmulgee, OK; Member of Consortium for Manufacturing Competitiveness
  Ball-bearing model based on a drawing by Leonardo da Vinci; Photo: Brian Merrett. Collection of The Montreal Museum of Fine Arts
  Detail from Leonardo da Vinci Madrid MS 1. f.20v, courtesy of Biblioteca Nacional, Madrid

Cover Design by Judi Orozco/The Drawing Board

10 9 8 7 6 5 4   XXX 99 98 97 96 95 94 93

Library of Congress Cataloging-in-Publication Data

Hacker, Michael.
  Living with technology/Michael Hacker, Robert A. Barden. — 2nd ed.
      p.   cm.
  Includes index.
  Summary: A textbook examining the history of technology and its impact in such areas as communication, industry, transportation, and medicine. Also discusses possible technology of the future.
  ISBN 0-8273-4907-6
  1. Technology — Juvenile literature. [1. Technology.] I. Barden, Robert A. II. Title
T47.H253   1992
600 — dc20
                                        91-25707
                                           CIP
                                           AC

CONTENTS

SECTION ONE   INTRODUCTION: WHAT IS TECHNOLOGY?   1

(Courtesy of New York Convention and Visitor's Bureau)

SECTION TWO   COMMUNICATION 87

(Courtesy of Positron
Industries, Inc.)

SECTION 3   PRODUCTION

207

(Courtesy of Cincinnati Milacron)

SECTION FOUR   ENERGY, POWER, AND TRANSPORTATION   371

(Courtesy of Amoco Corporation)

SECTION FIVE   CONCLUSION: LOOKING INTO THE FUTURE   463

(Courtesy of NASA)

PREFACE

Technology has been part of human life for over a million years, but in recent decades technology has caused more remarkable change to occur than ever before in history. Today, we all are *Living With Technology.* We now are completely surrounded by technological systems. We have become dependent upon the products and services modern technology provides. All industries and all people will continue to be greatly affected by new technological developments. Ours is a highly technological society.

No matter where we live, technology affects us in our everyday lives. (Courtesy of Pat Morrow)

TECHNOLOGY AND INDUSTRY

The impact of technology on industry is visible everywhere. Automobile manufacturers are increasingly making use of robots to paint and weld auto bodies. Computer-aided drafting (CAD) has increased the productivity of drafters in architectural and engineering firms. In the printing and publishing business, typesetting has become almost entirely computerized. Within the airline industry, technology continues to spur progress. A comprehensive airline network connects our nation. Most cities are now served by commercial jet services. Jet planes like the supersonic transport (SST) travel from Paris to New York in three and one-half hours.

TECHNOLOGY EDUCATION

Today, success in industry hinges upon effective use of technology. (Courtesy of Chrysler Corporation)

Technology Education is the means through which education about technology is provided as a part of all students' general education. The goals of other technically or occupationally oriented programs are intended to provide students with job-specific skills. A significant distinction must be drawn between programs specifically designed to provide vocational training, and those designed to provide technological literacy as a part of a fundamental, liberal education for all people.

School is the ideal place to begin to foster an understanding of technology, and the role it plays in shaping our culture. Students should learn, at an early age, that technology is a human endeavor. Whether technology is used to benefit people or to destroy our society is entirely a human decision. While learning about technological systems and the resources they use, students can also learn about human responsibility in the control and application of technology.

ORGANIZATION OF THIS BOOK

Living With Technology is designed to help students become technologically literate. The text is divided into five sections comprising sixteen chapters. The first section (Chapters 1-3) introduces the student to the impact of technology on our lives, provides an overview of generic technological resources, and focuses on problem-solving methods as applied to technological systems.

The second section is devoted to a study of communication technology. Chapters 4-7 cover electronics, computers, graphic communication, and electronic communication.

Section Three (Chapters 8-12) is devoted to production technology. Material processing, manufacturing, construction, and managing production are addressed in detail.

In Section Four (Chapters 13-15), students examine how technology is used to provide energy, power, and transportation.

The final section (Chapter 16) presents a look at how the future will be affected by developments in communications, manufacturing, construction, energy, and biotechnology.

SPECIAL FEATURES

Living With Technology includes many special features to assist the reader in becoming technologically literate.

- The use of four-color printing in the 500 photographs and illustrations throughout the book helps to clarify the explanation of technological concepts.
- Each chapter begins with a set of major concepts. These prepare the reader to be aware of key ideas while reading.
- The major concepts are repeated in the margin adjacent to the description in the text.
- A series of carefully chosen activities provides motivational connections between technological concepts and practical applications.
- Mathematics and science concepts are explained throughout the text.
- Key words are highlighted.
- Complete summaries are included at the end of each chapter. These review each of the major concepts.
- Information about careers within each of the major technological clusters is provided, as well as an overview of the future of the workforce in the United States.
- The text includes boxed inserts containing features of special interest.
- A glossary of terms with accurate definitions of words is provided.
- A Technological Time Line is included for historical reference.

■ Opportunities for student youth leadership and participation in special projects and events are discussed in the Technology Student Association section.

ACKNOWLEDGMENTS

We would like to offer grateful thanks to our colleagues in Technology Education, in New York and across the nation, from whom we have learned so much, and who consistently inspire us with their dedication and professionalism. For their assistance in reviewing the manuscript for this edition, grateful acknowledgement is given the following people:

John Anderson
Ingram Tom Moore High School
Hunt, Texas

Tom Barrowman
Queensbury Middle School
Queensbury, New York

Robert Bauer
Springhill Junior High School
Akron, Ohio

M. James Benson
Dunwoody Institute
Minneapolis, Minnesota

Robert Daiber
Triod High School
Marine, Illinois

Denmark Garcia
Washington Middle School
Cairo, Georgia

Anthony T. Gordon
Education Inspector for Design and
   Technology
Staffordshire, United Kingdom

Rodney Gould
Unadilla, New York

Clint Isbell
California State University at Long Beach
Long Beach, California

Courtney Kennicutt
Muscatel Junior High School
Rosemead, California

Robert Laffer
H.B. Thompson Junior High School
Syosset, New York

Donald P. Lauda
California State University at Long Beach
Long Beach, California

David Magnone
Matoaca Middle School
Matoaca, Virginia

David Pullias
Richardson Independent School District
Richardson, Texas

John Ritz
Old Dominion University
Virginia Beach, Virginia

Margaret Rutherford
Howell Intermediate School
Victoria, Texas

Terry Starkel
Paulding Middle School
Arroyo Grande, California

George Trombetta
West Hollow Junior High School
Melville, New York

Peter Tucker
Highland High School
Highland, Illinois

Robert Warren
Hidden Valley Junior High School
Roanoke, Virginia

We wish to express our deep appreciation to the Delmar staff, particularly to our friend, Associate Editor Chris Worden, who was instrumental in rewriting sections of the manuscript, obtaining photo permissions, and most importantly, in providing us with the constant support necessary to sustain the drive to write.

Thanks are also warmly given to Chris Chien, our project editor, who worked untiringly to assure the high quality of the manuscript.

Finally, we would like to thank Larry Stiggins and Margaret Rutherford for their contributions to Chapter 11, and Jennifer Norris for her contribution on Artificial Intelligence in Chapter 16.

ABOUT THE AUTHORS

Michael Hacker is a twenty-year veteran of secondary school teaching. His commitment to Technology Education has shaped his career. As early as 1969, his technology-based junior high school program had received national attention. He has authored a dozen articles in national journals and has presented at numerous state, national and international conferences. He is past president of the New York State Technology Education Association and has served on and chaired various International Technology Education Association (ITEA) committees on behalf of the Technology Education profession. In 1985, he was named an Outstanding Young Technology Educator by the ITEA. In his present capacity as Associate State Supervisor for Technology Education at the New York State Education Department, his responsibilities include the development and implementation of Technology Education curricula and staff development programs.

Robert A. Barden is an electronics engineer specializing in the design and development of high capacity data, voice, and video communication systems. His work includes the integration of fiber-optic, microwave, and satellite technologies. Mr. Barden was the chairman of the New York State Futuring Committee, which recommended the establishment of Technology Education as a mandated discipline in New York. As a curriculum team leader for the New York Technology Education curriculum project, he was instrumental in the conception and development of the state syllabus. On the national level, Mr. Barden has served as a member of the National Advisory Council of the ITEA and has published articles and presented seminars on systems and technology for teachers and teacher trainers. He is a senior member of IEEE and has served on its Committee on Precollege Mathematics, Science and Technology Education.

ACTIVITY ACKNOWLEDGMENTS

Because technology implies application of knowledge, a study of technology without an applications phase does not present a sufficiently clear interpretation of its dimensions. In order to make the study of technology exciting and relevant to students, a laboratory-based, activity-oriented approach should provide the vehicle through which content is presented. *Living With Technology* has been written to provide the conceptual base necessary to support such a hands-on instructional program. The text includes an outstanding series of student activities that reinforce major technological concepts and enhance problem-solving skills. These activities additionally provide an opportunity to apply mathematics and science concepts within a laboratory setting.

The activity contributions of the following individuals have made this fine series of activities possible.

Thomas Barrowman
Queensbury Middle School
Glens Falls, New York

Now and Then; Tug O' War; Computers in Industry; International Language; Beam that Signal; Cuttlebone Casting; Checkerboard; Prefab Playhouse; Laser Construction; Troubleshooting; Scrambler; Satel-loon; Pole Position; Glassmaking; Cycloid Curve; Hovercraft

Jim Cast
Sachem High School North
Lake Ronkomkoma, New York

Revision of Dome Construction

Henry Harms
Lake Grove, New York

The Great Spinoff

Alan Horowitz
Felix V. Festa Junior High School
West Nyack, New York

It's About Time!; Low-Power Radio Transmitter; Team Picture; Morse Code Communications; The Missing Link; T-Square Assembly Line; Dome Construction; Bridge Construction; One, if by Land; Hot Dog!; A Penny for Your Thoughts!; My Hero!; Repulsion Coil; You're on the Right Track; Dust or Bust!; Hurricane Alley; The Medusa Syndrome; Space Community

Robert Laffer
H.B. Thompson
   Junior High School
Syosset, New York

Learning About Cameras and Film Development

Ethan Lipton
California State University at Los
   Angeles
Los Angeles, California

Communicating a Message

Grant Luton
Schrop Middle School
Akron, Ohio

Robotic Retriever

Doug Polette
Montana State University
Bozeman, Montana

Production Company

Fred Posthuma
Westfield High School
Westfield, Wisconsin

Photograms; Muscle Power

A.R. Putnam
Indiana State University
Terre Haute, Indiana

Model Rocket-Powered Spacecraft; An Entrepreneurial Company; Installing Electrical Systems

Margaret Rutherford
Howell Intermediate School
Victoria, Texas

Space Station; Air Flight

Neal Swernofsky
Farmingdale, New York

Plop, Plop, Fizz, Fizz

Kenneth Welty
Illinois State University
Normal, Illinois

Mapping the Future

SECTION

1

(Courtesy of New York Convention and Visitor's Bureau)

INTRODUCTION: WHAT IS TECHNOLOGY?

CHAPTER 1

TECHNOLOGY IN A CHANGING WORLD

MAJOR CONCEPTS

- Technology affects our routines.
- Science is the study of why natural things happen the way they do.
- Technology is the use of knowledge to turn resources into goods and services that society needs.
- Science and technology affect all people.
- People create technological devices and systems to satisfy basic needs and wants.
- Technology is responsible for a great deal of the progress of the human race.
- Technology can create both positive and negative social outcomes.
- Combining simple technologies can create newer and more powerful technologies.
- Technology has existed since the beginning of the human race, but it is growing at a faster rate today than ever before.

INTRODUCTION

For most of us, life is made up of **routines**. At a certain time every morning, we wake up, wash up, and eat breakfast. Then we go to school or work. In the afternoon or evening, we come back home for dinner, work or relax or both, and go to sleep. Bedtime for most of us is the same every night. The cycle of routines is finished in one day and begins again on the following day.

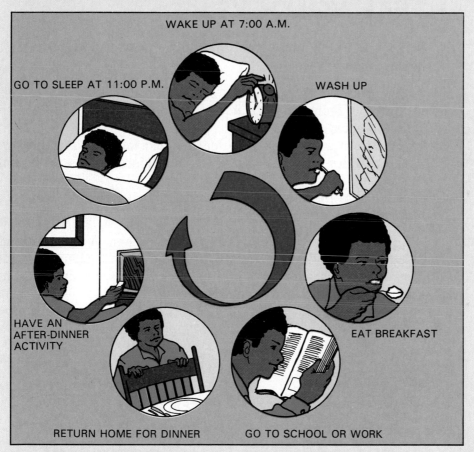

Diagram of a twenty-four-hour cycle: a common daily routine.

Why do we follow the routines that we do? For most of us, almost every part of our routine depends on, or is affected by, our **technology**. For example, when we wake up and when and how we wash up depends on technology. Some cultures have a primitive technology. People awake when the sun rises. They wash up when they can in nearby lakes or streams. In our culture, artificial lighting makes it possible to be up and busy before dawn. We shower in warm water simply by turning on a faucet, anytime we like.

People in some parts of the world base their routines upon the solar cycle. (Photo by Michael Hacker)

This book is about technology and how it affects people's routines and lifestyles. Our routines and the way we live are greatly affected by the devices, products, and services provided by technology.

WHAT IS THE DIFFERENCE BETWEEN SCIENCE AND TECHNOLOGY?

Science is the study of why natural things happen the way they do.

Science and technology are different. However, they are related in the following ways:

- Scientists learn how rocks and minerals in the earth were formed. Technologists use these materials to make useful objects.
- Scientists study space to learn basic facts about the sun, the planets, and the stars. Technologists build and launch space shuttles and satellites.
- Scientists discover how the human body works. Technologists make artificial hearts and limbs.

Technology is the use of knowledge to turn resources into goods and services that society needs.

Scientists and technologists work together. What scientists discover, technologists put to use. Biologists, chemists, and physicists are scientists. Architects, engineers, product designers, and technicians are technologists.

Science and technology affect all people.

Technology is interpreted differently by different people.
(Courtesy of Feedback, Inc.)

Scientists and Technologists

SCIENTISTS

DO RESEARCH

ASK QUESTIONS ABOUT EVENTS THAT OCCUR IN THE NATURAL WORLD

PROPOSE NEW THEORIES

EXPERIMENT UNDER CAREFULLY CONTROLLED CONDITIONS

CONFIRM OR DENY THEORIES

TECHNOLOGISTS

DEVELOP SYSTEMS TO COMMUNICATE INFORMATION AND IDEAS

CONSTRUCT BUILDINGS, BRIDGES, AND TUNNELS

MANUFACTURE PRODUCTS

TRANSPORT PEOPLE AND GOODS

BREED NEW FORMS OF PLANT AND ANIMAL LIFE

Technology Is . . .

- The sum of human knowledge, used to change resources to meet people's needs.
- Making things work better.
- A way of helping our species survive.
- The means by which people control or change their environment.
- "The application of knowledge and the knowledge of application."—Melvin Kranzberg
- "That great growling engine of change."—Alvin Toffler
- A process that uses many kinds of resources to meet people's needs.
- Our way of adjusting to our environment.

WHY STUDY TECHNOLOGY?

People create technological devices and systems to satisfy basic needs and wants.

Technology affects the lives of all of us. The telephone, television, automobile, refrigeration, new medicines, polyester clothing—the products of technology are all around us. Technology fills our needs and makes our lives more comfortable, healthy, and productive.

To use technology wisely, we must understand what it can and cannot do for us. It can give us tools to increase our powers. We can reach higher with ladders. We can swim under water with scuba tanks. We can travel quickly on the ground and in the air and in space. We can cure disease and heal injury. We have been able to shape our environment to fit our needs and wants. With technology, we create a different world than that we receive from nature.

Technology is responsible for a great deal of the progress of the human race.

But technology causes problems, too, such as pollution and crowded highways. Solving one problem with technology very often creates another problem.

WHEN DID TECHNOLOGY BEGIN?

People often think of our times as technological times and other eras as before technology. In fact, people have always used technology, as you can see from the technological time line on pages 494-497.

For at least a million years, people used tools and invented ways to use them on various materials. The kinds of tools that have been important in different times have given us a way to classify historical periods.

The **Stone Age** lasted from about 1,000,000 B.C. to about 3000 B.C. During this period stone was used for many tools. Other materials used for tools were bones and wood. The earliest known dugout canoe was made about 6500 B.C.

Morning Routines

MORNING ROUTINES NOW

(Courtesy of Kohler Co.)

Hot water for a bath or shower comes from a modern plumbing system. The system sends warm water through pipes to various places in the house.

(Courtesy of Kohler Co.)

Electrical appliances and new countertop materials make cooking and clean-up much easier.

MORNING ROUTINES THEN

In the middle and late 1800s, a charcoal-burning heater was placed in a tub of cold water. The heater was removed when the water was warm.

(Courtesy of Science Museum Library, London)

Meals were cooked on wood or coal stoves. Cooking a meal required starting a fire and was a job that took hours.

Technology Satisfies Our Needs

TECHNOLOGY SATISFIES OUR NEED TO PRODUCE FOOD

Agricultural Technology Now

(Courtesy of Sperry Corp.)

Farm machines can harvest enough wheat in nine seconds to make seventy loaves of bread.

Agricultural Technology Then

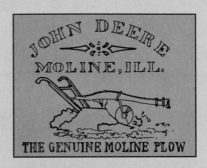

Years ago, farmers had to use human or animal muscle power to plow their fields.

TECHNOLOGY SATISIFIES OUR MEDICAL NEEDS

Medical Technology Now

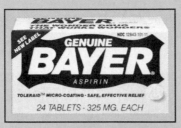

(Courtesy of Glenbrook Laboratories of Sterling Drug Inc.)

Many medicines are available for headache relief.

Medical Technology Then

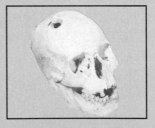

(Courtesy of Science Museum Library, London)

Early people thought headaches were caused by evil spirits in the head. To get rid of the spirits, holes were drilled in the skull with drills made of shark's tooth or flint. This is known as trepanation. Surprisingly, some patients survived more than one of these drillings.

TECHNOLOGY SATISFIES OUR NEED FOR MANUFACTURED ITEMS

Manufacturing Now

Manufacturing Then

(Courtesy of Renault, Inc.)

(Courtesy of Ford Motor Co.)

In a modern automobile plant, cars are produced at the rate of one every minute.

In 1885 in Germany, Karl Benz built the first gasoline-driven automobile. Henry Ford built his first car in 1896 and founded the Ford Motor Company in 1903.

TECHNOLOGY SATISIFIES OUR NEED FOR ENERGY SOURCES

Energy Sources Now

Energy Sources Then

(Courtesy of Bob Klein)

Modern technology produces energy using oil, gas, coal, and nuclear fuels.

In the Middle Ages (about A.D. 1100), water wheels provided most of the power for production. They were used to grind grain into flour.

TECHNOLOGY SATISFIES OUR NEED TO COMMUNICATE IDEAS

Communications Now	Communications Then

(Courtesy of NASA)

Today, satellites bring television signals from other countries into our homes. The signals are sent from ground stations to the satellites, which rebroadcast them throughout the world.

In 1774, in Geneva, Switzerland, George Lesage set up a telegraph using one wire for each letter of the alphabet. The telegraph sent a message along wires to another room.

TECHNOLOGY SATISIFIES OUR TRANSPORTATION NEEDS

Transportation Now	Transportation Then

(Courtesy of NASA)

(Courtesy of Smithsonian Institution—National Air and Space Museum)

Today the space shuttle and rockets make it possible to move objects and people between the earth and space.

In 1903 at Kitty Hawk, North Carolina, Wilbur and Orville Wright's biplane flew 852 feet and stayed up for 59 seconds.

Early agriculture became more efficient with simple plowing devices. (Photo by Edith Raviola)

During the **Bronze Age** (starting about 3000 B.C.), people made tools and weapons from bronze. Bronze is a mixture of copper and tin. Before the Bronze Age, copper was used for decorative purposes. Bronze Age people learned that copper could be heated with charcoal to yield pure copper. By melting other ores with the copper, stronger metals like bronze could be produced.

The **Iron Age** was the period when iron came into common use. It began around 1200 B.C. in the Middle East and about 450 B.C. in Britain. The process of making iron from ore is called **smelting**.

People have been using technology for over a million years.

The early iron-smelting furnace was a clay-lined hole in the ground. Iron ore and charcoal were placed in the hole. Air was pumped in with a bellows. The air made the charcoal burn hot enough to turn the ore into a spongy mass of iron. This spongy mass was hammered into shape while it was red hot.

Prehistoric people used fire for cooking meat and protection from wild animals. They used the bow for hunting. They made needles from splinters of bone to turn animal skins into clothing.

During the Stone Age, there were few villages. Most people lived nomadic lives, wandering from place to place. When they used up food sources, they would move to a new location. People hunted animals and gathered plants, fruit, seeds, and roots for food.

The plow, developed in Egypt, let people grow their own food. People began to settle into towns. They were no longer nomads. They became farmers who grew flax, which provided fibers to make linen cloth. They used oil lamps for light at night. They invented the wheel and vehicles with wheels, and they built roads and stone houses. They had systems for irrigation to increase plant production. They had sewage systems to safeguard health.

One of the most significant of the early inventions was the water wheel. Human muscle power was replaced by water power. Before the water wheel, people ground grain by hand, using two large stones. This was such hard work that people were sometimes made to do it as punishment.

The water wheel started the machine age. It provided power not only for grinding grain to make flour but for other purposes as well. It was used also in pumping water, making cloth, and smelting iron.

The use of machinery instead of hand tools was perhaps the most important technological development of the Middle Ages. In Britain, there were 5,624 water wheels—about one for every fifty families in the country at the time.

THE INDUSTRIAL REVOLUTION

Starting about 1750, many new devices and processes were invented. New ideas spread through the Western world. This marked the beginning of the Industrial Revolution and the factory system of work.

The Industrial Revolution got its name from the great changes that took place in the way products were made. Before this time, craftspeople used their own tools and their workshops to make things. With machines, however, factories could be set up. Products could be made faster and cheaper. Craftspeople could not

This water wheel operates a set of bellows for iron smelting.

This early auto plant shows assembly lines where each worker did a simple task in the manufacture of the final product (1914). (Courtesy of Ford Motor Company)

compete. Many of them went to work in factories. They worked for wealthy people who had the money to buy machinery and set up factories. Workers used their employers' tools and machines instead of their own and received wages for their work.

Henry Ford is often called the "father of mass production" because he was the first American to use the assembly line on a large scale. But the assembly line did not start with Ford. In England, more than a hundred years before Ford's assembly line, Richard Arkwright developed the first manufacturing system. He linked together machines of his own design. They changed raw cotton into thread in a sequence of steps. Each machine carried out one job and prepared the material to be processed by the next machine.

Arkwright was the inventor of the **factory system**. He built many mills, turning what had been hand work into work done by machines operated by people.

Arkwright's factory system produced cloth cheaper and faster. However, it also caused some harm. Men, women, and children worked fourteen hours a day under crowded and un-

Technology can create both positive and negative social outcomes.

This machine helped convert raw cotton into thread.
(Photo by Michael Hacker)

safe conditions. Workers and others pushed for changes in the way workers and their families were treated.

The Industrial Revolution brought about social changes as well as technological change. Trade unions were organized. Laws were passed about working conditions, hours, and wages. Child labor laws were passed, forbidding factory owners to hire children below a certain age. Parents were often gone from the home all day, so schools were built to educate and care for children during the workday.

Before the Industrial Revolution, change had taken place slowly. After it started, things happened quickly. People began to expect change.

Patent laws were developed to protect inventors. People who invented a new device or improved on an old one could patent their ideas so no one could use them without paying for them. The profit motive began to push people to invent and improve, and change became planned.

Combining simple technologies can create newer and more powerful technologies.

The widespread use of the printing press also encouraged technological change. Books and manuals provided people with the ideas of others, ideas they could use, build on, and combine. Transportation systems helped by spreading printed materials all over the world. The sharing of knowledge allowed people to combine ideas. A few simple ideas could be used as building blocks for newer and more powerful technologies.

EXPONENTIAL CHANGE

During prehistoric times, technological change came very slowly. It took many thousands of years to change from stone tools to metal tools. As time passed, people had new ideas, and invented new tools and devices. These ideas could be combined to come up with more new tools and devices. The more ideas there were, the faster new tools and devices were invented.

The rate of change in technology became faster and faster. Today it is faster than it has ever been before. Some people say our knowledge is doubling every four years. We say there is an **exponential rate of change** because changes are happening at a faster and faster rate.

What does "exponential rate of change" mean? Let's look at an example. Maria found a store that was selling cassette tapes at a very good price. Her mother agreed to let her buy ten cassettes a month. Her brother, Steven, wanted some, too. He got his mother to agree to this plan: he would buy two cassettes the first month, and double the number he bought each month thereafter. Who do you think would have more cassettes after six months?

Combining Technologies

Shipbuilding techniques + the steam engine = the steamship

Optics + chemistry = photography

Telegraph + printing technology = the newspaper

Internal combustion engine + wagon and carriage construction technology = the automobile

Synthetic materials + medical technology = the artificial heart

Kite and glider technology + light-weight gasoline engine = the airplane

New materials (titanium) + jet engine technology = spy aircraft

Photographic technology + satellite technology = exploration of the earth

Robert Fulton's steamboat, *Clermont*, sailed from New York City to Albany in the early 1800s.
(Courtesy of The New York Public Library—Astor, Lenox and Tilden Foundations)

Cameras carried by satellites can determine the best locations to prospect for oil or natural gas.
(Courtesy of NASA)

At the end of the first month, Maria owned ten cassettes. Each month, she bought the same number of tapes as she did the month before. After six months she had sixty cassette tapes. Her tape supply increased by the same rate (10 tapes) each month. Therefore, the change in the number of tapes was a **linear rate of change** (like a straight line).

Steven started out by buying two tapes. He doubled his purchases each month thereafter. In the second month, he bought four and in the third, eight. Steven's tape supply increased faster each month, while Maria's increased at the same rate every month. His supply increased exponentially. Their mother

MONTH NUMBER	NUMBER OF TAPES PURCHASED EACH MONTH	TOTAL NUMBER OF TAPES OWNED
1	10	10
2	10	20
3	10	30
4	10	40
5	10	50
6	10	60

Maria's tape purchases:
a linear rate of change.

MONTH NUMBER	NUMBER OF TAPES PURCHASED EACH MONTH	TOTAL NUMBER OF TAPES OWNED
1	2	2
2	4	6
3	8	14
4	16	30
5	32	62
6	64	126

Steven's tape purchases: an
exponential rate of change.

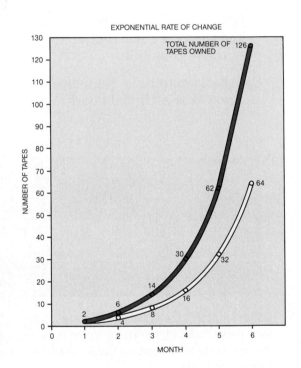

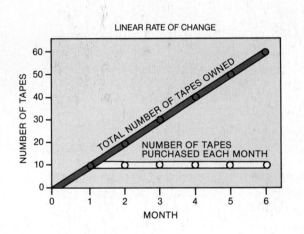

Technology has existed since the beginning of the human race, but it is growing at a faster rate today than ever before.

soon realized she would be spending all her money on tapes for Steven, and put an end to the arrangement.

When something changes at an increasing rate, we say that it changes exponentially. This is true of technological knowledge. It took about a million years to go from using stone tools to using tools from bronze, but only about 5,000 years to go from using bronze tools to using machines. The growth of technological change is still getting faster and faster.

You can get an idea of how fast technology has changed by looking at a time line of technological change. A time line is a type of graph. It lists events that have occurred over a given period of time. Over the last hundred years, technological change has come even faster than before.

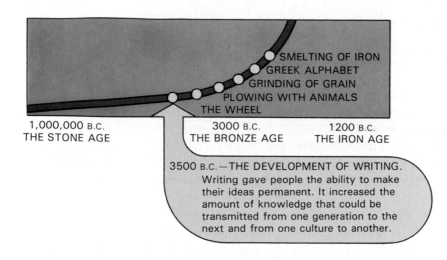

SMELTING OF IRON
GREEK ALPHABET
GRINDING OF GRAIN
PLOWING WITH ANIMALS
THE WHEEL

1,000,000 B.C.
THE STONE AGE

3000 B.C.
THE BRONZE AGE

1200 B.C.
THE IRON AGE

3500 B.C.—THE DEVELOPMENT OF WRITING.
Writing gave people the ability to make
their ideas permanent. It increased the
amount of knowledge that could be
transmitted from one generation to the
next and from one culture to another.

Time line: From Stone Age
to Iron Age. During the prehistoric period (1,000,000
B.C. to 3,500 B.C.), technology changed exponentially,
but at a very slow—almost
linear—rate. After 3,500 B.C.,
the rate of technological
change began to increase.
It is still increasing today.

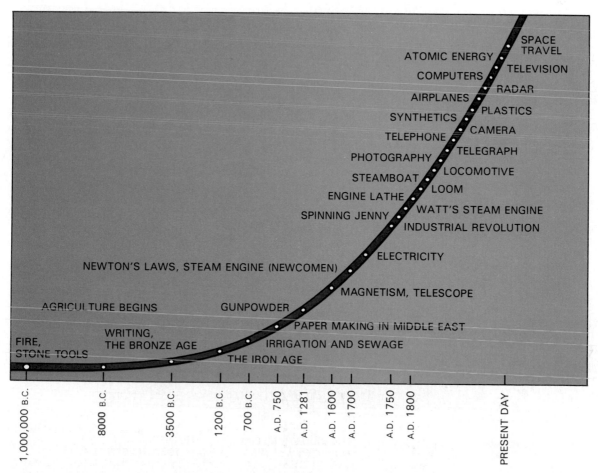

SPACE TRAVEL
ATOMIC ENERGY
TELEVISION
COMPUTERS
RADAR
AIRPLANES
PLASTICS
SYNTHETICS
CAMERA
TELEPHONE
TELEGRAPH
PHOTOGRAPHY
LOCOMOTIVE
STEAMBOAT
LOOM
ENGINE LATHE
WATT'S STEAM ENGINE
SPINNING JENNY
INDUSTRIAL REVOLUTION

ELECTRICITY

NEWTON'S LAWS, STEAM ENGINE (NEWCOMEN)

MAGNETISM, TELESCOPE

AGRICULTURE BEGINS   GUNPOWDER

PAPER MAKING IN MIDDLE EAST

WRITING,
THE BRONZE AGE

IRRIGATION AND SEWAGE

FIRE,
STONE TOOLS

THE IRON AGE

1,000,000 B.C. | 8000 B.C. | 3500 B.C. | 1200 B.C. | 700 B.C. | A.D. 750 | A.D. 1281 | A.D. 1600 | A.D. 1700 | A.D. 1750 | A.D. 1800 | PRESENT DAY

Technological time line: 1,000,000 B.C. to present day

THE THREE TECHNOLOGICAL ERAS

Human history can be divided into three technological periods. The first was the **agricultural era**. Most people lived off the land. Many tools and discoveries had to do with growing and harvesting crops. The **industrial era** began with the Industrial Revolution in the late 1700s. During this era, many new machines were invented. Today, we are in an **information age**. Many of today's inventions are based on electronics and the computer.

During the agricultural era, most people were farmers. They grew their own food. They used their own muscle power or that of animals to do jobs like pumping water and plowing fields.

During the industrial era, many people were employed in factories. Machines replaced human and animal muscle power.

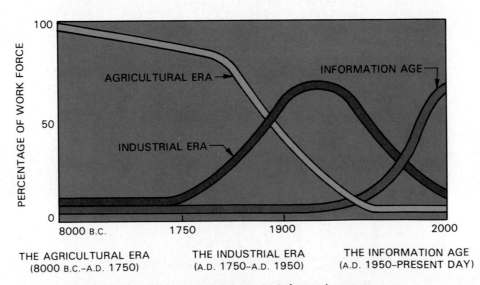

Shift from agricultural era to industrial era to information age

Steam and electricity were used to run motors, which ran machinery.

We have now entered the information age. Many jobs depend on workers being well-educated and staying informed about changes in technology.

TECHNOLOGICAL LITERACY

Because technological change has increased so quickly, technology is an important force in our society. To make sense of our world, we must understand technology and how it affects us. We must become **technologically literate**.

A person who is literate in English can read and write. A person who is literate in technology understands technology. Technologically literate people know that technology is not magic. They understand how processes work, and how products are made. They know that technology is created by people to fill human needs. They are able to make informed decisions about technology.

What kinds of decisions are these? One is choosing from among all the products and services that are available. All of us are consumers. We buy the products of technology.

Another kind of decision has to do with our role as citizens in a democracy. We can affect how technology is used in this country. We can write letters, vote, and speak out about what is happening. We can encourage the use of helpful technologies. We can oppose uses of technology that might harm us or the environment.

A technologically literate person is a good consumer of technology. (Courtesy of Tandy Corp.)

SUMMARY

Technology is as old as the human race. Since prehistoric times, technology has filled people's needs. Technology has filled our needs for food and medical care, our needs for shelter, clothing, and manufactured products, and our need to communicate information.

We can classify historical periods by the kind of technology that was available at different times. During the Stone Age, people used tools made of stone. During the Bronze Age and the Iron Age, tools and other items were made of metal. The Industrial Revolution began with the development of machines.

Before the Industrial Revolution, technological change took place slowly. As time passed, the profit motive encouraged invention of new devices and improvement of old ones. Technological change became very rapid.

Technological change is increasing at an exponential rate. Each new technological development can be the start of new ideas, resulting in more invention, more changes.

Human history can be divided into three technological periods. In the agricultural era, most people were farmers. In the industrial era, most people worked in factories. In the present era, called the information age, most people use computers and communications in their places of work. This book will help you become more technologically literate, so you can live successfully in our technological world.

REVIEW QUESTIONS

1. Explain the difference between science and technology.
2. Describe how technology affected your routine this morning.
3. List five needs that people have and explain how technology helps to satisfy those needs.
4. Explain two ways in which technology satisfies our need to communicate ideas or process information.
5. Give two examples of technologies that have developed from more simple technologies.
6. Draw a technological time line that illustrates how technology is growing at an exponential rate.
7. Describe one major example of how technology has made life easier for people.
8. Define agricultural era, industrial era, and information age.

KEY WORDS

Agricultural	**Exponential**	**Mass production**	**Technologically**
Bronze Age	**Industrial**	**Resources**	**literate**
Change	**Revolution**	**Routines**	
Communications	**Information Age**	**Science**	
Construction	**Iron Age**	**Stone Age**	
Energy	**Manufacturing**	**Technology**	

**SEE YOUR TEACHER FOR
THE CROSSTECH PUZZLE**

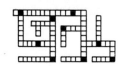

NOW AND THEN

Setting the Stage

An open house is being planned for the tool manufacturing company where you are employed. You have been asked to set up a display showing how your firm designed tools in the past and how it is done now.

Your Challenge

Research the subject of drills and drilling machines. Gather information on how drills were made, and the materials that were used. Examine the types of drilling machines that have been used in the past. Gather information on how drills are made today and on the machines that utilize drills. Organize the data on a **NOW AND THEN** chart. Using the research data, forge an historic spade drill. Test the spade drill using modern hand drills, or power drills.

Procedure

RESEARCH

1. Find out more about drills by finding information on the following:

steel—	carbon, high speed, tungsten
drill parts—	body, flute, shank, point, clearance angle
drill shape—	twist, auger, spade
heat treating—	hardening, tempering, annealing, case-hardening
hand drills—	bow, brace, crank, power
drilling machines—	press, radial, gang, CNC

2. Arrange the data on a **NOW AND THEN** chart. Be sure to use color, pictures, and real materials where possible.

APPLICATION—FORGING A SPADE BIT

CAUTION: Be sure to wear all the proper safety equipment and safety glasses.

1. Form teams of two students. Use a hacksaw and cut a 10" length of ¼" or 5⁄16" round milled steel.
2. The first student forges one end of the 10" steel rod flat. Rotate the stock to make sure the flat forged section is at the center line of the stock. Use a propane torch or gas forge.

Suggested Resources

Milled steel (¼" or 5⁄16")
Nails
Propane torch
Vise grips
Metalworking texts
Books on blacksmithing
Museums
Library

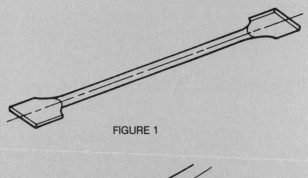

FIGURE 1

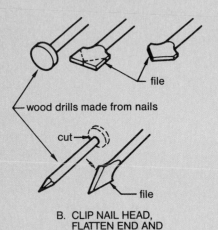

A. FLATTEN NAIL HEAD FOR WIDE DRILL.

file

← wood drills made from nails

cut →

file

B. CLIP NAIL HEAD, FLATTEN END AND FILE.

FIGURE 3

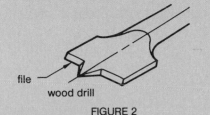

file

wood drill

FIGURE 2

3. Cool the stock and allow your partner to forge the other end of the stock. (see Figure 1)
4. Cut the stock in half. Each student will now have a 5" forged blank.
5. Use a file and shape the point and clearance angle. (see Figure 2)
6. Follow your teacher's directions and harden the steel or case-harden the spade bit. (The drill may not have to be tempered because tool steel is not being used.)
7. Test the spade bit by drilling wood.

Nails can be used to produce many different size drills. Use vise-grips to hold the nails when forging. Keep in mind that dull drills will heat up as they spin and may be very hot after use. (see Figure 3)

Technology Connections

1. Check your **NOW AND THEN** chart to see if there are examples of technological systems that developed from more simple technologies.
2. Was the original drill developed because of a want or a need? Did this want or need change with the modern version?
3. How might the tool or drilling process change in the future?
4. What is the most recent method of making holes in materials?

Science and Math Concepts

▶ Many machines and processes make use of the principles of the six simple machines: lever, wheel and axle, pulley, screw, wedge, and inclined plane.

▶ The revolutions per minute (RPM) of a drill is determined by the drill being used and the material being drilled. Cutting speed is expressed in feet per minute. The cutting speed for wood is approximately 300 fpm.

$$RPM = \frac{4 \times \text{cutting speed}}{\text{drill diameter in inches}}$$

THE GREAT SPINOFF

Setting the Stage

Tops are among the oldest toys known. Children in ancient Greece played with tops, and tops remain popular today all over the world. The most common top receives its motion from a string that is wrapped around it and then pulled. A similar spinning motion is used by the gyroscope to guide and stabilize ships, airplanes, and missiles.

Competitions involving tops date back to the 1700s. Contests involving the decoration, speed, musical sound, and duration of spin were held. In China during the 1800s professional top spinners entertained large audiences with tops that performed tricks such as jumping up steps, and walking up and down an incline.

Your Challenge

Construct a top and enter the Great Spinoff competition to be held for your class. The goal is to produce the top that spins the longest. Each student in the class will construct the same kind of handle. Use the problem-solving process (see page 49) to determine the optimum (best):
1. diameter and thickness for the top.
2. kind and length of string.
3. length of dowel and kind of point for it.

Procedure

NOTE: Throughout this activity wear eye protection and follow the safety procedures taught by your teacher.
1. Follow directions provided by your teacher to make the handle.
2. Use a compass to lay out two tops of different diameters. Use both ½" and ¾" stock. Make sure you leave a mark at the center of the circle.
3. Cut out both tops. Sand the edges, making sure that each top remains round.
4. Drill a ⅜" hole in the center of each top.
5. Cut a piece of ⅜" dowel for each top. Put a point on each dowel using one or more of the techniques demonstrated by your teacher.
6. Drill a ⅛" hole in the dowel for the string.
7. Assemble the dowel and top.
8. Place in the handle, wind up the string, and test.

Suggested Resources

½" and ¾" softwood
⅜" dowel
Compass
⅛", ⅜", and ⁷⁄₁₆" drill bits
String

24

9. Apply the problem-solving process (see pages 49-60) to improve the length of time your top remains spinning. Keep a log to record your progress. Use sketches and brief written descriptions to explain each change you made.
10. Participate in your class's Great Spinoff.

Technology Connections

1. List three changes you made to your top that helped increase the length of time that it remained spinning.
2. Compare your top to the one that remained spinning the longest in your class. What changes could you make to your top that might help it spin longer?
3. Explain why the gyroscope is more than a toy.

Science and Math Concepts

▶ A compass is a tool that can be used to draw a circle of desired size.

▶ The diameter of a circle is two times the radius.

▶ Gyroscopes are accurate navigational aids used to guide ships, submarines, and airplanes.

CHAPTER 2

RESOURCES FOR TECHNOLOGY

MAJOR CONCEPTS

After reading this chapter, you will know that:

- Every technological system makes use of seven types of resources.
- The seven resources used in technological systems are people, information, materials, tools and machines, energy, capital, and time.
- Since there is a limited amount of certain resources on the earth, we must use resources wisely.
- Solving technological problems requires skill in using all seven resources.

TECHNOLOGICAL RESOURCES

Resources are things we need to get a job done. Think about hamburgers. McDonald's restaurants have sold over fifty billion of them. McDonald's uses resources to cook and serve its hamburgers.

What resources are needed? First, we need **people**. To make hamburgers, we need people to raise and butcher cattle, to grind up the meat and cook the hamburgers.

We need **information**. We must know how to feed and take care of cattle, how to keep the meat fresh, how to cook it. We need to know how to season the meat, and how long and at what temperature to cook it.

We need **materials**. The materials we process to make a hamburger are meat, spices, and seasoning.

We need **tools**. Some of these tools are a stove and cooking utensils.

We need **energy**. It will take energy to cook the meat. McDonald's uses electricity, but at home we might use gas or charcoal to do the job.

We also need to buy the meat and the tools, and pay the people. We need money. Money is a form of **capital**.

Finally, **time** is a resource, too. Cooking a hamburger takes time.

You can see that making hamburgers requires the use of seven kinds of resources. They are: people, information, materials, tools and machines, energy, capital, and time. The same seven resources are needed to build a skyscraper or make a jet plane. In fact, **every technological process involves the use of these seven resources**. Whether you are plowing a field, cooking a hamburger, or using a telephone, the seven resources are needed.

Every technological system makes use of seven types of resources.

People eat their hamburgers and create a demand for the product. (Courtesy of McDonald's Corporation)

The seven resources used in technological systems are people, information, materials, tools and machines, energy, capital, and time.

We need information about how to keep cows healthy. (Courtesy of Cetus Corporation)

Tools are an important resource for preparing food. (Courtesy of McDonald's Corporation)

People's needs for exercise have caused the development of clothing that makes running easier. (Courtesy of NASA)

PEOPLE

Let's take a closer look at the seven technological resources. First, people are needed. Technology comes from the needs of people. People create technology and people consume its products and services.

People bring about technology in the first place. People have many needs that are filled by technology, as you learned in Chapter 1. Sometimes, governments start programs that make technology grow. For example, the Soviet Union sent the first satellite, Sputnik, into space in 1957. The United States government decided to match this achievement. In 1958, NASA (National Aeronautics and Space Administration) was created to direct the space program. In 1969, U.S. astronauts landed on the moon.

People use what they know, try to learn more, and develop technologies. NASA scientists had to combine their knowledge with new ideas to come up with a space vehicle and a way to get it to the moon and back safely.

Of course, people provide the labor on which technology depends. Many workers are needed to provide the products and services we use every day.

People are also the consumers of technology. It is people who eat the hamburgers, drive the cars, watch the television sets, and travel the roads and airways.

(Courtesy of NASA)

INFORMATION

Technology requires information. We need to know what to do and how to do it. Technology has grown quickly during the last few decades because of an explosion of information. Information is now doubling every five years. It is shared throughout the world because of new and better ways to communicate.

Only people have knowledge. People create knowledge from information.
(Copyright IBM Corporation, 1983)

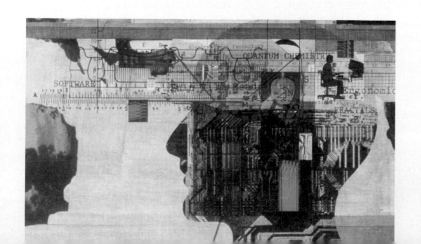

We use information in many different ways. A surgeon must know what tools to use during an operation. A farmer must know what corn will grow best in local soils. A factory worker must know how to operate a machine.

Everyone in our technological world uses information. Information begins as data, raw facts and figures. Data is then collected, recorded, classified, calculated, stored, and retrieved. It becomes information. **Data processing** is the act of turning data into information.

Information can be found in many places—in computer files, books, films, and museums. But information is not valuable until we make use of it. We process information by collecting it, thinking about it, and applying it to meet our needs and wants.

MATERIALS

When people hear the word "resources," they think of materials first. Materials are a very important resource for technology. **Natural resources** are materials that are found in nature.

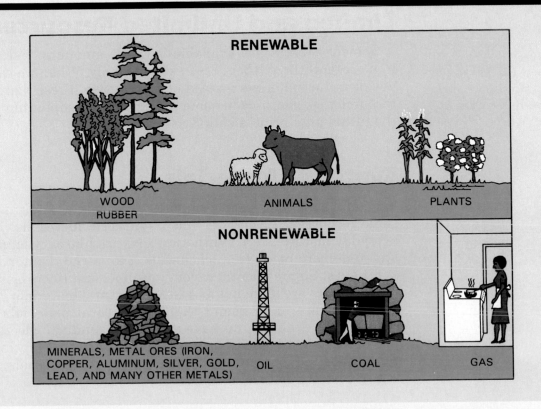

Renewable and Nonrenewable Raw Materials

RENEWABLE

WOOD
RUBBER   ANIMALS   PLANTS

NONRENEWABLE

MINERALS, METAL ORES (IRON,
COPPER, ALUMINUM, SILVER, GOLD,
LEAD, AND MANY OTHER METALS)   OIL   COAL   GAS

These include air, water, land, timber, minerals, plants, and animals. Natural resources that will be used to make finished products are called **raw materials**.

Countries that are rich in natural resources have lots of raw materials. The United States is rich in some natural resources but must import others. We have a great deal of timber, oil, coal, iron, and natural gas. However, we must import most of our chromium, platinum, and industrial diamonds from South Africa. Our nickel comes from Canada and Algeria. Our cobalt is imported from Africa and Europe. Our aluminum comes from Jamaica, South America, and Australia.

Raw Materials

There are two kinds of raw materials: **renewable raw materials** and **nonrenewable raw materials**. Renewable raw materials are those that can be grown and therefore can be replaced. Wood is a renewable raw material. Natural rubber comes from a tropical tree. It, too, is a renewable raw material. Animals and plants are renewable resources.

Nonrenewable raw materials cannot be grown or replaced. Oil, gas, coal, and minerals are nonrenewable. Once we use up our supplies of these resources, there are no more.

Limited and Unlimited Resources

Since there is a limited amount of certain resources on the earth, we must use resources wisely.

Some resources are available in great amounts, like sand, iron ore, and clay. Others are in short supply. When we can, we use plentiful materials instead of scarce ones. Fresh water is a resource that is scarce in some places. Some people think that the future may bring a shortage of water.

Synthetic Materials

People have long used technology to make substitutes for some resources. These are called **synthetic materials**. Many everyday materials are synthetics. Plastics like acrylic, nylon, and Teflon are made from chemicals. Industrial diamonds are synthetics. So are dacron, rayon, gasoline, and fiberglass.

Synthetics are often not as costly as natural materials. Many synthetics are more useful than the natural materials they replace. For example, we have glass that conducts electricity, plastics that last longer than metal, and fabrics that repel water. Synthetics can also be used in place of scarce materials, helping to save our natural resources.

Sails made from synthetics (Mylar™ and Kevlar,™ helped speed the yacht "Freedom" to victory in the America's Cup races. (Courtesy of DuPont Company)

New synthetic fibers provide bright colors and exciting styles for clothing. (Courtesy of DuPont Company)

The largest fabric structure in the world is the Haj Airline Terminal in Saudi Arabia. (Courtesy of OC Birdair)

TOOLS AND MACHINES

People have been using tools for more than a million years. Tools include hand tools and machines. Tools extend human capabilities. Some of them let us do jobs faster and better. Others let us do jobs we couldn't do at all without them.

Although some forms of animal life can use tools, only human beings can use tools to make other tools.

We use tools to fix things around the house. (Photo by Michael Hacker)

We use kitchen tools to prepare food. (Photo by Michael Hacker)

Six Simple Machines

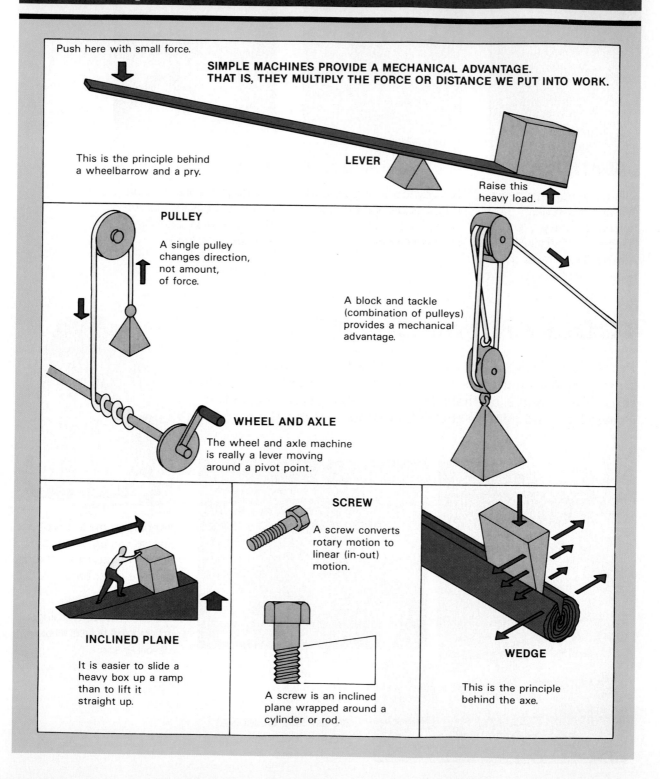

Push here with small force.

SIMPLE MACHINES PROVIDE A MECHANICAL ADVANTAGE. THAT IS, THEY MULTIPLY THE FORCE OR DISTANCE WE PUT INTO WORK.

This is the principle behind a wheelbarrow and a pry.

LEVER

Raise this heavy load.

PULLEY

A single pulley changes direction, not amount, of force.

A block and tackle (combination of pulleys) provides a mechanical advantage.

WHEEL AND AXLE

The wheel and axle machine is really a lever moving around a pivot point.

INCLINED PLANE

It is easier to slide a heavy box up a ramp than to lift it straight up.

SCREW

A screw converts rotary motion to linear (in-out) motion.

A screw is an inclined plane wrapped around a cylinder or rod.

WEDGE

This is the principle behind the axe.

Hand Tools

Hand tools are the simplest tools. Human muscle power makes them work. They extend the power of human muscle.

Machines

Machines change the amount, speed, or direction of a force. Early machines were mechanical devices. They used the six **simple machines**: lever, wheel and axle, pulley, screw, wedge, and inclined plane. Early machines used human, animal, or water power.

Many modern machines have moving mechanical parts. Some, such as televisions and stereos, use electrical energy. Some machines use electricity to move mechanical parts (for example, those that have electric motors). These machines are called **electromechanical** devices.

Automatic machines do not need people to operate them. They must only be started and watched by workers to make sure they are working properly.

(Courtesy of Stanley Tools, Division of the Stanley Works, New Britain, CT 06050)

An electric sewing machine is an example of an electro-mechanical device. (Photo by Michael Hacker)

All this early jukebox machine needs is for the human to put two cents in the slot. Quite a bargain! (Courtesy of Smithsonian Institute)

This welding robot can follow a seam between two pieces of metal. (Courtesy of General Electric Research and Development Center)

Electronic Tools and Machines

Some electronic tools are used for testing electrical circuits. The computer is an electronic tool. Computers are used to process information. They are also used to run factory machinery. Computers are used in many machines, saving greatly on energy and labor.

This computerized system controls the flow of over one-half millon gallons of fuel oil through pipelines in Texas. (Courtesy of Dupont Company)

Optical Tools

Some optical tools extend the power of the human eye. Lenses magnify objects, making them easy to see and study. Microscopes and telescopes are optical tools. Today, optical tools help us learn more about the genes that direct human growth and function.

Another optical tool is the **laser**. Lasers send very strong bursts of light energy. The light energy can be used to measure, cut, and weld materials. It can also be used to send messages over long distances. Lasers are accurate tools. They can be used to cut through pieces of metal, or repair damage in a human eye.

ENERGY

The United States uses a huge amount of energy. Energy is used to make products, to move goods and people, and to heat, cool, and light the places where people work and live. The United States has only about 6 percent of the world's population. But it uses about 35 percent of the energy used in the world. Some energy resources are in great supply. Others are in limited supply and can get used up.

This powerful microscope can magnify the surface of a piece of metal as much as 140,000 times. (Courtesy of General Electric Research and Development Center)

Hot laser pulses cause a metal surface to soften and vaporize. (Courtesy of General Electric Research and Development Center)

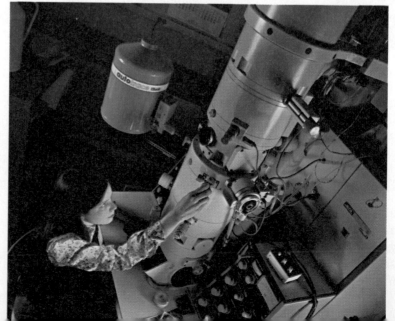

Renewable energy sources are those that can be replaced. Human and animal muscle power and wood are examples of renewable energy sources. Limited energy sources are those that cannot be replaced once we use them up. These sources include coal, oil, natural gas, and nuclear fission (atomic energy). Most of the energy we use comes from limited energy sources. Unlimited energy sources are those that we have more of than we can ever use, at least in a practical way. These sources include solar, wind, gravitational, tidal, geothermal, and nuclear fusion.

Many forms of energy start with the sun. People and animals get their energy from the foods they eat. The source of all food is plants, which use sunlight and carbon dioxide for growth. Coal, oil, and gas come from decayed plant and animal matter. The heating of air masses by the sun causes winds.

There are six different kinds of energy sources. They are: human and animal muscle power, solar energy, gravitational energy, geothermal energy, chemical energy, and nuclear energy.

Human and animal muscle power is still in use today, especially in developing nations. Solar energy provides wind energy, heat, and light energy. Chemical energy comes from sources such as wood, and fossil fuels like coal, oil, and gas. Chemical energy can also be stored in batteries. Gravitational energy comes from tides and falling water. Heat deep inside the earth provides geothermal energy. Nuclear energy comes from the conversion of radioactive matter into energy. We can use these sources of energy directly. We also can convert them into other forms of energy, such as mechanical, electrical, and light energy.

The sun is the original source of much of the energy on earth. We cannot create more energy. We can only change matter into energy or change one form of energy into another form.

Wind energy is actually a form of solar energy. (Courtesy of U.S. Department of Energy)

CAPITAL

Capital is one of the seven technological resources. To build homes or factories, to make toasters or automobiles, to move people or goods, capital is needed. Any form of wealth is capital. Cash, stock, buildings, machinery, and land are all capital.

A company needs capital to operate. To raise capital, a company may sell stock. Each share of stock has a certain value. When people buy the stock, this money goes to operate or expand the business. These investors become part owners (shareholders) in the company. Shareholders hope that the company will do well, and their stock will become more valuable. The company may turn back some of its profit to investors in the form of dividends.

Capital resources are necessary for any technological act. (Courtesy of PPG Industries)

Companies also borrow money from banks. Banks charge **interest**. This means that the amount of money paid back is more than the amount borrowed. A company borrows money with the hope that its profits will help pay the loan and the interest.

TIME

Early man measured time by the rising and setting of the sun and the change of seasons. It was much later that clocks were used to measure time periods less than a day.

When most people lived by farming, time was measured in days. In the industrial era, time became more important. It began to be measured in hours, minutes, and seconds. In today's information age, tasks are done in fractions of seconds. Computers process data in nanoseconds (billionths of a second). Time has become an increasingly important resource in our information age.

SUMMARY

Every technological activity involves the use of seven resources. They are: people, information, materials, tools and machines, energy, capital, and time.

People's needs drive technology. Humans design and create technology using their knowledge and intelligence. People can make policies that promote technological growth, and people use the products and services of technology.

Information is needed to solve problems and to create new knowledge. Information comes from raw data, which is processed by collecting, recording, classifying, calculating, storing, and retrieving it. People turn information into knowledge by giving it meaning.

Materials found in nature are called raw materials. Raw materials can be made into useful products. Renewable raw materials are those that can be grown and therefore replaced. Nonrenewable raw materials are used up and cannot be replaced. Synthetic materials are human-made materials. They can be produced with useful characteristics natural materials do not have.

Tools extend the capabilities of people. Hand tools extend the power of the human muscle. Optical tools extend the power of the eye. Computers extend the power of the brain. Machines are tools that change the amount, speed, or direction of a force. Most modern machines have moving parts. Machines that use electrical energy to move mechanical parts are called electro-

Time Measurement Throughout the Ages

When people lived by farming, they needed to know when to plant seeds. They did not need the precise time of day. A sundial or burning rope clock was adequate. A ring of huge stones at Stonehenge, England, is believed to have been built in ancient times to be used as a calendar. Stars and planets seen through spaces between the stones told the time of year.

During the Middle Ages, monks invented the water clock for telling time. In the industrial age, people used mechanical clocks to tell time.

In today's information age, it is sometimes necessary to measure even small fractions of a second. Tools used for these measurements include the quartz crystal clock, the atomic clock, and the oscilloscope.

Stonehenge (Photo by Susan Warren)

An oscilloscope (Courtesy of Tektronix, Inc.)

SUNDIAL

WATER CLOCK

PENDULUM CLOCK

An atomic clock (Courtesy of Hewlett-Packard Company)

mechanical devices. Automated machines can operate without much human control. Electronic tools, particularly the computer, save huge amounts of time, energy, and labor.

Energy sources are either renewable, limited, or unlimited. Renewable energy sources include human and animal muscle power and wood. Limited energy sources include oil, gas, coal, and nuclear fission. Unlimited energy sources include solar, wind, gravitational, tidal, geothermal, and nuclear fusion.

Capital is any form of wealth. Capital can be cash, shares of stock, buildings, machinery, or land.

Time is an important resource in the information age. Electronic circuits carry huge amounts of data in billionths of a second.

The age we live in is a complex one. If we understand how technological resources are used and develop the ability to use them wisely, we will be better able to function as creators and consumers of technology.

Solving technological problems requires skill in using all seven resources.

REVIEW QUESTIONS

1. What are the seven resources common to all technologies?
2. Define a machine in your own words. Then use your definition to determine whether the following items are machines:
   a. a baseball bat
   b. software for a video game
   c. a radio
   d. a ramp for wheelchairs
   e. a hand-operated drill
   f. a wrench
3. Wood is a renewable resource. Does that mean that we can cut down all the trees we need? Explain your answer.
4. What are two advantages of synthetic materials over natural materials?
5. Name three of the limited and three of the unlimited sources of energy.
6. If you wanted to start a company, how could you arrange to get capital?
7. How do knowledge and information differ?

KEY WORDS

Capital	Geothermal	Machines	Resources
Coal	Hydroelectricity	Material	Solar
Energy	Inclined plane	Nuclear energy	Synthetic
Finite	Information	Oil	Time
Gas	Laser	People	Tools

SEE YOUR TEACHER FOR THE CROSSTECH PUZZLE

PLOP, PLOP, FIZZ, FIZZ

Setting the Stage

Each day of our lives we come in contact with many technological systems. Each of these systems has been designed to satisfy a need or want, or to solve a problem. Large systems are usually composed of smaller systems called subsystems. When combined, the subsystems help the larger system achieve its goal. (You will read more about systems in Chapter 3.)

Have you ever played the game Mouse Trap? The goal of the game is to set up a zany contraption that will capture the mouse. We can look at the entire contraption as a system, with all of its parts as its subsystems. The system is designed to solve the problem of catching the mouse. To start the system a crank is turned. The crank moves a boot that kicks a bucket, sending a ball down a ramp. The ball hits a bathtub, flipping a man who triggers a cage to fall over the mouse. The crank, bucket, ball, man, tub and net are all subsystems of the mouse-trapping system. Each part by itself has little value, but when combined they become a powerful system used to solve the problem.

Suggested Resources

Wood pieces
Cardboard
Foam board
String
Rubber bands
Clothespins
Assorted fasteners
Wire
Dowels
Paper cup
Paper clips
Material processing
  equipment
Hot glue gun
Plenty of Alka-Seltzer

Your Challenge

Using the materials provided, design and build a transport system that will pick and deliver one Alka-Seltzer tablet into a glass of water placed three feet away. Be sure to stay within the following constraints:

1. You may only use the materials provided by your teacher for the construction of your transport system.
2. All parts of the transport system must stay within the delivery area as shown in the diagram.
3. You may provide the power for the system, but you may not touch the Alka-Seltzer at any time.
4. No part of the system can come in contact with the glass of water.

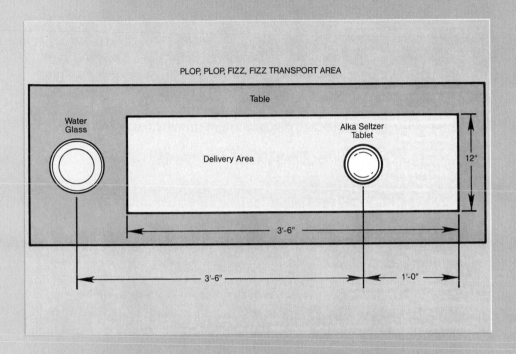

PLOP, PLOP, FIZZ, FIZZ TRANSPORT AREA

Procedure

1. Make sure you understand the problem and the constraints you must work within.
2. Divide the Alka-Seltzer delivery system into as many subsystems as you think are needed to solve the problem.
3. Brainstorm some alternative solutions for each of these subsystems.
4. Select the most appropriate solution and select appropriate materials to implement your solution.
5. Using the safety procedures described by your teacher, construct your solution.
6. Test your solution and make modifications if necessary.

Technology Connections

1. Describe two problems that had to be solved in order to get your Alka-Seltzer delivery system to work.
2. Describe each of the subsystems in your transport system.
3. Describe an alternative solution to the problem that you later considered inappropriate.

Science and Math Concepts

▶ When an object, such as the Alka-Seltzer tablet, is lifted, it is given *potential energy.* When it is dropped into the water glass, the tablet's potential energy is converted to *kinetic energy.*

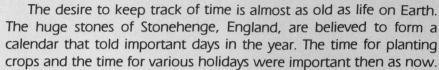

IT'S ABOUT TIME!

Setting the Stage

The desire to keep track of time is almost as old as life on Earth. The huge stones of Stonehenge, England, are believed to form a calendar that told important days in the year. The time for planting crops and the time for various holidays were important then as now.

Throughout history, people have viewed time as a valuable resource. Today we must often measure amounts of time as small as one-billionth of a second. As computers process more and more data at higher speeds, time as a resource becomes more and more important.

Your Challenge

Design and build a clock using a battery-operated quartz movement.

Procedure

NOTE—Do not use any tools or machinery until you have been told how to use them safely. Always wear safety glasses when working in the technology lab.

1. Using proper drawing techniques, design a clock body to be cut out of a piece of wood. Cut a full-scale *template* from heavy paper or cardboard.
2. If computer aided drawing (CAD) is available, transfer your hand-drawn sketch onto the system. Use the printed output as a template.
3. Make a detailed list of ALL the supplies and resources you need to make the clock. Estimate the amount and cost of: supplies, labor (minimum wage), and machinery and tools. Correct this list as the activity continues.
4. Make a detailed step-by-step list of procedures you will follow to make the clock. Again, correct the list as the activity continues.
5. Use the template you made to transfer the shape of your clock onto the wood.
6. Cut the shape out.
7. Drill a 3" diameter hole halfway through the clock body using a multispur drill bit.
8. Use a ⁵⁄₁₆" twist drill to make a hole the rest of the way through the clock body *concentric* to the 3" hole.
9. Use a file, sandpaper, sanders, etc. to shape and smooth the clock body. A router can also be used to shape the edges on the clock body. *A thorough sanding is very important.*

Suggested Resources

Safety glasses and lab aprons
¾" hardwood or softwood at least 6" wide
Multispur drill bit—3" diameter
Twist drill—⁵⁄₁₆"
Router
Jigsaw or band saw
Drill press
Stains and finishing supplies
Clock parts—quartz action, numbers, hands, washers, nuts, sawtooth hanger
'AA' alkaline battery

42

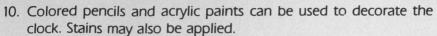

10. Colored pencils and acrylic paints can be used to decorate the clock. Stains may also be applied.
11. Apply at least two coats of polyurethane transparent finish to the clock body. Rub down the finish with #280 grit sandpaper between coats.
12. Adhere the self-stick clock numbers, install the quartz movement, clock hands, and saw-tooth hanger.

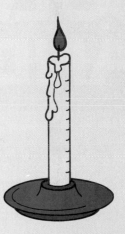

Technology Connections

1. The seven resources used in technological systems are people, information, materials, tools and machines, energy, capital, and time. Describe how you used each of the seven technological resources to design and build your clock.
2. Time is an important resource in the information age. The growing use of computers has made time even more important. Why?

Science and Math Concepts

▶ Some computers can process data in *nanoseconds*. A nanosecond is one-billionth of a second (1/1,000,000,000 or 10^{-9} seconds).
▶ *Concentric* circles have the same center.

CHAPTER 3

PROBLEM SOLVING AND SYSTEMS

MAJOR CONCEPTS

- People must solve problems that involve the environment, society, and the individual.
- A carefully thought out multi-step procedure is the best way to solve problems.
- A good solution often requires making trade-offs.
- Technological decisions must take both human needs and the protection of the environment into consideration.
- People design technological systems to satisfy human needs and wants.
- All systems have inputs, a process, and outputs.
- The basic system model can be used to analyze all kinds of systems.
- Feedback is used to make the actual result of a system come as close as possible to the desired result.
- Systems often have several outputs, some of which may be undesirable.
- Subsystems can be combined to produce more powerful systems.

PROBLEM SOLVING

Humans have always been faced with problems to solve. They have always needed food, clothing, shelter, and health care. These needs are met through technology. People solve their problems using available resources and knowledge.

Headaches, for example, have been a problem for humans for a long time. Do you remember trepanning, discussed in Chapter 1? People used tools to drill holes in a person's skull. This was supposed to let evil spirits escape. People did not know enough about the cause of headaches to solve this problem.

Early humans solved problems of food and shelter by using the materials around them. Caves were used as homes. People gathered roots, fruit, and seeds of plants to eat, and made tools to hunt animals for meat.

Today's problems are also those of human needs and wants, but there are many more problems and they are more complex than ever before. Some of these problems involve society and the environment, such as:

- How can we dispose of wastes without harming the environment?
- How can we produce enough energy to meet our increasing needs?
- How can we assure a continuing supply of clean, safe water?

Other problems have to do with the individual. For example:

- How can we improve the sound quality of recorded music?
- How can we help vision-impaired people to see better?
- How can automobile drivers communicate with each other?

People must solve problems that involve the environment, society, and the individual.

Waste disposal has become a major problem. (Photo courtesy Stephanie Zarpas/NYSDEC)

HI, YOUR LEFT TAILLIGHT IS OUT.

201-301

Will driver-to-driver communication of this sort ever be possible?

Extended-wear contact lenses are now available that can stay in the eye for a period of weeks. (Courtesy of Schering-Plough Corporation)

GOOD DESIGN IN PROBLEM SOLVING

Solving a problem is rarely quick and easy. It takes time and thought. We must understand exactly what is needed to solve the problem. We must make our solution as low-cost and easy to use as possible. We must figure out how long the solution will last. Very often, there are a number of different solutions to a problem. These solutions must be compared so that the best one is chosen. The best ideas are further refined and improved. Good solutions to problems are those that work well, are inexpensive, and cause little or no harm to the environment and people. When a technological solution causes harm, people must decide whether the solution's benefits outweigh the problems.

EXAMPLES OF WELL-DESIGNED TECHNOLOGICAL SOLUTIONS

Engineers, designers, and scientists solve a huge number of different technological problems. These can range from redesigning a stereo to creating new life forms like a plant that repels insects. Here are some well-designed technological solutions:

Telephones (Courtesy of Radio Shack, a division of Tandy Corporation)

The Dame Point Freeway Bridge in Jacksonville, Florida. (Courtesy of Brendrup Corporation)

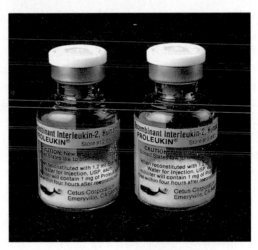

Crush-resistant tomatoes
(Photo courtesy Heinz USA)

Genetically engineered drugs
(Photo courtesy Cetus Corporation)

Personal stereos (Courtesy Sony Corporation of America)

Problems That Still Need Solving

Engineers and scientists are trying to solve problems in many fields. Just one example of these involves **superconductors**.

Materials that conduct electricity, like copper wires, all have electrical resistance. Electrical resistance opposes the flow of electricity. Resistance produces heat, so energy is lost as electricity flows. Resistance is caused by the movement of atoms in a conducting material. The moving atoms oppose the flow of electricity.

Superconductors are materials with no resistance. That means they are perfect conductors of electricity. When an electric current starts flowing in a superconducting wire, no energy is lost.

Using superconductors, very strong electrical currents can be made to flow. Powerful electromagnets can be made using these strong currents.

For many years, it was thought that superconductors could only be made at temperatures around −432° Fahrenheit and below. To cool materials this far required liquid helium and was too costly to be practical.

In 1986 and 1987, researchers around the world developed materials that became superconductors at much higher temperatures. Some worked at temperatures as high as −234° Fahrenheit. To reach these temperatures, liquid nitrogen can be used. It is cheap enough to make such a superconductor practical. However, these new superconducting materials are brittle. They are hard to make into wire. Also, scientists are not sure whether they can carry large electrical currents. What is needed is a material that can superconduct at room temperature. This is a problem that scientists and engineers are hoping to solve someday.

This small piece of superconducting material has been cooled to −284° Fahrenheit. At that temperature, it becomes superconducting and floats in the air above a magnet (the Meissner Effect). (Courtesy Bellcore & NYNEX; photo © Bellcore 1987)

This high-speed magnetic levitation (maglev) train works because electromagnets in the trains and tracks repel each other and provide a nearly frictionless ride. With superconducting magnets, the trains could be made to travel at speeds over 300 miles per hour. (Courtesy Magnetic Transit of America, Inc.)

THE TECHNOLOGICAL METHOD OF PROBLEM SOLVING

Problem solving is faster and easier, and results are better, if people follow a procedure. The procedure given below is only one of many. You may find that when you solve a problem, you go back and forth among the listed steps, and do not follow them in order. But the list covers the activities and thought processes that are always part of the problem-solving process.

There are seven steps in problem solving:

1. Describe the problem as clearly and fully as you can.
2. Describe the results you want.
3. Gather information.
4. Think of alternative solutions.
5. Choose the best solution.
6. Implement the solution you have chosen.
7. Evaluate the solution and make necessary changes.

A carefully thought out multi-step procedure is the best way to solve problems.

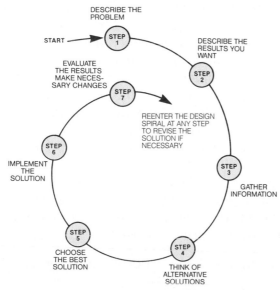

THE PROBLEM-SOLVING SPIRAL

Step 1: Describe the Problem Clearly and Fully

To solve a problem, we must first understand it. What has caused the problem? What situation caused the problem and requires us to think about finding a solution? A statement describing the problem gives you a way of thinking about the problem in a very clear way. Here are some examples of clearly stated problems:

- People with arthritis in their fingers have a hard time gripping small objects. They need an easy way to carry out such tasks as unlocking a door.
- Colored drawing pencils roll off a desk easily and break, and hunting for the right color of pencil in a box is a nuisance.

Once we know what the problem is, we can decide what to do about it. We might decide that the problem is just too big for us. It will have to wait until a group of engineers with enough money and time get interested in solving it. Or we might decide that the problem is uninteresting or unimportant. We might decide we don't want to work on it.

Most of the time, we need to solve problems that are presented to us. Sometimes we want to solve them because they are important to us. Sometimes we have to solve them because parents, teachers, or friends ask us to. Sometimes we want to solve problems because they are challenging and we think it will be fun to come up with a solution.

Let's consider a problem that might be presented in a technology class. Suppose we have to design and construct a rubber-band-powered vehicle. This vehicle must be able to carry a raw egg safely over a distance of 50 feet on a smooth, level surface. We want our vehicle to travel faster than other competing vehicles.

In this case, the problem is to win a school competition by constructing an egg-carrying device. To more clearly define the problem, however, we must consider it very carefully. We must recognize that winning the competition means:

1. We must design and construct a device powered by rubber bands.
2. The device must carry an egg without breaking it.
3. The device must be faster than any other student's device.

Once we really understand the problem, we are in a much better position to solve it.

Let's assume we have now clearly defined the egg transport problem. We understand that the problem is to win the competition by designing the fastest method of transporting a raw egg over the race course without breaking the egg.

Step 2: Describe the Results You Want

Once we decide to try to solve a problem, we have to decide exactly what it is we want to accomplish. We have to set goals. We may have several goals in mind for the egg transport problem. Perhaps we want

- to have fun.
- to improve our technical skills.
- to get a good grade.
- to impress our friends.

Our major goal, of course, is to build a device that will win the competition.

By setting clear goals, we determine what results we want to occur. These goals are our desired results. Setting goals is an important part of our problem-solving system. It helps us understand exactly what we want to accomplish and why.

The result you want is to provide a solution that works better than anyone else's solution.

Our goals should take into account any special requirements imposed by the problem. The list of specifications must include all the requirements of the problem. These requirements are called **design criteria**. If we were building a house, our design criteria would include the kinds of rooms, number of stories, and whether the house will have a basement and an attic.

Some of the design criteria for our egg transport problem might include the following:

1. The vehicle must carry a medium-size raw egg without breaking it.

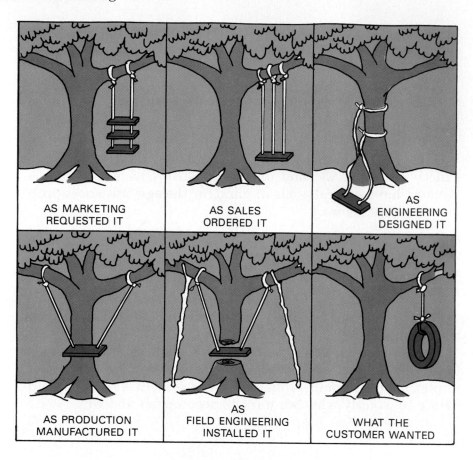

AS MARKETING REQUESTED IT	AS SALES ORDERED IT	AS ENGINEERING DESIGNED IT
AS PRODUCTION MANUFACTURED IT	AS FIELD ENGINEERING INSTALLED IT	WHAT THE CUSTOMER WANTED

This cartoon illustrates the need to state criteria exactly.

2. The vehicle must be painted attractively.
3. The vehicle must have an identification number.
4. The vehicle must travel faster than any other competing vehicle.

Can we try to get the results we want any way we please? Can we decide, for example, to build a device that uses a jet engine? It would certainly be the fastest vehicle, but would the solution be acceptable to the judges?

Problems generally have certain limitations. The specifications should include these limitations. The following are some of the limitations imposed by the egg transport problem.

1. The vehicle must cost no more than two dollars.
2. The vehicle must weigh no more than 1 pound.
3. The vehicle must be able to fit into a $12'' \times 6'' \times 4''$ container.
4. The vehicle must be powered by no more than four #6 rubber bands.

The specifications tell us what conditions the solution must meet. If we understand the problem specifications and have set our goals, we are in a good position to begin the problem-solving process.

Step 3: Gather Information

An important part of solving any problem is collecting information about it. This information gathering is called **research**. By knowing how other people have approached similar problems, you will learn about good and bad solutions. If a product is to be used by people, you may want to collect data from the library on people's heights, weights, length of reach, or other design factors that will make the product easier to use.

Some companies and government agencies constantly perform **basic research** into the nature of different materials and processes. They don't expect to produce any products immediately from what they learn, but they save the results and hope that the new knowledge will be useful at a later time.

Companies often do **market research** to determine if customers will like a new product. Companies may ask potential buyers to fill out a questionnaire to find out what they like or don't like. For example, if a company wants to develop a toothpaste for teenagers, the questionnaire might ask teens what they like or don't like about the toothpaste they're using now. Do they like the taste? Do they like the way it feels in their mouths? What kind of dispenser do they prefer to use, a tube or a pump? What colors do they prefer for the toothpaste, tube, and box? The company will use the results of this research to design the product so it appeals to the greatest number of people.

The library is a good place to go to do research.
(Photo by Paul Meyers)

Step 4: Think of Alternative Solutions

The research done in Step 3 may give you one or more possible solutions to the problem. There is almost always more than one solution to every problem. We can suggest several ideas, each one of which might do the job. These different ideas for solutions are called **alternatives**.

Developing new alternatives is one of the most important parts of the problem-solving process. How do we come up with them?

One way to develop alternative solutions is to use our **past experience**. When we do research as described in Step 3, our information comes from the past experiences of others; by using our own experience and thinking of how we might have solved similar problems in the past, we may find a new way to solve the problem.

Another way of coming up with alternatives is called **brainstorming**. During brainstorming, each person in a group can

Scoring the Alternatives

One way of deciding which alternative is the best solution is to score the alternatives. A sample of scoring is shown below. In this case, a rating of 0 means a poor score, 1 is fair, 2 is good, 3 is very good, and 4 is excellent.

When we compare the actual results of the three alternatives with the desired results (goals), we find that the best solution is to build the vehicle out of styrofoam. Of the three alternatives, the styrofoam vehicle best meets the specifications. It is therefore the best solution.

SPECIFICATION	WOOD	STYROFOAM	METAL
Carries egg safely	3	4	2
Painted attractively	4	3	4
Weighs no more than 1 lb.	4	4	0
No larger than 12″ × 6″ × 4″	4	4	4
Has identification number	4	4	4
Faster than other vehicles	2	4	1
Uses four #6 rubber bands	4	4	4
Total score	25	27	19

suggest ideas. One person writes all the ideas down; no one is allowed to laugh at or criticize any idea, no matter how foolish or unusual it might seem.

The brainstorming process is used to help people think more creatively. People feel free to share any wild ideas they may have. Sometimes one person's wild ideas will open up someone else's mind to a totally new approach. After many ideas have been proposed, the group reviews them all. The best ideas are then developed further.

A third way to develop alternatives is by **trial and error**. This is the way most people do jigsaw puzzles. When putting together a puzzle, we are really solving a problem by trying out different ways of placing the pieces. Eventually, all the pieces are put in the correct places and the problem is solved. When solving real problems by trial and error, the end result may not fit together as perfectly as a completed jigsaw puzzle, but the process used to solve it is similar.

A fourth way to develop alternatives is to use what psychologists call **insight**. Have you ever had an idea just pop into your head? These sudden ideas are usually followed by the "Aha!" response ("Aha! I've got it!"). Insight comes from being thorough in researching the problem, and from being creative in thinking about the problem from many different angles. Even when you are not consciously thinking about the problem, your brain may still be working on it.

Still another way alternative solutions are discovered is by **accident**. Some of the most important discoveries, like penicillin, occur when the inventor goes as far as possible and still doesn't solve the problem. A chance happening then provides the answer. In other cases, the solution to a problem is discovered by someone who is looking for the solution to another problem. It takes a person with insight to recognize when a solution has been discovered by accident.

Step 5: Choose the Best Solution

Once you have developed a list of alternative solutions to the problem, you need to select the best possible solution. Each alternative must be examined to see if it meets the design criteria and constraints that were defined in Step 2. Usually, you can throw away the alternatives that don't meet the criteria or constraints.

The alternatives that are left must then be examined to see which is best. This step may involve more research. For each alternative, you may draw on knowledge from other technological areas, or from other areas such as science, math, and his-

Even Thomas Edison Had His Problems

Thomas Edison invented many electrical devices including a lighting system. He had to develop a light bulb that could burn continuously for hours. He tried hundreds of different materials for the light-bulb filament without success. Finally, he tried carbonized (burned) thread, and it worked. Edison used the trial-and-error problem-solving method. He was successful because he took careful notes and used feedback from each trial to change what he did next.

Thanks to Thomas Edison, you can do your homework at night!

Thomas Edison used feedback from his failures to come up with a successful solution. He used trial-and-error methods to solve the problem of finding the proper filament for this lightbulb.
(Courtesy General Electric Hall of History Foundation)

tory, or from other areas of society, such as economics or social science. This may take more research in a library.

Another way to do further research is by testing the resources each alternative may require. For example, factors such as weight, strength, and density might be important to know when selecting the best solution to building a new kind of boat. If not enough is known about a new kind of structure for the boat, you may have to do some testing. The results of these tests must be recorded and compared with the results from other tests so that a fair and accurate decision can be made about which solution is best.

Sometimes, the testing will suggest that if we change one alternative slightly or combine two or more alternatives, we will wind up with a better solution. The process of changing or combining alternatives to improve them is called **optimization**. By optimizing the alternatives, we can get the best possible solution to the problem.

Often, different alternatives may be better in different ways.

Optimizing an alternative

Many technological limitations had to be overcome for a man to be put on the moon. (Courtesy of NASA)

For example, one material may be stronger but a second material may cost less. In such cases, we must decide which criteria are the most important, and arrive at the best overall solution to the problem. This selection of the best overall solution, even though it may not be perfect in every way, is called making a **trade-off**.

A good solution often requires making trade-offs.

Step 6: Implement the Solution

A model or prototype of the best solution must be built for evaluation.

Once we choose the best solution, we can begin to put it in place. We are ready to try the solution under actual conditions. This step is often called **implementation**. Implementation means actually building or creating the proposed solution.

Most often a **prototype** or **model** of the solution is made. This is particularly important if the proposed solution is very large and costly, or if many of the final products must be made, or if the proposed solution presents risks to people or the environment.

A model can be full sized or it can be a smaller scale version of the proposed solution to the problem. For example, a small scale model of a new airplane would be built to test in a wind tunnel before the first actual plane was built. The first functioning plane to be built full size would then be the prototype. Skilled craftspeople are often employed to make prototypes or models before full-scale construction or production is started.

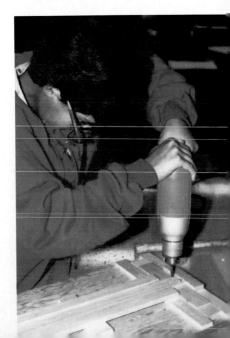

Modeling Design Solutions

When solving problems, we must develop and test alternative solutions. Sometimes, however, it is costly or dangerous or both to carry out such tests. To test alternatives without trying them, **models** are often used.

Suppose that there are several alternatives for the design of a large power plant. It will take years and millions of dollars to build such a plant. It's not possible, then, to build and test each alternative design. Instead, the planners use models. Models are used to test ideas without risking a great amount of time, capital, or public safety. There are five kinds of models.

1. **Charts** and **graphs** describe how an alternative solution might work.
2. **Mathematical models** show how an alternative will work by use of mathematical equations that predict performance.
3. **Sketches, illustrations, and technical drawings** show the ideas in picture form so they can be understood by others. Drawing a design often brings up ideas to improve it. The same thing often happens when you discuss the design with others.
4. **Working models** show how an alternative would work. A working model can be partly functional (only part of the idea is modeled) or fully functional. It can be made of the material that will be used, or of a different, more easily worked material. They can be full size or made to scale (larger or smaller than the alternative).
5. In **computer simulation**, a computer does mathematical modeling. The computer may display a picture of the idea on the screen. Computer simulation is most useful when a large number of calculations must be carried out.

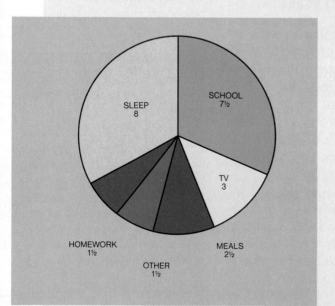

This pie chart describes the number of hours a student spends on various activities.

SLEEP 8
SCHOOL 7½
TV 3
MEALS 2½
OTHER 1½
HOMEWORK 1½

$$V = C \log_e \frac{M_o}{M_t}$$

V	= ROCKET VELOCITY
C	= EXHAUST VELOCITY
M_o	= INITIAL MASS
M_t	= MASS AT TIME "t"

This equation predicts the velocity of a rocket during flight.

Men creating a model of an automobile. (Photo courtesy of General Motors)

An example of a drawing used to convey ideas. (Reprinted from MECHANICAL DRAFTING by Madsen, Shumaker, and Stewart, © 1986 by Delmar Publishers Inc.)

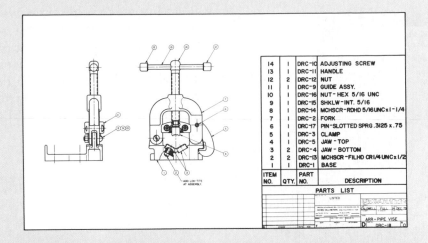

ITEM NO.	QTY.	PART NO.	DESCRIPTION
14	1	DRC-10	ADJUSTING SCREW
13	1	DRC-11	HANDLE
12	2	DRC-12	NUT
11	1	DRC-9	GUIDE ASSY.
10	1	DRC-16	NUT - HEX 5/16 UNC
9	1	DRC-15	SHKLW- INT. 5/16
8	1	DRC-14	MCHSCR-RDHD 5/16 UNC x 1-1/4
7	1	DRC-2	FORK
6	1	DRC-17	PIN-SLOTTED SPRG .3125 x .75
5	1	DRC-3	CLAMP
4	1	DRC-5	JAW - TOP
3	2	DRC-4	JAW - BOTTOM
2	2	DRC-13	MCHSCR-FILHD CRI/4 UNC x 1/2
1	1	DRC-1	BASE

PARTS LIST

ARR - PIPE VISE
D DRC-18

This model tests wind effects on the city of Boston, Massachusetts. Engineers used data from the model to design buildings that would not create harmful wind effects in the city. (Reprinted from TECHNIQUE magazine, Summer 1985, with permission. Copyright Data General Corporation)

A computer simulation used to model the "blind spot" experienced by the driver of a 120-ton truck. (Courtesy Komatsu Presser and Structural Dynamics Research Corporation)

Step 7: Evaluate the Solution and Make Necessary Changes

Once we have tried our solution by building a model or prototype, we must study it and test it to see how well it satisfies the requirements described in Step 2. Observing (monitoring) the results of the tests may suggest how we can improve the design or construction of the solution. The feedback we get allows us to compare our actual results with the desired results.

I SEE YOU'VE GOTTEN SOME FEEDBACK.

Then we can know what changes we must make.

Once we are satisfied with the solution, we can build the full-scale structure, or start mass-producing the product. Evaluation must be a continuing process. We should seek and use feedback over the life of the product or solution to make sure that it continues to meet the needs stated in the original design brief. If necessary, we can make additional changes to the product during its life.

SOLVING REAL-WORLD PROBLEMS

The problems a student might solve in a school technology class require the same methods used in the outside world. Solving such problems helps prepare students to solve harder problems outside the classroom.

Social and Environmental Concerns

Engineers and designers must keep in mind what effect their solutions will have on society and the environment. For example, suppose a new airport is being planned. It cannot be built too near a residential area. The noise would disturb and upset people.

In the real world, the needs of society or the community must be considered. A good technological solution meets the needs of people and preserves the environment.

Politics

Often, solutions to real-world problems are affected by politics. Groups of people have special interests. For example, some people oppose the building of nuclear power plants. They say that radioactive material could poison the environment in case of an accident. They point out that there is no safe way to get rid of radioactive waste.

Other groups favor nuclear power plants. They believe that nuclear power can provide the energy our country needs. They think it will make us self-sufficient so that we don't have to depend on other countries for oil to fuel our power plants. They think the risks of an accident are small. They are willing to trade these risks for the benefits of a reliable source of energy.

Cost versus performance is a trade-off we often experience.

Risk/Benefit Trade-Offs

A common trade-off made in solving large problems is a risk/benefit trade-off. To obtain wanted benefits, we accept some risk. We try to keep the risk as low as possible. We may not implement a solution if risks are too high. When you travel by car, you accept a very low risk of being hurt in an accident. You receive the benefit of traveling quickly and comfortably.

Need for Continued Monitoring

Often, solutions to real-world problems must be monitored over many years to make sure there are no unwanted outcomes. For example, between 1958 and 1961, many pregnant women took a drug called thalidomide to help them relax. After several years doctors began to see that the drug had harmful side effects. Some of the women who took the drug had babies with birth defects. The birth defects were later traced to the drug.

When thalidomide was first given, it seemed to be a fine solution to the problem of helping pregnant women relax. Only after years had passed did people realize that it was not the best solution. All the effects of a technological solution may not be known until long after the solution is implemented. That's why it's necessary to keep on monitoring and studying results.

Values

Our values influence our decisions. The way we feel about something makes us decide in favor of or against it. If we think of automobiles only as transportation, we might decide to buy a basic car that gets good gas mileage. If we feel that automobiles are neat and driving is fun, we might decide to buy a sports car or a luxury car.

Our values affect our choices. (Courtesy Bob Thomas & Associates, Inc.)

Technological decisions must take both human needs and the protection of the environment into consideration.

Most problems that can be solved in a school technology class do not involve politics, the environment, or cultural traditions. Class problems are not as complex as the technological problems of the real world. Real-world problems mean more limitations—limitations that are related to social, environmental, and political factors.

SYSTEMS

People design technological systems to satisfy human needs and wants.

A **system** is a means of getting a desired result. A technological system does this through technology. For example, an automobile is a technological system for traveling from one place to another. A radio lets us listen to music or news. A computer lets us do calculations quickly. A system can be huge, such as the space shuttle. It can also be small, like a pocket calculator.

All systems have inputs, a process, and outputs.

Technological systems are all alike in one way. Each has **inputs**, a **process**, and **outputs**.

THE BASIC SYSTEM MODEL

The basic system model can be used to analyze all kinds of systems.

All systems include inputs, a process, and outputs. Feedback is added to provide a better way of controlling the system. The **basic system model** can be used to describe any technological system. A **system diagram** can be drawn to show how these parts work together in a system.

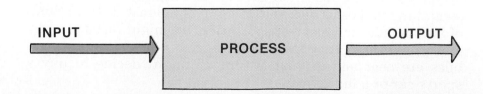

Diagram of a basic technological system.

Inputs

The **input** is the command we give a system. It is also the **desired result**. When we turn on a television set, we are giving it a command. That command is: "Give us picture and sound."

Let's look at another example. A car moves when we tell it to by stepping on the gas. The input command (or desired result) might be: "Go 30 miles an hour."

Other system inputs are the resources needed by the system (see Chapter 8). The seven kinds of resources used by technological systems are people, information, materials, tools and machines, energy, capital, and time.

The Process

The **process** is the action part of a system. It combines the resources and produces results.

In an automobile, the process involves both the car and the driver. The seven technological resources are used in the process. Energy is stored in the gasoline. The machine is the car. People (the driver), information, time, materials, and capital work together to make the car go 30 miles an hour.

Outputs

The **output** is what is produced. It's the **actual result**. We hope that the output matches the command input. That is, we

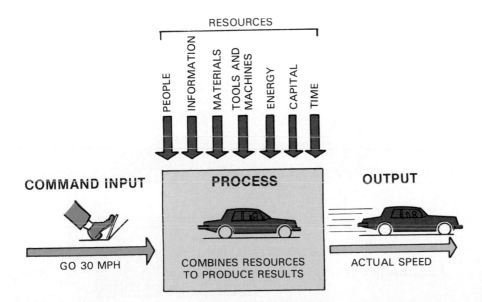

The process combines the seven technological resources to produce the desired result. The output of the system is the speed that the car actually goes.

hope that our car will go 30 miles an hour when we step on the gas. Most systems have more than one output.

Feedback

How does the driver know when the car is going 30 miles an hour? The driver checks the speedometer. The speedometer gives the driver **feedback**. Feedback is information about the output that can be used to change it. When the car's speed reaches 30 miles an hour, the driver lets up on the gas. The driver then pushes only hard enough to keep the car going at 30 miles an hour.

The speedometer is a **monitor**. A monitor gives feedback about output. It lets us compare the actual result to the result we want. We can **control** the system, if needed, to get the output we want. Systems with feedback are sometimes called **control systems** or **feedback control systems**.

An example of a technological control system is a sump pump. A sump pump is used to pump water out from under a house before the basement floods in times of heavy rainfall. It can be turned on and off by a person. When the water level gets high, the pump is turned on. When the level goes down, the pump is turned off. The person provides the feedback that controls the system. In some sump pumps, this is done automatically. A float turns the switch on or off. A person isn't needed for the job.

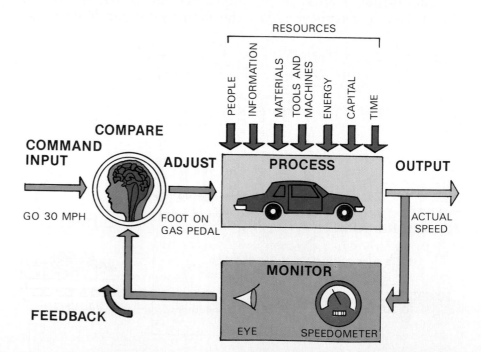

The combination of the speedometer, the driver's eye, and the driver's brain forms the feedback loop.

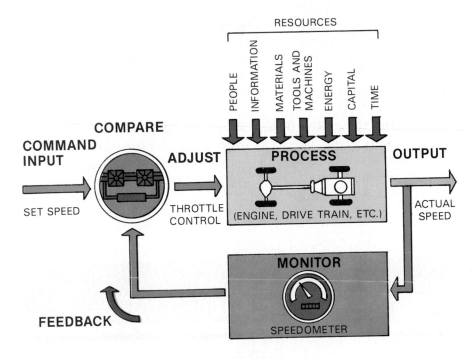

If a car has an automatic speed control system, the driver is removed from the feedback loop. The speed is monitored automatically and compared to the desired speed set by the driver.

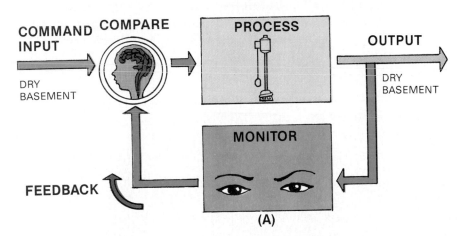

(A)

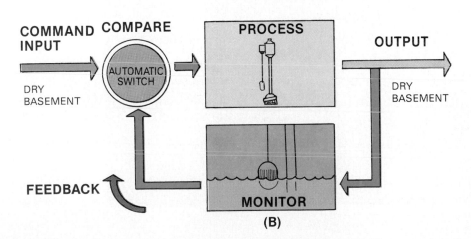

(B)

The system diagram looks the same, whether a person provides feedback and control of the pump (A) or the feedback and control are supplied automatically by a float and switch (B).

A control system is being used to help you learn. Your teacher uses homework and tests as monitors to see how well you are learning. Your teacher grades and returns homework and tests. Both of you use this feedback to find out where you are doing well, and where you need more work or perhaps some help.

Feedback is used to make the actual result of a system come as close as possible to the desired result.

Systems that have feedback are called **closed-loop systems**. Feedback "closes" the loop from input to output. Some systems don't use feedback. They are called **open-loop** systems. A person who wears a blindfold while trying to draw a picture of a dog is an example of an open-loop system. Without feed-

Instant Feedback, Medieval Style

In the Middle Ages, teaching machines were used to train knights. A knight on horseback would charge a wooden figure mounted on a pivot. If he struck the figure in the center, it would fall over. If not, the figure would swing around and hit the knight with a club. It was instant feedback and instant learning.

back, the person cannot compare the output to the input. When the blindfold is removed, the person can draw the picture more accurately. Now we have a closed-loop system.

Even our own bodies contain systems. For example, our bodies maintain a temperature of about 98.6° Fahrenheit. The input command to the body's temperature regulation system is the desired temperature, 98.6° Fahrenheit. Maintaining that temperature involves the action of the muscles, skin, blood, and the body "core." The output is the actual body temperature.

IN HOT WEATHER, EVAPORATING SWEAT COOLS THE BODY DOWN. IN COLD WEATHER, SHIVERING WARM THE BODY UP.

Sweating and shivering are part of the body's feedback control system that maintains a constant temperature.

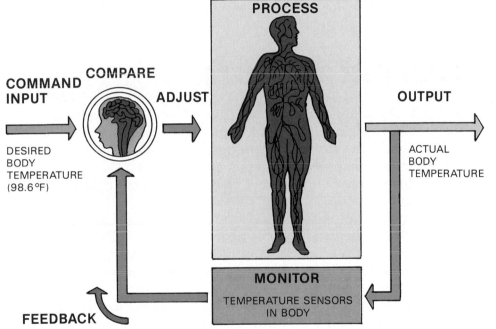

A human system

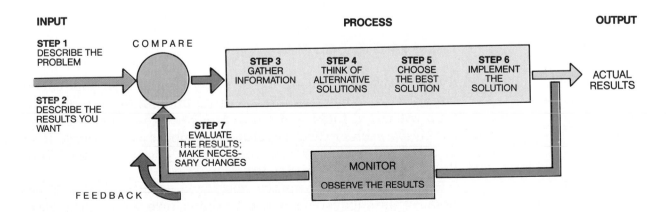

The problem-solving system has the same system diagram as technological systems.

The body has many other control systems. There are systems that regulate sugar level, heartbeat, oxygen collection, and other important activities. These control systems keep our body conditions just about the same, even though outside conditions may be changing.

You can perform a feedback experiment using a pencil. Place the pencil on a table. Close your eyes, turn around once, and try to pick up the pencil without opening your eyes. You probably can't do this easily. You have no visual feedback (you can't see the pencil). You may find that if you feel around you can get the pencil. You will be using tactile (touch) feedback. You use tactile feedback when you use your fingers to pick up or hold something.

MULTIPLE OUTPUTS

Systems often have several outputs, some of which may be undesirable.

A system may produce several outputs. They can be desirable, undesirable, expected, or unexpected. This may be true even if we designed the system to produce only one desired output. A coal-burning power plant is designed to produce electricity. However, it also produces heat, smoke, ash, noise, and other outputs.

Sometimes extra outputs are useful. Heat produced by a power plant can be used to heat nearby buildings. Other outputs such as noise or smoke, may be unwanted. We may have to take steps to reduce or eliminate them, even if we get less electricity when we do so.

When designing systems, a person must consider unexpected outputs as well as expected outputs. Sometimes, designs must be changed. We may lose some of the desired output when we reduce the unwanted outputs.

SUBSYSTEMS

Subsystems can be combined to produce more powerful systems.

Systems are often made up of many smaller systems called **subsystems**. When you are trying to understand a large system, you might find it helpful to break it into subsystems. You can study each of them separately. Suppose you want to look at a transportation system that carries goods by truck from Los Angeles to New York City.

You could break down the large system into smaller ones. Some of the subsystems would be the vehicle system, the management system, and the communication system. Each of these could be broken down further into more subsystems. You would create a subsystem tree.

Four Kinds of Output

Outputs from a system can be of four types. A power plant's outputs could include all four.

1. The expected, desirable output from a power plant is electricity. The added output of heat is also expected. If something useful is done with it, it is also desirable.
2. The expected, undesirable output from the power plant is noise and smoke.

3. An unexpected, desirable output was found at one power plant. The plant discharged some of its heat into a river, warming the water. Tropical fish flourished in the river near the plant, creating an attraction.
4. An unexpected, undesirable output of some plants is acid rain. Acid rain is caused by the pollution power plants produce.

This power plant produces all four kinds of output.

Subsystem tree diagram for a large transportation system. Each subsystem can be broken down into smaller subsystems.

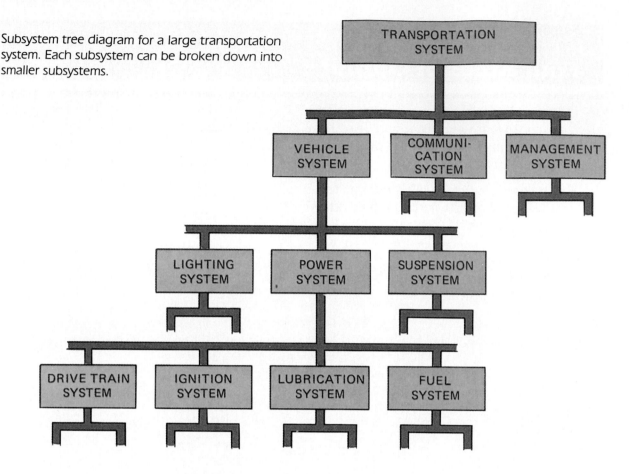

SUMMARY

People have always been problem solvers. Human needs have caused people to use technology to make life easier. There are still problems. They involve society, the environment, and the individual.

Good solutions must be carefully thought out and designed. There is usually more than one good solution. Alternatives must be compared to choose the one that works best, is most economical, and causes least harm to people and the environment.

Problem solving is most effective if a step-by-step procedure is used. One such procedure has seven steps: 1. Describe the problem clearly and fully. 2. Describe the results that are wanted. 3. Gather information. 4. Think of as many alternative solutions as possible. 5. Choose the best solution. 6. Implement the solution you have chosen. 7. Evaluate the results of trying your solution and make changes, if necessary.

Five ways of finding alternative solutions to a problem are using past experience and the experience of others, brainstorming, trial and error, insight, and accidental discoveries.

Modeling is a problem-solving technique. Models are used to test ideas without risking a great deal of time and capital or endangering the public.

Once the best solution has been chosen and implemented, it should be monitored over the life of the product or solution for any possible bad side effects.

The technological problems presented in school are less complex than real-world problems. Real-world problems involve political and environmental issues, as well as those relating to values.

Technological systems are made by people to satisfy human needs or wants. A system is a method of achieving the results that we desire.

All systems have inputs, processes, and outputs. The input is the command we give a system. The input command is also called the desired result. The process is the action part of a system. It combines the resources and produces results. The output is the actual result delivered by the system.

Feedback is used to make the actual result of a system come as close as possible to the desired result. Feedback is made up of a monitor that observes the actual result, a comparator that compares the actual result with the desired result, and a controller that changes the process to make the output closer to the desired result.

Systems with feedback are called closed-loop systems. Systems that do not have feedback are called open-loop systems. Open-loop systems cannot be controlled as well as closed-loop systems.

Large systems are often made up of smaller subsystems. Examining each subsystem by itself can be useful in understanding a large, complex system.

Systems often have multiple outputs. When we design a system, we must think about any possible undesirable outputs. We may have to modify a system design to reduce or eliminate the undesirable outputs.

REVIEW QUESTIONS

1. Give one example each of problems involving society, the environment, and the individual.
2. Propose a workable and economical solution to a problem involving a personal issue.
3. What are the seven problem-solving steps listed in this chapter?
4. What are five ways of coming up with alternative solutions?
5. Your city has run out of land for landfill (refuse disposal). City government has chosen to build a very expensive incinerator to handle the garbage problem. What are some trade-offs that were made in reaching this decision?
6. Give an example of how a person's values might affect his or her decision about the kind of car to buy.
7. List five important parts of a technological system.
8. What does the process part of the system do?
9. Why is feedback important in a system?
10. Give an example of
    a. feedback you've received recently in school.
    b. feedback you've received from a friend.
    c. feedback you can receive when riding a bicycle.
    d. feedback in a technological system.
11. Give an example of feedback in a body system.
12. Name some subsystems that make up a large railroad system.
13. Using the basic system model, model the operation of a nuclear power plant. Indicate the input (desired result), the process, the output (actual result), monitoring, and comparison.
14. The automobile has become a very important system of transportation. Identify an output resulting from the development of the automobile that is:
    a. expected and desirable.
    b. expected and undesirable.
    c. unexpected and desirable.
    d. unexpected and undesirable.

KEY WORDS

Actual results
Alternatives
Basic research
Basic system model
Brainstorming
Closed-loop system
Control

Design brief
Design folder
Desired results
Feedback
Implementation
Input
Insight

Market research
Model
Monitoring
Open-loop system
Optimization
Output
Problem solving

Process
Prototype
Research
Subsystem
System
Trade-off
Trial and error

SEE YOUR TEACHER FOR
THE CROSSTECH PUZZLE

MODEL ROCKET-POWERED SPACECRAFT

Setting the Stage

When an unmanned spacecraft is launched on a mission, feedback control systems are operating on board the spacecraft. These systems cause the spacecraft to go where we want it to, and return to be recovered and flown again.

Several subsystems must work together to make the mission successful. First, a low-speed guidance system must control the craft until it gains speed. Then, a high-speed guidance system must take over. When the craft reaches its destination, a system must turn it around for the return trip. Finally, a recovery system must bring it back to earth safely.

Your Challenge

Build a model rocket-powered spacecraft with on-board feedback control systems. These systems must allow the spacecraft to fly successfully and be recovered to fly again.

Suggested Resources

Paper mailing tape—2" wide and 20" long
One wooden dowel rod—¾" in diameter and 12" long
Two pieces of wooden dowel rod—¾" in diameter and ½" long
One paper soda straw—2" long
One strip of tagboard—1½" × 10"
Three pieces of heavy thread (crochet thread is good)—each 10" long
One sheet of light plastic (bags from drycleaners are a good source)—12" × 12"
Six pieces of masking tape—½" × ½"
Two cork stoppers—#4 and #6 sizes
Soft elastic cord—⅛" wide and 10" long
One model rocket engine (Estes A8-3 or B6-4)

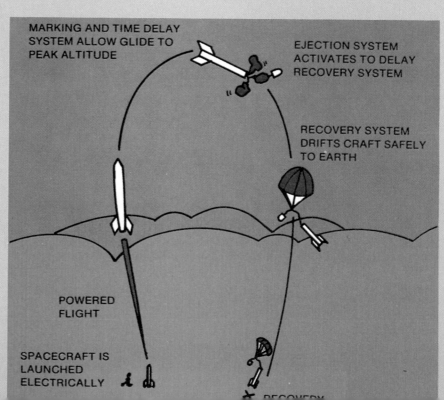

MARKING AND TIME DELAY SYSTEM ALLOW GLIDE TO PEAK ALTITUDE

EJECTION SYSTEM ACTIVATES TO DELAY RECOVERY SYSTEM

RECOVERY SYSTEM DRIFTS CRAFT SAFELY TO EARTH

POWERED FLIGHT

SPACECRAFT IS LAUNCHED ELECTRICALLY

Procedure

1. A few safety rules must be followed:
   a. Engines must only be ignited electrically and by remote control. Each package of engines contains instructions.
   b. Rockets must never be fired indoors or in a congested area. A launch rod must be used, and no one should stand closer than ten feet to the launch area.
   c. Rockets should never be recovered from power lines or dangerous places.
   d. All vehicles should be tested for flight stability before being flown for the first time.
2. To make the body tube, tear or cut a sheet of notebook paper in half so that you have two sheets, each 4¼" × 11".
3. Carefully roll one piece of paper around the 12" dowel rod and glue it together with white glue. You have a paper tube 11" long. Do not glue the tube to the rod, and do not remove the rod.
4. Cut one end of the mailing tape at an angle of 45 degrees.
5. Wet the tape (do not soak it) and carefully spiral the tape around the paper tube on the dowel. The angled edge should be started along the top edge of the paper tube. Be careful not to glue the tape to the rod. As you reach the lower end of the tube, slide the rod up inside the paper tube and trim the tape along the edge of the paper. Remove the finished body tube from the rod to dry.
6. To make the nose cone, glue the two corks together and to one of the ½" dowel pieces as shown. When dry, shape the nose cone with sandpaper.
7. Cut the plastic into an 8" hexagon and attach the shroud lines (crochet thread) at the corners with the masking tape squares. This is the parachute.
8. Drill a ¼" hole in the remaining dowel piece, and glue it firmly inside the body tube, 2½" from the bottom of the tube.
9. Using the fin pattern, cut three fins of tagboard. Glue them near the end of the body tube. When dry, reinforce the joints with more white glue.
10. Glue the straw to the body tube between two fins.
11. Attach the elastic shock cord to the top of the body tube. Staple the free end of the shock cord and the parachute shroud lines to the nose cone.

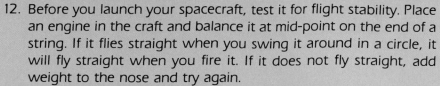

12. Before you launch your spacecraft, test it for flight stability. Place an engine in the craft and balance it at mid-point on the end of a string. If it flies straight when you swing it around in a circle, it will fly straight when you fire it. If it does not fly straight, add weight to the nose and try again.

SAFETY NOTE: Prepare and fly your rocket only as directed by your teacher and using the instructions that came with the engine. Use flame-proof material for wadding.

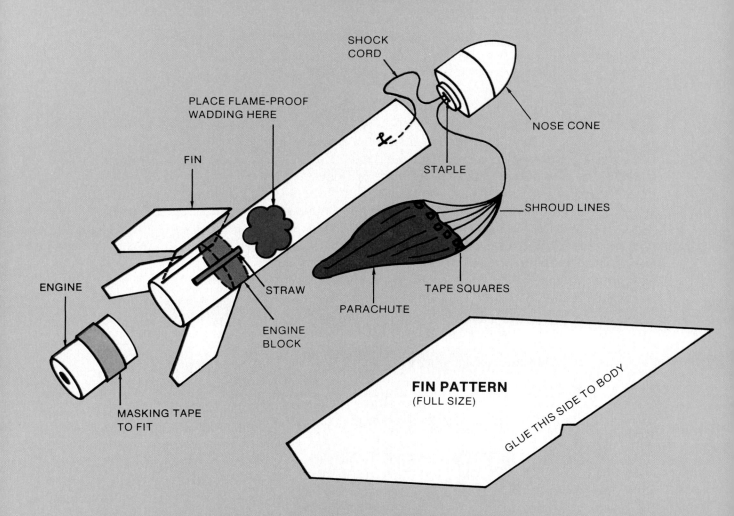

SHOCK CORD

PLACE FLAME-PROOF WADDING HERE

NOSE CONE

FIN

STAPLE

SHROUD LINES

ENGINE

STRAW

TAPE SQUARES

ENGINE BLOCK

PARACHUTE

MASKING TAPE TO FIT

FIN PATTERN
(FULL SIZE)

GLUE THIS SIDE TO BODY

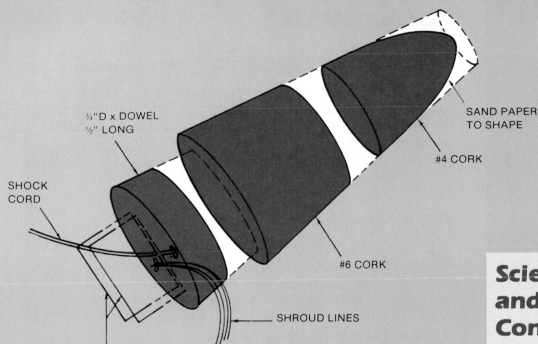

¾"D x DOWEL
½" LONG

SAND PAPER
TO SHAPE

#4 CORK

SHOCK
CORD

#6 CORK

SHROUD LINES

2 STAPLES

Technology Connections

1. Which part of your craft acts as the low-speed guidance system? The high-speed guidance system? The recovery system? How is feedback provided to the recovery system when it is needed?
2. Systems with feedback control are used by most industries today. What kind of feedback does the entertainment industry use? What about the advertising industry?
3. Some outputs of some systems are undesirable. What are some undesirable outputs from the air transportation industry?

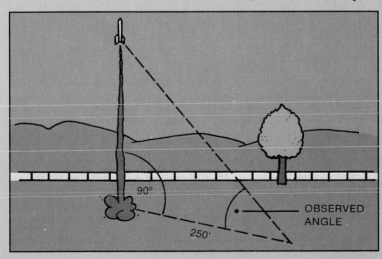

90°

250'

OBSERVED
ANGLE

Science and Math Concepts

▶ Systems are sometimes complex combinations of many other systems.
▶ To find the maximum altitude your spacecraft obtains in flight, a principle of trigonometry can be used which states that all of the angles and sides of any triangle can be found if any three of the parts, including one side, are known. Measure a distance of 250 feet from the launch site and track the flight with a protractor. Observe the angle of the maximum altitude of the flight from that spot. Look in a table of trigonometric functions and find the tangent of the angle. Multiply the tangent of the angle times 250 (the distance from the launch site) to calculate the altitude.

TUG O' WAR

Setting the Stage

The county fair is coming up this weekend. One of the organized activities you have entered is the tractor pull. With only 20 seconds to win, you must pull the opposing tractor over a center line, using a tow line fastened to the rear of the tractors. Because you are the defending champion, you find yourself out in the hot sun, making sure your tractor is ready to compete.

Your Challenge

Using the problem-solving system outlined in Chapter 3, design and construct a vehicle that can pull another student's vehicle across a center line, using an attached line. The vehicles must begin the competition near the center line. Tow lines are attached to the rear of each vehicle. At the end of 20 seconds, the marked center of the string will be checked to determine the winner.

Procedure

1. Make a full-size drawing of the top view of your vehicle.
2. Draw the motor placement and pulley sizes. (Hint: You can reduce the rpm of the final drive pulley by increasing its size. This will also increase the torque or pulling power at the wheels.)
3. Make the chassis for your vehicle.
4. Turn the wood wheels and pulleys on the metal lathe, using the jig supplied by the teacher.
5. Mount the motors on the chassis by bending sheet metal strips over the motor and fastening them to the chassis. Be sure that the strips are long enough to be attached to the chassis.
6. Consider bearing surfaces. Mount the pulleys and wheels. Soft copper tubing can be used for bearings. Welding rod makes excellent axles.
7. Run motor wiring neatly to the rear of your vehicle. Color code your wires so that when the control is hooked up, switches will start the motors in the same direction.
8. Design a towing subsystem that will make your vehicle better than the other vehicles.
9. Hook your vehicle to the challenger's vehicle and test your design skill.

Suggested Resources

2 toy dc motors
2 battery packs
8 'C' cells
Rubber bands (belts)
Sheet metal
Acrylic
Wood
Assorted fasteners
¼" OD soft copper tubing

78

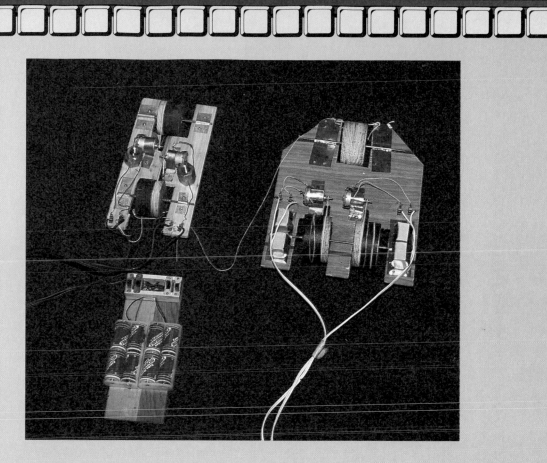

Technology Connections

1. Problem solving begins by identifying the problem. In this activity, what was the problem?
2. What goals did you set? What specifications did you have?
3. What alternative solutions did you come up with?
4. Why did you choose your solution?
5. What feedback did you receive? How would you change your solution for the next time?
6. Lubricants help reduce friction. Are there areas on your vehicle where you could apply lubricating compounds? What type of lubricant would you use?
7. Increasing the weight of the vehicle may give you an advantage. How will this help? What vehicles are designed with heavy chassis?

Science and Math Concepts

▶ The rate of doing work is called **power.** The basic unit of electrical power is the watt. 746 watts = one horsepower.

▶ The speed ratio of one pulley to another is found by dividing the diameter of the small pulley into the diameter of the large pulley. If the drive pulley is the smaller pulley, the result is a speed reduction. If the drive pulley is the larger pulley, there will be a speed multiplication.

SECTION ACTIVITIES

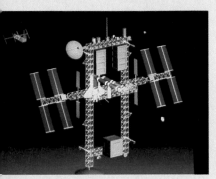

(Courtesy of NASA)

Equipment and Supplies

Model lumber
Toothpicks
Empty plastic pop bottles
Straws
Lego® Systems
Aluminum foil
Aluminum foil trays
Laminated foil or mylar
Glue sticks
White glue
PVC glue
Latex paint
Spray paint
L'eggs® pantyhose containers
Construction paper
Cardboard
PVC pipe
Transfer letters
Cylindrical containers
Sandpaper
Background music tapes
Blank VCR tape
VCR camera
Tape recorder
Glue gun
Coping saw
Scissors
Computer

SPACE STATION

Objectives

When you have finished this activity, you should be able to:
- Identify the modules and main components of the space station.
- Describe the function of modules and components of the space station.
- List justifications (reasons) for the space station.
- Design and construct a model of the space station.
- Discuss international cooperative efforts in the planning and construction of the space station.

Concepts and Information

Rockets, space shuttles, space stations, and the national aerospace plane all are a part of the Space Age. During the Space Age, technologies have increased at a very high rate. Prior to this time in history, technologies existed from the very simple ones of the Stone Age to the more complex during the Industrial Age. Just as in the past, technological systems in this Space Age require resources. These resources are people, information, materials, tools and machines, energy, capital, and time. The space station, a transplant of science and technology in outer space, is one of our most advanced technological systems.

Skylab was the United States' first space station. It was a converted third stage of a moon rocket. Three crews of astronauts visited Skylab during its existence.

The Soviet Union has a space station in orbit that they intend to maintain permanently. The Soviet space station is known as Mir, a Soviet word for peace. It is to become a complex of space-based factories, construction and repair facilities, and laboratories.

On January 25, 1984, President Ronald Reagan announced a ten-year plan to develop a permanent space station. Along with the United States, Japan, Canada, and the European Space Agency would contribute in this international effort to launch a space station in early 1990s.

Maintaining United States leadership in space is the main reason for our commitment to this endeavor. NASA (National Aeronautics and Space Administration) sees the space station as a facility in space with many purposes. The space station will be made up of laboratories for scientific research, observatories to study the earth and the sky, and a garage-like facility to repair and service satellites and spacecrafts.

The space station will have as one of its modules a manufacturing plant that will produce metallic super alloys for construction. This plant will also produce pure glass for laser and optical uses, super-pure pharmaceutical chemicals, and superior crystals for electronic systems. Another important reason for the space station is to further develop space-based communication systems. It also will serve as a construction site to assemble structures too large to be carried by a space shuttle. In the future, it can serve as a base for vehicles that will send and retrieve payloads to and from a higher orbit.

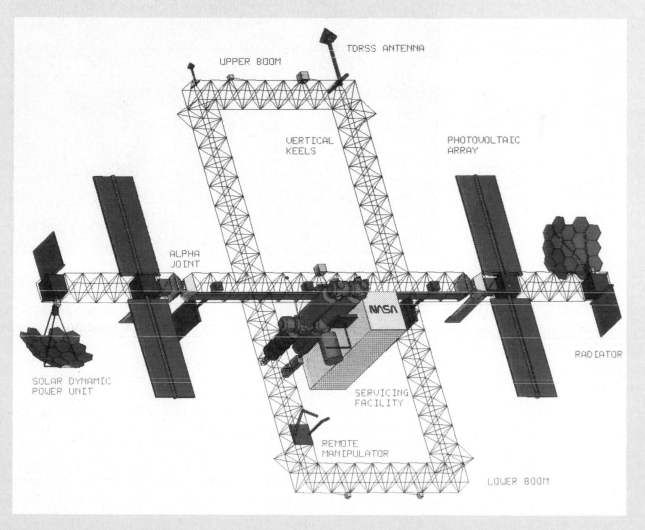

(Courtesy of NASA)

As shown, the space station features a dual keel or latticework beam structure. The two vertical beams are joined at the top and bottom by horizontal beams. Near the middle is a long horizontal beam that supports the arrays of solar cells, which convert sunlight into electricity. It also supports a solar dynamic power unit that is located at the end of the horizontal beam. This system is made up of hexagonal mirrors that collect solar heat. Solar heat drives an electricity-generated turbine. Attached to the upper boom is the TDRSS (Tracking and Data Relay Satellite System) antenna. This is part of a satellite communication system that makes voice exchange and record data flow possible. Radiators for dissipating heat are attached to the horizontal beam that supports the array of solar cells (photovoltaic array).

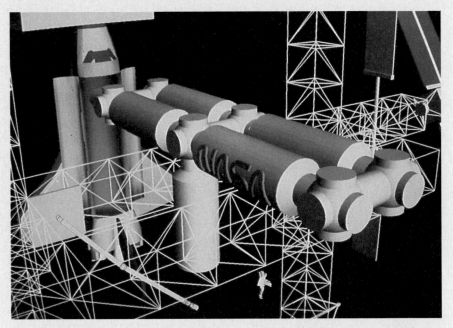

(Courtesy of NASA)

Near the center of the dual keels are the pressurized modules. These modules are linked together with external airlocks and tunnels. The modules, which are identical in external shape, are about 13.6 meters (45 feet) long and 5 meters (15 feet) in diameter. With atmospheric conditions near that of the earth, these cylindrical modules will serve as a habitat (living quarters) and laboratories. Astronauts will be able to work in shirt sleeves. Near the modules is the servicing facility where repair and assembly will occur.

Japan, Canada, and the European Space Agency are cooperating with the United States in the development of the space station. Japan is designing a research and development laboratory. The European Space Agency is also designing a laboratory and a platform. Canada is designing a mobile servicing center equipped with a manipulator arm.

This remote manipulator arm will be used to assemble and maintain the space station.

The space station is a venture into the future where vehicles will roam through space collecting and transmitting information back to earth, lunar, or space stations. As an international effort, it will be the beginning of a mission to Mars. The space station will be a future factory where pharmaceuticals, pure glass, super metallic alloys, and superior crystals are produced. As an outpost in space, it will continue the exploration of the newest frontier.

Activity

Space stations are similar to a service station. You can go there to refuel your vehicle, have it serviced or repaired, or get supplies. Parts of the service station are operated by people. Other parts of the service station are maintained automatically. Like a service station, space stations have communication and energy systems. A service station is usually contained on a pad of concrete and asphalt. Gravity holds all the parts onto the concrete and asphalt. Space stations exist over 300 miles above the earth where gravity is very weak. Modules and components must be attached to some form of framework. All parts of the station in the sky must be shuttled up in a fixed position in space. Using this information, design and build a model of a space station that could be used in a proposal you present for a real space station.

(Photo by Dennis Moller)

Procedure

Space Station Design

After you have read the concepts and information, you will become a member of a team. As a team you are to:

1. Study the concepts, information, and literature provided.
2. Select a name for your space station team. Each member of the team is to submit one design. As a team, choose one of the designs. One member of the team is to sketch the final form of the design the team has selected. Use the computer to generate a drawing of the space station.
3. Decide upon materials, tools, and equipment needed. List the materials needed and get them from your instructor or bring them from home.
4. Whether it be a manufacturing plant on earth or a space station in outer space, when a company wishes to construct the structure or some component, a proposal or bid is submitted. Your team will go through a similar process. As you formulate your ideas, begin a proposal for your team's concept of a space station. Include the following:
   a. Front cover for the proposal (be sure you have chosen a name for your space station team).
   b. List of subcontractors (family members or a member of the community who helps you in any manner).
   c. Drawing of the space station.
   d. List of all materials, tools, and equipment you will need to use.
   e. Procedure you will follow in constructing the space station.
   f. List of all modules and components, and functions of each.
   g. List the desirable and/or unique features of your space station.
5. After receiving proper instruction on safety and approval from your instructor, construct the framework to which all modules and components will be attached. Wear safety goggles.
6. Construct modules and components for the space station.
7. Paint all structures, modules, and components of the space station. (Follow manufacturer's requirements for ventilation.)
8. Attach transfer labels to identify your space station and its parts.

Space Station Proposal

1. Using the materials collected under Item 4, have a member of the team use a word processor and graphic program to write up your proposal.
2. Write up a script you can follow in presenting your concept of the space station on videotape.
3. Design and construct a setting for the videotape presentations. (One setting can be used by all teams.)
4. Rehearse the presentation. Have your instructor or a member of the team videotape the presentation.

(Photo by Dennis Moller)

(Photo by Dennis Moller)

Review Questions

1. What are the functions of the following modules and components of the space station: habitat; laboratories; servicing facility; solar dynamic power unit; vertical keels; photovoltaic arrays; remote manipulator; radiator; and TDRSS antenna.
2. List eight possible uses of the space station that would justify its existence.
3. Which foreign countries are involved with the United States in the construction of the space station? What are the contributions of each?

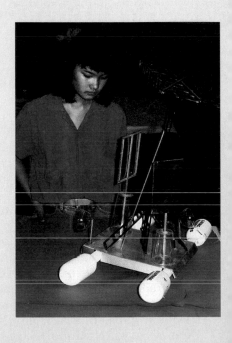

(Photo by Dennis Moller)

EXAMPLES OF WORKERS WITHIN OCCUPATIONAL CLASSIFICATIONS

Production Workers

Laborers
Machine operators
Assemblers
Welders
Machinists

Management, Administrative, and Clerical Workers

Managers
Proprietors
Clerical workers
Computer operators
Retail trade workers
Finance workers

Service Workers

Fast food workers
Hospital workers
Security guards
Personal service workers (hair stylists, tour guides, etc.)

Technical and Professional Workers

Programmers
Engineers
Technicians
Teachers
Lawyers
Health care workers

The graph shows the continuing decrease in workers engaged in production, an increase in management and administrative workers, average growth for service workers, and a steadily increasing growth in technical and professional jobs. (Data from Dr. Dennis Swyt, National Bureau of Standards.)

TOMORROW'S JOBS

In Chapter 1, the shift from an agriculturally based to an industrially based to an information-based society was described.
During the industrial age, many jobs required people to do physical labor, such as working on factory assembly lines operating large, noisy machines. In the information age, many good jobs require people with a great deal of knowledge. The jobs that pay the most are those that require people to use their heads, not their muscles. For example, engineers and computer programmers are paid more than clerks and fast food workers.

WHAT THE FUTURE WORK FORCE WILL LOOK LIKE

Workers can be divided into four categories. These categories are production workers, management and administrative workers, service workers, and professional and technical workers. During the industrial age, more people worked in production than in any other category. Today, there are fewer production workers, but more management and administrative workers, and more professional and technical workers. These workers have jobs that require knowledge and a good education.

WHAT EMPLOYERS LOOK FOR

Besides looking for workers with knowledge and skills, employers want to hire people who have good work attitudes. A good work attitude includes the ability to get along with other people, the desire to do a good job, and the ability to get things done on time. Sometimes, employers feel that a good work attitude is even more important than good technical skills. Employers can often teach their workers how to do technical things, but an employee with a good attitude toward work will always be an asset to a company.

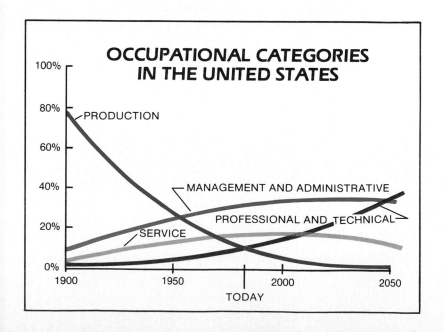

86

SECTION

2

(Courtesy of Positron Industries, Inc.)

COMMUNICATION

CHAPTER 4

THE ELECTRONIC COMPUTER AGE

MAJOR CONCEPTS

- The use of electronics has completely changed our world in the last hundred years.
- Electric current is the flow of electrons through a conductor.
- Electronic circuits are made up of components. Each component has a specific function in the circuit.
- An integrated circuit is a complete electronic circuit made at one time on a piece of semiconductor material.
- Computers are general-purpose tools of technology.
- Computers use 1s and 0s to represent information.
- Computers have inputs, processors, outputs, and memories.
- Computers operate under a set of instructions, called a program. The program can be changed to make the computer do another job.
- Computers can be used as systems or can be small parts of larger systems.

ELECTRONICS

The use of electronics has changed our world during the last hundred years. People have learned to use electricity to work with information. Electrical signals can carry information quickly over wires or through the air by radio. Electronics also lets people communicate with machines, making machines even more useful.

The use of electronics has completely changed our world in the last hundred years.

Electronics in Our World

The electric light has extended our day. (Courtesy of General Signal Corporation, Stamford, CT)

Electric appliances in the kitchen allow us to keep our food longer and prepare it more quickly. (Courtesy of Maytag)

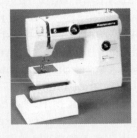

Other electric appliances have reduced the amount of time we spend on work, giving us more free time. (Courtesy of Sears Roebuck & Company)

Electronic entertainment has changed the way we spend our free time. (Courtesy of RCA)

(Courtesy of Eastman Kodak Company)

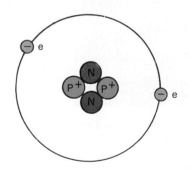

A helium atom has two protons and two neutrons in its nucleus. The atom also has two electrons in a shell (orbit) around the nucleus.

THE SMALLEST PIECES OF OUR WORLD

All materials are made up of tiny particles called **atoms**. Materials made up of atoms of only one kind are called **elements**. Iron and carbon are examples of elements. Only 104 elements are known to exist. An atom is the smallest part of an element that can exist and still have all the properties of that element. Atoms are so small that you cannot see them, even with the most powerful optical microscope.

Atoms of different kinds may be combined to make materials called **compounds**. When a compound is formed from two or more elements, it has properties all its own. It may be nothing like the elements it is made of. For example, sodium, a poisonous metal that reacts violently when it touches water, makes a compound with chlorine, a poisonous gas. The compound is sodium chloride, or common table salt. Because elements can be combined in many ways, millions of compounds can be formed from the 104 elements.

Atoms are made up of even smaller particles. These particles do not have the properties of the element. They have their own properties. Atoms have a center part called a **nucleus**. The nucleus is made up of **protons** and **neutrons**. Smaller particles called **electrons** circle the nucleus very rapidly.

The number of protons in an atom determines the kind of element it is. For example, atoms with 13 protons are aluminum atoms. Atoms with 29 protons are copper. Other elements you know are oxygen and nitrogen, which make up the air we breathe, and metals such as gold, nickel, and lead.

Protons and electrons have electric charges. Protons are positive and electrons are negative. Neutrons have no charge. In most natural atoms, the number of protons equals the number of electrons. The positive charges equal the negative charges. The atom, therefore, has no charge.

Particles with opposite charges are attracted to each other. Particles with the same charges repel each other (push each other away). Negative electrons are attracted to their nucleus because of the protons' positive charge. Their rapid motion around the nucleus keeps them from falling into it.

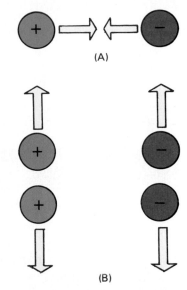

Objects with different charges attract each other (A). Objects with similar charges repel each other (B).

ELECTRIC CURRENT

In some atoms, the electrons are held tightly to the atom. In other atoms, some of the electrons are easily pulled away. They may move from one atom to another. Materials whose atoms give up some electrons easily are called **conductors**. Materials that hold tightly to their electrons are called **insulators**. In a conductor, electrons can move from one atom to another. In an insulator, each atom's electrons are tightly held, and electrons are not free to move between atoms.

Electrons can flow through a thin wire or a piece of solid material, or even through the air, as in a lightning bolt. The flow of electrons is called **current**. The measure of current flow is the **ampere** or **amp**. One amp is equal to about six billion billion electrons flowing past a point in one second.

When you want to move a chair, you have to push on it. You have to exert a force. In the same way, to get a current to flow, a force has to be applied. This force, called an **electromotive** force, is measured in **volts**. Without voltage, no current will flow.

Electric current is the flow of electrons through a conductor.

A battery provides electromotive force. A battery has a positive terminal and a negative terminal. When the terminals are connected to the opposite ends of a wire, electrons start moving. They are attracted to the positive terminal and repelled from the negative one. This sets up a current, or flow of electrons.

Electrical Current Flow

The flow of current through a wire is much like the flow of water through a pipe. In the electric circuit shown in (A), electromotive force comes from the battery. In the water pipe shown in (B), the force comes from a person pushing a piston.

In both cases, a greater force will make a larger current flow. More water will flow through a larger water pipe, as shown in (C). More current will flow through a larger wire, because a larger wire has less resistance.

Ohm's Law is an equation that describes the flow of electrical current.

$$\text{Current (amps)} = \frac{\text{Voltage (volts)}}{\text{Resistance (ohms)}}$$

If voltage gets larger, current gets larger. If resistance gets larger, current gets smaller.

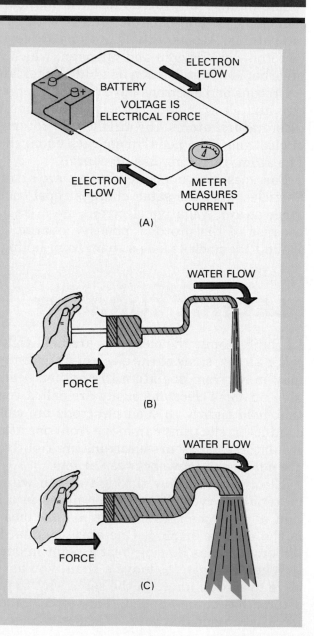

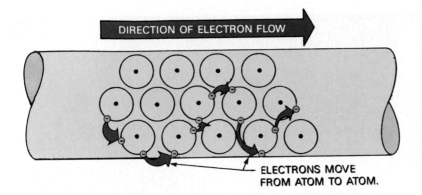

DIRECTION OF ELECTRON FLOW

ELECTRONS MOVE
FROM ATOM TO ATOM.

In a metal wire, electrons are free to move from one atom to the next. Electric current is the flow of electrons through the wire.

Some conductors are better than others. For a given voltage (force), more current flows through a good conductor than a poor one. **Resistance** is the opposition to a flow of current. It is the measure of how good a conductor is. A material with high resistance is a poor conductor. A material with low resistance is a good conductor. The unit of resistance is the **ohm**.

ELECTRONIC COMPONENTS AND CIRCUITS

Electronic **components**, or parts, control the flow of electricity (electrical current). They carry out many useful tasks. Components are connected together in different ways to form **circuits**. A circuit is a group of components connected together to do a specific job. Designers show plans for circuits using drawings called **schematics**. In these drawings, each component has its own **symbol**.

Electronic circuits are made up of components. Each component has a specific function in the circuit.

One of the simplest components is the **resistor**. A resistor has a known resistance value. It is used to control current flow. Resistors come in a wide range of values, from less than one ohm to tens of millions of ohms.

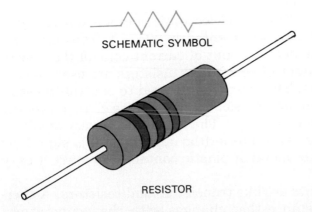

SCHEMATIC SYMBOL

RESISTOR

On many resistors, color-coded bands indicate the resistance in ohms.

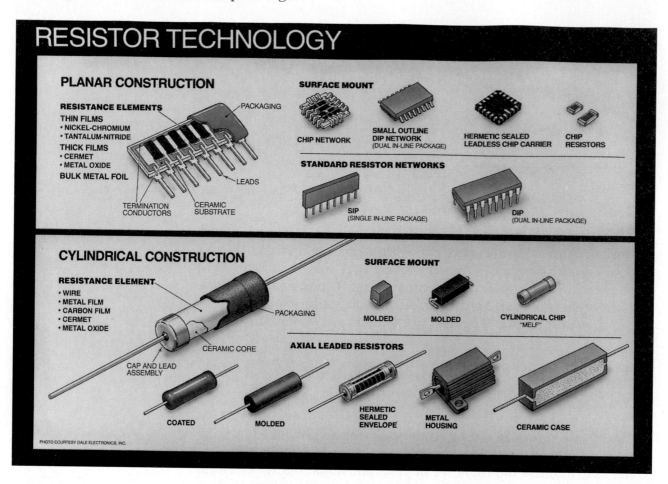

Resistors come in many shapes and sizes. They are used in many different types of circuits. (Courtesy of Dale Electronics, Inc., Columbus, NE)

Semiconductors are materials that are neither good insulators or good conductors. The most common semiconductor material is **silicon**. One kind of component made using semiconductors is the **diode**. A diode lets current flow in one direction but not the other.

One of the most important electronic components today is the **transistor**, which was invented in 1947. A transistor is a resistor that lets a small amount of current control the flow of a much larger amount of current. Transistors are used to control electric motors. They can also be used to control the storage of a small amount of electric charge used to represent information, as in a computer. The transistor is very small. It is a square wafer a few thousandths of an inch on a side. It is packaged in a larger metal or plastic container to make it easy to handle.

Other components are like transistors and resistors. A **thermistor** has a resistance that changes with the temperature.

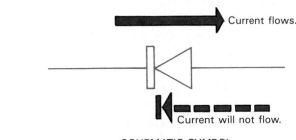

Current flows.

Current will not flow.

SCHEMATIC SYMBOL

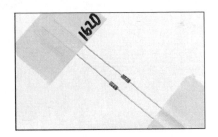

Small diodes are used in digital circuits and in radio detection circuits. Large diodes are used in circuits that supply power or control large currents. (*Courtesy of Radio Shack, a division of Tandy Corporation*)

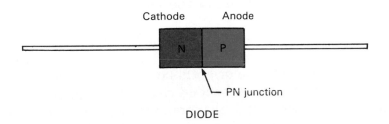

Cathode   Anode

N   P

PN junction

DIODE

A diode is made when a P-type semiconductor and an N-type semiconductor meet at a PN junction. Electron current will flow across the junction in one direction, but not in the other.

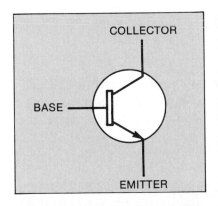

COLLECTOR

BASE

EMITTER

A small amount of base current in a transistor can control a large amount of collector current. Transistors are used for making small signals larger (amplification) and for controlling electrical devices. (*Photo courtesy of Hewlett-Packard Company*)

Thermistors can be used to make electronic thermometers. They can also be used as part of the control system of refrigerators or ovens. A **photoresistor** has a resistance that changes with the amount of light hitting it. Photoresistors can be used to turn on lights when it gets dark. They also can be used to measure light.

Many other components are used in building circuits. Batteries, switches, motors, and generators are a few of these.

Printed Circuits

Circuits are groups of components connected together to do a specific job. Components are often connected by wires.

Soldering is a method of joining two wires together. A metal called solder is melted on them, forming a connection. Solder has low resistance. It makes a good connection.

Care is taken to make sure wires in a circuit do not accidentally touch. This would set up an unintended flow of current (a short circuit). To prevent this, wires often have a covering of insulation. The insulation prevents short circuits.

Early circuits used large components that were connected to each other by several wires. Each wire was soldered by hand. Components became smaller over the years, and hard to solder. Also, a way was needed to make the same circuit over and over again, without mistakes.

The **printed circuit board** solved both problems. A printed circuit board is a thin board made of an insulating material, such as fiberglass. On one or both sides, a thin layer of a good conductor, often copper, is bonded right on the board. Patterns etched in the copper form paths for electricity. Holes for mounting components are drilled in the board. The components are then soldered to the conducting paths on the board. The conducting paths are photographically placed on the board, so many boards can be made with exactly the same circuit. Once the components are mounted on the board, they can all be soldered at once by an automatic soldering machine.

Integrated Circuits

An integrated circuit is a complete electronic circuit made at one time on a piece of semiconductor material.

One of the most important inventions of the twentieth century is the integrated circuit. An **integrated circuit** provides a complete circuit on a tiny bit of semiconductor. Integrated

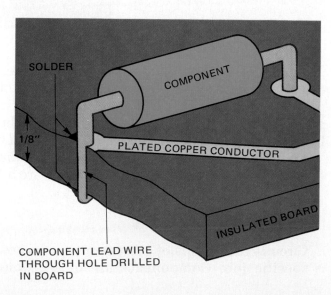

A typical component mounted on a printed circuit board. (From Barden & Hacker, COMMUNICATION TECHNOLOGY, copyright 1990 by Delmar Publishers Inc.)

SOLDER

COMPONENT

1/8"

PLATED COPPER CONDUCTOR

INSULATED BOARD

COMPONENT LEAD WIRE
THROUGH HOLE DRILLED
IN BOARD

This printed circuit board has many components mounted in a tight space.
(Courtesy of Metheus Corporation)

A soldering iron melts the solder, joining the wires to the component terminals. Soldering provides a good mechanical and electrical connection. (Photo courtesy of Cooper Industries, Inc., copyright Tom Watson Photography)

circuits are often less than one-tenth of an inch long by one-tenth of an inch wide. This **chip** contains components and conducting paths.

A chip is designed by an engineer, who makes a drawing of it several hundred times larger than it will be. The drawing is photographically reduced, forming a **mask**. The mask is used to put patterns on a wafer of semiconductor material. Many identical circuits are made at once on a round wafer several inches across.

Computers are built using large integrated circuits. Computers that took up rooms of space twenty years ago now fit on a desk top because of integrated circuits. Chips have replaced large, bulky circuits in many other systems, as well.

Chips use less material, take up less space, and are cheaper to manufacture. Thus, the cost of electronic products came down quickly when chips came into use. If the same thing had happened over the last ten years in the automobile industry, a Rolls-Royce would now cost $500 and get 1,500 miles per gallon.

Analog and Digital Circuits

Information can be represented by electricity in several ways. One way is to have a voltage change based on the information it represents. A voltage could represent a person's speech. It would get larger as the person talked louder. In this case, the voltage is an **analog** of, or similar to, the person's speech. It is called an **analog signal**.

An electronic circuit that works with analog signals is called an **analog circuit**. Voltages in such a circuit change smoothly, as do the things they represent, such as a person's voice.

Sometimes information must be very accurate or must be sent over long distances. Under these conditions, analog cir-

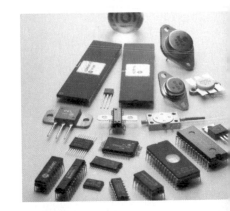

Integrated circuits, like transistors, are packaged in larger plastic or metal containers for protection and ease of handling. Often, the more complex the integrated circuit, the more input and output connections it needs. This requires the package to be larger. (Courtesy of Hitachi America, Ltd., Semiconductor & IC Division)

Size and Complexity of Integrated Circuits

Integrated circuits have become more and more complex since they were invented by Jack Kilby in 1958. Single circuits can perform more and more complex tasks. One measure of a chip's complexity is the number of transistors it uses. People often talk about four types of integrated circuits:

1. SSI—Small Scale Integration: several dozen transistors.
2. MSI—Medium Scale Integration: up to several hundred transistors.
3. LSI—Large Scale Integration: up to several thousand transistors.
4. VLSI—Very Large Scale Integration: one hundred thousand or more transistors.

Each of the squares on the round wafers in the photograph is a complete integrated circuit. Wafers are usually two to four inches in diameter and contain dozens or hundreds of integrated circuits.

(Courtesy of Matsushita/Panasonic)

The power of the computer is largely dependent upon the number of components that can be placed on an integrated circuit chip. In 1961, this integrated circuit had 4 transistors. By the year 2000, it is expected that chips will contain one billion components. (Courtesy of National Semiconductor Corporation)

cuits are not good enough. In these cases, **digital technology** is used.

In digital circuits, information is first coded into a series of 0s and 1s. A voltage above a certain value is coded as a 1. A voltage below that value is coded as a 0. Each 1 or 0 is called a **bit**, short for **binary digit**. Binary refers to the number system that has only two numbers, 0 and 1.

The Pascaline was a mechanical adding machine invented by Blaise Pascal in 1645.
(Courtesy of The Computer Museum, Boston, MA)

COMPUTERS

One field that electronics and integrated circuits have changed drastically is the field of computers. For thousands of years, people have used machines to help with calculations. The Chinese abacus is still used today. Napier's bones, invented in 1617, was used to multiply. The first mechanical adding machine was invented by Blaise Pascal in 1645. It used sets of wheels, moved by a needle, to add numbers and give a sum.

The first all-purpose calculator was developed in the mid-1800s by Charles Babbage. It could be instructed, or programmed, to do sets of calculations. Ada Lovelace, Babbage's co-worker, was the world's first computer programmer. A modern computer programming language, ADA, is named after her.

Herman Hollerith devised a way of automating the U.S. Census in 1890. Information was coded as holes punched into cards. The information could be tabulated by machine. Hollerith's method was a complete system. It had a machine to punch the cards (input). It had a tabulator for sorting the cards (processor). It had a counter to record the results (output). A sorting box rearranged the cards for reprocessing (feedback). In 1911, Hollerith's Tabulating Machine Company became a part of a

(Courtesy of Buick Motor Division)

(Courtesy of First Security Corporation)

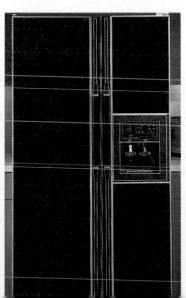

(Courtesy of Whirlpool Corp.)

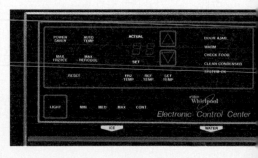

company that later became International Business Machines Corporation (IBM). IBM is the largest computer company in the world today.

Integrated circuits made computers smaller and cheaper. Computers have been used since the late 1940s. But not until computers could be put onto one chip did they come into household use.

Computers and microcomputers are used everywhere. Microcomputers are used in electronic games, including video games. They are used in automatic bank teller machines (ATMs) and cash registers. They are used in home appliances, such as micro-

Computer Viruses

Just as infections can attack the human body, can be contagious and spread, computer viruses can infect a computer program and spread to other software. A computer virus is a software program that attaches itself to other programs with which it comes in contact. When a virus infects a program, it can alter or delete files, or consume all the remaining computer memory.

Typically, viruses lodge themselves in the computer's main memory or operating system. Any other program that is run is then infected. When infected software is shared by other computer users, the virus spreads.

Computer viruses are a real threat to our information-based society. Criminals who wish to steal financial data, or who gain access to computer systems containing classified documents, could hurt our finance and defense industries. They could threaten our largest corporations. They could even jeopardize the nation's air traffic control system. The Federal Bureau of Investigation now is looking into computer virus cases. Developing a virus and threatening to destroy data is serious business. It is not a meaningless joke.

Computer programs are being developed to combat viruses. These immunization programs detect viruses by comparing actual program length to expected program length, or by checking for the presence of certain known viruses. These programs have names like "Disk Defender," "Interferon," and "Vaccine."

In this information age, knowledge is our most precious resource. It must be protected and treated with great respect.

(Courtesy of USA Today Magazine © January, 1989 by the Society for the Advancement of Education)

wave ovens and VCRs. They are also widely used in automobiles.

The computers described above are small, even though they might be powerful. But there are also very large computers that are used for large, complex jobs. Big computers record income tax information sent in each year by taxpayers. They help engineers design new airplanes.

WHAT IS A COMPUTER SYSTEM?

A computer does its work according to a list of instructions, called a **program**. The program can be changed at any time. A computer is therefore a general-purpose tool. A programmer makes it do a given job by providing instructions, but can change the instructions to make it do a different job. The computer is under **program control**.

Computers are general-purpose tools of technology.

Most of today's computers are digital, using 1s and 0s to represent information. Any number can be represented by a binary number, a group of 1s and 0s.

Computers use 1s and 0s to represent information.

Bits are organized into groups of eight to make them easier to work with. These groups of eight bits are called **bytes**. Each byte can represent one of 256 different characters (numbers, letters, punctuation, or other information). Data can be repre-

The ENIAC

The ENIAC (Electronic Numerical Integrator And Computer) used 18,000 vacuum tubes. It was ten feet tall, three feet deep, and 100 feet long. The vacuum tubes gave off light and heat that attracted moths. The moths became trapped in the wires and moving parts of the computer. People had to clean the moths out, a process known as "debugging." Modern computers don't have problems with moths. But people say they are "debugging" when they find and fix problems in a computer.

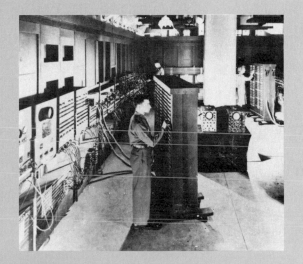

(Courtesy of Sperry Corporation)

DECIMAL	BINARY
0	0000 0000
1	0000 0001
2	0000 0010
3	0000 0011
4	0000 0100
5	0000 0101
6	0000 0110
7	0000 0111
248	1111 1000
249	1111 1001
250	1111 1010
251	1111 1011
252	1111 1100
253	1111 1101
254	1111 1110
255	1111 1111

This chart shows some conversions from decimal (base ten) numbers to binary (base two) numbers. Eight-bit binary bytes are shown.

sented by bytes, kilobytes (one kByte = one thousand bytes), or megabytes (one MByte = one million bytes).

The Computer Processor

All computers have some parts in common. The first is the **processor**. The processor controls the flow of data, its storage, and what the computer does with the data. The processor reads the program and changes the instructions into actions. The actions might be to add two numbers or to store a number or letter.

The **power** of a processor refers to how fast it is. Personal computers can carry out hundreds of thousands of instructions in a second. Large business computers can carry out millions of instructions per second (MIPS). Very fast computers can handle hundreds of millions of instructions per second.

Memory

The place where the program is stored is called the **memory**. The memory also stores the information being worked on. Most modern computers use integrated circuit memory circuits. A tiny chip can store more than one million characters.

The **random access memory** or **RAM** stores the program and the information currently being worked on. When a computer is referred to as a 640 kByte computer, the RAM can store 640 kilobytes. Personal computers have RAMs of 256 kBytes (lap-

(Courtesy of Radio Shack, a division of Tandy Corporation)

(Courtesy of Prime Computer, Inc.)

These three computers have very different main memory sizes. The small lap-top computer has 640 kilobytes of memory; the desk-top personal computer has 4 megabytes of memory; the large superminicomputer has up to 16 megabytes of memory.

top portables) to several MBytes (larger desktop computers). Very large computers have RAMs of many megabytes.

A computer must have another, much larger memory. This other memory, **storage** or **secondary storage**, stores information for use later. Storage is very large so that many different kinds of information or large amounts of the same kind of information can be stored.

Secondary storage includes floppy disks, hard disks, and magnetic tape. Floppy disks are thin, flexible magnetic storage disks that can be easily inserted into or removed from the computer. Hard disks are thick, rigid magnetic storage disks that are permanently mounted in the computer.

On all three, data are stored magnetically. The surface of the disk or tape (called the **medium**) is coated with a thin layer of iron oxide, a magnetic material. A tiny electromagnet, or **head**, is placed near the tape or disk as it moves. A voltage applied to the head magnetizes tiny bits of iron oxide. Information is stored as magnetic fields. This storage process is called "writing to disk" or "writing to tape." Information can also be taken back from the disk or tape by the head. The magnetic fields in the disk or tape are changed back into electrical impulses. This is called "reading from disk" or "reading from tape."

Secondary storage can hold an unlimited amount of information. When one disk or tape is full, it can be replaced by another. A floppy disk used in some personal computers can store more than one MByte of information, equal to more than 600 pages of typed text. A small hard disk, which is also used in personal computers, stores up to 20 MBytes, or 10,000 pages of typed text. There are hard disk drives containing several large disks that can store hundreds of MBytes.

Tape storage is much the same as with floppy disks, except that the information is stored on tape that looks similar to audio reording tape. The tape is often held in cassettes for ease of loading, unloading, and storage.

This fixed disk unit contains several disks stacked one on top of another. There is a separate head for each disk. (Courtesy of Pertec Peripherals Corporation)

A single optical disk, 8 inches in diameter, can store as much information as 15,000 sheets of paper. The disk and its drive can retrieve the information within 0.5 second. (Courtesy of Matsushita/Panasonic)

The **optical disk** is now also being used for memory storage. Optical disks are used to store data in audio compact disks (CDs) and video disks (see Chapter 8). In computers, they are able to store billions of bytes of information, or gigabytes (GBytes).

Computer Input

Information stored in and processed by the computer must be exchanged with people or other machines. This exchange is called **input/output** or **I/O**. Many I/O methods are in use because of the many ways computers are used.

Information provided to a computer is called **input**. You are probably familiar with computer input through a **keyboard**.

Computers have inputs, processors, outputs, and memories.

Bar Code Readers

The bar code reader is an input device used in supermarkets. It reads labels on boxes and bottles of store products.

A special code, called the Universal Product Code (UPC), is used. The UPC is made up of vertical lines of different thicknesses. At the check-out counter, a device called an **optical scanner** picks up light reflected from the white spaces between the bars of the UPC. The black-and-white stripes are changed to on/off pulses of electricity.

The computer uses the code to tell what the product is, how much it costs, and whether to charge tax for it. The computer might also keep a record of how many of that product have been sold and how many should be ordered from the supplier.

The Universal Product Code (UPC) uses thick bars, thin bars, and blank spaces to encode information about a product. (From THE WAY THE NEW TECHNOLOGY WORKS by Ken Marsh)

A keyboard is similar to a typewriter keyboard. People use a keyboard to program a computer. A keyboard can also be used to provide data to a computer. The data are then processed through a program already stored in the computer. Communicating with a computer by means of a keyboard is called an **interactive** process. Input through the keyboard is followed quickly by output from the computer.

Tapes, hard disks, and floppy disks can also provide input to a computer. Tapes and disks can hold a program or data. The computer can move, or load, the data into its main memory. People can write new programs on their computers, storing them on tape or disk. These tapes or disks can then be copied and sold to others.

A device called an optical character reader can transfer input from the printed page directly to the computer. It changes letters and numbers into a code of bytes. In this way, many pages of text can be put into a computer's secondary storage for later use.

Input can also be in the form of human speech. Special devices can recognize some spoken words (up to a few hundred) and change them into bytes. This technology is still being improved. Someday it may be an important source of computer input.

Computer Output

Computer output appears in many forms. You probably have seen the most common, the **video monitor**, or **CRT screen**. CRT stands for cathode ray tube. A cathode ray tube changes electrical signals to light images. CRTs are used in televisions to produce the picture you watch. They are also used in test equipment called oscilloscopes.

Video monitors can be used to display text, like that on this page, or graphics (pictures), or both at the same time. They can be black-and-white or green-and-white, or full-color.

Often, a keyboard is used with a monitor. The result is a system that can provide input to the computer (through the keyboard) and display output from the computer (through the monitor). The combination is called a **terminal**. Sometimes, other input devices are added to the terminal such as the **mouse**, the **light pen**, and the **touch-sensitive screen**.

A **printer** is another common computer output device. A printer records output on a piece of paper. Such a paper record is called **hard copy**. Two kinds of printers used with computers are **dot matrix printers** and **daisy wheel printers**. Dot matrix printers are used to make drawings as well as print letters and numbers. Because these printers use dots, not lines, the pictures and letters are sometimes not very clear.

A mouse combines output with input. (Courtesy of Apple Computer, Inc.)

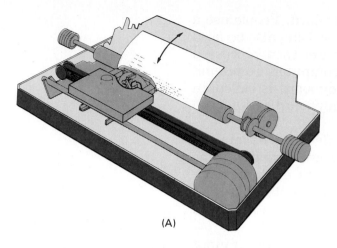

(A)

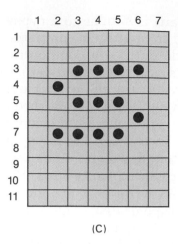

(C)

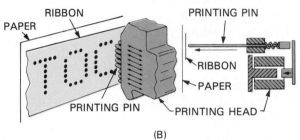

(B)

(A) A dot matrix printer has a print head that contains a group of pins. (B) The pins can be moved by electromagnets to strike a ribbon, making impressions on paper. (Parts A and B from Brightman & Dimsdale, USING COMPUTERS IN AN INFORMATION AGE, copyright 1986 by Delmar Publishers Inc.) (C) The letter "s" is made by activating a number of pins in the right pattern. The matrix shown here is 11 × 7. Other matrix sizes are used.

Daisy wheel printers, on the other hand, print clearly. But they cannot print pictures. Daisy wheel printers are usually more costly than dot matrix printers. They are also slower.

Large computers use printers that can print much faster than dot matrix or daisy wheel printers. They can print whole lines or pages at a time. Another kind of printer used with both large and small computers is the **laser printer**. The laser printer can print both pictures and text very quickly.

Like a printer, a plotter marks on paper. Plotters are output devices that use one or more pens to make drawings. Plotters are often used in systems that make, change, and store drawings, such as CAD, or computer-aided design systems.

Audio output takes the form of tones, beeps, music, and voice. Tones and beeps signal that the end of a page has been reached. They can tell the operator that an instruction is unknown to the computer. Music and voices can be made inside the computer using a device called a **synthesizer**. A synthesizer can produce a wide range of tones, volume, and even drum-like sounds. Voice synthesizers reproduce speech. They are used by telephone companies to give customers telephone numbers or the time of day.

Computers can be connected to each other. They can also be connected to terminals far away, a process called **data commu-**

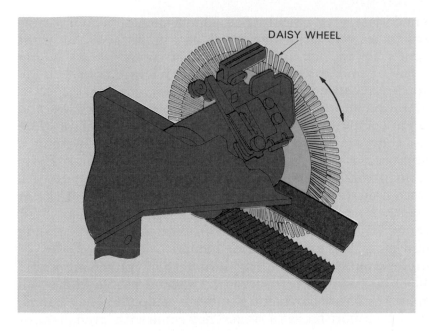

DAISY WHEEL

A daisy wheel contains many "petals." Each petal has a raised character on it. A daisy wheel printer positions the correct character, and strikes it. This pushes the character onto an inked ribbon, which leaves an impression on the paper. (From Brightman & Dimsdale, USING COMPUTERS IN AN INFORMATION AGE, copyright 1986 by Delmar Publishers Inc.)

nications. A special device called a **modem** is often used. Modems must be used in pairs. One modem converts the 1s and 0s into tones of two different pitches (frequencies) that can be sent on the telephone lines. The modem at the other end changes the tones back into 1s and 0s. An inexpensive modem can send the information on one typed page in seconds.

COMPUTERS, LARGE AND SMALL

Computers come in all sizes. They range from a chip less than one inch square to a room full of equipment. Computers also have all sizes of capability. Some are slow processors, while

This LaserJet III si printer produces high-quality copies at 17 pages a minute. (Courtesy of Hewlett-Packard Company)

A plotter may be used to make multicolored drawings. Photo courtesy of Houston Instruments, a Summagraphics Company)

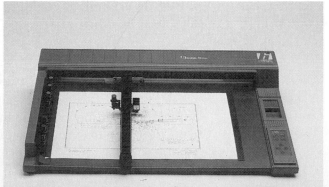

A *microcomputer* (Courtesy of NCR Corporation)

others do jobs very quickly. Some have a small memory while others have a very large memory. A user must choose the right computer for the job. You can think of computers as falling into one of four categories. They are: microcomputer, minicomputer, mainframe computer, and supercomputer.

Microcomputers are found in appliances, automobiles, and personal computers. They can be as small as one chip. More often, they are a group of integrated circuits including a microprocessor chip. Their memories can be small (one kByte) or large (several MBytes, as in some "supermicrocomputers"). Microcomputers handle data or instructions 8, 16, or 32 bits at a time (1, 2, or 4 bytes at a time). They may be called "8-bit machines" or "16-bit machines," or "32-bit machines," depending on how many bits at a time they handle.

Minicomputers are slightly larger than microcomputers. Minicomputers are often shared by several people in a small company, or one department of a large company. They handle 16, 24, 32, or more bits at a time. They come with large disks or tapes for secondary storage.

Mainframe computers are the large computers used by large companies, government agencies, and universities. They are used to make out payroll checks, keep personnel records, keep track of orders, or keep lists of warehoused items. These large computers handle data and instructions 32, 36, 48, and 64 bits at a time. They may have very large secondary storage devices such as hard disks and tapes. Mainframes can carry out millions of instructions per second.

Supercomputers are the fastest and largest computers. They are most often used for research, for analyzing huge amounts of data, or for other very large jobs. Supercomputer speed is measured by the number of multiplications or divisions (floating point operations) per second (FLOPS) the computer can carry out. (A floating point operation might be $1.23 \times 2.6 = 3.198$.) The largest supercomputers can carry out billions of floating point operations per second (GFLOPS). Supercomputers are costly to buy and use.

This supercomputer is very fast. It can store up to 256 million words of memory and is used for artificial intelligence experiments. (Photo by Paul Shambroom, courtesy of Cray Research, Inc.)

Computers are becoming more powerful all the time. The power of a supercomputer from twenty years ago is now available in a desktop personal computer. This trend toward more power in a smaller package may continue through the year 2000 and beyond.

COMPUTER SOFTWARE

Computers can be used for many different jobs. How they are used depends on input/output devices and how they are programmed. A computer program is called **software**. There are three important kinds of computer software. They are: operating systems, applications programs purchased for use, and applications programs written by the user.

The computer's **operating system** lets a user control the computer and its components. It also makes the components available to other kinds of software. An operating system is chosen to fit the computer and the job it must do. Sometimes more than one operating system is available for a particular computer. The user must choose the right one for a job. Examples of operating systems used in personal computers are MS-DOS and OS/2.

An applications program tells the computer the steps to follow to carry out a specific task. These programs include computer games, word processors, and car engine control programs. Applications programs are stored on tape or disk. They can be bought for use with personal or mainframe computers.

A user must make sure a program will work (is **compatible** with) the operating system. Many programs can be used with several different operating systems. They can be used on different computers.

Sometimes no program exists to do a job. In this case, a program will have to be written. This may be easy and quick,

```
10 INPUT "What is your name ";N$
20 INPUT "Please tell me a number";A
30 INPUT "Please tell me another number";B
40 PRINT "Thank you,";N$;", the product of";A;"and";B;"is :";A*B;"."
50 PRINT "The Quotient of";A;"and";B;"is:";A/B;"."
60 PRINT "The sum of";A;"and";B;"is :";A+B;"."
70 PRINT "The difference between";A;"and";B;"is :";A-B;"."
80 END
```

A) This simple BASIC program instructs the computer to record the name of the operator and to ask for two numbers. The computer will then multiply, divide, add, and subtract the numbers.
(Program courtesy of R. Barden, Jr.)

```
RUN
What is your name ? Mary
Please tell me a number? 8
Please tell me another number? 2
Thank you,Mary, the product of 8 and 2 is : 16 .
The Quotient of 8 and 2 is: 4 .
The sum of 8 and 2 is : 10 .
The difference between 8 and 2 is : 6 .
```

B) The actual exchange between the operator and the computer is shown here. The entries in red are made by the operator. All others are output from the computer. The entry "RUN" starts the program.

or it may be a long, hard effort. Some programs take years to write. An applications program is written in one of many programming languages. Each language has features that make it best for writing certain kinds of programs.

One common programming language is **BASIC** (Beginner's All-purpose Symbolic Instruction Code). It is used by students, businesspeople, and hobbyists. It is fairly easy to learn and use. BASIC can be used on most small personal computers as well as on large mainframe computers.

Pascal is a language that is becoming more and more popular. It is often the language students learn after they learn BASIC. Pascal is named after Blaise Pascal, who invented the first mechanical adding machine.

Some languages have been invented to help computers "think." **Artificial intelligence** is the imitation of human thought by computers. Programming in most computers uses complete information to arrive at clear answers. In artificial intelligence, information may not be complete. Answers may, or may not, be correct. The computer is able to learn from its mistakes.

COMPUTERS AND THE SYSTEM MODEL

It is helpful to think of the computer in terms of a system model. The terms used in describing how a computer works are system terms. Input devices provide command inputs and

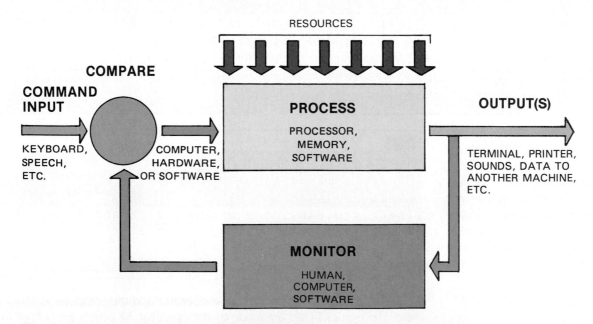

The general system diagram can be readily applied to computers.

resource inputs. For example, a user at a terminal types in a program (command input). He or she then types in data (resource input).

The computer's processor acts on the resources in response to the command. The processor is the process in the system model. The output of the computer is the output of the system. Feedback may come from a person, or through hardware or software.

Computers are sometimes used as stand-alone systems. Very often, however, a computer is part of a larger system. In this case, the computer is only a subsystem. It may provide part of the larger system's feedback, process, or comparison. It may provide the command input to the larger system. Computers come in many sizes and can be programmed to do a wide variety of jobs. Because of this, they are one of the most useful and widespread tools of technology.

Computers can be used as systems or can be small parts of larger systems.

SUMMARY

The use of electronics has changed technology greatly over the last hundred years. Electricity can help represent, store, change, and communicate information.

All materials are made from atoms. Atoms contain smaller

(Courtesy of NCR Corporation)

Computer Applications

Computers are often parts of other, larger systems. In a manufacturing system, a computer may supply command inputs to a production line. It might also compare the actual output to the desired output. Then it can order any necessary changes. In a system that addresses and mails thousands of letters a day, the computer is the process part of the system. Its output is addressed envelopes, letters, and bills.

A computer is often used to help people form a feedback loop. For example, a computer can be a central control center in a transportation system. It can help switch trains from track to track or bring planes in to land safely.

A computer can have several roles. In a microwave oven, a microcomputer sets the energy level based on the cook's input. It can turn the oven on. It can sense when food is done and shut the oven off or keep it on at lower power to keep the food warm.

A control computer for automated manufacturing and warehousing systems. (Courtesy of Gould, Inc.)

The control center for Buffalo, NY's light rail transit system. (Courtesy of General Signal Corporation, Stamford, CT)

particles called protons, neutrons, and electrons. Protons have a positive electric charge, while electrons have a negative electric charge. Particles with the same charge repel each other. Particles with opposite charges attract each other.

Materials whose atoms give up electrons easily are called conductors. Materials whose atoms hold tightly to their electrons are called insulators. Electric current flows when electrons move through a material. Electromotive force makes the electrons flow, forming a current. The measure of how strongly a conductor opposes current flow is called resistance.

Electronic components include resistors, diodes, and transistors. Components connected together to do different jobs are called circuits. Printed circuits and integrated circuits make it possible to put more circuits into smaller spaces.

Analog circuits work with signals that vary smoothly as the information they represent changes. Digital circuits work with information that has been converted into binary codes (1s and 0s). Digital circuits are best for sending information over long distances, or for ensuring accuracy.

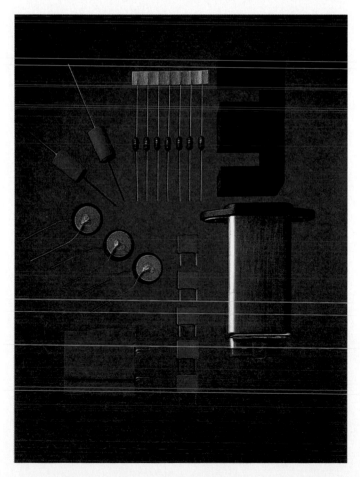

(Courtesy of Siemens Components, Inc.)

Computers are general-purpose tools of the information age. They can be programmed, or instructed, to do many different jobs. They have processors, main memory, secondary storage, and input/output components. Computing power has greatly increased during the past fifty years, while the cost of computer systems has fallen.

Computers can be classed as microcomputers, minicomputers, mainframe computers, or supercomputers. These classes are constantly changing as computers become more powerful.

Computer software is divided into operating systems and applications programs, which can be purchased already written, or be written by the user.

The computer may be easily described by the general system model. Computer terms are much like system terms.

Computers come in many sizes. They can be programmed to do many different jobs. Because they are so useful, and because their cost has gone steadily down, they are widely used. They are used in appliances and automobiles, as well as in word processing, science research, manufacturing, and business.

REVIEW QUESTIONS

1. Name three particles found inside of atoms.
2. In an electronic circuit powered by a 9-volt battery, one ampere of current flows. If the 9-volt battery is replaced by a 20-volt or higher battery, does more or less current flow? Why?
3. Name five electronic components that can be used to build circuits.
4. Why was the invention of the integrated circuit important in the history of technology?
5. Based on your own experience and observation, give one example each of how the use of electronics has changed manufacturing, transportation, communication, and health care technologies.
6. Should a telephone be an analog or digital instrument? Why?
7. Name four parts of a computer.
8. Describe the difference between operating system software and applications software.
9. A computer can be used for mailing letters to thousands of people. List the major components that you would expect to find in such a computer system. Draw the system using a general system model.
10. Do you think it is a good idea to have a totally automated system with no involvement by people? Why or why not? Give an example to support your answer.

KEY WORDS

Ampere	Conductor	Memory	Random access
Analog	Current	Operating system	memory (RAM)
Bit	Digital	Printed circuit	Resistance
Byte	Electron	board	Semiconductor
Circuit	I/O	Printer	Supercomputer
Component	Insulator	Processor	Transistor
Compounds	Integrated circuit	Program	Voltage

SEE YOUR TEACHER FOR THE CROSSTECH PUZZLE

COMPUTERS IN INDUSTRY

Setting the Stage

Computers are an important tool for industry. They allow us to simulate real-life situations and to test ideas. They are also frequently used for computer-aided drafting. As a member of a design team, for example, you might be involved with computer designing of a new car. How can a computer help you develop and test your design before it is modeled?

Your Challenge

Operate a computer, disk drive, printer, and joystick or mouse. Use programs that require you to input information to make a more informed decision concerning technology projects. Examples include "The Factory," "Car Builder," and "Blazing Paddles."

Procedure

1. Insert "The Factory" disk into the disk drive and load the program. Use all three levels or files. The experience you gain from learning how to operate the machines, design a product, and understand how a product was built at the factory will help you in other technology activities.

   File 1: Test a Machine
   - a. A punching, rotating, or striping machine is available for testing.
   - b. Use the arrow keys to choose the process and input your choices with the RETURN or ENTER key.
   - c. Once you have learned how to use each machine you will then be able to build a factory using the second file.

   File 2: Build a Factory
   - a. Using the arrow keys, put up to eight machines together in an assembly line to produce a finished product.
   - b. Once your factory is assembled, erase the assembly line, leaving the finished product. Then, you or a partner should attempt to reestablish the assembly line that produces the product.

Suggested Resources

Computer
Disk drive
Printer
Joystick or mouse
"The Factory"
"Car Builder"
"Blazing Paddles"

File 3: Make a Product

You will be shown a product that has been made by several machines. Reconstruct the sequence of machines and processes used in the construction of the project.

2. You have just experienced how a computer can help people in choosing processing techniques and sequence of operations. Now try to use a program for computer-aided drafting (CAD) and for testing a product. Load "Car Builder" into the computer.

File 1: By following the design sequence, design and construct a car. Chassis length, engine placement and size, type of steering, body shape, and types of tires are a sampling of decisions you will have to make.

File 2: The next file on "Car Builder" will test your car in a wind tunnel. The drag form factor will also be displayed for the car you designed.

File 3: Using the final file, road test the vehicle you designed. By following the directions on the disk, save and/or print your CAD vehicle.

3. Now try a program that will allow the printer to become a graphics plotter and instant drafting machine. Load "Blazing Paddles" into the computer.

By using a joy stick or mouse and following the directions, you will be able to produce quality drawings in a short time. There are hundreds of programs on the market, each with their own system of commands and operations to be performed. Many of them are complex, so stick with the ones that meet your requirements. "Blazing Paddles" will allow you to draw any plans you might need for the activities in later chapters.

Technology Connections

1. After using "Car Builder," model the body you designed. Test it in the lab wind tunnel.
2. Name and properly hook up all the computer accessories that you used for the above programs.
3. List some uses for the computer in our technological world.
4. What other communication systems are used in combination with the computer?

Science and Math Concepts

▶ One disk can hold more than one million magnetic charges or bits of information. There are eight bits in a byte of information. The middle section and two other small areas of the disk are exposed so the computer can read and write to the disk.

LOW-POWER RADIO TRANSMITTER

Suggested Resources

Safety glasses and lab apron
1 copper clad circuit board—2" × 3"
Direct etching dry transfers (Radio Shack #276-1577)
Etchant
Shallow pan for etching
Plastic funnel
Carbon paper
Steel wool (000)
Wire cutters
Soldering pencil and solder
Drill and drill bits
Aluminum or plastic case

The following electronic components:
T1—2N3906 PNP transistor
R1— 130 K ohm resistor
C3 & C4—.022 μfd capacitor
C2—.0047 μfd capacitor
C1—100 pfd ($\mu\mu f$d) capacitor
L1—Adjustable tapped loopstick antenna coil for broadcast band
L2—10 or 15 turns of #30 enameled wire around L1
B1—9 volt alkaline transistor battery with 9 volt battery snaps
M1—1000 ohm magnetic-type earphone or microphone with ⅛" phone plug
S1—Miniature spst toggle switch
ANT—30" telescoping antenna
⅛" miniature phone jack—open circuit

Setting the Stage

Electronics and radio communications were developed by people like Edison, Morse, DeForest, and Marconi. The devices used to transmit and receive data have since been much improved. Supersensitive receivers with huge antennas can now pick up weak radio signals from spacecraft millions of miles away.

Your Challenge

Construct a small radio transmitter that can send a message through an AM radio.

Procedure

1. Be sure to wear safety glasses and a lab coat.
2. Cut a 2" × 3" piece of single-sided copper clad circuit board with a squaring shear or fine-toothed saw. Clean with 000 steel wool.
3. Duplicate the printed circuit layout on the circuit board with direct etching dry transfers.
4. Etch the circuit. This takes about 20 minutes.
5. Remove the resist material and wash the circuit board in water. Again clean with 000 steel wool.
6. Drill ¹⁄₃₂" (or #52) holes in the board on the donut dots so that pigtail leads and components can be mounted. Also, drill ³⁄₁₆" diameter mounting holes in each corner of the board.
7. Wrap 10 or 15 turns of #30 enameled wire around L1.
8. Solder all components with a small soldering pencil. CAUTION: Excess heat will cause the copper to lift from the board and can destroy electronic components. Use a small alligator clip as a heatsink whenever possible.
9. When wiring the battery snaps in place, watch the polarity (+ or −). The transmitter will not work if the battery is wired incorrectly. DOUBLE CHECK your wiring.
10. Connect the antenna, microphone, and battery.
11. Tune an AM radio to a spot where there is no station.
12. Turn on your transmitter (S1) and adjust the tuning slug of L1 (the adjustable tapped loopstick antenna coil) until you hear a whistle in the AM radio.
13. Now speak directly into the microphone. You should hear your own voice.
14. If there is a problem: Recheck all wiring. Look for short circuits (a piece of steel wool across two points), open circuits (a small

crack in the copper foil), and poor solder connections. Also, make sure your battery isn't dead or its polarity reversed. Try a different microphone if possible.

15. If everything works fine, you may wish to construct a small aluminum box for the transmitter.

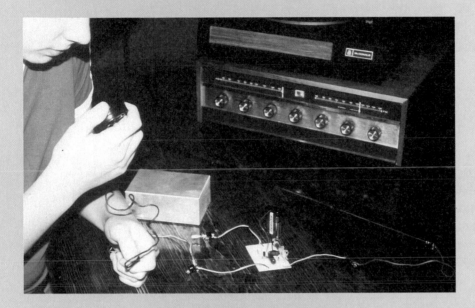

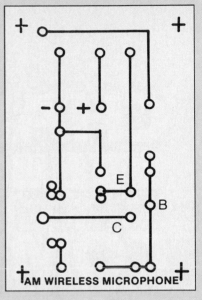

VIEW FROM THE FOIL SIDE
OF THE CIRCUIT BOARD

BLACK IS COPPER

Technology Connections

1. Electronic circuits are made up of *components*. Each component has a specific function in the circuit. What is the function of the microphone in the transmitter? The battery?

2. The use of electronics has revolutionized all aspects of technology. What would your life be like without electricity? What things would you miss the most?

3. What is it called when many components of a circuit are miniaturized and produced on one piece of semiconductor material?

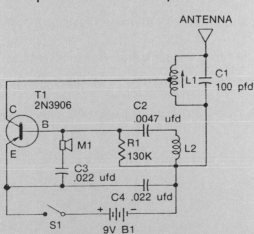

Science and Math Concepts

▶ A *capacitor* is made from a combination of conducting plates separated by an insulator. It can store an electric charge.

▶ Semiconductors are made from materials such as germanium or silicon. Their electrical resistance is somewhere between conductors and insulators.

CHAPTER 5

COMMUNICATION SYSTEMS

MAJOR CONCEPTS

After reading this chapter, you will know that:

- Communication includes having a message sent, received, and understood.
- Humans, animals, and machines can all communicate.
- A communication system has an input, a process, and an output.
- The communication process has three parts. They are: a transmitter, a channel on which the message travels, and a receiver.
- Communication systems are used to inform, persuade, educate, and entertain.
- Communication systems require the use of the seven technological resources.
- Two kinds of communication systems are graphic and electronic.

WHAT IS COMMUNICATION?

Humans have always needed to communicate. To help them get what they must have to live and to stay safe and well, people have had to make their needs and wants known to each other.

Spoken and written languages are used by people to communicate. Hundreds of different languages are spoken throughout the world. In the United States, Canada, the British Isles, and South Africa, the common language is English. Yet there are differences in English in these countries. A "truck" in the United States is a "lorry" in Great Britain. A "flat" in South Africa is an "apartment" in the United States.

It is sometimes hard for people to communicate even when they are speaking the same language. When people who speak different languages try to communicate, it is even more difficult.

To communicate, we must be sure that what we are saying is understood by the other person. We must be sure that our words have the same meaning to that person as they do to us.

Communication includes having a message sent, received, and understood.

TYPES OF COMMUNICATION

Person-to-Person Communication

People can communicate with each other in many ways. Most often, we use speech. Sometimes, however, we communicate without speaking. When you are happy, you smile. When you are sad, your face tells everyone how you feel. You might wink if you are sharing a joke or a secret. People communicate with each other through their facial expressions.

People also use body language. If you are angry, you might cross your arms in front of you. If you are bored, you might shift about in your seat and look around. You may not know that your body language is telling someone else how you really feel.

People use their senses to communicate. Of course, sight and hearing are important in communication. But so are touch and smell. A child's mother tells him she loves him with a hug. Using perfume or cologne tells other people that you want to be pleasant to be around.

Some people claim that they can send their thoughts or receive thoughts from others. They call themselves **psychics**. Some psychics claim that they can predict the future. Some say they know things about the past that others do not know. Nobody is sure whether or not these people have special powers. They may just be good at making guesses.

Animal Communication

People can communicate with animals. You know that people can communicate with their pets. A dog knows when his

People come from many different backgrounds, but they all need to communicate.
(Courtesy of Southern California Edison)

owner is ready to take him for a walk. Perhaps he knows the word "walk" or he knows what to expect because of his owner's tone of voice. The dog's owner knows when the dog is hungry. The dog may stand next to his food bowl and whine or wag his tail.

Animals can also communicate with other animals. When bees find a source of food, they come back to the hive. There, they crawl in a figure-eight pattern among the bees crowding around them on the comb. Their motion tells other bees how far and in what direction to fly to find nectar.

Some chimpanzees have been taught a human language called sign language. One chimpanzee learned sign language and could "talk" with her trainers. Later, when she had babies, she taught them sign language, too.

Animals communicate with each other in many ways. This bee is showing the direction and distance of a food source.

Machine Communication

People can also communicate with machines. When you play a video game, you're communicating with a machine. You move the joystick or paddle and your motion is changed into electrical signals in the game. Machines can communicate with people, too. The output of a computer is its message. Output can be printing on paper, or sounds from a voice synthesizer, or light on a screen.

Machines often communicate with each other. In more and more factories, computers control machines. For example, a robot arm spray-paints automobiles in a large automobile plant.

As automation becomes more widespread, machine-to-machine and machine-to-human communications become more important.
(Courtesy of Allen-Bradley, a Rockwell International Company)

Humans, animals, and machines can all communicate.

A computer controls the robot arm. It tells the robot arm what to paint and for how long to paint it.

Machines also communicate with each other to heat a house. A person sets the thermostat at 72°. The furnace heats the room to this temperature. Then the thermostat sends a message (an electrical signal) to the furnace to turn off.

You have seen that people communicate with animals, with each other, and with machines. Animals communicate with animals. Machines communicate with machines. Here is something for you to think about: Could a machine and an animal communicate? When would this kind of communication be useful? Can you think of some forms it could take?

COMMUNICATION SYSTEMS

When people speak to each other, they create a **communication system**. In Chapter 3, you learned that a **system** is a way to get desired results. Every system has an **input**, a **process**, and an **output**.

A communication system has an input, a process, and an output.

A communication system could be two people talking. In such a case, the **input** is the desired result. The input is the message you want to send to the other person. The process is how you communicate the input. In a conversation between two people the process is speech. The output is the message that the other person gets. **Feedback** tells you whether the person has understood what you said.

How do you get feedback when you are speaking to someone? How do you know that the message you sent was received and understood? You might ask the person, "Do you understand?" Or you might look at the person's face and body lan-

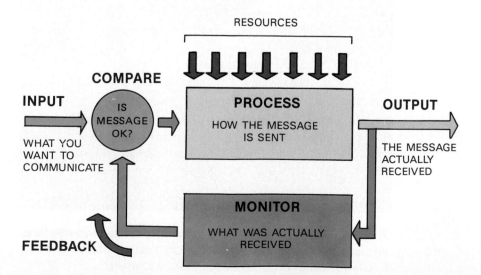

The general system design for a communication system

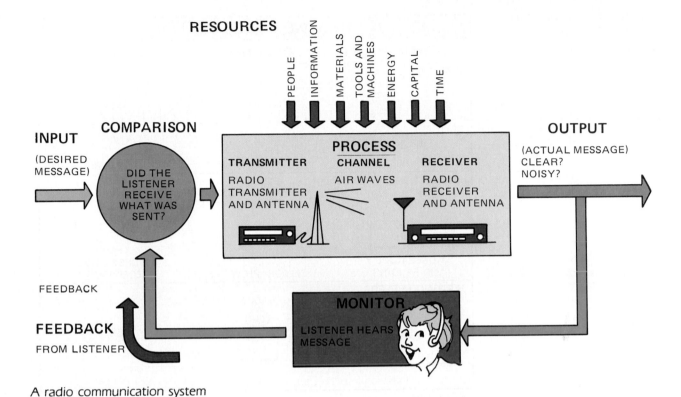

RESOURCES

PEOPLE INFORMATION MATERIALS TOOLS AND MACHINES ENERGY CAPITAL TIME

INPUT
(DESIRED MESSAGE)

COMPARISON
DID THE LISTENER RECEIVE WHAT WAS SENT?

PROCESS
TRANSMITTER
RADIO TRANSMITTER AND ANTENNA

CHANNEL
AIR WAVES

RECEIVER
RADIO RECEIVER AND ANTENNA

OUTPUT
(ACTUAL MESSAGE)
CLEAR?
NOISY?

FEEDBACK

FEEDBACK
FROM LISTENER

MONITOR
LISTENER HEARS MESSAGE

A radio communication system

guage. A smile or a nod could show that the message is understood. A frown or a puzzled expression could show that your message has not gotten through.

THE PROCESS OF COMMUNICATION

All communication systems are alike in some ways. All of them have inputs, processes, and outputs. They must have feedback to be sure the message is understood.

The communication **process** has three parts. There must be a means of **transmitting** (sending) the message. There must be a **channel**, or route the message takes. There must be a **receiver** to accept the message. All three of these parts are present in every communication process.

The communication process has three parts. They are: a transmitter, a channel on which the message travels, and a receiver.

DESIGNING THE MESSAGE

Before we communicate, we must think about what we want to accomplish. Each message has a purpose. It must be designed

The communication process consists of a transmitter, a channel, and a receiver.

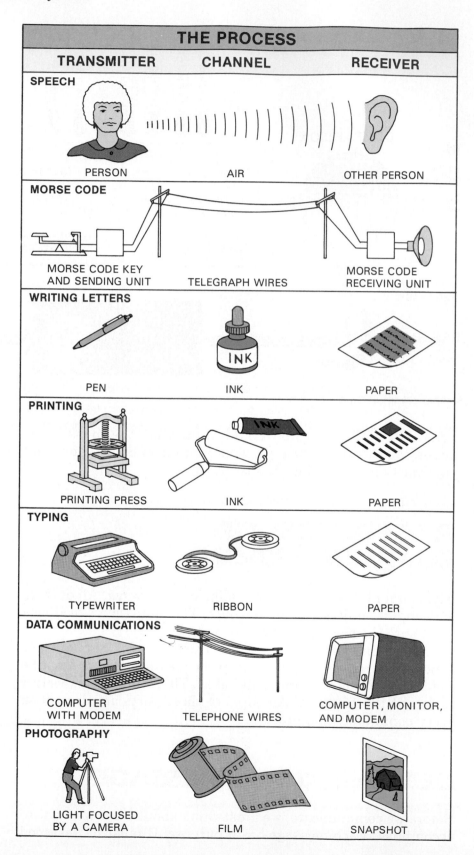

THE PROCESS

TRANSMITTER	CHANNEL	RECEIVER
SPEECH		
PERSON	AIR	OTHER PERSON
MORSE CODE		
MORSE CODE KEY AND SENDING UNIT	TELEGRAPH WIRES	MORSE CODE RECEIVING UNIT
WRITING LETTERS		
PEN	INK	PAPER
PRINTING		
PRINTING PRESS	INK	PAPER
TYPING		
TYPEWRITER	RIBBON	PAPER
DATA COMMUNICATIONS		
COMPUTER WITH MODEM	TELEPHONE WIRES	COMPUTER, MONITOR, AND MODEM
PHOTOGRAPHY		
LIGHT FOCUSED BY A CAMERA	FILM	SNAPSHOT

Television communication is often used to entertain.
(Courtesy of National Broadcasting Company)

to fit this purpose. Sometimes we want to **inform** people. We want to give them information. Sometimes we want to **persuade** people. We want to convince them to do something. We also may want to **entertain** people. And we communicate with others to **educate** them.

A communication system is chosen because it best fits a purpose. To inform, you might choose a newsletter. To persuade, you might use a telephone and speak to a person. Cartoons on television are used to entertain. Charts and drawings can be used to educate. Sometimes, a system is used to both entertain and educate at the same time.

There may be several good ways to communicate. Your choice will be based on the audience you wish to reach. If you are selling a new kind of toothpaste, you will want to reach the general public. You will most likely use one of the **mass media**, like radio, television, or newspapers. Mass media are those that reach large numbers of people. If you want to persuade a small group of businesspeople, you will choose a different form of communication. You might send a letter to each person, or present your ideas in a meeting.

Communication systems are used to inform, persuade, educate, and entertain.

RESOURCES FOR COMMUNICATION SYSTEMS

Communication systems make use of the seven types of resources.

Communication systems require the use of the seven technological resources.

A favorite form of entertainment provides communication careers for many people. (Courtesy of General Electric)

People

People design the systems. They decide on the message that is sent. They help to deliver the message, and they receive it. Actors and camera operators are needed for television shows and films. Writers write books, scripts for radio and television, and newspapers. Artists and photographers produce illustrations. Printers run machines that turn out many copies of books, newspapers, and magazines. People are needed to run and repair communication systems.

Information

Information is needed about the audience that will receive the message. Advertisers want to find out what will make people buy their products. What works for one group of people will not work for everybody. For example, teenagers like one kind of music, older people another. Book publishers need information about what people want to read. What people need and want to know will determine which books are published.

Information is also needed about how to communicate at low cost while keeping quality high. That means knowing how to choose everything from the best writers to the best quality paper. To keep communication systems going, engineers and technicians need information of many kinds.

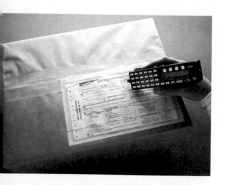

Federal Express keeps track of its packages with a Super Tracker. (Courtesy of Federal Express Corporation)

Materials

Materials such as paper, film, and tape are needed to carry the message. Materials are constantly being changed and

This LaserCard™ is a new credit card that can store the amount of information contained in two 400-page books. (Courtesy of Drexler Technical Corporation)

Tools like this 28-ounce portable terminal can be used to communicate with a central computer by radio. (Courtesy of Motorola Inc.)

improved to make communication faster, cheaper, and better. New camera film makes it possible to take pictures in very low light. Paper and inks can give book covers and printing the look of silver or gold. New optical disks store a large amount of information in a small space.

Tools and Machines

Printers and artists use hand tools like airbrushes and rulers, pens, and pencils. Machines such as computers, printers, cameras, printing presses, tape recorders, and radio transmitters are used in communication systems. These machines are used to design, send, receive, and store messages.

Energy

Energy is used to move the message from place to place. Electricity powers radio and television transmitters and receivers. It also runs computer systems and word processors. Motors run printing presses and electric typewriters. In computer printers, electricity is changed into magnetic energy by **electromagnets**. Electromagnets operate the printhead. Light energy is used to create images on photographic film.

High capital expenses are required to finance a newspaper plant. (Courtesy of Gannett Co. Inc.)

Capital

Capital is needed to set up and run a communication system. Machines and tools must be bought. People must be paid

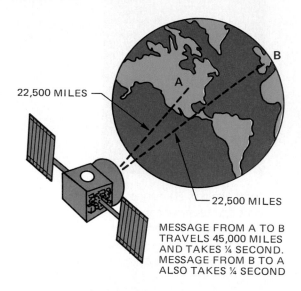

22,500 MILES

22,500 MILES

MESSAGE FROM A TO B
TRAVELS 45,000 MILES
AND TAKES ¼ SECOND.
MESSAGE FROM B TO A
ALSO TAKES ¼ SECOND

for their work. Work spaces such as television studios and print shops must be built or rented. Light and heat must be provided.

Time

Moving a message takes time. It must travel from the transmitter to the receiver. The time needed depends on the length of the message and the rate at which the message is sent. Sound travels at 1,096 feet per second. Electrical signals travel at the speed of light (186,000 miles per second). If you telephone someone in a distant country, your message will probably travel by way of a communications satellite. Satellites orbit the earth at an altitude of about 22,500 miles. It takes about ¼ second for a message to go from one place on earth to another by satellite; it takes another ¼ second for the response to return. Therefore, a person talking on the telephone to someone halfway around the world can expect a delay of at least ½ second between the times he or she asks a question and receives an answer.

CATEGORIES OF COMMUNICATION SYSTEMS

Two kinds of communication systems are graphic and electronic.

For many thousands of years, people have communicated with each other using many different methods. These include speaking, writing, signaling, and drawing. Today, all forms of communication fall into one of two categories. They are **graphic communication** and **electronic communication**. In graphic com-

Interference—Noise in the System

In communication systems, a channel is not perfect. It affects the information sent by the transmitter. Often, something that is wrong with the channel affects how clearly we get the message.

One kind of problem is **noise**. Noise is anything that interferes with communication. The static you hear on the radio during a thunderstorm is noise. But noise does not have to be something you hear. When an airplane flies over, it can affect a television picture. The picture may flutter. Dust on a record can cause noise. A smudge on a drawing is noise because you can't see the picture clearly. When engineers design communication systems, they try to keep the noise at a minimum.

Television "ghost" images are a form of noise. (Photo by Michael Hacker)

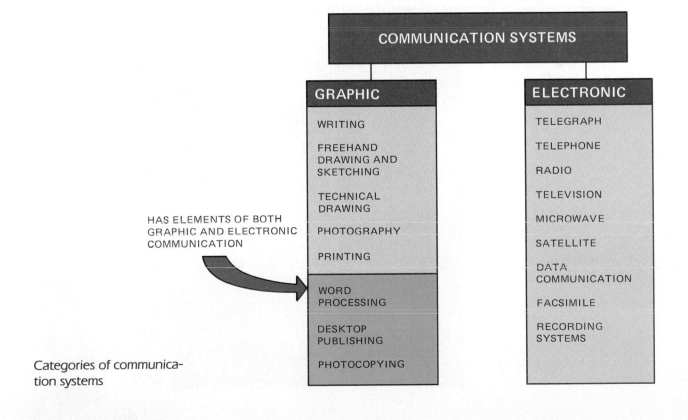

Categories of communication systems

HAS ELEMENTS OF BOTH GRAPHIC AND ELECTRONIC COMMUNICATION

COMMUNICATION SYSTEMS

GRAPHIC
WRITING
FREEHAND DRAWING AND SKETCHING
TECHNICAL DRAWING
PHOTOGRAPHY
PRINTING
WORD PROCESSING
DESKTOP PUBLISHING
PHOTOCOPYING

ELECTRONIC
TELEGRAPH
TELEPHONE
RADIO
TELEVISION
MICROWAVE
SATELLITE
DATA COMMUNICATION
FACSIMILE
RECORDING SYSTEMS

munication, the channel carries pictures or printed words. In electronic communication, the channel carries electrical signals. In the next chapter you will learn about graphic communication. Chapter 7 will cover electronic communication.

SUMMARY

Humans, animals, and machines communicate among themselves and with each other. Communication includes sending a message and having it received and understood. In a communication system, you know that the message was received and understood through feedback.

All communication systems have inputs, processes, and outputs. The communication process includes a transmitter, a channel on which the message travels, and a receiver.

We use communication systems to inform, persuade, entertain, and educate. The choice of a communication system is based on the type and size of our audience. Like other technological systems, communication systems make use of the seven types of resources.

Modern communication systems can be divided into two categories: graphic communication and electronic communication. In graphic communication, the channel carries images or printed words. In electronic communication systems, the channel carries electrical signals.

(Courtesy of Hewlett-Packard)

(Courtesy of International Business Machines Corp.)

REVIEW QUESTIONS

1. What is communication? Define it in your own words. Then use your definition to tell which of the following are not communication, and why not.
   a. a baby crying for its mother
   b. the sound of glass being broken accidentally
   c. a car horn
   d. a railroad car screeching on the tracks
   e. a bird chirping
   f. static on the radio
2. Give an example of animal-to-human communication.
3. Give an example of machine-to-human communication and an example of human-to-machine communication.
4. Choose a communication system you use and tell how it uses the seven technological resources.
5. What are four purposes of communication?
6. What are the three parts of the process of a communication system?
7. Give two examples of noise that you do not hear.
8. Draw a diagram of a person-to-person communication system. Label the transmitter, the channel, and the receiver.
9. What kind of communication system would be best for each of the following:
   a. selling a used stereo
   b. asking for money for cancer research
   c. letting people know you are looking for a part-time job
   d. entertaining a large audience
10. Describe the difference between graphic and electronic communication. Give one example of each kind of communication.

KEY WORDS

Channel	Educate	Noise	Receiver
Communication system	Electronic communication	Machine communication	Transmitter
Graphic communication	Entertain	Mass media	
	Inform	Persuade	

SEE YOUR TEACHER FOR THE CROSSTECH PUZZLE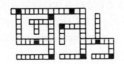

INTERNATIONAL LANGUAGE

Setting the Stage

Chin Lee is the business manager of a large firm that manufactures watches that are sold all over the world. A set of instructions printed in various languages is included with each watch. He could save the company a lot of money and possibly earn himself a pay raise if he could devise a small pamphlet containing pictured instructions to be understood by everyone. This pamphlet could be included with every watch, saving the company so many different printings.

Your Challenge

Using the international language of pictures, assemble a booklet of directions for an activity of your choosing.

Procedure

1. Study the example of picture directions provided by your teacher. Translate the directions by writing them down.
2. Look for directions that come with purchases and bring in examples of picture directions. For example, these might include how to install a VCR. Share these picture directions and build a file for later use in the classroom.
3. Assemble a list of examples of international symbols used to provide information. These will help you when you begin your task.
4. Choose a procedure that you are familiar with. Outline the procedure in writing. Use short sentences. Your procedure should reflect safety in each step.
5. Your outline might be long. Now you must begin to see how many ideas can be presented in one drawing. "One picture is worth 1,000 words." Group the ideas you would like presented in each drawing.
6. Produce your first picture using drawings, photography, computers, or clip art and ask fellow students to interpret it. Use feedback they give you to modify and change areas that are not clear. Color can be added to emphasize important points.
7. Repeat step #6 until you have finished describing how to do the activity.
8. Check your booklet by having another student write a set of directions while he or she looks at your picture directions.

Suggested Resources

Colored pencils
Markers
Stick figures
Stencils
Drawing equipment
Overhead projector
Opaque projector
Photographs
Computers
Clip art

Technology Connections

1. Communication includes having a message sent, received, and understood.
2. The communication process consists of a transmitter, a channel over which the message travels, and a receiver. In this activity, what is the transmitter? The channel? The receiver?
3. What purpose (inform, persuade, educate, or entertain) does your communication system accomplish?
4. How did you use each of the seven technological resources to create your communication system?

CHAPTER 6

GRAPHIC COMMUNICATION

MAJOR CONCEPTS

After reading this chapter, you will know that:

- In a graphic communication system, the channel carries images or printed words.
- Pictorial drawings show an object in three dimensions. Orthographic drawings generally show top, front, and side views of an object.
- The five elements needed for photography are light, film, a camera, chemicals, and a dark area.
- Four types of printing are relief, gravure, screen, and offset.
- Word processing improves office productivity.
- Desktop publishing systems combine words and pictures.

INTRODUCTION

The word **graph** means "to draw" or "to write." Graphic communication systems use images or printed words to carry a message.

A graphic message is designed for a particular audience. The first step is to decide who the audience is. Next, a communication process is chosen that will send the message at the least cost. That is, the most cost-effective process is chosen.

Suppose you are starting a lawnmowing business. You want to let people know about it. Your audience is the people whose lawns you want to mow, your neighbors. Although you could advertise in the newspaper, handing out a printed flyer might be more cost-effective.

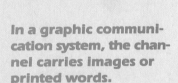

In a graphic communication system, the channel carries images or printed words.

Advertisements are designed to appeal to specific audiences. (Courtesy of Pepsi Cola, USA)

(Courtesy Maxell Robots)

PLANNING AND DESIGNING THE MESSAGE

Graphic communication starts with planning and design. To design a graphic message, a person chooses words and pictures and places them creatively on paper. Ink colors, paper, and sizes and styles of lettering (type fonts) must be chosen.

Design elements like lines or bars across the page may be added.

There are many graphic communication systems. Some of these are: writing, freehand drawing and sketching, technical drawing (drawing using special tools), photography, printing, and photocopying.

Word processors are electronic tools. But they are also graphic communication systems. In word processing, the message is made up of images and printed words on paper.

WRITING

The earliest writing we know about is **cuneiform writing**. It was first used by people who lived in the Middle East about 6,000 years ago (4000 B.C.). Cuneiform writing was done by pressing a wedge-shaped tool into wet clay. A symbol made up of these wedge-shaped marks stood for a word or idea. Later, the Egyptians used a writing method called **hieroglyphics**.

Elements of Design

Eight elements help to communicate designs effectively. These elements are shape, line, texture, color, proportion, balance, unity, and rhythm.

Shapes can include geometric figures, like squares and triangles, or can include irregular shapes such as those found in nature. **Lines** put boundaries around space and form objects. **Texture** refers to the way the surface of an object looks and feels. **Color** makes designs exciting and more interesting. Color can also make objects appear larger or smaller, heavier or lighter, or closer or farther away. **Proportion** and **balance** refer to the sizes within a design and how they relate to one another. Some designs have symmetry. That is, all parts of the design have corresponding parts (a mirror image) on the other side of the center of the design. **Unity** refers to the way all parts of a design produce a simple effect. **Rhythm** relates to the way the eye of the viewer moves around the entire design.

Hieroglyphic symbols are pictures of things. Hieroglyphics were carved into stone, or painted on stone or paper.

The first alphabet came from people living in the Middle East. The Hebrew alphabet started with the letters "aleph" and "bet." Later, the first two letters of the Greek alphabet were "alpha" and "beta." These letters together give us the word **alphabet**.

Hieroglyphics from the pyramid at Nur-Sudan. (Courtesy of Egyptian Tourist Authority)

THE INVENTION OF PAPER

Paper was first made from the papyrus plant by the Egyptians around 2500 B.C. The fibers of the plant were soaked in water. They were then mashed together and matted to form thin sheets. Paper like the paper we use today was invented by the Chinese about 2,000 years ago. But it was not until about A.D. 1400 that paper of really good quality was made. Lightweight, low-cost paper made it easier for people to record their ideas and share them with others. Technology boomed once people could share ideas. People could learn from what others had done. They could build on the ideas of others and improve on them.

FREEHAND DRAWING AND SKETCHING

In prehistoric times, people drew pictures on cave walls. Most of these cave pictures were hunting scenes. They showed people, animals, and weapons like spears and arrows. Perhaps these early artists thought their drawings had magical powers. They may have drawn hunting scenes to improve their luck in hunting.

People began to use drawings for decoration. They scratched and painted designs on weapons and pottery. As technology changed, people found many more uses for designs and pictures.

A drawing can be simple or complex. Generally, drawings begin as **sketches**. A sketch is a simplified view of an object or place. It gives the outline and a few details.

Better drawings were necessary when people needed to communicate the true sizes and shapes of objects. Craftspeople had to work from drawings to make objects. During the period called the Renaissance (about A.D. 1350-1500) methods of drawing improved greatly.

An early cave drawing

A simple sketch

TECHNICAL DRAWING

Technical drawing communicates true size and shape. It is a way of producing highly accurate drawings using special tools. Architects draw buildings and designers draw new products using technical drawing.

In technical drawing, a **drawing board** and drawing **instruments** are used. Some of these instruments are the T square, the plastic triangle, and pencils of many kinds.

The T square is held tightly against the edge of the drawing board and is moved up or down. In this way, parallel horizontal lines can be drawn. The plastic triangle is placed against the

In technical drawing, a relatively small number of tools are used to produce complex drawings. (Courtesy of Keuffel & Esser Company, Parsippany, NJ 07054)

By moving the T square and triangle on the drawing board, horizontal, vertical, and angled lines can be drawn.

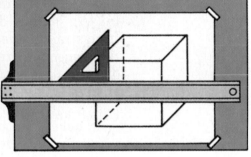

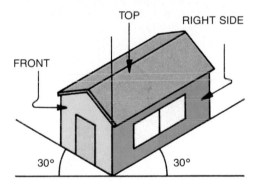

A three-dimensional view (an isometric drawing) of a house.

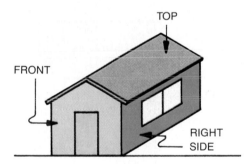

In an oblique drawing, the object is drawn with a straight-on view of one surface.

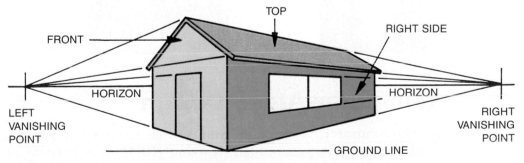

A perspective drawing makes an object look natural. If the horizontal lines on the drawing are extended, they will meet at two points called **vanishing points.** This is an example of two-point perspective.

long edge of the T square. It is used as a guide to draw vertical lines or lines at an angle. Using these instruments, a person can draw lines in many directions. Drawings of objects can be made to look very real.

Technical drawings can show objects in two ways. One way is to draw the object in three dimensions. This is called a **pictorial** drawing. Three types of pictorial drawings are isometric, oblique, and perspective drawings.

An **isometric** drawing is drawn within a framework of three lines. These are called an isometric axis. They represent three edges of a cube that meet at one corner. Two of the lines of the axis are always drawn at an angle of 30 degrees to the horizontal. An **oblique** drawing shows one side of the object as seen from straight ahead. The other two sides are shown at an angle. A **perspective** drawing is the most real-looking. In this kind of drawing, parts of the object that are farther away are drawn smaller than nearer parts.

A second kind of technical drawing is **orthographic**. Here, each side of an object is shown in a separate picture. Three views (front, side, and top) are often enough to show the object clearly.

Pictorial drawings show an object in three dimensions. Orthographic drawings generally show top, front, and side views of an object.

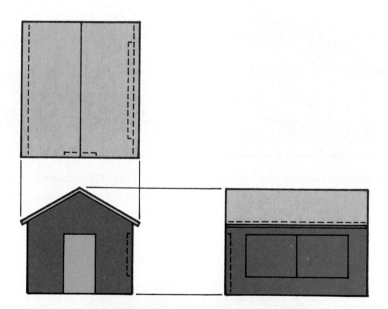

An orthographic drawing of a house. Three views are enough to completely describe its shape and size.

Computer-Aided Design

The computer has brought about great changes in drawing and design. **Computer-aided drafting** (CAD) has become an important tool of engineers, drafters, and designers. CAD stands for computer-aided design or computer-aided drafting. CADD stands for computer-aided design and drafting.

A plotter uses pens with different color inks to make drawings. (Courtesy of Hewlett-Packard)

A CAD operator using a CAD system to model an automobile. (Courtesy of Ford Motor Company)

Computers are changing technical drawing. With computer-aided drafting (CAD) systems, drafters can create, change, and document more complex drawings than ever before. (Courtesy of Autodesk)

A CAD system is made up of people, software, and hardware. The people who run the CAD system may be drafters, engineers, or technicians. It depends on the kind of job that is being done.

CAD software are computer programs that make the computer carry out needed tasks. Programs can be used to draw lines and arcs, put symbols on a drawing, turn it around or upside down, or zoom in for a closer look at one part of it.

CAD hardware includes a keyboard, mouse (a device used to point to things on the screen), display screen, drawing tablet, and plotter. The person at the keyboard can type in commands, use the mouse, or draw directly on the tablet. Sometimes, seeing the design on the display screen is all that is needed. If a hard copy (finished drawing on paper) is wanted, the pen plotter is used.

Using CAD, a designer can create drawings on a screen that are then stored in the computer's memory. CAD drawings may show mechanical parts, or they may show buildings or electronic circuits.

A CAD system can also help to find a design's strengths and weaknesses. It can show how an electronic circuit will work. It can tell whether a mechanical part will hold up under use. In addition, many CAD systems will list parts needed for a design, along with their cost.

Here are some ways CAD systems are better than hand-drawn designs:

1. Doing design and drafting together saves time.
2. Doing other jobs at the same time as design and drafting (such as providing lists of parts) reduces the chance of a mistake.
3. CAD makes it possible to save time on drawing. It takes two to eight times as long to do a drawing by hand as it does to do it using CAD.

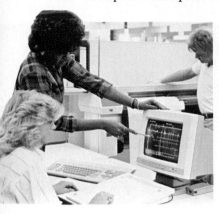

CAD systems come in all sizes. This is a small system being used in a school. (Courtesy of Texas Instruments, Inc.)

4. A design change or improvement can be made more quickly using CAD.
5. Drawings are more accurate and consistent from one to the next using CAD.

CAD has greatly increased the productivity of people who do design work. They can spend more time thinking about their designs and less time doing the actual drawings.

PHOTOGRAPHY

Artists use their eyes, minds, and hands in creating a picture. In photography, light and chemicals put the picture on the paper. The word **photography** means "to write with light."

All cameras have at least five parts in common: a dark chamber, a lens, a mechanism (usually a shutter) that lets light in for a controlled amount of time, a viewfinder for previewing the placement of an object, and a place for film.

The earliest camera-like device was first used in Italy in the 1500s. It was called the **camera obscura**. In Italian, this means "dark chamber." The camera obscura was just that—a room with no windows. It had a tiny lens set in the wall facing the street. The only light in the room came through this lens. This was a beam that cast an upside-down image of whatever was outside onto the wall. An artist put a canvas on the wall across from the lens so the image appeared on it. Then the artist traced and painted over the image.

In 1839, a Frenchman named Louis Daguerre presented a new process he had invented. It was the first true photography. His film was a copper sheet coated with silver and silver iodide. Silver iodide is sensitive to light. A chemical change takes place when light strikes it. This change formed an image on Daguerre's film. Making a photograph this way took a long time. A person had to sit very still in front of the camera for about half an hour. The pictures were called **daguerreotypes**.

A nineteenth-century daguerreotype of feminist Lucy Stone. (Courtesy of National Portrait Gallery, Smithsonian Institution, Washington, D.C.)

In the late 1800s, George Eastman introduced the Kodak camera. Until then, photography had been only for professionals. They had the costly equipment and studios needed for the job. The Kodak camera changed all that. Suddenly, anybody could take pictures. The company advertised, "You press the button, we do the rest." The camera came with a roll of film that could take 100 pictures. A Kodak owner sent the camera and film to the Kodak company for processing. New film was loaded into the camera and it was returned to the owner. Soon, every family owned a camera and a collection of snapshots.

The Five Elements of Photography

Five elements are necessary for photography:

1. **light** (the sun, a light bulb, or a flash);
2. **film** (color or black and white);
3. a **camera** (large or small, with all 5 parts);
4. **chemicals** (for developing film and printing pictures);
5. a **darkroom** to develop the film in.

All photography requires **light**. Light reflected by an object is recorded on light-sensitive film. Early photographs were generally taken indoors. A source of very bright light was needed. For this, magnesium powder was burned. It did give off a bright light, but it was smoky and dangerous.

Today, **film** is made from an acetate (a plastic) base, covered with silver and other substances. There are different kinds of film for different purposes. There are films for taking pictures in color and in black and white. There are films (infrared) that give an image of the heat coming from objects. Some films can be used to take pictures at night, or in places where there is almost no light.

Film is coated with tiny grains of silver bromide, which is sensitive to light. When the camera shutter opens, the lens focuses light on the film. The grains are exposed to light. When they are developed, the exposed grains turn parts of the film black. The parts that were not exposed to light are washed away during fixing. They leave clear areas on the film. In this way, a **negative** is made.

There are four major types of **cameras**. The **view camera** is the simplest. It has a lens at the front and film at the back. A shutter to control the time that light comes in lies just behind the lens. Behind that is a dark chamber called a bellows. It is

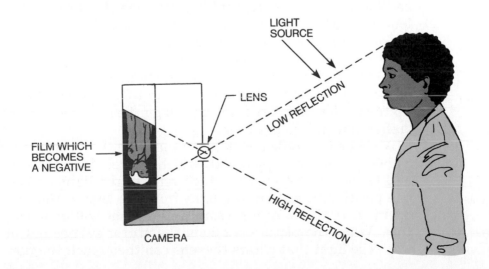

LIGHT SOURCE

LENS

LOW REFLECTION

FILM WHICH BECOMES A NEGATIVE

HIGH REFLECTION

CAMERA

Formation of a negative image on film.

A view camera is large and bulky, but can be used to take high-quality pictures. (Courtesy of Zone VI Studios Inc.)

A twin-lens reflex camera that has interchangeable lenses. (Photo by Joseph Schuyler)

made so it can be stretched out or made smaller to focus through the lens. The camera is very large. It must be supported by a three-legged stand called a tripod, but produces very large negatives of very high quality.

In a view camera you look through the back of the camera to see what you are photographing. In a **viewfinder camera**, you look through a separate viewfinder. Instamatic® cameras and disk cameras are viewfinder cameras.

A **twin lens reflex camera** uses two lenses. One is for viewing. The other is for focusing light on the film. This kind of camera also has a mirror that reflects the light from the viewing lens up to the top for a right-side-up image. That's where the name "reflex camera" comes from.

A **single lens reflex camera** is much like the twin lens reflex camera. It has only one lens, which is used for both viewing and focusing. The mirror, which reflects the light, moves. In one position, it reflects the light from the lens to the viewing opening. In this way, a person can see what will be in the picture. When the picture is taken, the mirror swings out of the way. The light that enters the lens can then reach the film.

The five elements needed for photography are light, film, a camera, chemicals, and a dark area.

A single lens reflex (SLR) camera. (Courtesy of Minolta Corp.)

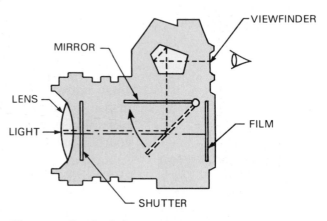

Diagram of a single lens reflex camera. (From Dennis, APPLIED PHOTOGRAPHY, © 1985 by Delmar Publishers Inc. Used with permission)

Chemicals are used to develop film. They are also used to print photographs. Three kinds of chemicals used are **developer, stop bath**, and **fixer**. Developer turns the exposed silver bromide grains black. Stop bath stops the developing. Fixer washes away all the unexposed grains. It clears those parts of the film that light did not touch.

Photographic paper and film are very sensitive to light. For that reason, developing is carried out in a dark area. This can be a corner of a room that can be completely darkened. It can be a closet. A room used for developing is called a **darkroom**. A home darkroom can be very small and simple. Professional darkrooms are filled with costly and complicated equipment.

A darkroom is used to develop photographs. (Photo by Michael Hacker)

THE DEVELOPMENT OF PRINTING

One of the most important advances in graphic communication took place in Germany around A.D. 1450. Johannes Gutenberg invented a way to make separate letters (movable type). He poured hot metal into molds. Before Gutenberg's invention, letters had to be carved one at a time. This was slow and costly.

With Gutenberg's type, books could be printed more quickly and cheaply. His printing press was soon used in many other countries. More people learned to read and they learned from what they read. Today millions of books and magazines are printed. People in the remotest places can share the knowledge of the world.

Newspapers were the first mass communications medium. They were being published in America as early as 1704. The first colonial newspaper was the *Boston News-Letter*. Most early newspapers were printed on hand-operated presses. About 150 years passed before companies were using machine-run presses. As late as 1837, Harper and Brothers, a company in New York, still printed books using a press powered by a mule.

Toward the end of the 1800s, newspapers became very popular. By then, machines had been developed that could print large numbers of newspapers very quickly. Newspapers brought people closer together. People could read about events in the rest of the world. They could read about them soon after the events took place.

Newspapers have had to change with the times. In 1840, the largest paper in the country, the *New York Sun*, printed only 40,000 newspapers a day. Today, the *New York Times* prints 1.5 million Sunday papers. News stories are written using word processors instead of typewriters. The pages are optically scanned by lasers and sent to printing plants by satellite. Huge printing presses use enormous spools of paper.

Some newspapers, like the *Wall Street Journal* and *USA Today*, are printed in several different places. Pages are transmitted by satellite to cities around the country. The papers are then printed locally and distributed by trucks. This is faster and less costly than printing the papers in one city and sending them out by truck or airplane to other cities.

With the help of satellite communications, newspapers like **USA Today** can be printed and distributed at several locations. (Courtesy of Scott Malay/Gannett Co. Inc.)

Johannes Gutenberg and the Printing of Books

In Mainz, Germany, about 50 years before Columbus discovered America, Johannes Gutenberg invented a new and faster way to print books. This invention was a huge leap forward for communication technology. It changed all aspects of society.

When Gutenberg was a young man, he studied using books that had been handwritten. He watched monks as they worked for years to make copies of the Bible.

Gutenberg wanted everyone to be able to own books. He felt there should be a way to make copies more quickly than writing them out by hand. He began to think about mechanical printing. He knew that wooden blocks were used to print playing cards. He also knew of metal stamps used to press markings onto metal coins.

Gutenberg knew that printing books

Johannes Gutenberg, inventor of the mechanical printing press.
(Courtesy of Inter Nationes)

Gutenberg's printing press
(Courtesy of Inter Nationes)

mechanically would mean making separate, movable pieces of type for the letters. He knew that it would take a long time to carve wood into printing letters. Besides, wood is soft, and would wear out quickly. He decided to make letters of metal. For each letter, Gutenberg made a steel stamp. He pressed the steel stamp into a block of softer copper, making a mold. Into this mold he poured molten metal, an alloy of lead and other metals. He could produce as many pieces of type as he wanted from one mold for a letter.

Making an endless supply of type with which to print was not enough. Gutenberg needed a way to hold the type in place during the printing process. He used a screw press (like the kind used to squeeze grapes) to do the printing. He also had to find an ink that would stick to the metal type.

By 1455, after three years of hard work, Gutenberg had printed about 200 copies of the Bible using his new press. He printed thirty of them on vellum, a paper made from animal skin. For the vellum, the hides of almost 10,000 calves were used.

Gutenberg invented the first printing system. The system had a press and good paper and ink. Its metal type could be used to print the words on one page of a book, then removed and reset to make the words on another page. With his press, people could make large numbers of books. Books became less expensive, so the average person could own books. Soon, many people were using Gutenberg's invention to print books. More books allowed knowledge to spread to all corners of the earth.

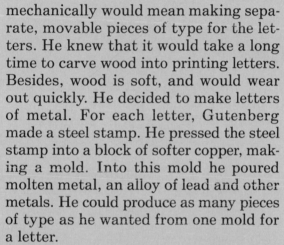

One of the original Gutenberg bibles (Courtesy of Inter Nationes)

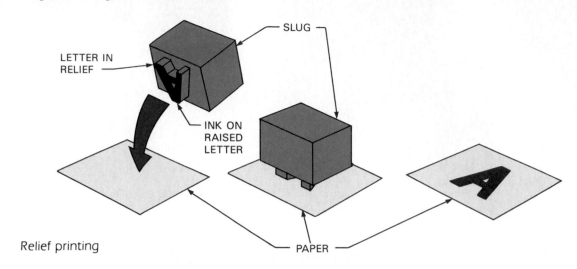

Relief printing

Relief Printing

Gutenberg's printing method used raised surfaces. This method is called **relief printing**. In relief printing, only the raised surfaces of the letters are inked. The lower surfaces are not inked. When the letter is pressed against a piece of paper, only the inked surface prints.

Relief printing is also known as **letterpress printing**. It is still used today, with a few improvements. Newspapers and greeting cards are printed using this method.

Most typewriters use relief printing. The letters that print on the paper are raised surfaces. When the letter strikes the ribbon, it transfers ink to the paper. Typewriting is a middle step between handwriting and printing.

Gravure Printing

It is also possible to print from a lowered surface. First, a line is scratched into the surface of a piece of metal. The surface is inked, and then wiped dry. The ink stays in the scratch. When a piece of paper is pressed against the metal surface, the paper pulls the ink out. This type of printing is called **gravure**, or **intaglio printing**. Gravure is used to print some magazines. It is used to print the magazine section of most Sunday newspapers.

Screen Printing

To print posters and T-shirt designs, a stencil is used. The stencil lets ink pass through some areas, and keeps ink from

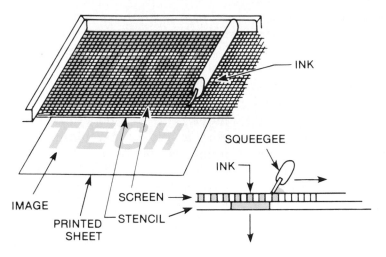

Open image areas allow ink to pass through the screen onto the paper below.
(Reprinted from Barden & Hacker, COMMUNICATION TECHNOLOGY, © 1990 by Delmar Publishers Inc. Used by permission.)

passing through others. A stencil, often made from plastic, is attached to a silk screen. The silk screen is stretched tightly on a wooden frame. The screen touches the paper or fabric to be printed, transferring the ink. This method is known as screen printing.

Four types of printing are relief, gravure, screen, and offset.

Offset Lithography

Today, most printing is done by **offset lithography**. **Lithography** means writing **(graphy)** on stone **(litho)**. It is based on the fact that oil and water do not mix.

Lithography was invented by a German artist, Alois Senefelder. He drew a

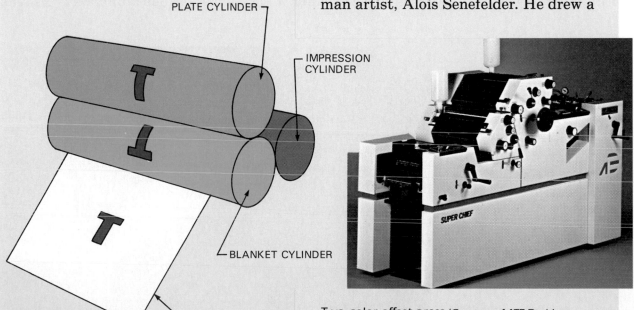

Offset printing

Two-color offset press (Courtesy of ATF-Davidson Company, Whitinsville, MA 01588)

line with a waxy crayon on a smooth, flat piece of limestone. He wet the entire surface, then applied an oil-base ink. The ink would stick only to the crayon lines. When the limestone surface was pressed against a piece of paper, only the inked crayon lines would print.

Today's offset printing uses metal sheets rather than pieces of limestone. The idea, though, is the same. Using a photographic process, a greasy print of the image to be printed is placed on a sheet of aluminum. The aluminum sheet is called an **offset plate**. The plate is wrapped around a metal cylinder. The cylinder is wetted.

Next, the plate is inked. Ink sticks only to the greasy image, not to the rest of the plate. As the plate turns on the cylinder, it presses against another cylinder. This second cylinder is covered with a thin rubber blanket. The inked image is transferred (or offset) to the rubber blanket. The image is now reversed. The rubber blanket turns, and paper goes through the press. The image is offset again, this time to the paper. Now the image reads correctly.

WORD PROCESSING

Word processors combine the typewriter and the computer. What you type on the keyboard is stored in the computer. You can see what you are typing on the video display screen. If you make a mistake, you can type over it to correct it. Only after every word is the way you want it do you print the text on paper. All your corrections are made before you print out the page.

Word processors have many other useful capabilities. If a typist spells a word wrong throughout a letter, she or he can use the **search and replace** command. The word processor then hunts for the word each time it was used in the letter, and corrects the spelling. To move paragraphs around, a typist can

Word processing improves office productivity.

Word processing is rapidly replacing typing in most offices (Courtesy of Michael Hacker)

152

use the **move** command. To copy a chart from one page to another, the typist can use the **copy** command. In most offices, word processors are being used instead of typewriters. Word processors save time and help typists do better work.

DESKTOP PUBLISHING

Desktop publishing lets a person turn out a book or newsletter, page by page. This includes text, headlines, and pictures. Desktop publishing uses a computer, special software, a mouse, and a laser printer.

Desktop publishing permits you to compose a page layout using a computer. The finished layout is then output by a printer. (Courtesy of Aldus Corporation)

The system lets you place the words and pictures on the screen just as you want them to appear on paper. The image you see is called a **WYSIWYG image**. WYSIWYG is pronounced "whizzy-wig," and it stands for "what you see is what you get."

Companies can use desktop publishing to turn out their own newsletters and advertisements. The software is easy to use. Generally, a person chooses the width of the column and the size of the type and its style. Graphics are then placed on the page. These can be pictures, designs, or even photographs. Using a **scanner**, any photograph can be made to appear on the screen.

The text of the page is then placed on the screen by moving it from a word processor. The page can be rearranged by moving pictures and text around, at the touch of a key.

Desktop publishing systems combine words and pictures.

Only one copy of each page is printed from a desktop publishing system. If only a few copies of it are needed, a copying machine can be used to print them. Most of the time, many copies are needed. To do that, offset printing is used. The page is reproduced photographically on an offset plate. An offset printing press produces the number of copies needed. For this reason, desktop publishing is called a pre-press operation.

Today, some newspapers use a process called **pagination** to make up their pages. The whole page can be viewed on a screen,

Samples of materials generated by the desktop publishing process. (Courtesy of Aldus Corporation)

A computerized phototype-
setting machine (Courtesy of
Compugraphic Association)

or a person can zoom in on one column or sentence. Once the page is ready, it is sent electronically to a **phototypesetter**. This machine works like a computerized printer. It makes a high-quality copy of the newspaper page. From this copy an offset plate is made, and printing begins.

COMPUTER PRINTERS

Mechanical typewriters gave way to electric machines in the 1940s. A popular electric typewriter of the 1960s and 1970s, the IBM Selectric, needed about 1,500 mechanical adjustments, as many as some automobiles.

The newest typewriters are **electronic**. Many of the mechanical tasks have been taken over by integrated circuits. (To read about integrated circuits, see pages 96-97.) Electronic machines are easier to maintain and adjust. They can do more than old machines, as well. Many electronic typewriters have a memory. They can store many pages of information. They can also center text and underline words automatically.

Computer printers have also improved. Three types of printers are **daisy wheel**, **dot-matrix**, and **laser** printers. A daisy wheel printer uses a daisy-shaped printhead with many "petals" carrying the letters, numbers, and other printing characters at their tips. When a typewriter key is pressed, the daisy wheel spins, moving the proper petal into position. The petal hits the paper to print the letter. The quality of this kind of printing is excellent. It is called "letter quality" because it is good enough to use on business letters.

Dot-matrix printers are often less costly than daisy wheel printers. They use a different printing technology. The dot-matrix printhead is a rectangular group of pins. When a letter on the keyboard is pressed, some of the pins stick out to form the letter. These press into a ribbon, printing the letter on the paper (see Chapter 4). Dot-matrix printers can form all kinds of

A daisy wheel (Courtesy of
Michael Hacker)

shapes, not just letters and numbers. They can be used to produce graphs, charts, and drawings.

Laser printers can print both letter-quality text and graphics. They provide better quality printing than either daisy-wheel or dot-matrix printers.

Laser Printers

Laser printers are often used in desktop publishing. They can turn out high-quality pages of both text and pictures very quickly.

At the heart of a laser printer is a **photosensitive drum**. The drum is made from aluminum. It looks like a soda-pop can. The drum is coated with material that is sensitive to light.

The drum turns. As it turns, it passes under a wire that is as long as the drum and fixed in a position above it. The wire carries electricity. It is called a **corona wire**. (A corona is the bright light you see when lightning flashes. The air around the lightning ionizes. That is, it becomes charged with electricity and can conduct electricity.) The air space between the corona wire and the drum also ionizes. The air then conducts electricity. An electrical charge flows from the corona wire to the surface of the drum.

After it turns past the corona wire, the drum has a charge over its surface of 600 volts of static electricity. This is a high negative charge.

A laser beam then focuses light on parts of the drum. The drum becomes positively charged when the laser light strikes it. Now the drum has negative charges where there was no light and positive charges where the laser light struck it. The drum carries the image to be printed in the form of positive and negative charges.

Information to be printed is sent from the computer to the laser as a series of electric **pulses**. The laser pulses go on and off according to the computer data. The pulses of light go through a lens and then the beam hits a six-sided mirror. The mirror turns, making the laser beam move in an arc. The beam is focused by another lens. Then it bounces off another mirror. Finally, the beam sweeps across the drum in a horizontal line. It creates sections of positive charge along the line as it pulses.

The drum keeps turning. Horizontal lines of charge are added until the whole

Laserjet II printer (Courtesy of Hewlett-Packard)

A negative static charge is applied to the surface of the drum.

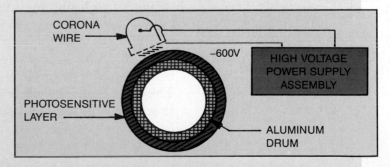

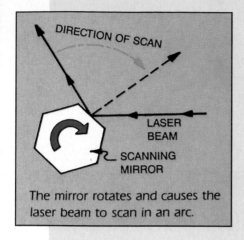

DIRECTION OF SCAN

LASER BEAM

SCANNING MIRROR

The mirror rotates and causes the laser beam to scan in an arc.

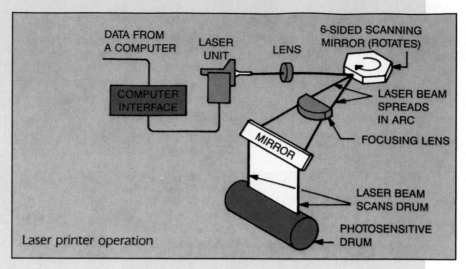

DATA FROM A COMPUTER

LASER UNIT

LENS

6-SIDED SCANNING MIRROR (ROTATES)

COMPUTER INTERFACE

LASER BEAM SPREADS IN ARC

FOCUSING LENS

MIRROR

LASER BEAM SCANS DRUM

PHOTOSENSITIVE DRUM

Laser printer operation

surface of the drum has been covered.

Toner, a black powder made of iron grains and plastic resin, is put onto the drum. The toner is negatively charged. Opposite charges attract each other. The toner sticks to the positively charged areas.

Paper is charged positively by another corona wire. The image on the drum then is pulled off onto the paper. As a last step, the toner is melted. It is forced into the paper by heat and pressure, fixing the image on the paper.

PHOTOCOPYING

In the Middle Ages, copying was done by hand. Monks knew how to read and write, so the job of copying documents fell to them. In 1937, a New York City law student named Chester Carlson came up with a fast way to make copies. He called it **xerography**, which means "dry writing." In 1959, the Xerox Company produced a copying machine that could easily be used in an office. It could make copies without messy inks or fluids.

Copying machines make use of photography and static electricity. You create static electricity when you walk across a rug on a cold, dry day and then touch a doorknob. You build up an electrical charge on your body. The charge is discharged when you touch an object with a different charge. Similar charges (two negative charges or two positive charges) repel each other. Unlike charges (positive and negative) attract each other.

Copying machines use a metal plate with a coating that is sensitive to light (see 1 in the diagram below). The metal plate gets a positive charge as it passes under a wire in the copying machine (2). The paper to be copied is exposed to a very bright light (3). The light is reflected by the white areas. It is not reflected by the areas that are dark with printing or writing. The light from the white areas wipes out the positive charge on the metal plate. The positive charge remains where the light

An early form of copying

156

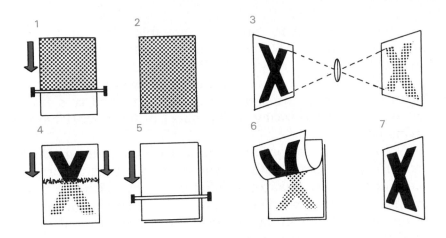

Diagram of the xerographic process (Courtesy of Xerox Corp.)

was not reflected. A negatively charged black powder called **toner** is dusted over the plate. It sticks to the positively charged areas (4). Another sheet of paper is charged positively (5). It attracts the toner (6). Last, the paper is heated. The heat bonds the toner to the paper and makes a finished copy (7).

SUMMARY

In a graphic communication system, the channel carries images or printed words. Some types of graphic communications systems are writing, freehand drawing and sketching, technical drawing, photography, printing, word processing, and photocopying.

The design of a graphic message includes choosing the words and pictures to be used. It also includes selecting appealing colors, design elements, and sizes and styles of lettering.

Cuneiform writing started around 4000 B.C. Later, the Egyptians developed hieroglyphics. They also made paper from the papyrus plant.

Generally, drawings begin as sketches. A sketch is a simplified view of an object or place.

Technical drawing is a way of recording and passing along ideas and information in a drawing. While many technical drawings are made by hand with instruments, computer aided drafting (CAD) is being used more and more by engineers, drafters, and designers.

Pictorial drawings show an object in three dimensions. Orthographic drawings generally show separate top, front, and side views of an object.

The five elements needed for photography are light, film, a camera, chemicals, and a dark area. Four types of cameras are the view camera, the viewfinder camera, the twin lens reflex camera, and the single lens reflex camera.

Johannes Gutenberg invented movable type and the printing press around 1450. Since then, printing technology has changed and improved greatly. Relief printing is printing from a raised surface. Gravure printing is printing from a lowered surface. Screen printing uses a stencil attached to a fine silk screen. In offset printing, a flat sheet of light-sensitive material is used.

Word processors combine typing with computing. Desktop publishing systems combine words and pictures to form complete documents. Desktop publishing starts with WYSIWYG images on a computer display screen. The elements of the image of an entire page can be changed and moved around. A high-quality copy is then printed.

Three kinds of computer printers are daisy wheel, dot-matrix, and laser printers. Laser printers print high-quality graphics and text.

Photocopiers make use of photography and static electricity. Negatively charged toner is attracted to a positively charged piece of paper and fused to it by heat.

REVIEW QUESTIONS

1. What is graphic communication?
2. Make an isometric and an orthographic drawing of a 2" x 2" x 1" block.
3. List two ways CAD has changed technical drawing.
4. Using the library as a resource, name five careers that require technical drawing.
5. What five elements are needed for photography?
6. How is a single lens reflex camera different from a viewfinder camera?
7. How did Johannes Gutenberg improve communication technology?
8. Give an example of something printed by each of the following processes:
   a. relief printing
   b. gravure printing
   c. offset printing
   d. screen printing
9. How does desktop publishing differ from word processing?
10. How is static electricity used in laser printers and copying machines?

KEY WORDS

CAD	Gravure printing	Orthographic	Screen printing
Daisy wheel	Isometric	Perspective	Technical
Desktop	Laser printer	Phototypesetter	drawing
publishing	Negative	Pictorial	
Dot matrix	Offset printing	Relief printing	

SEE YOUR TEACHER FOR THE CROSSTECH PUZZLE

TEAM PICTURE

Setting the Stage

It's only the first day of track practice and already the team is looking depressed. Every other team got brand new uniforms. Because of a budgeting mistake, the track team will have to wait until next year.

"Isn't there something we can do to get uniforms by ourselves?" asked Marty. "How about making our own!" said Amy.

Your Challenge

Design and make a stencil or iron-on transfer using a computer and graphics software. Use it to personalize a T-shirt or sweatshirt.

Procedure

1. Be sure to wear safety glasses and a lab coat.
2. Look through books, magazines, etc. for design ideas.
3. Use a computer to draw the image you want printed on the T-shirt.
4. If you are using a *graphics tablet,* it may be possible to digitize your design by 'tracing' it into the computer memory.
5. If you are using a *video camera* as the input device, it may be possible to digitize your own portrait! This requires special equipment and software such as Computereyes® or MacVision®.
6. If you are using software such as Print Shop®, many graphics are already included in a Graphics Library.
7. Once you are satisfied with your graphic, print it out on a dot matrix printer.
8. If you are using the Underware® direct transfer iron-on printer ribbon, and text is included in your design, FLIP YOUR DESIGN HORIZONTALLY to produce a mirror image *before* printing it out.
9. Iron the image directly onto a T-shirt. The transfer is safe and washable.
10. If you are using thermal screens to produce a stencil with the thermofax machine, do *not* flip your design into a mirror image. Instead, print it out using a dark printer ribbon.
11. To make a stencil using the thermal screens, simply pass the computer printout, together with a piece of thermal screen, through the thermofax machine.

Suggested Resources

Safety glasses and lab aprons
Computer with software for graphics and printing
Graphics tablet, light pen, mouse, or other input device
MacVision® digitizer (requires a video camera)
Computereyes® (requires a video camera)
Dot matrix printer
Thermal screens—9" × 11⅜"
Plastic frames—7¾" × 10½"
Squeegees—7⅜" wide
Screen mounting tape, double-faced, ¼" × 60 yds.
Hinged frame
Versatex textile paints—assorted colors
Thermofax machine
Underware® ribbons—direct iron-on transfer ribbons (available for most printers)

12. Now mount the thermal screen stencil on a hinged frame using double-sided tape.
13. Using a squeegee, press textile paint through the thermal screen stencil directly onto a T-shirt.

Technology Connections

1. Computer-generated graphics, including animation, are important in today's communications. How is this technology used by the entertainment industry? What about the advertising industry?
2. Scientists and engineers use computer-generated graphics and computer aided drawing (CAD) to help plan and test new automobile and aircraft designs. How does this help to keep design costs down?
3. Computer graphics and text are often combined in *desktop publishing*. What is desktop publishing? Do you think it will play an important part in the communications field?

Science and Math Concepts

▶ Graphic communication has been around since prehistoric times. Prehistoric people recorded their experiences on cave walls using natural pigments for color.
▶ Computer animation is done by drawing and erasing the object over and over. Each time the object is redrawn it is moved to a slightly different location.

LEARNING ABOUT CAMERAS AND FILM DEVELOPMENT

Setting the Stage

For approximately 150 years, photography has worked hand in hand with an ever-changing technology to allow a continuous flow of "Modern" cameras to be produced. Each generation of these cameras was a step forward; they became easier to operate, less effort was required to produce a technically excellent negative, and they became more fun to use.

However, because the final result of each step is a camera to be used by individual people, there have always been, and will always be disagreements about which is the finest quality, most esthetically pleasing, easiest to use, or most versatile of these image producers.

Your Challenge

Construct a chart or graph comparing many different aspects of a number of chosen cameras; use this chart or graph to decide which of these cameras is the most desirable to own or use.

Load, expose, develop, and print a foil of black-and-white film. Analyze your photograph.

Procedure

Part 1

1. Bring a camera (any kind) or an advertising brochure (available at any camera store for no charge) to school. (Any school cameras would be helpful, as well as teacher-acquired brochures.)
2. Distribute a checklist to each team of 2-4 students (a graph may be substituted or used in conjunction with the checklist).
3. After handling the cameras or carefully reading the paperwork, the checklist or graph should be used, comparing each of the categories used in the sample checklist.
4. The team should rate the cameras, deciding which one is the most desirable to use, and these results should be reported to the class.

Part 2

Follow the instructions on the handout from your teacher.

Suggested Resources

Various cameras and camera brochures
A metric ruler
A checklist of various camera parts
(No darkroom required)
Graph paper
Handouts from teacher

Technology Connections

1. Advances in optics have reduced size and weight of the camera, increased the ease of focusing and the brightness of the viewing screen, and allowed for auto focus and remarkable zoom lens production.
2. How has the creation of new plastics and other man-made materials affected the size, weight, and strength of more modern cameras?
3. Do you think that the use of computers, both for design and within the camera itself, has affected the types of cameras produced today?

Science and Math Concepts

▶ A normal lens has a focal length (in mm) roughly equivalent to the diagonal of the negative. A portrait lens is two times as long as a normal lens, while a wide-angle lens is between ½ and ¾ the length of a normal lens. A proportion can be used to compare various focal lengths and film sizes.

▶ The larger the film size, the better the quality of the negative produced. A larger negative requires less enlargement to produce the same size photo.

163

PHOTOGRAMS

Setting the Stage

A photogram is a silhouette picture made on a piece of photographic paper. Objects are placed on the paper and exposed to white light. When the picture is developed, we see that the place where the objects were laid is white. The other areas are black. This is because light cannot penetrate these objects, thus producing a white image. The areas exposed to light turn black.

Your Challenge

Create a unique photogram. Use your photogram to convey a message or describe an emotion.

Procedure

1. Locate all materials in your darkroom.
2. If not already mixed, mix the developer, stop bath, and fixer according to the instructions on the package. Wear rubber gloves, eyeglasses, and apron. Place each chemical in a separate tray. Be sure to remember what is in each tray! Your instructor can help you out in mixing the chemicals if you are having problems.
3. Place water in the fourth tray.
4. Turn the safelight on, and turn off all white lights in the room. It will take a little while for your eyes to get used to the dark.
5. Take one piece of photographic paper out of its protective cover. Remember that this paper is sensitive to all light except your safelight. *Do not* expose the paper to the white room lights at this time!
6. Place the photographic paper with the shiny side up on a flat surface under your light source. This could be an enlarger or some other white light source.
7. Place your items for the photogram on top of the photographic paper. Arrange them in a unique way. Try to describe an emotion (love, hate, anger, etc.) or convey a message.
8. Turn on the enlarger or other light source and make the exposure. You may have to experiment with the amount of time the light is on, depending on the intensity of the light hitting the photographic paper.
9. Take the exposed piece of photographic paper and place it in the paper developer tray exposed side up. Rock the tray gently. You should see an image appear on the paper. Depending on the type of developer used, the time will vary. Typical time would be

Suggested Resources

Darkroom or equivalent with running water

Photographic paper—black and white 8.5″ × 11″ (resin coated)

Enlarger (or some other light source)

Photo chemicals
—paper developer
—stop bath
—paper fixer

Four chemical trays (to fit the paper size)

Safelight (for black and white photo paper)

Squeegee

Timer (wall clock or watch)

Objects to create photogram, such as rings, string, nails, etc.

Rubber gloves, safety glasses, and apron

around 1 minute and 20 seconds in the tray. *Note:* If the print turned out too dark, you need less exposure time. If the print turned out very light, you need more exposure time.

10. Next place the print in the stop bath. This is normally for around 10–15 seconds. This stops the development.

11. Place the print in the fixer. Fixing time is typically 5 minutes. The fixer preserves the image by hardening it on the paper. If not fixed properly, the print will turn brown in a period of time.

12. Next, place the print in the water tray. It is good if the water is running slowly in the tray. This removes any excess chemicals from your print. Normal wash time for resin coated paper is 4 minutes.

13. Place your photogram on a flat surface and squeegee off any excess water. Be careful not to scratch the surface of the print.

14. Place your newly created photogram in a print dryer, or just let it air dry.

Technology Connections

1. What are some commercial and industrial uses of photography?
2. How has current technology altered photography? Hint: What about camera types, styles, and uses? Instant photography?
3. How do you think large photographic processing companies process your film and prints?
4. Why is photography a unique communication process as compared to other methods of communication?
5. Why did some objects cause the paper, when processed, to appear gray, not really black or white?

Science and Math Concepts

▶ The photographic process requires certain chemicals to process film and photographic paper.

▶ Silver particles on the surface of photographic paper or film are sensitive to light. The chemical developer turns exposed silver particles black. The stop bath stops developing action. The fixer washes away unexposed silver particles.

CHAPTER 7

ELECTRONIC COMMUNICATION

MAJOR CONCEPTS

After reading this chapter, you will know that:

- In an electronic communication system, the channel carries an electronic or electromagnetic signal.
- Electricity and electronics have greatly changed communication technology.
- The telephone is the most commonly used form of electronic communication.
- In radio communication, the message is sent through the air from a transmitting antenna to a receiving antenna some distance away.
- Computing and communication technologies are being used together to make powerful new tools for working with information.
- A number of computers or computer devices joined together is called a network.

WHAT IS ELECTRONIC COMMUNICATION?

In Chapter 5, you learned that all communication systems have three parts. They are: a transmitter, a receiver, and a channel that carries the message from the transmitter to the receiver. In systems described in Chapter 6, the channel was ink or photographic film. If the channel uses electrical energy to carry the message, it is said to be an **electronic communication system**.

Many graphic communication systems use electronics to make them work better. A microcomputer in a camera may aid in focusing or opening and closing the shutter. A copying machine uses both a microprocessor and electronic circuits. However, neither the copying machine nor the camera are electronic communication systems. Their channels do not carry electronic signals. In a camera, the channel is film. In a copier, the channel is toner.

Electronic communication has created the information age, much as steam engines brought about the industrial age. Today, we can watch live TV broadcasts from other countries. We can speak on the telephone with people who are thousands of miles away. We use automated teller machines to bank after banking hours. All of this is possible because electricity and electronics are used in communication systems.

In electronic communication systems, the message can be sent through cables (as in a telephone system). It can be sent through the air (as on radio). It can be stored (as on recording tapes or compact disks), and moved from place to place. Systems that send messages immediately are called **transmitting and receiving systems**. Systems that store messages electronically are called **recording systems**.

In an electronic communication system, the channel carries an electronic or electromagnetic signal.

Electricity and electronics have greatly changed communication technology.

Electronic communication systems allow these financial traders to have the latest prices from all over the world displayed instantly.
(Courtesy of Positron Industries, Inc.)

TRANSMITTING AND RECEIVING SYSTEMS

The Telegraph

The first electronic communication system to be widely used was the **telegraph**. During the first half of the 1800s, telegraph systems were set up in Europe and the United States. In 1843, Samuel F.B. Morse received $30,000 to build a telegraph line from Washington, D.C. to Baltimore. Morse's first system used a pen that made marks on a piece of paper. He soon replaced it with with a telegraph sounder, a machine that made clacking sounds. The sounds were a code for letters. An operator who knew the code would write down the letters. In 1858, the first telegraph cable was laid across the Atlantic Ocean from England to America. The Morse code, though somewhat changed, is still used today.

The Telephone

There are over 150 million telephones in the United States today. That makes the telephone the most commonly used form of electronic communication. The crank-box telephone of the late 1800s has been replaced today with instruments like TouchTone® phones that have many useful features.

Alexander Graham Bell, the inventor of the telephone, was a teacher of the deaf. He knew a great deal about the way the human ear works. He used this knowledge to invent the telephone. Another inventor, Elisha Gray, patented a device much like Bell's telephone a few hours after Bell did. For several years, Bell and Gray fought in court over who had the patent. Finally, Bell won.

A telephone mouthpiece contains tiny carbon grains. When you speak into it, the sound of your voice presses on these grains. When you speak loudly, the pressure is greater, and the grains become tightly packed. This lets more electric current flow through the telephone circuit. When you speak softly, the grains are more loosely packed. Less electric current flows. The current that flows through the telephone line changes as you change the way you speak.

Electricity flows through the telephone earpiece on the receiving end. It makes a thin piece of metal vibrate. These vibrations change in strength as your speech changes. In this way, what you are saying is exactly reproduced.

Using a Telegraph System

A simple telegraph system has four parts. They are: a telegraph key, a power source, a buzzer or sounder, and wires to connect the sending station to the receiving station.

The operator sends the message by pressing down and letting up on the key. The key can be held down for a short period or time or a long period of time.

Groups of shorts and longs (dots and dashes) stand for letters, numbers, and punctuation marks. These are received by the operator at the other end, who writes down the message. The Morse code is the most commonly used code of this type. It can also be used for signaling with lights.

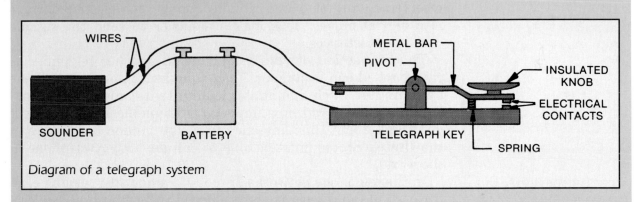

Diagram of a telegraph system

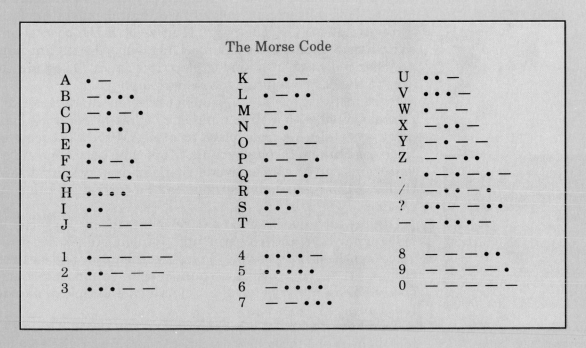

The Morse Code

A	• —	K	— • —	U	• • —
B	— • • •	L	• — • •	V	• • • —
C	— • — •	M	— —	W	• — —
D	— • •	N	— •	X	— • • —
E	•	O	— — —	Y	— • — —
F	• • — •	P	• — — •	Z	— — • •
G	— — •	Q	— — • —	.	• — • — • —
H	• • • •	R	• — •	/	— • • — •
I	• •	S	• • •	?	• • — — • •
J	• — — —	T	—	—	— • • • • —

1	• — — — —	4	• • • • —	8	— — — • •
2	• • — — —	5	• • • • •	9	— — — — •
3	• • • — —	6	— • • • •	0	— — — — —
		7	— — • • •		

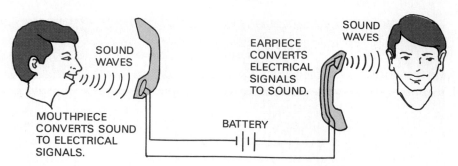

A telephone converts sound to electrical signals and electrical signals back to sound.

The telephone is the most commonly used form of electronic communication.

Sometimes people talking to each other on the telephone are separated by many miles. The electric current must be increased by devices called amplifiers or repeaters to reach the receiver. Some telephone circuits change the electric current into digital pulses. This makes it easier to send the signals over long distances.

The connection of your telephone to another telephone is called **telephone switching**. Telephone switching is now done by computer. Such a computer is built to do only that one job. You can understand how important telephone switching is if you think about this: any one of the 150 million telephones in the United States must be able to call any other telephone in the world.

In the telephone networks of today, a smoothly varying electric current (analog signal) is produced by the mouthpiece microphone. This current is changed into digital pulses much like computer data. The pulses are then sent to the central office switching computer. At the receiving end, the digital pulses are changed back into analog electric current. They are then sent to the earpiece of the receiving telephone.

Since many people are talking on telephones at once, switches are connected with a large number of wires. Fiber optic cables carry some signals from place to place. Microwave relay stations send others through the air. More than one thousand conversations can be carried over a single microwave signal. More than ten thousand conversations can be carried over one optical fiber.

Digital technology makes it possible to use services like call forwarding and call waiting. It also makes the use of voice synthesizers possible. Voice synthesizers are electronic circuits that put together sounds that sound like human speech. These provide telephone numbers and time of day over the phone.

Telephone technology is changing all the time. The cordless telephone is one fairly new device. It contains a radio transmit-

A cordless telephone. (Courtesy of Tandy/Radio Shack)

ter. The transmitter sends a signal to a nearby telephone, which then carries the conversation as usual.

More and more people have telephones in their automobiles. The **cellular radio** is used for car telephones. Like cordless phones, automobile telephones send radio signals. Cordless phone signals travel only short distances. Cellular radio signals let a person in an automobile communicate over a much larger area, such as a city.

In the future, the telephone will be even more useful than it is now. A home telephone will be connected to a computer. You won't need a telephone book to look up a number. Your telephone will call for help automatically when you need the police, an ambulance, or firefighters.

The Automatic Telephone Switch: An Invention Born of Necessity

Inventions often come from people who are in great need of them. In the late 1800s Almon Strowger was a funeral home director in a small town in the Midwest. The town's telephone operator was the wife of the owner of another funeral home. When people called the operator for a funeral home, she would connect them with her husband's.

Mr. Strowger saw his business failing. To save it, he invented a device that would connect telephones without an operator. The switch he invented was the first automatic system to be used in a public exchange. Strowger switches are still in use today in some telephone offices.

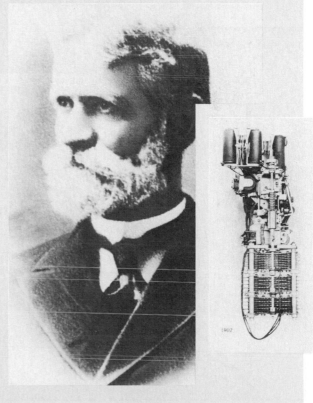

Almon Strowger and his automatic telephone switch
(Courtesy of Science Museum Library, London)

(Courtesy of AT&T Bell Laboratories)

Radio

During the mid-1800s, James Maxwell, a Scottish physicist, showed on paper that it was possible to send signals to other places through the air. Not until the new century, however, were devices built that would send and receive radio waves.

The first truly long-distance radio transmission took place on December 12, 1901, in a deserted old hospital building in Newfoundland, Canada. Guglielmo Marconi heard the three shorts of the Morse code for the letter S. The code had been sent across the Atlantic Ocean over radio waves and picked up by his receiver. People were excited by the invention, called the wireless. Wires were no longer needed to send messages!

Ships were the first to use radio communication. No wires were needed for ship-to-ship or ship-to-shore messages. Ships could send routine messages or calls for help. New inventions such as the vacuum tube allowed voices and music to be heard over radio. Regular radio broadcasts began in the 1920s at

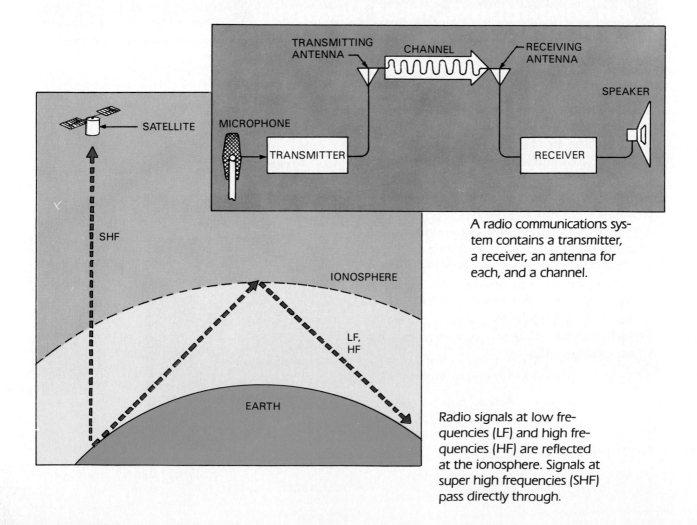

A radio communications system contains a transmitter, a receiver, an antenna for each, and a channel.

Radio signals at low frequencies (LF) and high frequencies (HF) are reflected at the ionosphere. Signals at super high frequencies (SHF) pass directly through.

KDKA in Pittsburgh. Today, there are dozens of radio stations in almost every part of the country.

Radios let us listen to music, news, and sporting events. They give us two-way communication between cars, boats, airplanes, and homes. We can use them to communicate with people in space.

Most radios are built the same way. Radio transmitters create an electric voltage that changes direction from positive to negative (alternates) many times each second. The number of times that it changes each second is called its **frequency**. Frequency is measured in **cycles per second**. One cycle per second is called one hertz.

When alternating voltage from the transmitter is sent to an antenna, an **electromagnetic wave** is launched into the air. Radio signals are electromagnetic waves. Radio signals with low frequencies have **long wavelengths**. Radio signals with high frequencies have **short wavelengths**. Radio waves travel outward in all directions away from the antenna.

Signals of different wavelengths travel differently through the atmosphere. The right wavelength must be chosen for each kind of radio communication. High frequency (HF) radio waves bounce off the atmosphere's upper layer, the **ionosphere**. They can be used for communication between two points on the earth that are very far apart. Super high frequency (SHF) radio waves are used for satellite communication. They travel straight through the ionosphere.

In radio communication, the message goes through the air from a transmitting antenna to a receiving antenna some distance away. The channel is the part of the electromagnetic spectrum used for the signal. Because each transmitter uses a different frequency, many transmitters in the same area can send messages at the same time. That is why you can choose among a number of TV or radio stations.

Radio communication systems can be used in different ways. One transmitter can send out a signal to many listeners. This kind of operation is called **broadcasting**. You know about AM and FM radio broadcasting. If a transmitter is meant for only one receiver, the service is called **point-to-point**. Point-to-point transmissions are useful for communicating with remote places (such as fire-ranger towers) or for mobile users (such as an appliance-repair truck).

Television

In television, an image is changed into electrical signals. The signals travel across a distance. They are changed back into an

In radio communication, the message is sent through the air from a transmitting antenna to a receiving antenna some distance away.

This broadcast antenna system covers an area that includes more than ten million people. (Courtesy of The Port Authority of New York and New Jersey)

Wavelength and Frequency

Electromagnetic waves are waves of energy that travel through space. Radio and TV signals are electromagnetic waves. They travel from one antenna at the transmitter to another antenna at the receiver. Light is also a form of electromagnetic wave. All electromagnetic waves travel through space at the same speed. You may already know what this speed is. Electromagnetic waves travel at the speed of light, about 186,000 miles (or about 300 million meters) each second. So a wave sent out from a radio transmitter (or a light) is 186,000 miles (or about 300 million meters) away one second later. This is true no matter what the frequency of the wave is.

During that same second, the radio transmitter generates the number of wave cycles defined by its frequency. A 10 MHz (Megahertz) transmitter will generate 10 million cycles in one second. These 10 million cycles cover 300 million meters in one second. Therefore, the **wavelength**, or distance covered by one cycle, is:

$$\text{Wavelength} = \frac{300 \text{ million meters per second}}{10 \text{ million cycles per second}}$$

$$\text{Wavelength} = 30 \text{ meters}$$

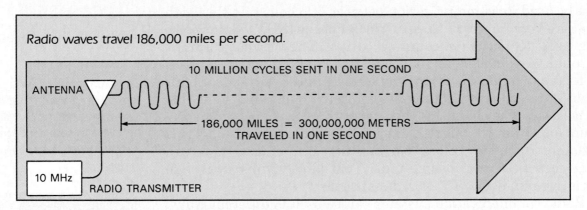

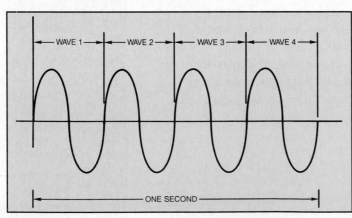

The diagram represents an electromagnetic wave with a frequency of four cycles per second. A wavelength is the distance from one point on one wave to the corresponding point on the next wave. Frequency refers to the number of wavelengths in one second.

Amateur Radio

Radio amateurs, or "ham" radio operators, were among the first to experiment with radio. They made many discoveries that led to the use of shortwave radio and improvements in equipment. Today many ham radio operators still build their own equipment. They can also buy a wide variety of equipment in stores. To use this equipment, they must first pass a written test. They are then issued a license by the Federal Communications Commission.

Today's radio amateurs include people of all ages, from children to grandparents. They use their radios to talk to other amateurs around the world, as well as those across town. Frequently, they provide a public service by making it possible to communicate in an area hit by a natural disaster such as an earthquake or tornado.

Amateur radio ("ham" radio) is a hobby that allows private operators to talk to other hams around the world. This is another example of point-to-point communication. (Photo A courtesy of QST October 1986, Photo B courtesy of American Radio Relay League)

image on a screen. Television is a broadcast communication system. It is much like radio except that the information being carried is seen as well as heard.

The television camera is in the transmitter part of the system. The camera changes the scene into electrical signals **(video).** A device then either stores or transports the video signals. This device is the communication channel. Last, a monitor changes the video into images on a screen. This is the receiver, which is watched by the viewer.

Video signals may be stored in video recorders (for example, a videocassette recorder, VCR). Video may also be sent directly by cable (as in closed-circuit TV). It may be sent by cable TV. It may be sent over the air using TV transmitters.

Cameras change the scene into video signals. The signals can be black and white, or color. Color signals break down light into red, blue, and green for transmission. These signals are reassembled at the monitor.

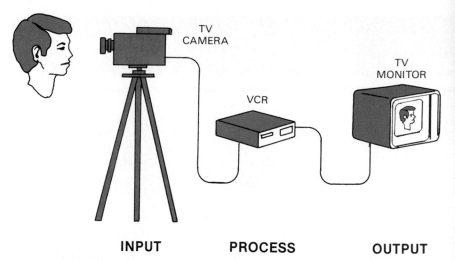

INPUT   **PROCESS**   **OUTPUT**

A TV system converts a visual image into an electrical video signal. The signal can be stored in a video record or broadcast live.

Using a closed circuit TV system, security guards can watch many areas at once.
(Courtesy of ADT, Inc.)

In closed-circuit TV, the camera is connected to the monitor with a cable. This kind of TV is used to allow people to watch a concert or lecture when there is not enough room to seat everyone. Closed-circuit TV also lets security guards watch several areas at the same time.

Broadcast TV is the most common television system. In broadcast TV, each transmitter has its own frequency, on which it sends the video. This is called a carrier frequency. Each TV channel is assigned a carrier frequency. TV receivers (TV sets) are monitors with tuners. The tuners are used to choose a TV channel. TV transmitters send sound at the same time as the picture.

Television has a limited range. People in remote areas often cannot receive any TV stations. To make it possible to receive TV transmissions from a distant place, cable TV is sometimes used. Cable systems use very high antennas or relay stations to receive distant signals. The system delivers all the channels received to subscriber homes on a single cable.

Cable can carry broadcast TV. It can also carry movies, sporting events, concerts, and community news. Because of this extra programming, there are cable TV systems in most large cities, even where regular TV reception is good.

Microwave Communication

FM and AM radio, TV, microwave radio, and fiber optic communication are alike in one way. They all use electromagnetic waves to send a message from the transmitter to the receiver. Radio waves, microwaves, and light waves are all electromag-

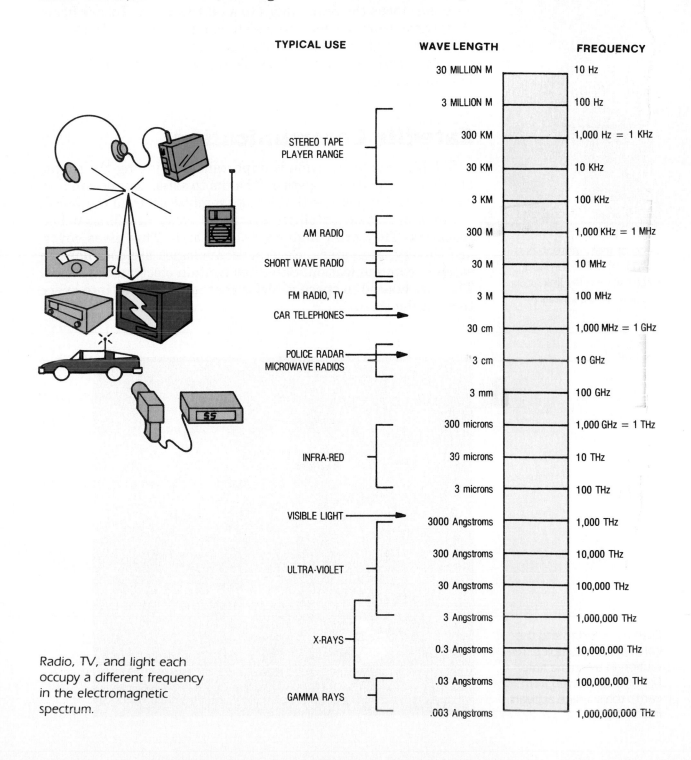

TYPICAL USE	WAVE LENGTH	FREQUENCY
	30 MILLION M	10 Hz
	3 MILLION M	100 Hz
STEREO TAPE PLAYER RANGE	300 KM	1,000 Hz = 1 KHz
	30 KM	10 KHz
	3 KM	100 KHz
AM RADIO	300 M	1,000 KHz = 1 MHz
SHORT WAVE RADIO	30 M	10 MHz
FM RADIO, TV	3 M	100 MHz
CAR TELEPHONES	30 cm	1,000 MHz = 1 GHz
POLICE RADAR MICROWAVE RADIOS	3 cm	10 GHz
	3 mm	100 GHz
	300 microns	1,000 GHz = 1 THz
INFRA-RED	30 microns	10 THz
	3 microns	100 THz
VISIBLE LIGHT	3000 Angstroms	1,000 THz
	300 Angstroms	10,000 THz
ULTRA-VIOLET	30 Angstroms	100,000 THz
	3 Angstroms	1,000,000 THz
X-RAYS	0.3 Angstroms	10,000,000 THz
	.03 Angstroms	100,000,000 THz
GAMMA RAYS	.003 Angstroms	1,000,000,000 THz

Radio, TV, and light each occupy a different frequency in the electromagnetic spectrum.

Each of these antennas is used in a point-to-point microwave relay link. (Courtesy of Andrew Corporation)

netic waves. All occur at different frequencies. As the frequency gets larger, the wavelength of the wave gets smaller.

Microwave radios are radios that use higher frequencies than FM radios or TV broadcasts. Because their frequencies are higher, their wavelengths are shorter. They are therefore called microwave or "little wave." The small wavelength lets small antennas focus the radio waves to a narrow beam. In this beam they travel from one microwave station to another. Microwave radios are used to send telephone conversations from one telephone central office to another. They are used to send TV signals to remote places.

Satellite Communication

Satellite communication is important in bringing the people of different countries together. Thanks to satellites, we can now communicate quickly with the most remote places in the world.

Communication satellites are radio relay stations, called **repeaters**. They orbit high above the earth. This gives coverage to very large areas. Several technologies are combined in satellite communication. Satellites contain electronic systems. They are housed in space vehicles that must be sent into space to orbit the earth.

Both the satellite and the earth make a complete revolution in the same time (24 hours). Viewed from the earth, the satellite appears not to move.

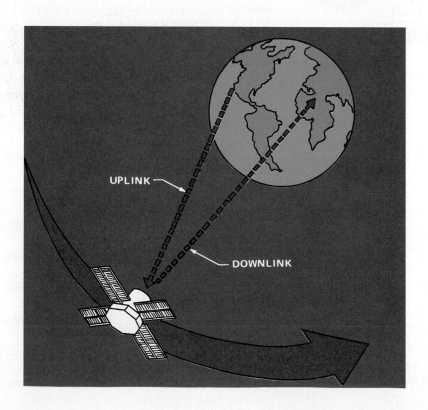

Perhaps you have tried tying a rope to a bucket of water and swinging the bucket over your head. If you swing it too slowly, the water falls out when the bucket is upside down. If you swing the bucket faster, the water stays. It seems to be stuck to the bottom of the bucket.

A satellite can be thought of as swinging around the earth. Gravity is the "rope" that holds the satellite to the earth. When it is close to the earth, the satellite must go around the earth very quickly to stay up. At about 22,500 miles above the earth, the satellite needs to move only once around the earth every 24 hours to stay up.

Suppose a satellite circles the earth just above the equator once every 24 hours. To a person on the equator, it will look as if it is staying in the same place. The earth is turning along with the satellite as the satellite moves around. When a satellite stays above a place on earth, it is said to be in **geosynchronous orbit**. (**Geo** means earth and **synchronous** means together.)

Geosynchronous satellites are useful. An antenna pointed at such a satellite never has to move. Because the satellite is very high, its signals can be picked up over a large area of the earth.

A transmitting station on the earth sends signals to the satellite on one frequency. This is called the **uplink**. The satellite receives the signal and changes it to a different frequency. The satellite then sends this changed signal back toward the earth. This is called the **downlink**. Anyone with a satellite receiver in the covered area can pick up the transmission. Some systems let people receive satellite transmissions at home at low cost.

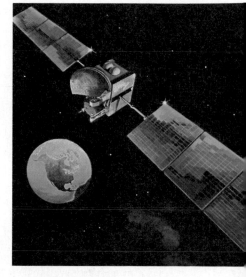

Spacenet I (Copyright 1984 GTE Spacenet Corporation. Spacenet is a registered trademark of GTE Spacenet Corporation)

Fiber Optic Communication

Telephone switches are connected by wires that are many miles long. These wires run underground or are strung on telephone poles. Because of the many conversations that can go on at the same time, a large number of wires are needed on these long routes. These wires have long been made of copper, a costly metal. A lot of copper wire is needed to carry so many conversations. A modern technology that uses light instead of electricity is changing all that.

More and more telephone and data networks now use light to carry information. The basis of this system is cable made of very thin strands of coated glass fibers. Called **fiber-optic cable**, it can guide light around corners. It can carry light for long distances (up to 60 miles) without having to amplify it. Generally, there are many fibers in one bundle.

A very bright light source that can be controlled is needed for a transmitter in a fiber optic system. This can be a **laser** or

Optical fibers used in communications are very small. Each point of light in this picture is the end of an optical fiber. (Courtesy of United Telecom)

a **light emitting diode (LED)**. Information is put onto the light wave by changing the voltage powering the laser or LED. As the voltage changes, the light becomes brighter and darker, creating a code that represents the information. The fiber optic cable is the channel. The receiver is a light-sensitive semiconductor device called a **photodiode**. The photodiode changes light into an electrical signal that represents the information.

Light is very high frequency electromagnetic radiation. It has a frequency far above radio waves in the spectrum. (This means that it has a very much shorter wavelength.) It has a large bandwidth, meaning it can carry large amounts of information. One of the fibers in a multiple-fiber cable can carry over 10,000 telephone circuits, or more. A single cable may have more than 144 such fibers. Most major cities now use fiber optic cable in their telephone systems. Fiber optic cables now span the continent and both the Atlantic and Pacific Oceans.

DATA COMMUNICATION SYSTEMS

Data communication is communication between computers or between a computer and another device. Such a device, called a "peripheral" (outside) device, could be a terminal or a printer. During the early years of the computer, most data communication took place in a computer room. This form of data communication is called **centralized computing** because all processing is done by a central computer. Terminals and printers were connected to it.

Today's computers are smaller, less costly, and more powerful. Computers can now be used where people live and work. They can be connected to larger computers in other places. Some computing can be done on small computers. Small computers can share work with other computers or send larger, more difficult jobs to a large computer. This arrangement is called **distributed computing**.

Computing and communication technologies are being used together to make powerful new tools for working with information.

Advances in communications and low-cost computers have made distributed computing possible.

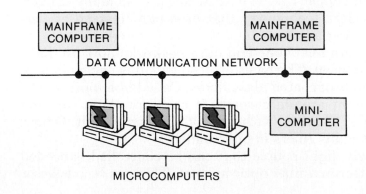

Character	ASCII Code
<	0 111 100
=	0 111 101
>	0 111 110
?	0 111 111
@	1 000 000
A	1 000 001
B	1 000 010
C	1 000 011
D	1 000 100
E	1 000 101
F	1 000 110
G	1 000 111
H	1 001 000

Part of the ASCII code

Computer Codes

Computers and other digital equipment send messages back and forth using codes. In digital codes, a group of bits (called a character) stands for a letter, number, or punctuation mark. Characters are generally five to eight bits long.

ASCII (pronounced *as-key*) is a code that many computers and computer devices use. Another common computer code is **EBCDIC** (pronounced *ebb-sa-dick*). The letters stand for **Extended Binary Coded Decimal Interchange Code**. The codes are used in the same way but they are different codes. When a computer that uses ASCII has to communicate with one that uses EBCDIC, one code has to be changed into the other.

Modems

Telephone lines are often used to carry data communication. Digital equipment cannot directly use telephone lines because data signals are different from telephone voice signals. A device called a **modem** must be used. The modem is hooked up between the digital equipment and the telephone line. A modem turns data signals into sounds that the telephone line can carry. This process is called **modulation**. At the other end, another modem turns the sounds back into data signals. This is called **demodulation**. The word "modem" means **mo**dulator-**dem**odulator.

Computers can be connected to each other using modems and telephone lines. In this way, it is possible to send data from home to home, home to office, and office to office. Many people use modems to reach **electronic bulletin board** services.

Acoustic couplers are modems that connect computers to the telephone system through a telephone handset. (Courtesy of Anderson-Jacobson, Inc.)

Direct-connect modems link computers via the telephone system. (Courtesy of Hayes Microcomputer Products, Inc.)

A traveling executive receives messages from his office electronic mail system by means of a hand-held computer and modem at a public telephone. (Courtesy of GE)

An electronic bulletin board is a computer that you can call using your telephone, computer, and modem. You can store messages on the bulletin board for others to look at and receive messages that they have stored.

Another form of data communication is **electronic mail**. You get an "electronic mailbox" that others can put messages in just for you. You can arrange it so other people get copies of these messages, just like memos in an office. Workers can sort through the messages in their electronic mailboxes quickly. They can throw away messages they don't need by erasing them. They can save messages they do want by storing them electronically. If they wish, they can send answers by electronic mail. No paper ever has to be used. However, a printer can be used to make a paper copy. Electronic mail systems are used in large companies. These are private mail systems. Public mail systems can be used by small companies and people at home. They can use modems and small computers to communicate through electronic mail.

Data Networks

A number of computers or computer devices joined together is called a network.

A number of computers or computer devices joined together is called a **network**. There are computer networks that have thousands of terminals attached to many large computers. Com-

Ticket agents can make reservations on an airline's computerized reservation system from anywhere in the world through data networks that serve thousands of agents at a time. (Courtesy of United Airlines)

Many office functions are now automated through a combination of computer and communication technologies. (Courtesy of NCR Corp.)

puter networks are used to make airline reservations quickly from anywhere in the world. They are used to operate automatic teller machines for banking after a bank closes.

In many offices today there are small data networks. Called **Local Area Networks**, they allow small computers throughout an office to share data. Computers can also share a printer, a modem, or a large amount of memory. Other machines can be added to such a network. They include typewriters, copiers, and other office machines that contain microprocessors and data communications connections. Using these networks, the usefulness of office equipment can be greatly increased. For example, a typewriter connected to a computer can work either as a typewriter or as a computer printer. The term **office automation** is used to describe the use of computers and communications in the office.

Facsimile

Facsimile (FAX) is a way of sending pages of text and pictures electronically. Newspapers use FAX to send news photos from one place to another. Weather maps have been sent this way since the 1920s. In the last few years, FAX has become a very important way to communicate. Many companies are now using FAX machines to send pictures and words over long distances.

Facsimile transmission starts by breaking up an image into

Facsimile machines enable people to send replicas of documents and graphics around the world. (Courtesy of Pitney Bowes, Inc.)

patterns of black and white. To do this, an optical scanning device moves across the page. The white and black areas are changed to electrical impulses. The impulses are sent over wires to a FAX machine in another place. That machine reverses the process. It turns the impulses into a black-and-white image of the page.

RECORDING SYSTEMS

Electronic communication systems that store the message are called **recording systems**. Magnetic recording tape is one medium on which the message could be stored. Other storage media include magnetic disks, phonograph records, optical disks, and other devices. Whatever the medium is, it can be taken from one place to another. The message can then be played back, or reproduced. In this way, the message can be replayed many times. This is true even though it was recorded ("sent") only once. Recording systems can store sound, video, or data. Data storage has already been described in Chapter 4. Here we will focus on sound and video recording.

Phonograph Records

Sound recording has come a long way since Thomas Edison invented the phonograph in 1877. His device could both record and play back. To record, a metal needle scratched a groove

Stereo

Most recordings today are **stereophonic**. That means that they have two sound channels. Two microphones in different places are used to pick up the sound when the recording is first made. Each sound channel is amplified and recorded separately. The tape player that plays back the tape also amplifies each channel separately. Each of the two speakers plays what one of the two microphones picked up. Because people have two ears, stereo sounds much more natural and complete.

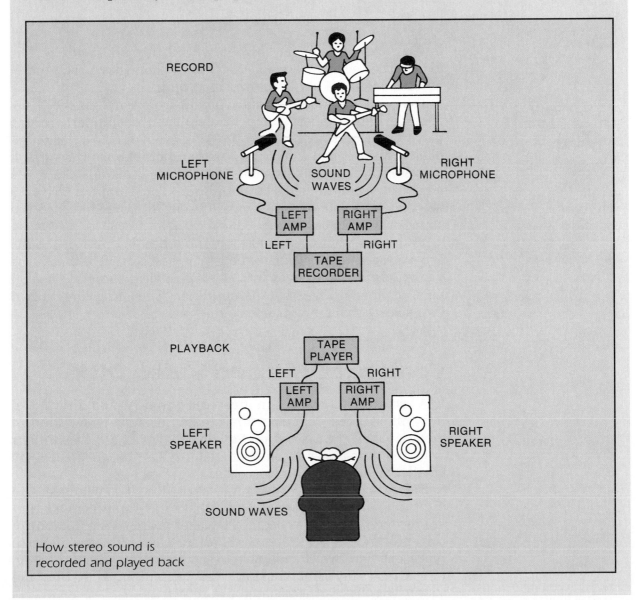

RECORD

LEFT MICROPHONE

SOUND WAVES

RIGHT MICROPHONE

LEFT AMP

RIGHT AMP

LEFT

RIGHT

TAPE RECORDER

PLAYBACK

TAPE PLAYER

LEFT

RIGHT

LEFT AMP

RIGHT AMP

LEFT SPEAKER

RIGHT SPEAKER

SOUND WAVES

How stereo sound is recorded and played back

Edison's phonograph was able to record and play back sound. (Courtesy of RCA)

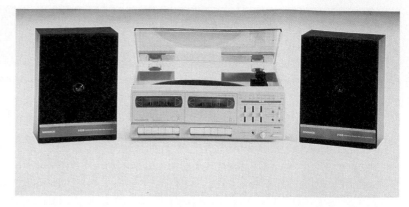

Modern phonographs produce high quality sound reproduction. (Courtesy of N.A.P. Consumer Electronics Corp.)

into a rotating cylinder covered with a thin sheet of tin. The louder the recorded sound, the deeper the groove. The metal needle could also play back the recording.

Today, phonograph records are made from vinyl plastic. They provide high-quality sound when played on modern record players. Records are made by pressing grooves into a flat round plastic disk. When a record is made, microphones turn sound waves into electrical signals. The electrical signals are made larger in a device called an **amplifier**. The amplifier drives a needle that makes grooves of different sizes that record the sound waves.

Your home phonograph has a pointed needle that rides in the grooves of a record. This needle is part of a cartridge that turns variations in the grooves into small electrical signals. The signals are made larger by the amplifier. Then they are turned into sound waves by the speakers.

Compact Disks and Video Disks

A record with grooves in it can pick up dust and dirt. When it is played, the dust and dirt create "noise." A new kind of record, called the **laser disk**, has no grooves at all. Laser disks are sometimes called **compact disks (CDs)** because they are smaller than phonograph records.

Before sound is recorded on a laser disk, it is changed into digital bits (see Chapter 4). Laser disks have spiral tracks that are recorded by a laser beam. The laser beam burns millions of tiny pits into the surface of the disk. Deep pits are made to represent "0s," while shallow pits represent "1s." Even the deep pits are so tiny that you can't tell by looking that they are there. The disk is then coated to protect it.

Compact disks combine optical and digital technologies to produce extremely high quality audio and video recordings. (Courtesy of Sony Corporation of America)

When a CD is played, a laser beam shines light on it. A light-sensing device "reads" the light reflected from the pits. A deep pit reflects a little bit of light. A shallow pit reflects more light. The reflected light is changed into digital pulses of electricity. The pulses are turned into sound.

Compact disks are widely used for stereo sound systems. Larger disks, called **video disks**, are used to store and record video. These disks also use lasers to read the information stored on the disk. Video disks are not as popular as videocassette recorders. This is because the disks can be used for playback only. There is currently no way to record on the disks at home. When a method is developed for home recording on the disks, video disks will probably become more popular.

Tape Recordings

A popular way to record sound, video, and data is on **magnetic tape**. Magnetic tape is a long, thin piece of mylar plastic that has been coated with a metal oxide. The oxide coating can

Modern tape players provide high quality speech and music reproduction. (Courtesy of N.A.P. Consumer Electronics Corp.)

be magnetized. The tape is pulled past an electromagnet called a **tape head**. The head creates a changing magnetic field when the voltage going to it changes.

In the recording studio, sound is changed into a varying electric voltage by a microphone. An amplifier boosts (increases) the small electric voltage from the microphone. The electrical signal is then sent to the recording head. The tape moves past the varying magnetic field in the tape head and the oxide coating on the tape is magnetized to a varying degree.

On playback, the process is reversed. The tape is moved past a playback head. The playback head picks up the changing magnetic field on the tape and changes it to a voltage. An amplifer boosts the voltage so that it is large enough to drive a speaker. The speaker changes the voltage back to sound waves.

Several different sounds can be recorded on one tape at the same time. Each is recorded on a different part of the tape. These are called **tracks**. Four-track tapes are common.

To store enough tape to last for an hour or more, reels are used. Tapes wound on open reels are called **reel-to-reel** tapes. These are not often used in home tape players, but they are in wide use in studios. Two reels enclosed in a plastic case, called a **cassette**, are more popular for home use. Both audio and video cassettes (often called videotapes) are in widespread use.

Cartridges use one reel and a continuous loop of tape. Tape is drawn out of the center of the reel past the heads, and wound back on the outside of the reel. A cartridge can play continuously. It cannot be rewound or backed up as reel-to-reel or cassettes can.

Recording tape comes packaged in different ways. One familiar package is the cartridge. (Courtesy of Ampex Corporation, Magnetic Tape Division)

MODERN TELECOMMUNICATIONS SERVICES

Teleconferencing

A **teleconference** is a conference held with people in different places. Travel costs are growing. It is far less costly to hold meetings in which people can communicate without having to be in the same place. A teleconference connects people by telecommunication lines. Several kinds of teleconferences are possible.

In the simplest kind of teleconference, only voice lines are used. People hear each other as if they were sitting in a group.

This is sometimes called a conference call. It can be set up using telephone lines. Each person uses his or her telephone. If a telephone with a loudspeaker is used, a group of people sitting together in one room can take part in the teleconference.

Sometimes it is useful in a teleconference for people to see as well as hear each other. In this case, television can be added. This kind of teleconferencing is called **videoconferencing**. Videoconferencing is costly. It is most cost-effective over very long distances, where travel costs for a meeting would be very high.

Telecommuting

Using powerful personal computers, some workers can stay at home to do their jobs. Programmers, word processor operators, and data-entry clerks, for example, can work at home. The finished work can be brought to the office on a floppy disk at the end of the day. Or the work can be transmitted in digital form to the company's computer by telephone lines and modems.

Some workers like telecommuting because they can work on their own schedule. Also, they don't have to travel to and from the office every day. Parents who work at home can be with their children. Businesses like telecommuting because they do not have to provide desks, workspace, and electricity.

As with any new system, there are undesirable outputs. Because a telecommuting worker has little contact with other workers, business may suffer. Telecommuting workers may not be able to work as efficiently at home because of telephone calls and visitors.

Effective data communications allows some information workers to work at home rather than in an office. (Courtesy of AT&T Bell Laboratories)

Automated teller machines allow customers to bank at any time of the day or night.
(Courtesy of First Security Corporation)

Electronic Banking

The combination of computing and communications has changed the way banking is done. **Automated teller machines (ATMs)** can be found almost everywhere. They are even outnumbering bank branches in some places. ATMs let people deposit money, withdraw money, find out account balances, and pay bills at any time, night or day.

ATMs are computer terminals connected by telephone lines to the bank's main computer. In many areas, groups of banks share ATMs. This is cheaper for the banks and makes it possible to provide many more ATMs.

Two-way Cable TV

At one time, cable TV systems could send signals only from the control center (the **head end**) to subscribers. Many new cable TV systems can carry signals back from the subscribers to the head end. These are called two-way cable systems.

Two-way cable TV has made several new services possible. With **pay-per-view**, customers are charged only for the programs they watch rather than paying a flat monthly fee. Sometimes billing is done automatically whenever the pay channel is on. In other systems, the viewer must ask for the program from the cable operator. This kind of system is used in many hotels.

Communications are changing the way we shop. (Courtesy of AT&T Bell Laboratories)

Shop-at-home lets customers learn about many kinds of products. A keyboard is used to request information. When a request is received, the product is shown on TV through a playback of a videotape or videodisk. The customer may then order the product.

Using **data base inquiry**, people can use computers to look at information stored in data bases. Data bases are maintained by many groups. Some of these are newspapers, organizations, and financial institutions. Such a service could be used to look through a newspaper such as *The New York Times* or the *Wall Street Journal*.

SUMMARY

The use of electricity and electronics in communication has created the information age, just as steam engines created the industrial age. A communication system is called an electronic communication system if the channel uses electrical energy to carry information. In electronic communication systems, messages are sent immediately or stored to send later.

One of the earliest and simplest electronic communcation systems was the telegraph. In telegraph systems, codes of long and short sounds (dots and dashes) are used to represent numbers, letters, and punctuation. While the telegraph was a fast way to communicate in its time, it is slow by today's standards. Only people who knew the Morse code could use it directly.

Today, telephone is the most commonly used electronic communication system. Most modern telephone systems change voice signals into digital data for switching and transmission.

Telephone switches, which automatically connect parties, are one-purpose computers. Conventional telephone technology has been combined with radio technology to produce new devices such as cordless and automobile telephones.

People first used radios to communicate with ships at sea. Radios send information through the air from a transmitting antenna to a receiving antenna located some distance away. Radio, TV, microwave radio, and light are all forms of electromagnetic energy, but each has a different frequency.

In television, images are changed into electrical signals that are sent through the air to a receiver that changes them back to images. Closed-circuit TV systems transmit video over cables instead of through the air.

Microwave radio is used to transmit thousands of telephone conversations from one telephone office to another. It is also used to send TV signals from one location to another. Satellite communication uses microwave radios that communicate through a satellite. The satellite is a radio repeater that circles the earth at the same rate that the earth turns, so that it remains above a fixed location on earth.

Fiber optic cable guides light from one end of the cable to the other. A light source at one end can transmit information to the other end of the cable. Fiber optic cables can carry the same amount of information as many larger and more costly copper cables.

Data communication is communication between computers or from a computer to a terminal, printer, or other peripheral device. In centralized computing, all processing is done in one large computer with peripheral devices attached to it. In distributed computing, the processing is done by many smaller computers located in different places.

Computer communication is carried out through data codes. Modems are used to change computer digital signals to sounds, and vice versa. Data communication over telephone lines usually requires a modem to turn the data signals into tones.

Many computers or computer devices joined together is called a network. Networks can cover a very large area and use telephone lines to communicate, or they can cover only one office.

Sound is recorded on magnetic tape, phonograph records, and laser disks (often called compact disks). Video is recorded on magnetic tape and video disks.

Quickly changing communication technologies have brought us new services. We now have teleconferencing, electronic banking, and various services provided by two-way cable TV.

REVIEW QUESTIONS

1. What is an electronic communication system? Define the term, and give three examples.
2. A newspaper uses electronic typesetting machines to help set its type. Is the newspaper an electronic communication system? Explain your answer.
3. Use the Morse code chart provided in the text to write "technology education" in Morse code.
4. Are telephone circuits analog or digital? Explain your answer.
5. What two new products were the result of combining radio and telephone technology?
6. A radio signal has a frequency of 30 MHz (million cycles per second). What is its wavelength in meters?
7. Do microwave radios operate at a higher or lower frequency than FM radios?
8. Why is fiber optic cable better than copper wire for large numbers of telephone circuits?
9. How has communication technology changed the way computers are used?
10. What is a modem? How does it work?
11. Why does stereo sound more real and natural than single speaker sound?
12. Would you like to be a telecommuter? Why or why not?

KEY WORDS

Amplifier	Distributed	Local Area	Telecommute
ASCII	computing	Network	Teleconference
Broadcast	Downlink	Modem	Telegraph
Cassette	Electromagnetic	Network	Telephone
Compact disk	wave	Office automation	Tracks
Data	Fiber optic	Stereo	Uplink
communication	Frequency	Tape head	Wavelength

SEE YOUR TEACHER FOR THE CROSSTECH PUZZLE

Suggested Resources

Safety glasses and lab apron

Copper magnet wire, enameled (single strand, 22 gauge, about 30' long)

Twin lead stranded wire

Electrical tape

Pine—¾"

Wire cutters

Hot glue

Spring brass

Drill, drill bits, countersink

6 flat head machine screws with hex nuts and wing nuts—1½" × ¼ #20

6 self-tapping screws—½" #6

25 gauge tin plate

35 mm film container cap

1 hex head, soft iron machine bolt with two nuts—3" long, ⅜ × 16 NC

Assorted woodworking and sheetmetal tools and equipment

6–12 volt DC power supply

MORSE CODE COMMUNICATIONS

Setting the Stage

A *code* can be defined as a set of signals or symbols that have a specific meaning to both the sender and the receiver of the message. Satellites in earth orbit use coded radio signals to send data back to earth. Computers with modems, teletype machines, and many other devices use coded signals to transmit data.

Your Challenge

Design and build a telegraphy device. Using this device and the Morse code, send a message to another student.

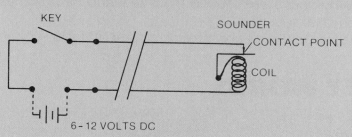

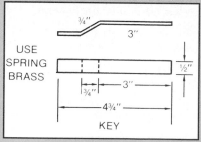

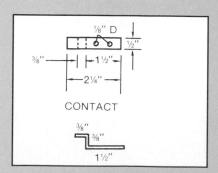

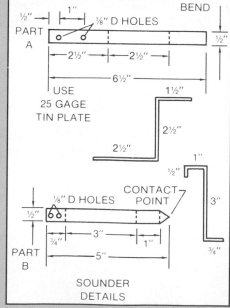

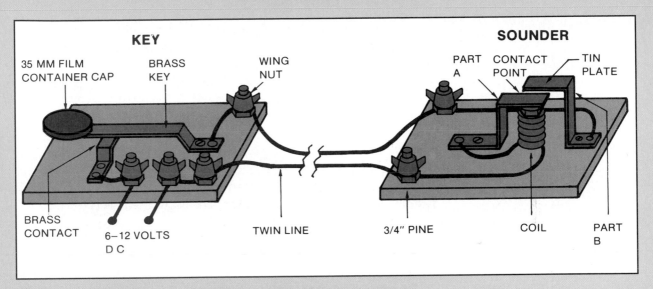

KEY — SOUNDER

35 MM FILM CONTAINER CAP · BRASS KEY · WING NUT · PART A · CONTACT POINT · TIN PLATE · BRASS CONTACT · 6–12 VOLTS D C · TWIN LINE · 3/4" PINE · COIL · PART B

Procedure

1. Be sure to wear safety glasses and a lab coat.
2. Cut and sand 4" × 6" pine bases.
3. Install the 3" machine bolt end nuts, and the six flat head machine screws and nuts.
4. Using the copper magnet wire, wrap a coil around the length of the 3" machine screw. Four to six layers of wire are okay. Start and finish the coil at the bottom of the bolt. Tape the bottom of the coil in place leaving 8–10" of extra wire at both ends.
5. Make Parts A and B of the sounder as shown and mount to base.
6. Make brass key and contact as shown. Mount to base. Hot glue film container cover to end of key.
7. Wire all parts as shown. The sounder pieces may have to be *slightly* bent for best results. You should hear a buzzing sound if everything is adjusted properly.
8. Send a message to another student.

Technology Connections

1. The communication process consists of a transmitter, a channel, and a receiver. In telegraphy, the Morse code key is the transmitter and the sounder is the receiver. What part of a telegraph circuit represents the channel, or route the message takes?
2. When telegraph lines are run long distances, relay stations are needed. Why?

Science and Math Concepts

▶ A wire carrying an electric current has a magnetic field around it. If the wire is turned into a coil, the magnetic field inside the coil becomes stronger than that formed by a straight wire.
▶ If a soft iron core is placed inside the coil, an *electromagnet* is formed.
▶ The strength of a magnetic field is measured in a unit called the *tesla*.

BEAM THAT SIGNAL

Setting the Stage

During the interview with your supervisor, you are informed that you must take a training session to learn about the manufacturing of semiconductors before you begin your public relations job. You are aware that a semiconductor laser is the smallest laser produced today. But how is it produced and why is it so useful in the field of communications?

Your Challenge

Simulate point-to-point transmission of radio communication systems with a helium-neon laser. The signal will be bounced off a satellite and received on the ground.

Procedure

1. Draw a horizontal line across the board 5" up from the bottom of the white board. This line will represent the earth.
2. In each corner of the board, project a line up to the top of the board near the center. This will form a triangle.
3. Measure each base angle and write the degrees near each angle. Use math to find the third angle. (The total number of degrees in a triangle equals 180°.) Check your work by measuring the third angle with a protractor.
4. Place a mirror at the top of the triangle.
5. Place the laser at the bottom of the board in one corner and the receiver in the other corner.
6. Obtain permission to turn on the laser. Adjust the mirror so the beam lines up on the sides of the triangle and hits the receiver.
7. Using the mirror for a guide, draw a line. Measure one angle between the mirror and the triangle. The other angle should be the same.
8. Play music from your tape recorder through the input jack of the laser. This will modulate the laser beam. Adjust the volume on the tape recorder for a clear sound.

Suggested Resources

4—4" × 4" mirrors mounted on ¾" thick plywood
Protractor
Ruler
Framing square
3' × 4' white board
Assorted markers
Audio-modulated helium-neon laser
Laser receiver and amplifier
Tape recorder

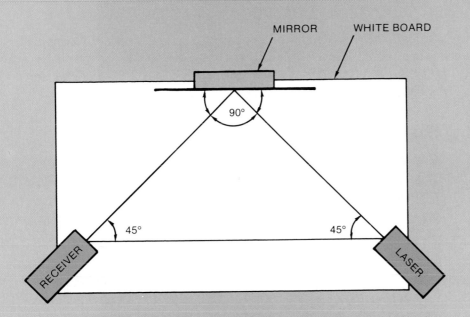

MIRROR   WHITE BOARD

90°

45°   45°

RECEIVER   LASER

Technology Connections

1. Hook a piece of fiber-optic cable between the laser and the receiver. Plug the tape recorder into the input jack of the laser. Again play the tape recorder. This will demonstrate fiber-optic communication.
2. Try the same experiment over a greater distance, such as 30 feet. Omit finding the angles. Keep all the equipment on the floor for safety. The laser beam must not hit your eyes.
3. How does a compact disc make use of a laser to record and play back information?
4. Fiber-optic cable is becoming increasingly common for what type of communication? How is the laser used in this type of communication?

Science and Math Concepts

► The angle of incidence equals the angle of reflection.
► Laser light is monochromatic (made up of only one color).
► The angle at which light spreads is called **divergence.** Laser light does decrease in its intensity as it travels further from the laser, but its divergence is much less than that of other light sources.

THE MISSING LINK

Suggested Resources

Computer with monitor
  and disk drive
Printer
Modem
Telephone line
Telecommunications
  software
Connecting cables

Setting the Stage

Did you know that computers can talk to each other? Not with the same words that people use but with languages of their own. One of these languages is called the *American Standard Code* for *Information Interchange,* or ASCII (pronounced as-key).

Your Challenge

Connect your computer to another computer using a *modem* (*MOD*ulator + *DEM*odulator = MODEM) and telephone lines. Then transfer some data back and forth between the computers.

Procedure

1. Read the instructions that came with the modem.
2. Proper modem connections between the computer and the telephone line are a necessity for successful telecommunications. The manufacturer's recommendations for connecting (interfacing) your hardware should be *carefully* followed.
3. Make sure the telecommunications *software* you are using is compatible with your computer and modem.
4. Get familiar with your software *before* you try to call another computer. Read the directions carefully! Watch for key words like: *baud rate* (transmission and reception speed of the modem), *dialing* a number (touch-tone or pulse dialing), *uploading* (sending a message), *downloading* (receiving a message), *full-duplex* (for connecting to a mainframe computer), *half-duplex* (for calling another microcomputer), disconnecting or hanging up, etc.
5. Use the computer, modem, and communications software to dial the phone number of another telecommunications system. If possible, call a student in another classroom or school.
6. Make sure both computers are set at the same *baud rate* (i.e., 300 or 1200) and in the *half-duplex* mode.
7. Once the connection has been established, take turns typing messages. When you are finished typing your message, send the word *GO*. This tells the other student to begin typing.
8. After your telecommunication is over, be sure to follow the *disconnect* procedure for your modem. *Don't just turn the computer off and walk away!*

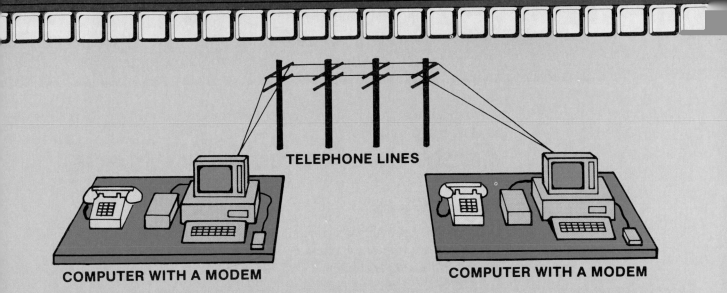

TELEPHONE LINES

COMPUTER WITH A MODEM   COMPUTER WITH A MODEM

Technology Connections

1. The communication process consists of a transmitter, a channel, and a receiver. In data communications, a computer with a modem is the sender, and another computer with a modem is the receiver. What part of the system represents the channel, or route the message takes?

2. A number of computers can be connected by telephone lines to form a *network*. What device is needed to connect a computer to a telephone line?

3. Why is it important for all computer manufacturers to use a standard code (such as ASCII) when designing new computers? What would happen if every computer used a different code?

Science and Math Concepts

▶ *Acoustics* is the science of sound.
▶ *Baud rate* refers to the speed at which a modem sends and receives data.

COMMUNICATING A MESSAGE

Objectives

When you have finished this activity, you should be able to:

■ Use a computer or word processor to input, store, and retrieve data.
■ Assemble text and graphic images for reproduction using manual paste-up or desktop publishing procedures.
■ Reproduce a sufficient number of copies using a photocopying process.
■ Communicate factual information using an audio medium.
■ Use an audio medium for persuasion (advertisement).
■ Communicate factual information using a video medium.
■ Use a video medium for persuasion (advertisement).
■ Identify strengths and weaknesses in communication using print, audio, and video media.

Concepts and Information

Computers and electronics are affecting all areas of our lives. Nowhere has this been greater than in communication technology. Computers have impacted the graphic communication and printing industry as tools for data storage, retrieval, and transmission. Computers are used to create and arrange both text (words) and graphics (drawings and photographs).

Equipment and Supplies

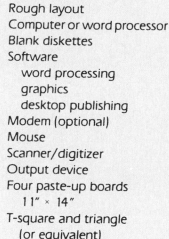

Newsletter

Rough layout
Computer or word processor
Blank diskettes
Software
  word processing
  graphics
  desktop publishing
Modem (optional)
Mouse
Scanner/digitizer
Output device
Four paste-up boards
  11" × 14"
T-square and triangle
  (or equivalent)
X-Acto® knife
Pencil, non-photo blue
Pen, black ballpoint
Ruler
Wax or rubber cement or
  glue stick
Photocopier

Audio Recording

Audio recorder
Microphone
Audio tape

Video Recording

Video recorder
Video tape cassette
Script blanks

Major newspapers and magazines throughout the country use this technology every day. Writers input their stories into computers using keyboards, modems, and optical character readers. Stories are then modified by editors and other staff writers. Photographs are included to help communicate the story to the reader. Many photographs are electronically transmitted. The wording and graphics for advertisements also may be electronically input and manipulated. Entire pages are then electronically assembled by editors and staff using large monitors, and sent to the presses.

Much of our communication uses the audio medium. The records and radio broadcasts we listen to are examples of this. Radio provides us entertainment, news and information. It involves us by allowing our imaginations to create "pictures."

(Courtesy of WRGB-Newscenter 6)

Television, movies, and video have become major parts of our lives. The combining of audio and visual images can help us get a clear understanding of the ideas being communicated. Television and videos entertain us. Advertisements persuade us to buy products. News programs allow us to see what's happening all over the world.

Activity

This project will provide opportunities to use various technical communication systems. You will be able to use current technology in the production of a newsletter, an audio presentation (simulating radio), and a video presentation (simulating television). You will design and communicate a message to inform and to persuade.

Procedure

Newsletter

1. The newsletter will consist of four 8½" × 11" pages. A rough layout may be secured from your instructor. It suggests the content and space available on each page for text and graphics: page 1—News, page 2—Features, page 3—Editorial and Advertisement, page 4—Sports. You may wish to develop your own layout.
2. Write articles. Keep in mind the appropriateness of the subject matter and approximate length (based upon the rough layout).
3. Completed articles should be carefully checked for content, correct spelling and grammar.
4. Write headlines.
5. Drawings may be created on your computer or hand drawn.
6. Each photograph must be converted into a halftone (made up of a series of dots). If you have the facilities you may do this yourself using a photographic process. If you have access to a scanner, photographs may be entered into a computer and digitized to produce a halftone.
7. Select a product or concept to advertise. Write copy and make appropriate graphics.
8. Input and store articles on a disk. (Note: The line length will be determined by examination of the rough layout.)
9. Set headlines and copy for your ad. Keep in mind the line length.
10. Output articles, heads, and graphics in galley form (columns).
11. Proofread the text and heads, carefully checking content, spelling, and grammar. Add or delete copy to fit the article and head to space provided on the rough layout. Examine graphics for appearance and size.
12. Make appropriate corrections.
13. Using electronic publishing, for each page:
    a. Arrange text and graphics. (Examine the rough layout carefully to determine the position of text, graphics, and advertisements.)
    b. Output pages.
    c. Adhere any graphics not generated by a computer following manual paste-up procedures **(step d)**.
    d. Add corner marks on each page (see **step f** in "manual paste-up procedures"). If there is not enough space on the ouput to add these corner marks, the output must be adhered to a paste-up board to allow more space.

(Courtesy of Aldus Corporation)

14. Using manual paste-up procedures, for each page:
    a. Output the corrected text, heads, and graphics.
    b. Using a T-square, align the paste-up board onto a drafting board (or light table). Use masking tape to secure each corner.
    c. Carefully measure and draw lines as indicated on the rough layout (paper lines, image lines, locations of articles, heads, and graphics) using a non-reproducing blue pencil, a T-square, and a triangle.
    d. Paste articles and heads in their proper positions using wax, rubber cement, or a glue stick. Use a T-square and triangle to carefully align elements according to rough layout. Make sure all lines are straight and be especially careful to smooth down elements without smearing and keep all work surfaces clean.
    e. Paste graphics (drawings and halftones) and advertisements as described in **step d**.
    f. Use a black ballpoint pen, a T-square, and a triangle to add corner marks (see diagram).
    g. Carefully double-check the alignment of all elements using a T-square and a triangle.
15. Photocopy each page and proofread it. This will be the last chance to correct errors in content, spelling, grammar, and position.
16. Tape a clean sheet of paper over the completed page for protection.
17. Photocopy as many copies of the completed page as desired.
18. Finish the newsletter by stapling the sheets together.

CORNERMARKS
(¾" LONG)

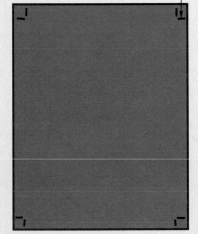

Audio Tape

The audio tape will simulate a radio broadcast. It will consist of two parts: (1) a factual or descriptive component and (2) an advertisement (for the same product as presented in the newsletter).

1. Identify the target population of the "broadcast" (age, gender, interests, etc.).
2. Decide the style to be used in the presentation (news, interview, dramatic, etc.).
3. Select the factual or descriptive content to be included. One of the stories from the newsletter could be used.
4. Examine the content of the advertisement used in the newsletter. How might it best be communicated in a radio broadcast?
5. Write a script. Keep in mind that an audio tape allows each listener to create "pictures" from the script.
   a. Outline the key topics.
   b. Write a specific narration (wording).
   c. Indicate the use of sound effects (music, special effects, etc.).
   d. Edit the script for appropriate content, grammar, and sequence.
6. Rehearse.
7. Produce a preliminary tape. Check your tape for background noise (unwanted sounds picked up by the microphone).
8. Review the preliminary tape. Revise the tape based on your review.
9. Record the "broadcast."
10. Review the final tape.

Video Tape

This medium will allow you to present a clear picture to the viewer, not just use words to help the "listener" create those images.

1. Identify the target population of the "broadcast" (age, gender, interests, etc.).
2. Determine the style to be used in the presentation (news, interview, dramatic, etc.). Think of television broadcasts you have seen to help get ideas.
3. Examine the content of the advertisement. How might it best be communicated using the video medium?
4. Outline the script.
5. Produce a preliminary storyboard. This will be an idea for each video image with accompanying script ideas.
6. Produce the script. Use script blanks (available from your teacher) to indicate each video image and accompanying audio.
   a. Each video image is represented by a rough sketch in the frame provided. This may also indicate camera angle and the depth of the picture.
   b. Exact wording should accompany each picture.
   c. Additional audio (music, sound effects, etc.) should be indicated.
   d. Review the script for appropriate content, grammar, and sequence.

7. Rehearse (check timing, script, and sequence).
8. Produce the preliminary video tape. Check for background "noise" (unwanted sounds or images).
9. Review the preliminary tape. Revise the tape on your review.
10. Record the "broadcast."
11. Review the final tape.

Review Questions

1. Discuss the roles of the seven technological resources in the completion of this activity.
2. How did the three parts of this activity attempt to inform, persuade, educate, and entertain?
3. What information is provided by a rough layout?
4. Discuss the advantages of desktop publishing and manual paste-up procedures.
5. In producing your newsletter, what methods were used to create graphics and to convert photographs to halftones?
6. List three methods that could have been used to input data for your newsletter.
7. What roles did electronic technology play in completion of the following activities: newsletter, audio tape, video tape?
8. What is "noise" in relation to audio and video? Why is it an important factor to consider?
9. What are the similarities and differences between a rough layout (newsletter) and a script (audio and video)?
10. What advantages and/or disadvantages did you discover in communicating using each of the following three media: (1) print, (2) audio, and (3) video?

_CAREER
_PAGE

CAREERS IN COMMUNICATION

The communication field includes a broad range of occupations having to do with research, writing, editing and production. They may be in the areas of education, journalism, publishing, television, business, advertising, public relations, photography, and speech.

OCCUPATION	FORMAL EDUCATION OR TRAINING	SKILLS NEEDED	EMPLOYMENT OPPORTUNITIES
ELECTRICAL ENGINEER AND TECHNICIAN— Electrical engineer designs, develops, tests, and supervises the manufacture of electrical and electronic equipment, such as radios, televisions, radar, industrial measuring and control devices, computers, and navigational equipment. Technicians build and service this equipment.	**Engineer:** Four-year college degree. **Technician:** Specialized training at technical institutes, junior and community colleges, and vocational and technical high schools.	**Engineer:** Excellent math skills, an analytical mind, and a capacity for detail. **Technician:** An aptitude for mathematics and science, and an enjoyment of technical work.	Much greater than average. There will be a strong demand for computers, robots, communications equipment, and electrical products for military, industrial and consumer use.
PHOTOGRAPHER— Takes pictures of a wide variety of subjects. Still photographers specialize in portrait, fashion, or advertising. Industrial photographers provide illustrations for scientific publications.	Entry-level jobs for photographers have no formal educational requirements. Special courses are available in universities, junior colleges, and high schools. Over 100 colleges offer a bachelor's degree.	Good eyesight and color vision, artistic ability and manual dexterity. Photographers should be patient, enjoy working with detail, and have some knowledge of chemistry, physics and mathematics.	Above average. The demand for photographers will be stimulated as business and industry place greater importance upon visual aids in meetings, stockholders reports, and public relations work.
PRINTING PRESS OPERATOR— Prepares and operates the printing presses in a pressroom or print shop.	Apprenticeship or training on the job. Courses in printing, communications technology, chemistry, electronics, and physics are helpful.	Mechanical aptitude is important in making press adjustments and repairs. An ability to visualize color is essential for work on color presses.	Average. Increased use of color printing will contribute to the growth of new jobs, computer-operated equipment will reduce labor requirements.

Data from *Occupational Outlook Handbook, 1986-87*, U.S. Department of Labor

SECTION

3

(Courtesy of Cincinnati Milacron)

PRODUCTION

CHAPTER 8

▢ ▢ ▢ ▢ ▢ ▢ ▢ ▢ ▢ ▢ ▢ ▢ ▢ ▢ ▢ ▢ ▢

PROCESSING MATERIALS

MAJOR CONCEPTS

After reading this chapter, you will know that:

- Processing materials is changing their form to make them more useful.
- The technological process brings about the changing of materials from one form to another.
- Technological systems change raw materials into basic industrial materials. Basic industrial materials are then changed to end products.
- Materials are processed by forming, separating, combining, and conditioning.
- Computers can control machines used to process materials.
- Materials are chosen on the basis of their mechanical, electrical, magnetic, thermal, and optical properties.

INTRODUCTION

To make material resources more useful, we process them. **Processing resources** means changing their form. For example, **raw materials** such as wood can be made into furniture. Cotton fiber can be made into thread. Thread can be spun and woven into fabric, which can be made into clothing. Paper can be made from wood chips. Animal hides can be made into shoes, handbags, and coats. Plants and animals can be processed into foods.

Processing materials is changing their form to make them more useful.

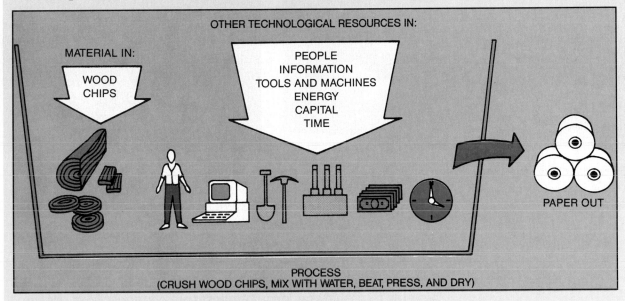

In a material conversion process, other technological resources are needed to convert materials from one form to another.

MATERIAL RESOURCES

Industries such as logging and mining are called **primary industries**. They produce our **primary**, or most basic, **raw materials**. Primary raw materials are taken from the earth and processed into **basic industrial materials**. Timber (from trees) is one example. It is made into wooden planks. These planks are then industrial materials. They are used by industry to make **end products** like furniture and houses.

Natural rubber (latex) is another raw material. It is changed

The technological process brings about the changing of materials from one form to another.

209

Some basic industrial materials (Courtesy of Commercial Metals Company)

The aluminum industry processes bauxite ore into many different products. (Courtesy of Aluminum Company of America)

Technological systems change raw materials into basic industrial materials. Basic industrial materials are then changed to end products.

to a basic industrial material by heating it with sulfur. The process is called **vulcanization**. Vulcanization makes the rubber able to withstand large temperature changes. Iron ore, limestone, and coke are made into steel. These materials are processed into steel slabs, sheets, rods, or beams. Crude oil is changed into chemicals from which plastics are made.

Most of our products are made from these basic industrial materials. We must use the other technological resources whenever one material is changed to another. Generally, value is added to a material each time we process it.

TYPES OF INDUSTRIAL MATERIALS

Wood, metal, ceramics, and plastics are industrial materials. Industrial materials like these are chosen on the basis of how well they suit a use. For example, plastic does not conduct electricity. For this reason, it can be used to cover (insulate) bare wires. Different kinds of wood are chosen for furniture-making because of their strength and beauty.

Wood

Wood comes in different forms. **Hardwood** comes from trees like maples, oaks, and poplars. These trees have broad leaves. They are **deciduous**. That is, they lose their leaves in the fall. **Softwood** comes from trees with needle-like leaves, such as pines and firs. These are **coniferous**, or cone-bearing, trees. Generally, hardwoods are hard and softwoods are soft. However, the terms have to do only with the kinds of leaves trees have. Balsa and basswood are hardwood trees, but their woods are soft.

Manufactured board, like plywood and particle board, is made from wood chips and sawdust. This is often stronger than the wood from which manufactured board is made. It will not warp or twist.

Wood is a renewable resource. It is cheap and plentiful. Most kinds of wood can easily be cut and shaped. Wood has beautiful colors and grain patterns, and can be quite strong.

Wood is a material often chosen by craftspeople and builders. (Courtesy of Boise Cascade Corp.)

Metal

Iron and the steel that is made from it are probably the most important metals used today. They are turned into end products like automobiles, skyscrapers, and machine tools. **Alloys** are combinations of metals. Metals that are more than half iron are called **ferrous** metals. Steel is a ferrous metal. Steel alloys can be made with special properties. For example, **stainless steel**, which contains chromium, resists rusting. Metals other than iron, and alloys without a large amount of iron, are called **nonferrous** metals. Nonferrous metals are aluminum, copper, magnesium, nickel, tin, and zinc. Brass is an alloy of copper and zinc. Bronze is an alloy of copper and tin. Pewter is an alloy of tin, antimony, and copper.

Electromagnetic ingot casting is being used to produce these aluminum ingots. (Courtesy of Alcoa Aluminum Corp.)

Ceramics

Ceramic objects are made from clay or similar inorganic (nonliving) materials. These include plaster, cement, limestone, and glass. In making clay products, clay is mined and mixed with other substances. It is then fired (heated) in an oven called a **kiln** to around 2,000° Fahrenheit. Firing makes the clay very hard. The clay can then be coated with a glass-like material called **glaze**. Glaze protects the surface of ceramics and gives them color. Ceramic dishes are common because clay is easy to obtain and costs little. Glazed ceramic objects like dishes are attractive and easy to clean.

How Steel Is Made

Steel is the world's most useful metal. It is used to make everything from paper clips to bridges. Steel costs little to make. It is produced in steel mills, from iron ore, which is a common material. Iron ore is found in the earth's crust.

To make steel, iron ore (iron oxide) is melted with limestone and coke in a **blast furnace**. The heat burns the oxygen from the iron oxide, leaving only molten (melted) iron. Some of the molten iron (called **hot metal**) is poured into molds. It cools and hardens into **pig iron**. Impurities in the molten iron rise to the top and are removed as **slag**.

Most of the hot metal is turned into steel in **basic oxygen furnaces (BOFs)**. Oxygen is blown into the top of the BOF at very high speed. There it combines with the carbon in the molten iron and changes the iron to steel. Steel is also made in **open-hearth furnaces** and **electric furnaces**. An open-hearth furnace is a shallow furnace that is heated by burning gases. An electric furnace produces heat using electricity. Small new mills, called **mini-mills**, use electric furnaces to make special kinds of steel.

Molten steel that comes from the furnace is processed in two ways. It can be cast into huge blocks called **ingots**. The ingots are then formed into steel shapes. These are rolled into end products like bars, rods, and sheets.

Molten steel can also be changed directly into basic steel shapes through a process called continuous casting. This method bypasses the ingot-making step.

(All photos courtesy of U.S. Iron and Steel Institute)

Coke is made by burning coal. When the coal is burned, gases, oils, and tar are removed. The coke that remains serves as fuel for the blast furnace.

In the blast furnace, a blast of air burns the coke. The resulting heat and gases remove oxygen from the iron ore. Pure molten iron collects in the bottom and is drawn off every few hours.

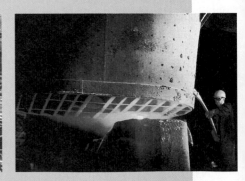

Huge ladles are used to pour molten steel into an ingot mold.

Electric furnaces like this one used to produce only special steels like tool steel and stainless steel. They now produce high volumes of regular (carbon) steel as well.

In this continuous casting process, an even flow of steel falls vertically down through rollers. The path of the steel becomes horizontal at the base. The steel slab is then cut into pieces.

Rolling mills convert ingots into basic shapes called slabs, billets, and blooms.

Slabs are further processed into steel sheets.

(All photos courtesy of U.S. Iron and Steel Institute)

Ceramics are common industrial materials. (Courtesy of Corning Glass Works)

Fiberglass is a ceramic material used in the manufacturing of this newly designed yacht called the Planesail. (Courtesy of Walker Wingsail Systems)

Ceramics generally do not conduct electricity well. They can be used as insulators. Wires carrying high-voltage electricity from power stations to your home use ceramic insulators. Ceramics are also used in light bulb sockets, switches, and other electric parts.

Ceramics can withstand high temperatures and remain strong. For this reason, mixtures of metal and ceramics are used inside some automobile and rocket engines.

Glass is a ceramic material. Most glass is made by melting sand, lime, and sodium oxide together at a temperature of around 2,500° Fahrenheit. This kind of glass is called **soda-lime glass**. It is used to make bottles, light bulbs, and window panes.

Fiberglass is a form of glass that is used for insulation. It is made by dropping molten glass onto a spinning steel dish. The dish has hundreds of tiny holes in it. Glass fibers are spun out of these holes as the dish turns.

Plastic

Plastics are made of long chains of molecules. These chains are called **polymers**. In the Greek language, "poly" means many and "meros" means parts. Most polymers are synthetic. That is, they are made by people rather than found in nature.

Thermoplastics are plastics that soften when heated. Like wax, they can be melted and shaped. When they cool, thermoplastics are hard again. Acrylic fibers (like nylon and Orlon) and polyethylene (used for plastic bags) are thermoplastics. So are polyvinyl chloride (or PVC, used for plumbing pipe and electrical insulation) and vinyl.

Thermoset plastics like bakelite and Formica do not soften when heated. They char and burn instead. They are less common than thermoplastics. "Unbreakable" plastic cups and dishes are made from malamine, a thermoset plastic.

PROCESSING MATERIAL RESOURCES

Four basic ways to process resources are forming, separating, combining, and conditioning. **Forming** a material means changing its shape without cutting it. **Separating** a material means removing a part of it, usually through a cutting or grinding process. **Combining** means joining two materials together. **Conditioning** materials changes their internal properties. There are many ways to accomplish each of these processes.

Materials are processed by forming, separating, combining, and conditioning.

FORMING PROCESSES

Forming a material means changing its shape without cutting it. For example, metal can be bent to change its shape. It can also be formed in other ways.

Casting

One way to form material is called **casting**. Castings are made from molds. When you walk on the beach and press your foot into the sand, you make a mold of it. If you melted metal, poured it into the sand mold, and let it cool, you would have a casting of your footprint. We use casting to make ice cubes. We pour water into an ice cube tray. When the water freezes, we can pop out ice cube castings.

Molds can be one piece or several pieces. The footprint is a one-piece mold. Another one-piece mold is a cake pan. We pour the cake batter into the mold. When baked, the cake hardens into the shape of the pan. This, too, is casting.

A two-piece mold can be used to cast ceramic (clay) objects. First, the mold is made from plaster. Then **slip** (liquid clay) is

The casting process is used to make pump and transmission housings. (Courtesy of Cross and Trecker Corp.)

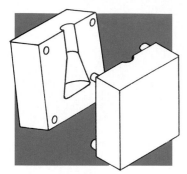

A two-piece mold for casting ceramic objects

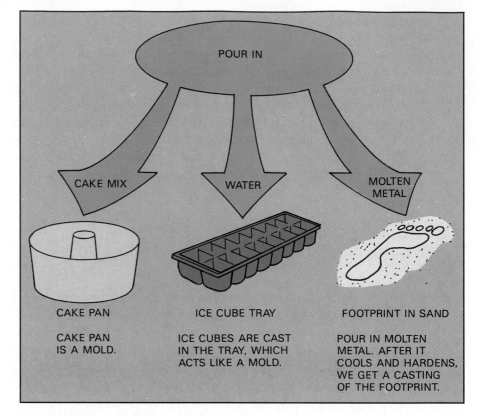

POUR IN

CAKE MIX

WATER

MOLTEN METAL

CAKE PAN

CAKE PAN IS A MOLD.

ICE CUBE TRAY

ICE CUBES ARE CAST IN THE TRAY, WHICH ACTS LIKE A MOLD.

FOOTPRINT IN SAND

POUR IN MOLTEN METAL. AFTER IT COOLS AND HARDENS, WE GET A CASTING OF THE FOOTPRINT.

Some common one-piece molds

poured into the mold. It is allowed to set (harden) for a few minutes. Then it is poured out again. The plaster absorbs water from the slip. This leaves a thin wall of clay inside the mold. When the clay dries, the mold is opened. The finished casting is removed.

Pressing

Pressing is like casting. It is used in many industrial processes. A measured amount of material is poured into a mold. A plunger with its own shape is lowered to force the material to spread out and fill the mold. The material is forced into the shape of the mold at the bottom and the shape of the plunger at the top. Then the plunger is pulled out, and the object is removed. When we make hamburger patties, we press the meat into shape with our hands. Waffles are pressed by waffle irons.

Sometimes powdered metal is pressed to make objects. The powder is put into the bottom of a mold. The top of the mold is lowered. Great pressure makes the powder into a solid. It is then heated to make the particles bond more tightly. This pressing process is called **sintering**.

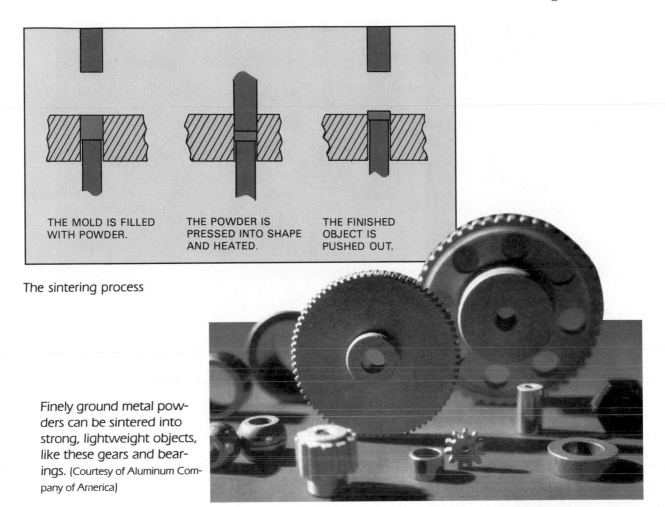

THE MOLD IS FILLED
WITH POWDER.

THE POWDER IS
PRESSED INTO SHAPE
AND HEATED.

THE FINISHED
OBJECT IS
PUSHED OUT.

The sintering process

Finely ground metal powders can be sintered into strong, lightweight objects, like these gears and bearings. (Courtesy of Aluminum Company of America)

Forging

A **forging** is a metal part that has been heated (but not melted) and then hammered into shape. Many metal parts are made by forging. Long ago, forging was done by hand. Blacksmiths forged horseshoes by heating pieces of metal and hammering them into shape.

Today, most metal forging is done by large machines. A piece of heated metal is placed in the lower half of a mold. A powerful ram presses the metal downward into the mold with as much as 2,500 tons of force.

Extruding

Extruding is another way of forming. Here, softened material is squeezed through an opening. It's much like squeezing a tube of toothpaste. The material takes the shape of an open-

These truck wheels are made from forged metals. (Courtesy of Alcoa Aluminum Corp.)

In days past, hand forging was a common method of forming tools and other useful items. (Courtesy of The Citizens & Southern National Bank of South Carolina)

A large forging press (Courtesy of Cerro Metal Products)

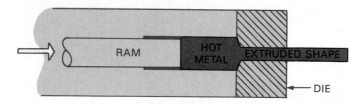

In extrusion, hot metal is forced through a hole called a die. The metal takes the shape of the die.

OTHER RESOURCES IN

MATERIAL RESOURCE IN

• CASTING
• PRESSING
• EXTRUDING
• FORGING
• BLOW MOLDING
• VACUUM FORMING

FORMED MATERIAL OUT

Some forming processes

ing. Suppose, for example, that the hole at the end of a toothpaste tube is square. The ribbon of toothpaste would come out in a rectangular block. Extruding objects can save work, because the end product does not require much more shaping and machining.

Blow Molding and Vacuum Forming

Blow molding and **vacuum forming** are processes used to form plastic. In these processes, a thin plastic sheet is heated until it is soft. In blow molding, air blows the plastic into a mold. Plastic bottles are made by blow molding. In vacuum forming, a vacuum pulls the warm, soft plastic down. The plastic clings to whatever it is drawn against. Vacuum forming is used to package products that hang on cardboard cards in supermarkets and toy stores. A plastic sheet is pulled down against the product in the package. This is known as blister packaging.

SEPARATING PROCESSES

Knives, saws, or scissors are used in separating one piece of material from another. We use a separating process when we cut food with a knife. Cutting is a separating process. Many different kinds of tools and machines are used for cutting. Some are designed to cut specific materials. There are cutting tools just for wood, metal, plastic, clay, leather, and paper. Tools and machines cut materials by **shearing**, **sawing**, **drilling**, **grinding**, **shaping**, and **turning**.

Shearing

Shearing is using a knife-like blade for separating. One blade can be used, as in a knife, or two blades can be used, as in a pair of scissors. In fact, another name for scissors is shears. In shearing, the sharp edge of the blade compresses the material being cut. When the force gets high enough, the material breaks along the line of the cut. The sharper the knife edge, the greater the force along the line on which the material is cut.

Sawing

Sawing is separating material with a blade that has teeth. Each tooth chips away tiny bits of material as the saw cuts. Two kinds of sawing processes are used to cut wood. **Ripping** is used to cut wood along the direction of the grain. **Crosscutting** is used to cut across the grain. Handsaws used to rip or cross-cut generally have between six and ten teeth per inch. Metal is cut by hand with a saw called a **hacksaw**. A hacksaw has a very hard steel blade. The blade generally has about eighteen teeth per inch.

Saw blades come in many forms. Some are made in circular shapes. Machine saws such as radial arm saws and table saws use circular saw blades. These blades are carefully made. Each tooth is very sharp. The blade spins rapidly, so many cuts per minute are made in the material being sawed.

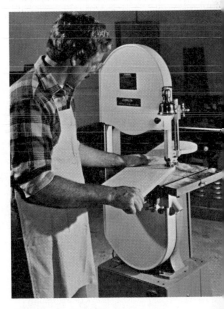

Operator using a band saw.
(Courtesy of Delta International Machine Corp.)

Drilling

Drilling is a separating process used to cut round holes in materials. A pointed tool with a sharpened end (twist drill) is turned very rapidly. Either a hand drill or an electric drill can be used to spin the twist drill. Drilled holes can be made small or large, from 1/10,000 of an inch to 3½ inches.

Grinding

Grinding is done by tools like grinders and sanding machines. Grinding tools make use of pieces of very hard material called **abrasives**. Abrasives are crushed into very small particles. These particles can be glued onto a flat sheet to make sandpaper or emery cloth. The particles can also be made into grinding wheels. As the grinding wheel turns, the abrasive particles rub against and cut away tiny pieces of the material.

We can sharpen tools like knives and scissors by grinding them. Grinding removes a tiny bit of material at a time. With skill, a blade can be sharpened to a fine edge.

Six Types of Cutting Machines

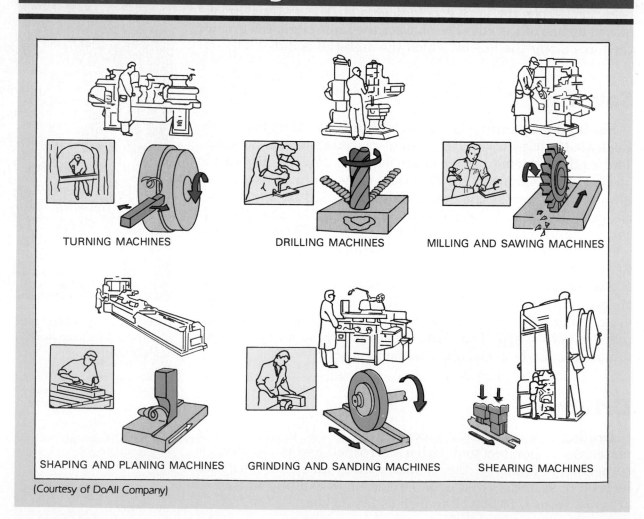

TURNING MACHINES

DRILLING MACHINES

MILLING AND SAWING MACHINES

SHAPING AND PLANING MACHINES

GRINDING AND SANDING MACHINES

SHEARING MACHINES

(Courtesy of DoAll Company)

Saws and Sawing

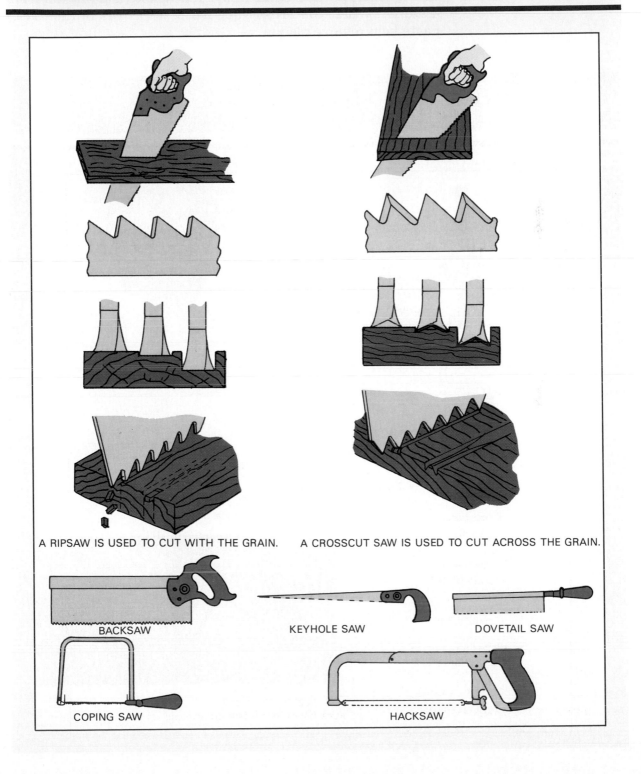

A RIPSAW IS USED TO CUT WITH THE GRAIN. A CROSSCUT SAW IS USED TO CUT ACROSS THE GRAIN.

BACKSAW

KEYHOLE SAW

DOVETAIL SAW

COPING SAW

HACKSAW

Polishing is another form of grinding. Polishes generally contain some very fine abrasive powder. When you rub an object with polish, you are removing tiny bits of it. This makes the surface smooth, clean, and shiny. Toothpaste is a fine abrasive material. When you brush your teeth, abrasives in the toothpaste help remove plaque.

Drills and Drilling

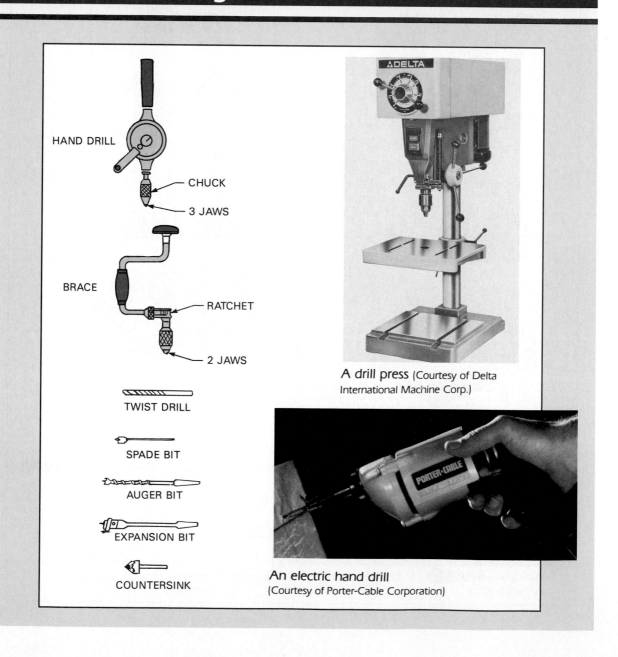

HAND DRILL

CHUCK

3 JAWS

BRACE

RATCHET

2 JAWS

TWIST DRILL

SPADE BIT

AUGER BIT

EXPANSION BIT

COUNTERSINK

A drill press (Courtesy of Delta International Machine Corp.)

An electric hand drill
(Courtesy of Porter-Cable Corporation)

Notice the safety shields over this grinding machine and the safety glasses worn by the operator. Sparks and tiny particles of material can fly into the eye unless proper safety precautions are taken. (Courtesy of Delta International Machine Corp.)

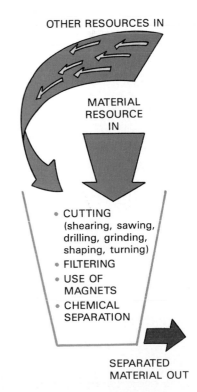

OTHER RESOURCES IN

MATERIAL RESOURCE IN

- CUTTING
  (shearing, sawing, drilling, grinding, shaping, turning)
- FILTERING
- USE OF MAGNETS
- CHEMICAL SEPARATION

SEPARATED MATERIAL OUT

Some separating processes

Shaping

Shaping is used to change the shape of a piece of material. Chisels and planes are hand tools used for shaping. Shaping tools have cutters with chisel-like edges that chip away material. Some shaping machines are jointers, planers, routers, and shapers.

Turning

Turning is another process that is used to shape materials. A turning tool is different from other shaping tools in that the tool itself doesn't move. Instead, the material to be cut (the workpiece) is moved. A lathe spins the workpiece. The cutting tool is held against the spinning workpiece and cuts material from it. When the cutting tool is moved closer to the workpiece, it reduces the diameter of the workpiece. Very complicated and beautiful shapes can be made using a lathe.

Wood lathes are used to make cylindrical objects, such as legs for tables and chairs. (Courtesy of Delta International Machine Corp.)

Other Separating Processes

Materials can be separated by means other than cutting. Materials can be separated **chemically**, as when water is separated into oxygen and hydrogen. Salt can be removed from water by letting the water evaporate. **Filtering** is a way of separating solids from liquids in a mixture. For example, you could separate the vegetables in a can of soup from the liquid by pouring the soup through a strainer. **Magnets** can be used to separate magnetic materials from nonmagnetic ones.

COMBINING PROCESSES

Sometimes we want to combine materials. We might want to **fasten** one material to another. We might want to **coat** a surface with a protective finish. We might want to make a **composite material** from two materials that is more useful than either of them alone.

Fastening Materials by Mechanical Means

Using nails, screws, and rivets, we can fasten materials together mechanically. Fasteners are made specifically for certain materials. Nails are used to fasten two pieces of wood. We would not use nails to fasten two pieces of metal.

Years ago, nails were made one at a time, by hand. The end of an iron rod was heated red-hot. It was hammered to a point, then snapped off at the length wanted. Nails were costly because it took a long time to make them. Most houses were put together without nails. Today, automatic machines make nails by the thousands. Partly because the price of nails has dropped, it has become cheaper and easier to build homes.

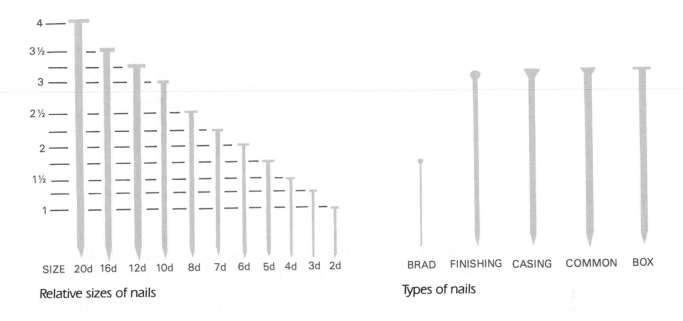

Relative sizes of nails

Types of nails

For the best holding power, nails should be driven into wood at a right angle to the grain. When you nail two boards together, the nail should be long enough to go two-thirds of the way through the bottom piece of wood. If the wood is very hard, the nail might split it. To avoid this, a hole is drilled in the wood that is slightly smaller than the nail's diameter. This hole, called a **pilot hole**, makes it easier for the nail to enter the wood.

The five most common types of nails are: brads, finishing nails, casing nails, common nails, and box nails. Nails are sold according to their size. Size is measured in **pennyweight**. Pennyweight used to refer to the cost of one hundred nails. An eight-penny nail (abbreviated 8d) cost eight cents per hundred. Now pennyweight refers only to the length of nails.

A screw can be used to pull one piece of material tightly against another. Screws provide more holding power than nails. They can be removed more easily. Different types of screws are used for wood and metal. The threads of wood screws start at the point and go about two-thirds of the way to the head.

Screws used to fasten pieces of thin sheet metal are called **sheet metal screws**. These are threaded all the way to the head. Pilot holes are drilled for sheet metal screws because a sheet metal screw can't start itself in a piece of metal. A pilot hole should be the size of the body of the screw without its threads. This is called the **root diameter** of the screw. Sheet metal screws cut a thread into the sheet metal as they are screwed in.

Machine screws and bolts do not have pointed ends. The thread is the same diameter from tip to head. Machine screws and bolts are held in place by a **nut** or a threaded hole. The nut

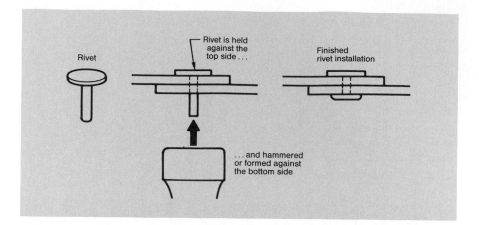

How two pieces of metal are held together with a rivet

has the same size thread as the machine screw or bolt. **Washers** are used between the nut and the material being fastened. Flat washers protect the material from being damaged by the nut. Lock washers keep the nut from loosening under vibration.

In driving screws, it is important to choose the right screwdriver. A screwdriver with too wide a blade will slip out of the screw slot and may hurt the material being fastened. A screwdriver with too narrow a blade could damage the screw slot and not provide enough power to turn the screw. **Never put your hand in line with the screwdriver blade because the screwdriver may slip.**

Riveting is often used in building aircraft. Rivets hold pieces of sheet metal together. One end of a rivet is already formed. The other end is hammered and formed after it is placed through the two pieces of metal to be fastened.

Fastening Materials with Heat

Soft soldering is joining metals with heat and soft solder. Soft solder is an alloy made from lead and tin. It melts at about 450° Fahrenheit. Soldering irons or guns are used to melt the solder. Soldering is the most common way to attach wires in electronic circuits.

Hard soldering involves the use of an alloy made from brass or silver. This material melts at about 1400° Fahrenheit. An acetylene torch provides the heat source. Hard soldering is sometimes referred to as brazing or silver soldering.

Welding is another way to use heat to join metals. In welding, the metals to be joined are heated high enough to fuse together. Welding rod is used like solder to help join the metals. Welding makes very strong bonds and requires temperatures of 6,000-7,000° Fahrenheit. The heat comes from a welding torch that burns a mixture of gas and air (gas welding). It can also come from a machine that uses high electrical current (arc welding).

Gluing Materials

Gluing is another way to fasten materials. In using glue, we are making use of the chemical properties of materials. The glue forms chemical bonds between itself and the materials being glued. Glues are made for many different kinds of material. For wood, white or yellow glues are used. For plastic, metal, and ceramic, epoxy or SuperGlue® are best.

Today, there is a glue for fastening almost every type of material. For example, for many years copper pipe was used

Types of Screws

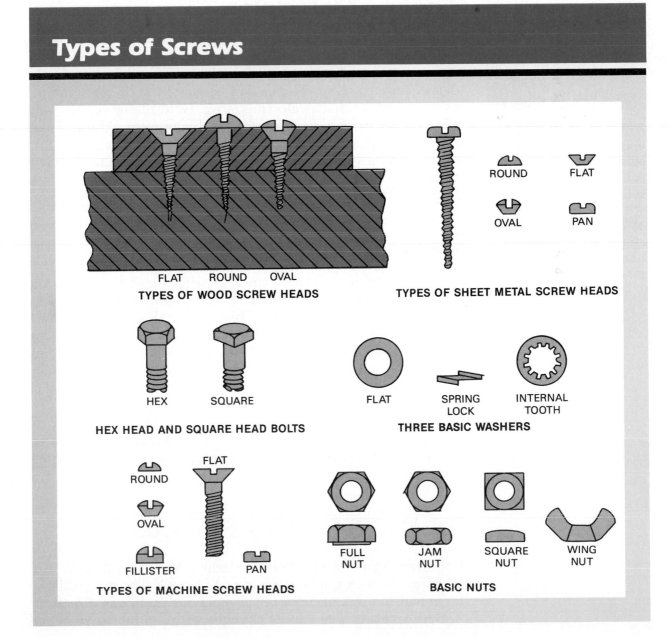

TYPES OF WOOD SCREW HEADS

TYPES OF SHEET METAL SCREW HEADS

HEX HEAD AND SQUARE HEAD BOLTS

THREE BASIC WASHERS

TYPES OF MACHINE SCREW HEADS

BASIC NUTS

Pennsylvania's Washington County courthouse has been restored to look as beautiful as it did when it was built at the turn of the century. The project required 450 gallons of paint, 15 gallons of stain, and 26 quarts of custom colorants. (Courtesy of PPG Industries)

for most plumbing jobs. The pipe was fastened by soldering the pieces together. Today, plastic pipe made of PVC (polyvinyl chloride) is used. Special glues are used to join pieces of PVC pipe. The glues bond the atoms of the two pieces of pipe.

A good glue joint is stronger than the material it joins. Hot glues are applied with glue guns. These glues are very strong and set rapidly, allowing quick fastening. Such glues are now being used to hold airplane parts together.

Coating Materials

To beautify or protect a surface, we can coat it with a finish. Paint, stain, and wax are finishes that can be used. Ceramic dishes are coated with glass-like glazes. The glazes make the dishes easy to clean. Metals can be coated with other metals by a process known as **electroplating**. Gold-plated jewelry and silver-plated tableware are made by this process. Aluminum is coated by a process called **anodizing**. Anodizing causes a thin oxide coating to form on the surface of the aluminum. **Galvanizing** is a process that coats steel with zinc to keep the steel from rusting.

Making Composite Materials

Thousands of years ago, the Egyptians added straw to the clay they used to make bricks. The straw made the bricks stronger. Technology has since brought forth many other composite materials. A **composite material** is a material made by combining several materials. The new material has special properties. For example, plywood is a composite material. Layers of wood are glued one on top of another. The result is a panel of very strong wood.

Fiberglass is a composite material made from glass and an epoxy resin. It can be stronger than steel. Fiberglass, however, weighs much less than steel. Fiberglass is used in making the bodies of some automobiles.

CONDITIONING PROCESSES

Conditioning materials changes their internal properties. For example, we can **magnetize** a piece of steel. The magnetizing force makes the molecules of the steel line up in one direction.

Heat-treating also causes changes within a material. When

The Electroplating Process

Electoplating combines chemistry with electricity. The part to be plated is connected to the negative terminal of a battery. A pure piece of the metal that is to do the plating is connected to the positive terminal. The part and the pure metal are put in a vat of plating solution. The solution for copper plating contains a chemical called copper sulfate ($CuSO_4$).

The copper sulfate solution breaks down into positively and negatively charged particles (ions) when electric current flows through it. In this example, the positively charged ions are ions of copper. They are attracted to the negative terminal, thereby plating it (covering it) with copper. Copper ions from the pure copper replace those used from the solution. Electroplating can be used to plate many different kinds of metals.

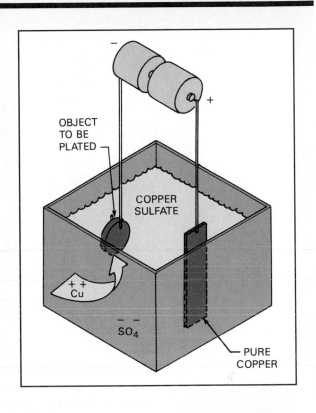

OBJECT TO BE PLATED

COPPER SULFATE

++ Cu

-- SO$_4$

PURE COPPER

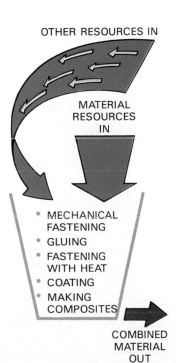

Composite materials are used in special-purpose planes, like the Lockheed SR-71 spy plane. (Courtesy of Lockheed-California Company)

OTHER RESOURCES IN

MATERIAL RESOURCES IN

- MECHANICAL FASTENING
- GLUING
- FASTENING WITH HEAT
- COATING
- MAKING COMPOSITES

Some combining processes

COMBINED MATERIAL OUT

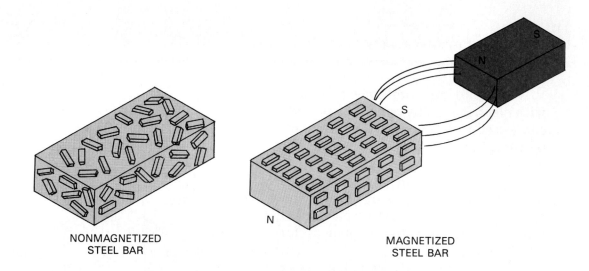

NONMAGNETIZED
STEEL BAR

MAGNETIZED
STEEL BAR

steel is heated red hot and quickly cooled in water, it becomes harder. This is called **hardening**. If we heat the steel again, not quite as hot, and cool it quickly, the steel becomes less brittle. This is **tempering**. If we heat steel red hot and allow it to cool very slowly, the steel becomes softer. This is called **annealing**.

When clay is fired in a kiln, it becomes harder and stronger. When a piece of metal is hammered, it becomes harder. This is called **mechanical conditioning**. The metal's crystal structure changes, getting longer and thinner. When we mix plaster and water, heat is given off because a chemical reaction takes place. The plaster hardens because of this **chemical conditioning**. In each example, the change takes place inside the material itself.

Other examples of conditioning are:

- light exposing photographic film
- chemicals developing photographic paper
- baking a cake
- cooking an egg
- freezing water
- boiling water
- melting ice
- putting metal in liquid nitrogen to turn the metal into a superconductor
- using radiation on a tumor
- making butter from cream
- sending electricity through the filament wire of a light bulb
- making wine from grape juice

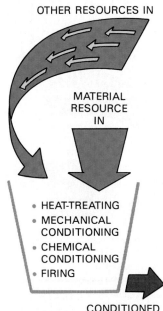

OTHER RESOURCES IN

MATERIAL
RESOURCE
IN

- HEAT-TREATING
- MECHANICAL CONDITIONING
- CHEMICAL CONDITIONING
- FIRING

CONDITIONED
MATERIAL OUT

Some conditioning processes

USING COMPUTERS TO CONTROL PROCESSING OF MATERIALS

Computers can be used to control machines that process materials. For example, computers are sometimes used in cooking. When food is heated in a microwave oven, the oven temperature and cooking time are controlled by a tiny computer. In some factories, machines that process materials are controlled by computers. Often the computer is built right into the machine. The computer can be programmed to make a machine tool cut material along a specified path. These computers can also be reprogrammed. A machine that makes parts for a tractor can be reprogrammed to make the part differently when the company decides to change the tractor's design. In the days before computer control, changing the way a machine worked could take a long time. A worker would have to spend hours or even days setting up and adjusting machines by hand.

Computer-numerical-controlled (CNC) machines and robots are two kinds of computer-controlled machines used for processing materials. Computers that direct the order of operations of

Computers can control machines used to process materials.

Computers can control machines used to process materials. In this two-machine/robot machining cell, computers control the machining of parts. (Courtesy of Cincinnati Milacron)

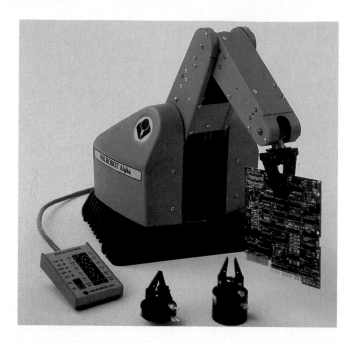

Here, a teach pendant is
used to program a robot.
(Courtesy of Microbot Inc.)

a machine can often be programmed using simple computer
languages. These languages use terms that are familiar to the
people who use the machines.

Robots are sometimes programmed by having a person "show"
the robot what it must do. With the robot in the "learn" mode
of operation, the person uses a "teach pendant" (remote controller) to move the robot through the movements needed to do
a job. The robot stores the motions in its memory. Then, when
commanded, the robot will go through the motions in order,
again and again.

PROPERTIES OF MATERIALS

*Materials are chosen on the
basis of their mechanical,
electrical, magnetic, thermal,
and optical properties.*

We choose our friends because they have characteristics we
like. We might like the way someone looks, or their sense
of humor. Materials are also chosen for their characteristics,
or **properties**. Properties of materials include strength, hardness, appearance, ability to conduct electricity, and resistance
to corrosion.

We use glass for windows because light comes through it.
We use plastic for dishes because it is strong and can be cleaned
easily. We make electrical wire out of copper because copper
conducts electricity well. We make phonograph needles using
small pieces of diamond because diamonds are hard enough to
last a long time. We make clothing out of nylon because it is
lightweight and attractive.

Mechanical Properties

Force applied to a material can make it bend or break. Certain kinds of material will bend more than others. A fishing rod made from fiberglass will bend quite a bit without breaking. Many kinds of wood break without bending much at all. Materials that can be bent without breaking are called **ductile materials**. When we make pots and pans, we start out with a flat sheet of metal. We then put pressure on part of the metal and form it into the shape we want. We may have to deform (change the shape of) the metal a great deal. When we make wire, we start with a thick rod and pull it through a small hole to make it thinner. This process, called **drawing wire**, works because the metal rod is a ductile material. It can be stretched very thin before it breaks. Any material that can be twisted, bent, or pressed into shape has a high ductility.

The opposite of ductile is brittle. A **brittle material** will not deform without breaking. Window glass is a good example.

Ductile materials are either **elastic** or **plastic**. A material that can bend and then come back to its original shape and size is elastic. It acts the way a piece of elastic does. Rubber bands, springs, and fishing rods are made from materials with high **elasticity**. Elasticity is the stiffness of a material.

A property similar to elasticity is **plasticity**. Plastic materials can be bent and will stay bent. The material we call plastic got its name because of that property. When we heat thermoplastic and bend it, it will stay bent after it cools. Modeling clay is a plastic material. So are certain metals. They stay deformed after the force that shapes them is removed.

When metal was in short supply during World War II, people made bicycles out of wood. (Courtesy of Smithsonian Institution)

You Can Try This

The following will help you understand the difference between elasticity and plasticity. Find a straight piece of steel rod, ¼ " in diameter. Bend it slowly. If you don't use too much force, the rod will straighten out again when you let go. This is an example of elasticity. Now bend the rod with more force. You will be able to bend it past its elastic limit. When you bend the rod past its elastic limit, it will stay bent. This is an example of plasticity.

Some materials are stronger than others. A material's strength is its ability to keep its own shape when a force is applied to it. Four kinds of force can be applied to materials. **Tension** is force that pulls on a piece of material. When we pull on a spring, it is under tension. **Compression** is the opposite of tension. It is a force that pushes on or squeezes a material. Squeezing a sponge and walking on rubber-soled shoes are examples of compression. **Torsion** is the twisting of a material. If we twist a piece of licorice candy, the material is in torsion. The twisting force itself is called **torque**. When a wrench is used to turn a bolt, torque is used. A **shear** force acts on a material like a pair of scissors. One part slides in one direction and the other part slides in the opposite direction.

Toughness is another mechanical property. It is the ability to absorb energy without breaking. For example, leather is tough. Sometimes meat is tough. It takes a lot of chewing to break down the fibers of the meat.

An important mechanical property is hardness. **Hardness** is a material's ability to resist being scratched or dented. A diamond is the hardest material known. Some metals are also very hard. Metal tools must be hardened to resist wear. Some synthetic materials, like tungsten carbide, are very hard. The teeth of circular saw blades are often made of tungsten carbide.

Electrical and Magnetic Properties

All materials resist the flow of electricity. Some, called **conductors**, offer very little electrical resistance. Most good conductors are metals. The very best conductor is silver. The next best is copper. Most wire is made from copper because silver is much more costly. People make a trade-off (performance for cost) when they choose copper instead of silver.

Properties of Materials

MECHANICAL PROPERTIES

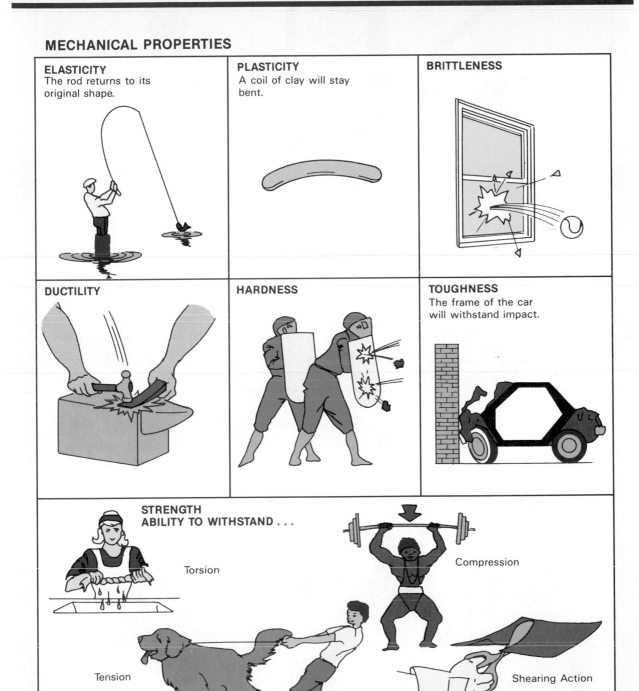

ELASTICITY
The rod returns to its original shape.

PLASTICITY
A coil of clay will stay bent.

BRITTLENESS

DUCTILITY

HARDNESS

TOUGHNESS
The frame of the car will withstand impact.

STRENGTH
ABILITY TO WITHSTAND . . .

Torsion

Compression

Tension

Shearing Action

OPTICAL PROPERTIES

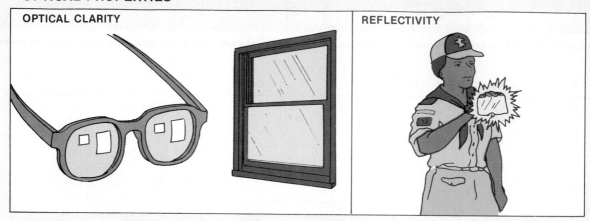

OPTICAL CLARITY

REFLECTIVITY

THERMAL PROPERTIES

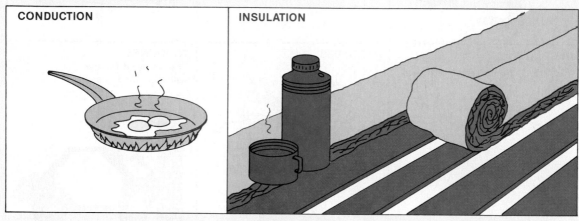

CONDUCTION

INSULATION

ELECTRICAL AND MAGNETIC PROPERTIES

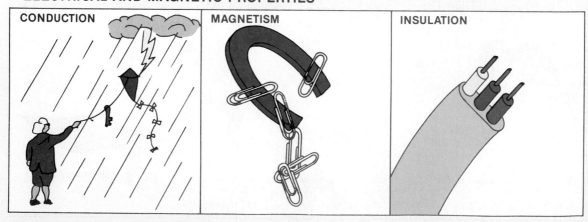

CONDUCTION

MAGNETISM

INSULATION

Materials that resist the flow of electricity most strongly are called **insulators**. Sometimes materials are chosen because they are good insulators. Wire is covered with plastic or rubber to protect people from electric shock. Plastic and rubber are used because they are insulators.

When electricity flows through a wire, a magnetic field is produced. An electromagnet can be made by wrapping wire around a piece of iron. When an electric current (for example, from a battery) flows through the wire, the iron piece becomes a magnet. Materials that can be attracted to magnets are **magnetic** materials. Iron, steel, nickel, and cobalt are magnetic materials. Copper, wood, glass, and leather are some nonmagnetic materials.

Thermal Properties

In the Greek language, "therm" means heat. Words like thermostat and thermos bottle name things related to heat. Thermal properties refer to a material's ability to conduct heat.

Metals are good conductors of heat. Copper and aluminum are two of the best. Other materials, such as rubber and fiberglass, do not conduct heat well. In building a house, materials are used that do not conduct heat well. A layer of material that does not conduct heat, called **insulation**, is used to prevent the movement of heat through the walls.

Optical Properties

Optical properties refer to a material's ability to transmit or reflect light. Some kinds of glass can transmit light well. Window glass transmits light well enough to see through, but not well enough to be used for scientific tools like telescopes. Special optical glass is used for telescope lenses. Plastic is lightweight and will not shatter. That makes it useful in contact lenses and eyeglasses. Very pure glass is used in making glass fibers that are used instead of wire in communication. Some metals reflect light very well. They are used in reflectors for headlights and flashlights.

DISPOSAL OF RESOURCES

We must also think about how we will dispose of end products when we are through with them. Often, instead of repairing something, we throw it away. We live in what has been called a "throw-away" society. Our soda comes in cans or bottles that we throw away. Our food comes in disposable plastic or paper containers.

When we throw away products, we bury them in landfills or burn them. But the materials these products are made of can cause pollution. Burning them can pollute the air. Storing them in landfills can pollute groundwater, and besides, landfills are overflowing. Toxic materials—lead and mercury, for example— and radioactive waste must be disposed of in a way that does

Material Decomposition Time

MATERIAL	TIME TO DECOMPOSE
Orange peels	1 week to 6 months
Paper containers	2 weeks to 4 months
Paper containers with plastic coating	5 years
Plastic bags	10 to 20 years
Feathers	50 years
Plastic bottles	50 to 80 years
Aluminum cans with flip-top tabs	80 to 100 years
Plutonium	24,390 years (half-life)
Glass bottles	Indefinite

Recycling is an important source of aluminum supply. (Courtesy of Aluminum Company of America)

To dispose of radioactive waste, technologists cover it with lead and then bury it in salt formations far underground. (Courtesy of Rockwell International Corp.)

Waste disposal is a major technological problem. (Courtesy of Sperry Corp.)

not pollute the soil, water, or atmosphere. Companies must work to make products of materials that will decompose (rot) to become part of the earth again. Those that will not decompose, like plastic or glass, should be **recycled** (reused).

SUMMARY

To make material resources more useful and more valuable, we process them. The other six technological resources are needed to process material resources.

Primary raw materials are processed into industrial materials. From industrial materials, end products are made. Materials are processed by forming, separating, combining, and conditioning them.

Forming a material means changing its shape without cutting it. Forming processes include casting, pressing, forging, extruding, blow molding, and vacuum forming. Separating processes separate one piece of material from another. Cutting is a separating process. We can cut materials by shearing, sawing, drilling, grinding, shaping, and turning. Combining materials means putting one material together with others.

Laser measurement system
(Courtesy of Hewlett-Packard
Company)

A polishing and grinding
line. (Courtesy of Allegheny
Ludlum Steel Corp.)

We can combine materials by fastening, coating, or making composite materials. Conditioning materials means changing their internal properties. Conditioning processes include magnetizing, heat-treating, mechanically working, and chemically processing a material. Computers can be used to control machines used to process materials.

Materials are chosen on the basis of their properties. Mechanical properties include: ductility (ability to bend without breaking); elasticity (stiffness); plasticity (ability to be bent and stay bent); strength (ability to withstand tension, compression, torsion, and shear); and hardness (ability to resist scratching or denting). Other properties are: electrical (ability to conduct electricity); magnetic (ability to be attracted to a magnet); thermal (ability to conduct heat); and optical (ability to transmit or reflect light). We can use technology to make materials with new properties. We should choose materials that decompose or can be recycled.

REVIEW QUESTIONS

1. Why must materials be processed?
2. Give an example of a food that is processed from animal or vegetable material. Give two reasons foods are processed.
3. What happens to materials in a technological process?
4. What is the role of computers in processing materials?
5. What are four ways materials are processed?
6. What processes would you use to make hamburgers from raw meat?
7. How do sawing, drilling, and grinding differ?
8. What kind of fasteners would you use to attach a metal bracket to a wooden shelf?
9. Why would you choose to weld two pieces of metal instead of gluing them or using screws?
10. Why might you use a different finish on wood than on metal?
11. What happens to the internal structure of a piece of steel when it is magnetized?
12. List five ways to condition materials.
13. Make a list of ten jobs in which materials are processed.
14. Explain why materials are chosen for products on the basis of their properties.
15. We plan to manufacture a jigsaw puzzle for four-year-olds. We want to sell it for under two dollars. What material might we make it from?
16. You need a screwdriver for electrical work. From what kind of material should the handle be made, and why?
17. Why must people think about the disposal of end products when choosing the materials from which they are made?

KEY WORDS

Brittle	Elastic	Insulator	Shaping
Casting	Extruding	Plasticity	Shearing
Ceramics	Fastening	Polymers	Tension
Coating	Ferrous metals	Pressing	Thermal
Combining	Forging	Properties of	Thermoplastics
Composites	Forming	materials	Thermoset
Compression	Gluing	Raw materials	plastics
Conditioning	Grinding	Recycle	Torsion
Conductor	Heat-treating	Sawing	Toughness
Drilling	Industrial	Separating	Turning
Ductile	materials		

SEE YOUR TEACHER FOR THE CROSSTECH PUZZLE

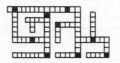

241

CUTTLEBONE CASTING

Setting the Stage

The hours of underwater searching did not yield the 8th cross, lost when the Spanish galleon went down off the Florida coast in the early 1700s. All 8 bead necklaces had been recovered, but only 7 center crosses. Since the jewelry was due to be displayed, the needed cross would have to be cast to fill in until the remaining religious artifact could be found.

Your Challenge

Cast jewelry using cuttlebone and an original pattern.

Procedure

1. Choose your pattern or model. Patterns can be constructed of wood, plastic, or metal.
2. Tape a piece of #220 abrasive paper on a smooth table. Using a circular motion, sand the inner portion of the bone to achieve a smooth, flat surface. Repeat this process with a second piece of cuttlebone.
3. Determine the approximate position of the pattern on the sanded cuttlebone surface. This position should be located at the thickest section of the cuttlebone.
4. Press three ³⁄₁₆" diameter wooden pegs into one of the cuttlebones. The wooden pegs should protrude approximately ⁵⁄₁₆" above the sanded cuttlebone surface, and be located at least ½" from the pattern. These pegs are used for alignment when the two halves of the mold are assembled.
5. Place your pattern in the predetermined area on the cuttlebone. Press the model halfway into the cuttlebone. Align the remaining prepared cuttlebone on the tapered wooden pegs, and press slowly against the first section until the sanded halves mesh. You may need to apply additional pressure with a padded vise.
6. Bind the two halves together with steel wire and saw off each end of the cuttlebone. Smooth each end with abrasive paper.
7. Carefully separate the mold and remove the pattern.
8. Cut a funnel shape in each half of the mold. This will be your reservoir for excess metal. Cut a channel from the funnel shape

Suggested Resources

Cuttlefish bone
Charcoal
Modern pewter
Abrasive paper (#220)
Steel wire
Propane torch
Small container of sand
³⁄₁₆" diameter dowel rod
Metal polishing materials
Graphite
Hard soldering flux
Sodium silicate

242

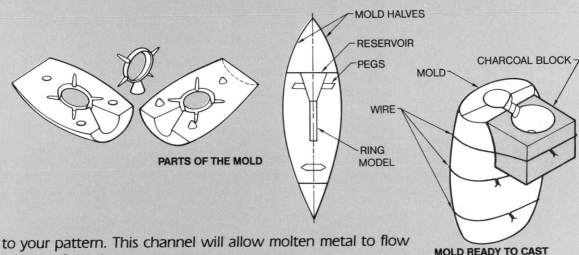

PARTS OF THE MOLD

MOLD HALVES

RESERVOIR

PEGS

RING
MODEL

CHARCOAL BLOCK

MOLD

WIRE

MOLD READY TO CAST

to your pattern. This channel will allow molten metal to flow from the funnel to your pattern.

9. Cut small thin channels from the pattern to near the outside of the mold. These will act as gas vents.

10. Paint the mold chamber with a heat-resistant solution of equal parts of hard soldering flux and sodium silicate (water glass). Another method is to dust powdered graphite on the mold surface and reassemble the mold with the pattern inside. This forces the graphite into the mold surface and produces a smooth casting.

11. Wire the mold together and place the mold upright in a shallow pan with some sand. The sand will hold the cuttlebone in position.

12. Your teacher will pour the molten metal into the mold using a ladle, or you may use a charcoal block wired to the cuttlebone to hold the metal. Use a propane torch to heat the pewter in the charcoal block.

13. Several castings can be obtained from the same mold if you use lead-free modern pewter. Sterling silver will pit the mold, allowing only one good casting.

14. Finish the jewelry using processes outlined by your teacher.

Technology Connections

1. What is an alloy? What metals are in modern pewter? Older pewter is an alloy of what metals?

2. Why have lead-based products been changed to lead-free products?

3. Identify the forming, combining, and conditioning processes you used in making your jewelry.

Science and Math Concepts

▶ The specific gravity of a substance is the ratio of the weight of a given volume of the substance to the weight of the same volume of water at the same temperature.

▶ The volume of irregular solids can be determined by using a water displacement method. Immerse your model in water in a graduated cylinder. Note the change in volume. Remove the model. Place casting metal in the cylinder to equal the volume change.

243

CHECKERBOARD

Setting the Stage

You have received a new contract with a local restaurant. They want some unique and practical tables. The owner thinks more people would come to the restaurant if they could eat and also socialize. How might you build a tabletop that is easily cleaned, and also serves as a gameboard before or after food is served?

Your Challenge

Design and construct a checkerboard table top that will resist wear and be easily cleaned.

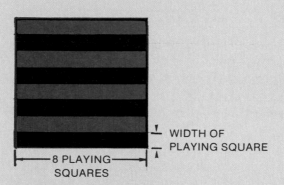

WIDTH OF
PLAYING SQUARE

8 PLAYING
SQUARES

|- LENGTH OF BOARD -|

CHECKERBOARD
ARRANGEMENT

Procedure

1. Cut material of two contrasting colors into eight strips as shown.
2. Glue the strips together.
3. Cut across the strips to form eight pieces, with eight contrasting squares each. Then, flip every other strip to create contrasting squares in the other direction, forming a checkerboard.
4. Glue the strips back together. If you chose to use thin plastic or ceramic material, glue the squares to a solid backing.
5. To add a three-dimensional quality to the checkerboard, cast a ⅜" to ¾" clear layer of polyester resin on the checkerboard. (Steps 6–11 explain how to do this casting.)
6. Cut and assemble a frame for the completed checkerboard. The height of the frame should be the thickness of the checkerboard plus the desired thickness of the polyester resin layer.
7. Apply finish and polyester resin wax release to the frame and the bottom of the checkerboard. Polyester resin will spill onto the frame and bottom of the board during the casting procedure. The resin wax release will prevent the resin from sticking to the frame and bottom of the board.

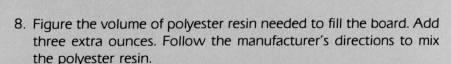

8. Figure the volume of polyester resin needed to fill the board. Add three extra ounces. Follow the manufacturer's directions to mix the polyester resin.

9. Carefully pour the polyester resin into the frame. Fill the checkerboard to the top of the frame.

10. Pour extra polyester resin in the center of the checkerboard. Immediately place a piece of plate glass that has been waxed and polished with a release agent over the checkerboard and resin. This will force any surface air bubbles to the outside of the board and make the surface smooth. (*Note:* Some resin will run out from the sides of the plate glass, so be prepared.)

11. When the polyester resin has hardened, remove the plate glass with the help of your teacher. Clean up the resin on the outside edge of the checkerboard.

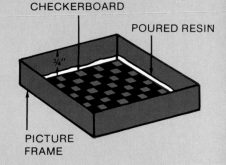

CHECKERBOARD

POURED RESIN

PICTURE FRAME

Technology Connections

1. Mylar will release from polyester resin. What other release agents might you use?

2. Identify all the tools and machines used in this lab.

3. Identify each material used as to whether it is renewable or nonrenewable.

4. List the procedures of material conversion that were used in this activity. These conversion processes can be listed under forming, separating, combining, and conditioning.

Science and Math Concepts

▶ Volume = length × width × height.

▶ Refraction of light is caused by a change in the speed of light as it leaves one medium and enters another. This is why the wood playing surface appears closer than it actually is when it is covered with the polyester resin.

CHAPTER 9

MANUFACTURING

MAJOR CONCEPTS

After reading this chapter, you will know that:

■ Production technologies fill many of people's needs and wants by means of manufacturing and construction systems.

■ Manufacturing is making goods in a workshop or factory. Construction is building a structure on a site.

■ Mass production and the factory system brought prices down. People were able to improve their standard of living.

■ Manufacturing systems make use of the seven types of technological resources.

■ There are two subsystems within the manufacturing system: the material processing system, and the business and management system.

■ Automation has greatly increased productivity in manufacturing.

■ Computers and robots have improved product quality while bringing manufacturing costs down.

PRODUCTION SYSTEMS

Our environment has been created by people. We live, play, learn, and work in structures built by people. Our food, furniture, clothing, and automobiles are made by people.

Production systems are the means by which our needs are met. There are two kinds of production systems. **Manufacturing** is making goods in a workshop or **factory**. **Construction** is building a structure on a site.

Construction systems are covered in Chapter 10. In this chapter you will learn about manufacturing systems.

Production technologies fill many of people's needs by means of manufacturing and construction systems.

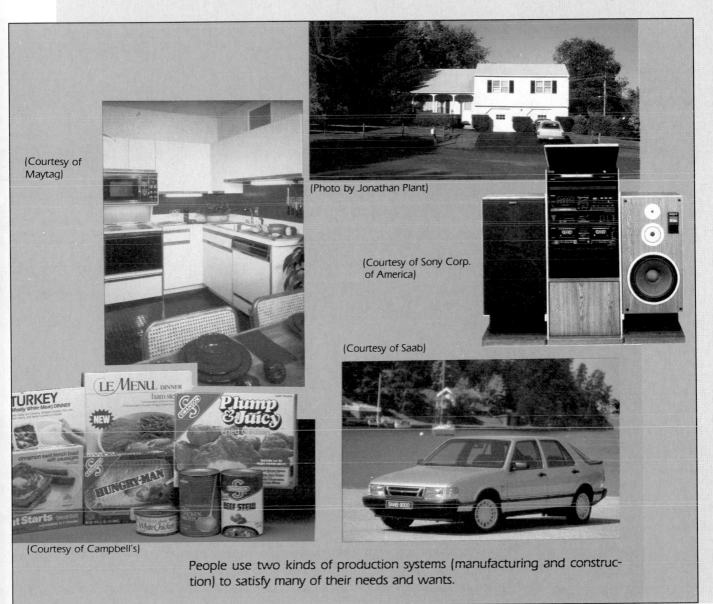

(Courtesy of Maytag)

(Photo by Jonathan Plant)

(Courtesy of Sony Corp. of America)

(Courtesy of Saab)

(Courtesy of Campbell's)

People use two kinds of production systems (manufacturing and construction) to satisfy many of their needs and wants.

The number of products to be manufactured is just one consideration when choosing the right manufacturing system. (Courtesy of Rockwell International Corporation)

MANUFACTURING SYSTEMS

Manufacturing is making goods in a workshop or factory. Construction is building a structure on a site.

People have used manufacturing technology for many thousands of years. Prehistoric people made use of natural materials to make weapons, food, and clothing. Stone, bone, wood, and clay were the materials most often used. Tools were made by chopping or scraping a piece of material to the desired shape and size.

Evidence shows that people were making pottery from clay over 30,000 years ago. The firing process was probably discovered by accident, when people found hardened clay under the ashes of their cooking fires. They then began to fire clay items on purpose. This is one of the first examples we have of manufacturing.

Natural metals, like copper, gold, and silver, were made into ornaments and tools. During the Bronze Age (starting about 3500 B.C.), people began casting metal.

Glass may have been the first synthetic (human-made) material. Among some early people, glass beads were considered to be very valuable. They were used as money in some places.

The Craft Approach

For centuries, objects were manufactured by people only for their and their families' use. Then people began to specialize. Shoemakers made shoes not only for family and personal use but for other people as well. In return, they received goods from other craftspeople. There were many kinds of craftspeople: candlemakers, weavers, spinners, glassblowers, silversmiths (who made tableware), coopers (barrel makers), gunsmiths, and tailors.

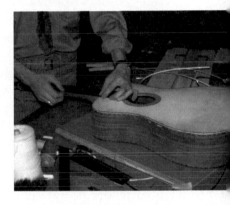

Many musicians have their instruments custom-made.
(Photo by Michael Hacker)

These craftspeople made their products one at a time, working alone from start to finish. Most often, they worked at home or in small workshops. Their tools were costly. Not everyone who wanted to become a craftsperson could afford to do so. Often, the master craftsperson hired young people who wanted to learn the trade. These young workers, called apprentices, were trained on the job.

People today still want one-of-a-kind products. We still have craft production. Of course, we pay more for products made by craftspeople. A hand-knit sweater, for example, is much more expensive than one made by machine in a factory.

Some products must be designed and made to meet particular needs. Handicapped people often buy **custom-made** items that make daily activities easier. Craftspeople today make pottery, jewelry, clothing, furniture, and many other items to suit individual needs and tastes.

The Factory System

As America grew, railroads, canals, and highways opened up new markets. More goods were needed.

During the Industrial Revolution, which started in the late 1700s, there were many new inventions. Machines such as the steam engine, the cotton gin, and the sewing machine helped with many tasks. Businesspeople used the new machinery to improve production. Soon goods were being made in factories by large numbers of workers. Over the years, the factory system replaced the craft system in the manufacture of most goods.

MASS PRODUCTION AND THE ASSEMBLY LINE

Mass production is the production of goods in large quantities by groups of workers in factories. In mass production, the pro-

Computers and Cowboy Boots

A modern-day industry that still employs craftspeople is the shoemaking industry. What is happening to the shoemaking craft in this modern technological age? It is an industry that is in the sunset of its life.

Because shoemaking requires skilled workers, labor costs are high. U.S. shoe manufacturers are finding it hard to compete with foreign competition. Today, most shoes that are purchased by people in the United States are made overseas. Between 1968 and 1986, the shoemaking industry in the United States lost about 100,000 jobs. Many companies have gone out of business.

Cowboy boots require fancy stitching.

It would be very expensive for companies to hire U.S. workers to do this stitching by hand. The handwork is now done by workers in Spain and Portugal, who provide labor at a lower cost.

Some years ago, the Shoe Machinery Group of Emhart Corporation developed computer-controlled stitching machines. Computerized stitchers are bringing the manufacture of cowboy boots back to the United States. Computer-controlled systems are being used for many other operations, including design. While the days of the cowboys and Indians may be over, it still looks good for cowboy boots in the United States.

This computerized stitcher is sewing a pattern on a cowboy boot. (Courtesy of Shoe Machinery Group—Emhart Corp.)

duction process is divided into steps. Each worker does one step, passing the item on for the next step. Work is carried out on an **assembly line**, a system by which the item is moved quickly from one work station to the next. Through the use of mass-production methods and the assembly line, more goods can be produced in a given period of time.

Mass Production and the Automobile Industry

One of the first moving assembly lines was at the Ford Motor Company in 1913. Auto parts were pushed from one worker to the next. This reduced production time by about one-half. By applying the same principle to the assembly of a total car, Henry Ford speeded up car production. A finished Model T Ford came off the assembly line every ten seconds.

The interchangeability of parts is one of the most important characteristics of a mass-production system. Modern automobiles, for example, are manufactured with interchangeable parts. Door latches for the Honda are alike. If one part breaks down, we can purchase another just like it from an automobile dealer.

A 1913 auto parts assembly line
(Courtesy of Ford Motor Company)

Workers making door latches
for Honda automobiles
(Courtesy of Rockwell International)

This student is using a jig. The jig holds a plastic strip in place so that the ends of the strip can be rounded evenly by a belt sander. (Photo by Michael Hacker)

Eli Whitney started one of the earliest assembly lines in 1789. Whitney signed a contract with the U.S. Army to make 10,000 rifles (a huge number in those days) in two years. He succeeded by making a large number of each kind of rifle part at once and keeping the parts in separate bins. The parts were **standardized**, exactly alike. This made them **interchangeable**—any of them could be used in assembly. Before this, rifles had been made one at a time, so the parts of a rifle would fit only that rifle.

Jigs and Fixtures

One way manufacturers make standardized parts exactly alike is to use **jigs** and **fixtures** on the machinery. A jig holds and guides the item being processed. It also guides the tool that does the processing. A fixture is used to keep the item being processed in the proper position.

IMPACTS OF THE FACTORY SYSTEM

Mass production and the factory system brought prices down. People were able to improve their standard of living.

The factory system produced a larger supply of goods. Luxury items became less expensive. More people could afford to buy the products of mass production.

The factory system also brought about other changes. New industries sprang up. The steel, automobile, and clothing industries provided millions of new jobs. Craftspeople and farmers became assembly-line workers.

Factories created wealth by adding value to the resources that were processed into goods. As a result, the standard of living improved for people who lived in industrialized nations.

Craft production and mass production were quite different. Craftspeople could stop working to take care of household chores. Factory workers, however, had to work without stopping. Time was very important. Manufacturing operations were **synchronized**. That is, one process had to be followed immediately by the next. If one step were delayed, all production would slow down.

Children were often used as factory workers in the late nineteenth and early twentieth centuries. They were often forced to work under harsh conditions and during evening hours. (Courtesy of the Bettman Archive)

Workers were often paid by piecework. They were paid for the number of items they completed each day. During the early 1900s, it was not unusual for people to work twelve hours a day. **Unions** were formed to protect the rights of workers. **Child labor laws** were passed to ensure that children were treated fairly.

During the craft era, families often worked together at home. Someone was always around to care for the children. When people began to work in factories, they had to leave home.

Finding a place for the children became a problem. The number and importance of schools increased partly because of the factory system.

THE BUSINESS SIDE OF MANUFACTURING

Until the 1930s, most businesspeople wanted only to improve the production process to make a product cheaper and faster. They wanted to be able to offer a standard product at a low price. A suggestion was once made to Henry Ford that he paint his Model Ts different colors. He replied, "Give it to them in any color, so long as it is black."

This attitude changed with competition. In the 1930s, General Motors started producing a new model of automobile every year. The way automobiles were advertised and sold was suddenly as big a concern as how they were produced. Marketing and business management became important systems in manufacturing.

Differences Between Craft Manufacture and Mass Production

CRAFT MANUFACTURE	MASS PRODUCTION
1. Workers are very skilled.	1. Workers need limited skill.
2. Workers make a product from start to finish by themselves.	2. Workers work on only one part of the product.
3. Work is varied and interesting.	3. Work is routine and often dull.
4. Craftspeople get satisfaction by seeing the finished product (like a completed chair).	4. Factory workers see only the one part that they produce (like the chair leg).
5. Each part is hand crafted so no two are exactly alike.	5. Parts are machine made and are interchangeable.
6. Only one item is produced at a time.	6. Many items are produced during the production run.
7. It takes a long time to produce each item.	7. The average time it takes to produce each item is reduced.
8. The cost of each item is high.	8. The cost of each item is lowered.
9. Quality depends mainly upon the skill of the craftsperson.	9. Quality depends mainly upon the accuracy of the machines and how well they have been set up by people.

Fire Escape Parachute
Patent No. 221,855
March 26, 1879

In March 1879, Benjamin Oppenheimer patented a fire escape parachute, complete with headpiece and sponge-bottom shoes.

THE ENTREPRENEURS

An **entrepreneur** is a person who comes up with a good idea and uses that idea to make money. An entrepreneur might improve a product, or improve the way a product is made, or even come up with an idea for a new product.

Some entrepreneurs are **inventors**. An inventor comes up with a totally new idea. The safety razor, the laser, and the contact lens are all inventions. Inventions can be protected by a patent. When a device is patented, no one but the patent holder can make and sell it for seventeen years. Many inventions are now in everyday use. Others, such as air-conditioned suits and hats with fans, did not catch on with the public.

Some entrepreneurs are **innovators**. An innovation is an improvement in an invention. Innovations lead to new uses. They can start new industries or change existing ones. The electric guitar is an innovation. A new music industry sprang up around the music played on this instrument. Other innovations are the diesel engine and power steering.

Manufacturing systems make use of the seven types of technological resources.

RESOURCES FOR MANUFACTURING SYSTEMS

Manufacturing systems use the seven technological resources to make a product. Value is added to these resources along the way. The finished product is worth more than the cost of the resources.

People

People design the products. They decide how to produce them. They choose the materials and the best tools and machines. People organize the production lines. People obtain the necessary capital. They advertise, distribute, and sell the products.

In the past, people provided more of the labor in manufacturing plants than they do today. In the 1950s, about 30 percent of workers in the United States worked in manufacturing jobs. Today, machines do many factory jobs. About 16 percent of the workforce works in manufacturing.

The roles of people in the manufacturing system have been changing. As workers have become more educated, they have asked to take part in decisions that affect the company. **Quality circles** are groups of workers and managers who get together during the work day. Workers discuss problems to be solved and ways to improve production. Management can explain prob-

Employees at Pittsburgh Plate Glass developed a better method for attaching the "button" that secures the rearview mirror to an automobile windshield. (Courtesy of PPG Industries)

lems to workers about costs, profits, and competition. Quality circles let workers and management discuss issues openly. The result is a better work environment and improved production.

American industries have had a hard time competing with foreign companies whose workers are paid much less. These industries have been forced to improve their production methods

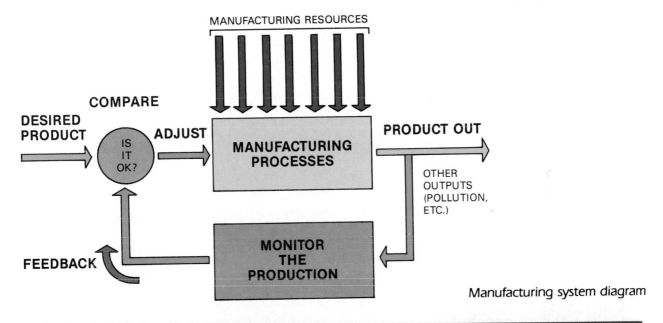

Manufacturing system diagram

Entrepreneurship and McDonald's Restaurants

One famous entrepreneur is Ray Kroc. Ray was a salesman who sold electric mixers, called multimixers, to restaurants. One of the restaurants he serviced was owned by two brothers. In 1954, Ray made an agreement with the two brothers to franchise the concept of the restaurant they were operating. The menu included 15¢ hamburgers, 10¢ french fries, and 20¢ shakes. The brothers were Mac and Dick McDonald. The restaurant was McDonald's. There are now close to 10,000 McDonald's restaurants worldwide.

Ray A. Kroc (Courtesy of McDonald's)

Here, information is being collected about how accurately the machine tool is performing. (*Courtesy of Deere & Co.*)

to remain in business. Some industries have been unable to do so. For example, U.S. steelworkers are paid six times as much as steelworkers in Brazil and eight times as much as Korean steelworkers. Between 1975 and 1990, about 300,000 American steelworkers lost their jobs. Workers who lose manufacturing jobs often have a hard time. They find that they can get work only in lower-paying service industries. They must be trained to do other kinds of work.

In years to come, many of the manufacturing jobs in the United States will center on the design and engineering of products. The assembly-line work will be done by automated machines or by workers overseas.

Information

Factories are often built in places where there are educated workers like engineers and computer programmers. Some companies build their plants near universities. Professors can then

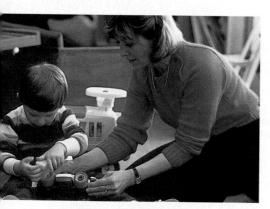

Toy manufacturers often make several prototypes of a product and observe children playing. Information about which toys are played with, for how long, and by whom is recorded to determine the best possibilities for future sales. (*Courtesy of Fisher-Price*)

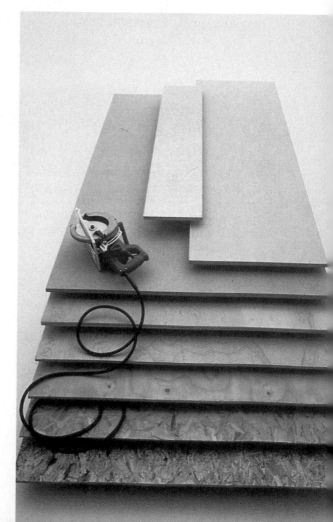

Plywood and chipboard material are made from wood, a raw material, but are manufactured into a more usable form. (*Courtesy of Weyerhaeuser Company Inc.*)

help company planners. Companies can also use university research to learn about new materials and production methods.

Companies must find out what people will buy and how their tastes are changing. They also gather information about the costs of materials. This information helps in choosing which materials to buy. Companies must keep track of production to help them adjust the manufacturing process.

Materials

Raw materials are made into basic industrial materials, which are made into finished products. For example, the steel industry uses coal, limestone, and iron ore to make iron ingots. Iron ingots are made into steel sheets. These steel sheets are made into finished products like automobile frames and bodies. (See Chapter 8.)

The cost of raw materials is important. The cost is not only the cost of the material itself, but other costs such as shipping. If a steel company in Indiana needs iron ore, should it buy ore from a mine in Wisconsin, where it is only 20 percent pure? Or should it buy the ore from Brazil, where it is 65 percent pure, and pay the extra shipping charges? This is the kind of cost-benefit trade-offs manufacturers must make in choosing materials.

Manufacturing systems sometimes require specialized tools. This mustard dispenser used by McDonald's employees puts the same amount of mustard on each hamburger. (Courtesy of McDonald's)

Tools and Machines

The tools used in modern factories are very advanced and precise. Most of them are automatic. Computer programs and sensing devices provide feedback and guide the machine operation.

Some machines, called **numerical control** machines, are controlled by punched tapes. The holes punched in the tapes direct the machines. A **control unit** receives and stores all the directions.

This machine is controlled by computer numerical control; the machine's control unit directs the machine's actions. (Courtesy of MHP Machines, Inc., Buffalo, New York)

Energy

About 40 percent of the energy used in the United States is used in manufacturing. Some of the biggest energy users are factories that make metals, chemicals, ceramics, paper, food, and equipment. Most manufacturers use electricity from fossil fuels (coal, oil, and natural gas). Other sources of electricity are hydroelectric and nuclear energy plants.

Factories are often built in places where energy costs are low. The glass industry grew up in West Virginia because the state had plenty of natural gas. Small steel mills using electric furnaces are built in places where electricity is cheap.

Some industries use the heat given off during manufacturing. The paper-making industry, for example, uses this energy to heat water and make steam. The steam turns steam turbines and produces electricity. This process of energy re-use is called **cogeneration**.

Capital

Companies must have capital to finance their operations. They must buy land, build factories, purchase equipment, pay

Materials to make products, like these rolls of aluminum used to make cans, must be purchased. (Courtesy of Reynolds Metal Company)

Workers in the finance department keep track of a company's money. (Courtesy of Union Pacific Corporation)

workers, maintain machines, and advertise their products. Capital is often obtained by selling shares of stock to the public. Stockholders become partners in the corporation. If the company makes a profit, the value of its stock may go up. Stockholders then make a profit, too.

Private companies may raise money from investors who contribute venture capital. A venture, like an adventure, is a trip into the unknown. **Venture capital** is money used to finance the costs of starting a new company. Investors take big risks. They expect to make big profits once a company starts production.

Time

In manufacturing, time is money. The faster products are made, the more profitable the company will be. **Productivity** is how quickly and cheaply a product is made. Since a large part of the cost of a product is the cost of paying workers, if workers do their jobs faster, productivity will increase.

Much thought has gone into improving productivity. In 1910, Frederick W. Taylor developed an idea called **scientific management**. His idea was to study every movement that a worker made. Then the worker's routine was changed to cut out any wasted movements. Such changes resulted in increased output without making people do any more work.

Today, companies try to make sure that products are constantly moving from one process to the next. The longer an item sits waiting for the next step in assembly, the lower productivity will be.

HOW MANUFACTURING IS DONE

Before a company starts making a product, it carries out **market research**. Market research helps the company find out what customers want in a product. Companies survey a sample group of people. They try to pick a sample that represents the people who might buy their product. Market researchers ask the sample group about the product. The feedback they receive helps the company decide whether to make the new product, or how to change it to make it better.

Using what has been learned from market research, product designers and engineers prepare drawings, sometimes using computers, and develop finished design ideas.

Research and Development (R & D) is done by product designers and engineers. R & D is used to come up with ideas

Expert craftspeople make a clay automobile model.
(Courtesy of Ford Motor Company)

There are two subsystems within the manufacturing system: the material processing system, and the business and management system.

OBTAIN MATERIALS

HEAT AND FORGE BLADE

ANNEAL (SOFTEN) BLADE BY HEATING TO CHERRY-RED COLOR AND COOLING SLOWLY

FILE TWO FACES OF BLADE

GRIND TIP TO PROPER ANGLE

REMOVE ALL SCRATCHES WITH EMERY CLOTH

HARDEN BLADE BY HEATING TO CHERRY-RED COLOR AND COOLING QUICKLY

CLEAN BLADE WITH EMERY CLOTH

TEMPER BLADE BY HEATING TO A STRAW COLOR AND COOLING QUICKLY

CLEAN BLADE WITH FINE EMERY CLOTH

BUFF BLADE

INJECTION-MOLD PLASTIC HANDLE

This flowchart shows the steps in making a metal screwdriver with a plastic handle.

for new products and improve ways of making old ones. R & D often leads to inventions or innovations.

Once designs are ready, management takes a close look at them. The company must decide whether the product can be made at a cost and sold at a price that will bring in a profit. If costs are too high, the product may be changed to use cheaper or different materials. Or a new production idea might help to lower costs.

When the engineers and businesspeople agree on a design, a model called a **prototype** is made. Craftspeople build these prototypes. Prototypes help in solving design and engineering problems. They are tested for a length of time before machinery is bought to begin factory production.

The last step in manufacturing is setting up the production line. Forming, separating, combining, and conditioning tools must be chosen. Operations must be organized to manufacture the product. A **flowchart** shows the operations of a production line in diagram form.

People who work in advertising must think of ways to sell the product. They create advertisements and commercials that will interest the public.

Salespeople sell and distribute the finished product. They are a very important part of the business side of manufacturing.

The company's job does not end when the product is sold. Products may need servicing or repair. Defective products may have to be replaced. Customer service departments help with these very important jobs.

ENSURING QUALITY IN MANUFACTURING

Companies want their products to be of the highest quality possible. Making sure that quality stays high during manufacture is the job of **quality control**. Quality control workers inspect

Quality Inspection by Laser

Lasers have been used in manufacturing as quality control inspection devices. The laser can be used to find flaws or mistakes in parts.

The simplest technique is shown below. The laser illuminates the part. Optical lenses focus the light on a sensor. The sensor sends information about the light pattern to a computer where the light pattern is compared with quality standards that have been programmed into the computer.

Laser inspection systems are highly precise and consistent in measurement. Many manufacturers use laser inspection systems to improve product quality.

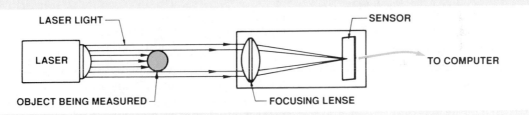

LASER LIGHT — SENSOR

LASER   OBJECT BEING MEASURED —   FOCUSING LENSE   TO COMPUTER

This is the simplest type of laser quality control inspection.
(Reprinted from MANUFACTURING TECHNOLOGY by Komacek, Lawson, & Horton, © 1990 by Delmar Publishers Inc.)

products to make sure they conform to the desired result. Feedback from quality control allows workers to change manufacturing processes when necessary. It also helps make sure that products are all alike, or uniform. **Uniformity** is an important concern of quality control.

Without quality control, many products would have to be thrown away. Good-quality products keep customers happy. Fewer items are returned or need repair.

AUTOMATED MANUFACTURING

Automation is the process of controlling machines automatically. For example, a robot can be programmed to pick up a part, move it a certain distance, and drop it into a bin. This kind of control is called **program control**.

Feedback control uses feedback to adjust the way a machine is working. Feedback control depends on the **sensor**, a device that gathers information about its environment. For example, a sensor "senses" when a drill has drilled deep enough. It then

In some factories, people inspect the parts by eye at various stages of the manufacturing line. (Courtesy of Sperry Corporation)

Automation has greatly increased productivity in manufacturing.

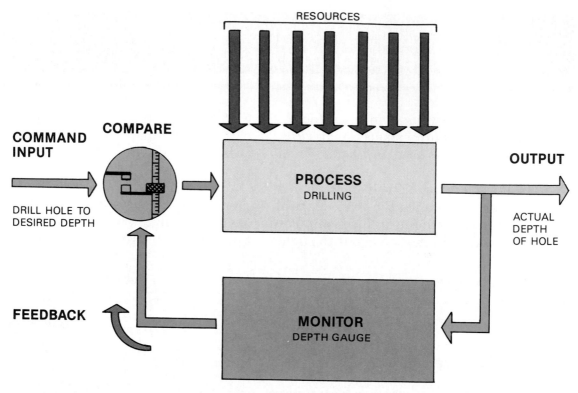

System diagram for an automatically controlled drill press. A switch activated by a depth gauge controls the drill press.

Automated machines attach heavy wheels to tractors. In the past it took three people to do this work. (Courtesy of Deere & Co.)

sends a signal to switch off the drill. A machine operator is no longer needed to turn the drill on and off. In automated factories, quality control is provided by sensors on machines. These sensors make sure the machines do their jobs exactly right.

Automation saves money on labor costs. To compete with lower-cost foreign products, more and more factories are being automated.

Robotics

Robots are automated machines that are controlled by computers. Many have sensors. Some of these robots can "feel." They can hold parts with just the right amount of pressure so they won't break. Other robots "see" with television eyes. They are able to tell the difference between parts of different shapes.

Robots are taking the place of people in many factories. Robots do almost all the work in one factory in Japan. People work there, too, making sure everything is operating the way it should. People are needed to install, service, and program robots.

Robots have allowed manufacturers to make products of higher quality at lower price. Robots don't take coffee breaks.

The Robot Revolution

Often we hear of the "robot revolution." Why is the use of robots a "revolution"? The Industrial Revolution replaced human energy (muscle power) with mechanical energy (machine power). Despite the new technology, human beings were still needed to operate the machines. Robots can actually replace human beings in a manufacturing plant. Although robots don't look human, they can act very much like people. They can perform movements just like a human arm, wrist, and hand. They can use sensors to "see" and "feel." Robots used in industry are called **industrial robots.**

This robotic hand is light and compact. It has three human-like fingers and fourteen joints. (Courtesy of Hitachi, Ltd.)

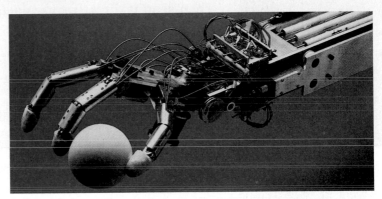

They can work twenty-four hours a day. Most of the jobs they do relieve people from dangerous, boring, heavy, or unpleasant work. Robots are used for welding, spray-painting, picking up parts and placing them into machines. They are used for loading objects onto platforms and conveyors.

Robots are better than ordinary machine tools because they can be **reprogrammed**. They can be programmed to weld a fender on one kind of car. Later, they can be programmed to do the same job on a different model.

CAD/CAM

CAD is **computer-aided design**. With CAD, a computer is used by designers, drafters, and engineers to do drawings and designs. The drawings are then stored in the computer. (See Chapter 6 for more on CAD.) CAD can also be used to test a design. In a **simulation**, a design is run through a series of tests, all on computer. The part itself is not needed.

CAM is **computer-aided manufacturing**. In CAM, computers are used to control factory machines. A computer might

Robots welding automobile parts. (Courtesy of Ford Motor Company)

In a CAD/CAM operation, a designer stores a drawing in a computer and sends it to a computer-controlled machine. There a prototype is produced. (Courtesy of Grumman Aerospace)

direct machines to drill holes or spray-paint a part.

CAD/CAM is a new technology that joins CAD and CAM. CAD/CAM lets a person create a design on the computer screen, then send it directly to a machine tool, which makes the part.

Computer-Integrated Manufacturing (CIM)

CIM is **computer-integrated manufacturing**. In CIM, computers are used not only for CAD/CAM, but for business needs as well. They are used to store information about raw materials and parts. They set times for the purchase and delivery of materials, report on finished goods, and do the billing and accounting.

Managers involved in purchasing, shipping, accounting, and manufacturing can get a total picture of all the factory conditions by looking at the computer screen. (Courtesy of International Business Machines Corp.)

Computers and robots have improved product quality while bringing manufacturing costs down.

CIM combines the manufacturing, design, and business functions of a company under the control of a computer system.

INVENTORY CONTROL

PRODUCT ANALYSIS AND DEVELOPMENT

OTHER FUNCTIONS

DESIGN

MAINFRAME COMPUTER

FINANCIAL REPORTING

EQUIPMENT CONTROL

MARKETING AND SALES

PRODUCTION SCHEDULING

INVOICE

SALES AND INVOICING

Flexible Manufacturing at Deere & Company

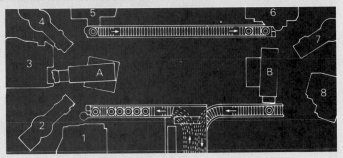

This plant makes construction equipment called backhoe loaders. Once a part enters the manufacturing system, it is tracked and controlled by a computer. It enters one end of the system and comes out the other end completely finished in as little as five minutes. The machines within the system are all computer-controlled. Each machine can be programmed to do many different kinds of machining jobs. Thus, the machines can turn out parts with different dimensions. An employee monitors the entire process.

The manufacturing system is diagrammed here to show part flow and system components. Parts progress from the number 1 machining center to the last machining stop at number 8. Parts move on automated conveyors until picked up by one of two robots (A and B). These robots feed parts to appropriate cutting machines (1, 3, 5, 6, or 8) at appropriate times. Stations 2, 4, and 7 are parts storage areas and automated tool carousels.

The entire manufacturing process is computer controlled.

A finished backhoe loader doing its job
(All photos courtesy of Deere & Co.)

Flexible Manufacturing

Flexible manufacturing is the efficient production of small amounts of products. Today, many products are made in batches of a hundred or a thousand, rather than millions of items. This is because customers have special needs. For example, the General Electric Company in New Hampshire makes 2,000 different versions of its basic electric meter. A John Deere factory in Iowa can make 5,000 different versions of its tractor for farmers with different needs. The same production line is used for all versions of a product. The machines are programmed to do different operations to make the different versions.

Just-in-Time Manufacturing

Raw materials come to factories by truck, train, or ship. They are most often delivered in large amounts that take up a lot of storage space. Companies must pay to rent, heat, and light warehouse space. They must pay people to move the materials and deliver them to the factory where they are needed.

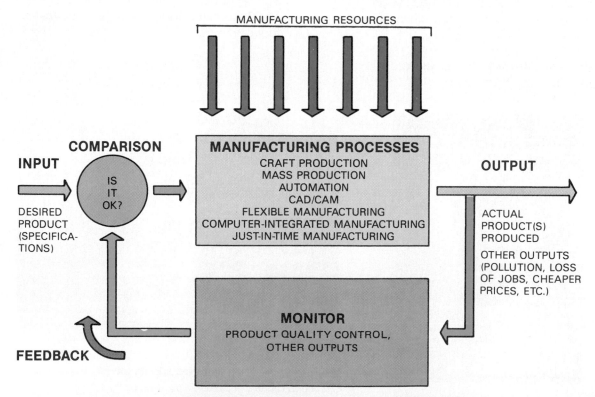

Well-designed manufacturing systems use modern processes to make products of good quality. The products must meet the desired specifications without harmful effects on people or the environment.

Just-in-Time (JIT) manufacturing is manufacturing in which materials and parts are ordered so that they arrive at the factory when they are needed. Also, the product is immediately shipped to the customer. With JIT manufacturing, there is no need for storage space and workers.

Reducing Design Time with Computer Models

Designing, producing, and testing scale model mock-ups and full-size prototypes can take weeks, months, or even years. To reduce the time involved in refining product plans, designers have turned to computer-generated models. Computer-aided drafting and design (CADD) systems speed up the design process. CADD systems are programmed with information on the properties and costs of materials; the operation of moving parts; and how various components work, such as electrical systems. When a product design is fed into the CADD system, the designer can specify materials and components. Then, simulated tests are performed on the design by the computer.

CADD systems are also programmed to calculate the total costs of manufacturing the product. Prices for individual components and materials are programmed into the computer. When the designer selects a component, the computer automatically creates a manufacturing cost estimate.

CADD systems give manufacturing companies a big advantage in beating their competitors to market. If a part does not work as planned, it can quickly be replaced on screen and retested. With actual prototypes, replacing parts can be a long, involved process. This reduction in design time helps companies get their products to consumers as fast as possible.

Designers can reduce the time it takes for the design engineering process by utilizing CADD systems to design and test products by computer. (Courtesy of Honeywell, Inc.)

(Reprinted from MANUFACTURING TECHNOLOGY by Komacek, Lawson, & Horton, © 1990 by Delmar Publishers Inc.)

SUMMARY

The two production systems are manufacturing and construction. Manufacturing is making goods in a workshop or factory. Construction is building a structure on a site.

For thousands of years, people made goods by hand. Craftspeople made items for their own and others' use. As the nation grew, people needed more goods. Factories began to mass-produce goods using the assembly line.

Assembly lines divide production into steps. Each worker does one job. The assembly line makes and uses standardized parts that are interchangeable.

The factory system improved the way Americans lived. It brought prices down. With the factory system, time became important since operations were synchronized.

The business side of manufacturing is important. Entrepreneurs start companies, invent new products, and change old ones. Many of today's businesses were started by entrepreneurs.

Manufacturing uses the seven technological resources. They are: people, information, materials, tools and machines, energy, capital, and time.

Automation has made factories much more efficient. More goods can be made in a shorter time with less labor cost. Automated machines are programmed to do a series of steps. They often make use of feedback from sensors. The sensors keep track of the manufacturing processes.

Making sure products are uniform and of high quality is an important goal for manufacturers. Quality control lowers costs and means fewer rejects and repairs.

Robots are being used in modern manufacturing plants. They do jobs that are dangerous or unpleasant for humans.

Computer-aided design and computer-aided manufacturing (CAD/CAM) link engineering and design with the factory floor. Designs for parts can be drawn using a computer. They can then be changed or stored for later use. The data can be sent to a machine that makes the part.

Computer-integrated manufacturing (CIM) uses the computer in engineering, production, and business. With flexible manufacturing, it is possible to produce special products for customers' special needs. Materials come in and products go out at exactly the right time in Just-in-Time manufacturing. These new methods lower costs and result in a better product.

REVIEW QUESTIONS

1. Give five examples of how manufacturing technology has helped satisfy people's needs and wants.
2. Explain how craft production differs from mass production.
3. How did mass production improve people's standard of living?
4. Draw a flowchart of an assembly line for making a greeting card.
5. What are two disadvantages of mass production?
6. What are the two subsystems that make up the manufacturing system?
7. Suggest an invention that would help you with your homework.
8. How might you innovate a soda can?
9. What would be a suitable product for your technology class to manufacture?
10. If you could form a quality circle with your classmates and teacher, what improvements would you suggest be made in the technology laboratory?
11. Why do manufacturers want their products to be uniform?
12. What could be two undesirable outcomes from a system that manufactures computers?
13. How is feedback used to ensure good quality in manufactured products?
14. Do you think that robots should be used instead of people on assembly lines? Explain why or why not.
15. How have computers affected the manufacturing industry?
16. Draw a system diagram for a system that manufactures chewing gum. Label the input command, resources, process, output, monitor, and comparison.

KEY WORDS

Assembly line	Factory	Just-in-time	Prototype
Automation	Feedback control	manufacturing	Quality control
CAD/CAM	Flexible	Manufacturing	Robot
CIM	manufacturing	Mass production	Uniformity
Custom-made	Interchangeable	Numerical control	Union
Entrepreneur	Inventor	Production	

SEE YOUR TEACHER FOR THE CROSSTECH PUZZLE

AN ENTREPRENEURIAL COMPANY

Setting the Stage

Entrepreneurs are people who come up with good ideas for new or improved products or services. They then use those ideas to make a profit. The ideas usually start with defining a need that someone has, then figuring out a way to fill that need.

For example, you and your classmates probably have been assigned lockers. It's not easy, however, to keep lockers neat. They tend to become cluttered and messy. Wouldn't it be a great idea if someone designed a locker organizer that would help keep items stored in an organized fashion?

Your Challenge

Form your class into a company to design a locker organizer that would be popular at your school. The organizer must provide a place for pencils, pens, and notebooks. You may also want to provide a way to organize other items you keep in your locker.

Procedure

1. Decide on a name for your company. Then, divide into R & D quality circles, four or five persons to each circle. Each circle will work independently throughout the design process.
2. Do market research to find out the preferred features for a locker organizer. Measure several different pencils, pens, and notebooks to determine size needs.
3. Make several rough sketches of your ideas. Consider materials best suited for the proposed designs.
4. Combine several ideas or select a good idea for your design.
5. Make a drawing of your design. Add dimensions.
6. Using cardboard as a substitute for the actual material you plan to use, make a prototype of your design. Color the prototype as you wish the actual product to appear.
7. Make a list of materials you would need to make each organizer. Determine the cost of the materials needed to produce your design. Use catalogs to compare different suppliers.

Suggested Resources

Sketch pad and soft lead pencils or felt pens
Ruler
Scissors
Transparent tape
Tagboard or thin cardboard
Tempera colors

8. Each circle will present its design to the class. Show the drawings and prototype, and discuss the features of the design that would make it popular. Tell how much it would cost to make.
9. Take a class vote on which organizer the company should make.

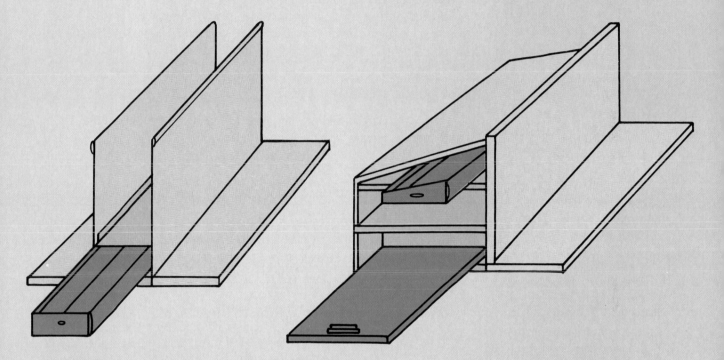

Technology Connections

1. Quality circles allow workers to become directly involved in decisions about the production process. What effect has this had on the workers and the companies?
2. Many of the products you use every day are manufactured by machines and automated equipment. How would your life change if everything you use had to be made by hand?
3. New production systems make increasing use of technologies such as robotics, CAD/CAM, and CIM, just to name a few. How will this affect you as a future worker and consumer?

Science and Math Concepts

▶ Control of modern production machines depends upon numerical data which counts in thousandths of an inch or less.

▶ Many modern production machines are combinations of electrical, hydraulic, and pneumatic systems.

271

T-SQUARE ASSEMBLY LINE

Setting the Stage

The newspaper clipping read: "Engineering firm needs designer/drafter helper for summer work: no experience necessary." You have always liked to draw, especially since you learned how to use drawing tools and a CAD system in your 7th and 8th grade Technology Education class.

You call the number and arrange for an interview. You're hired! Your first assignment? To help design, plan, and establish an assembly line to mass produce T-squares.

Your Challenge

With your class, set up an assembly line to mass produce a drawing tool known as a T-square.

Jigs and fixtures, which speed up the assembly line, can be built by the entire class.

Procedure

1. Be sure to wear safety glasses and a lab coat.
2. The teacher should precut the ½" × 1½" strips and ¼" × 1½" strips of clear cherry or other hardwood using the table saw, band saw, jointer, and planer.
3. Develop a flow chart of the assembly line. Be sure to include a foreperson, safety supervisor, and quality control check points.
4. Everyone in the class should help design and make the jigs and fixtures needed for the assembly line. Accuracy is very important at this stage.
5. Elect a foreperson to assign positions on the assembly line.
6. Rotate assembly line positions periodically.
7. When people switch jobs in the assembly line, they may have to be retrained for their new positions.
8. The miter boxes should be set up with stops to cut the head and blade pieces of the T-square to their proper length. The head is an 8" long piece of the ½" × 1½" strip. The blade is a 19½" long piece of the ¼" × 1½" strip.
9. In order to align the three pilot holes drilled in the T-square blade, use a student-made fixture clamped to the drill press. This technique is also used to drill the ⅜" hang-up hole in the other end of the blade. Two or more drill presses help prevent a log-jam at this point in the assembly line.
10. Accurate alignment jigs are needed to hold the pieces in place during the final assembly.

Suggested Resources

Safety glasses and lab aprons

Computer with software for computer aided drawing (CAD)

Dot matrix printer and/or laser printer

Pieces of clear cherry or other hardwood (for the head of the T-square)—½" × 1½"

Pieces of clear cherry or other hardwood (for the blade of the T-square)—¼" × 1½"

Miter boxes

Drill press

Power screwdrivers and/or variable speed electric drills with driver bits

Twist drills for the shank holes—⅛"

Twist drills for the pilot holes—1/16"

Round head wood screws—⅝" #4

Plywood (for the assembly jigs and fixtures)—⅜"

Heavy gauge aluminum strips (for quality control templates)—1½" × 19½"

Tri squares (for quality control checks)

11. Pilot holes of ¹⁄₁₆" diameter should be drilled in the head to facilitate the assembly process.
12. Use power screwdrivers and/or variable speed electric drills with driver bits to assemble the T-square. Do NOT overtighten the screws.

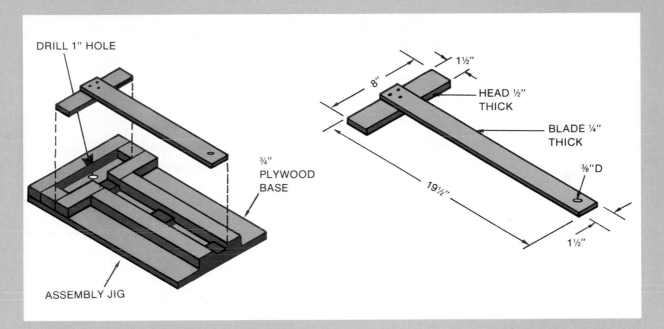

DRILL 1" HOLE
¾" PLYWOOD BASE
ASSEMBLY JIG
1½"
8"
HEAD ½" THICK
BLADE ¼" THICK
19½"
⅜"D
1½"

Technology Connections

1. What are some advantages of CAD?
2. Why is accuracy so important in designing and making the jigs and fixtures?
3. Why are quality control checkpoints important in an assembly line? Interchangeable parts?
4. There are two basic subsystems of the manufacturing system: (1) material processing and (2) business and management. Which subsystem does developing an assembly line flowchart fall into? Marketing? Final assembly?
5. Why is it important to use *standardized* measuring systems in manufacturing?

Science and Math Concepts

▶ The *metric system,* which is based on decimals, is a standardized measuring system used in science and technology all over the world.
▶ Threaded fasteners, such as screws, nuts, and bolts, use the principle of the *inclined plane.* This inclined plane, instead of going in a straight line, continually circles around the fastener in a spiral shape.

ROBOTIC RETRIEVER

Setting the Stage

The first things you notice as you enter the nuclear research building at Schleemer Enterprises, Inc. are the sirens and floodlights. Some men in white coats are huddled around a floorplan of the building. Fear is written on their faces. "Am I glad to see you!" says one of them as they notice your arrival. "Two units of Radium-X66 have melted through their canisters. There's not much time!"

Your Challenge

Using a teach pendant, program a robot to pick up and remove two Radium-X66 canisters from a designated area.

Procedure

1. Using the tape rule, T-square, and felt tip marker, measure and draw a grid made of 2" squares on the sheet of plywood. If done correctly, the plywood should have 24 rows of squares going each way.
2. The plywood will be the floor of the building. Make the walls using the lath material as shown.
3. Fasten the magnet to the bottom of the robot in a convenient spot. Epoxy cement may be used to make this more permanent.
4. Study the Model 603 Robot Manual and carefully follow the operating instructions.
5. Experiment with these commands by *measuring with the tape rule* how far the robot travels with each GO FORWARD command. Also, determine how far the robot turns with each TURN command.
6. Using the "building" you made earlier, place the robot in one of the corners opposite the door. Place one of the "canisters" in any one of the squares in the room, *except the squares along the edges of the wall.*
7. Using your graph paper, make a map of the room showing the location of the robot, the canister, and the door. Sketch on the graph paper the path the robot should follow to magnetically pick up the canister and carry it out the door. (*Hint:* Use only 90° turns at this time.)
8. On your sketch, write in the commands you must program into the robot's memory. Be very careful and take your time doing this.
9. Enter your program into the robot using the teach pendant. Replay the program and compare the robot's actual path with the path you sketched.

Suggested Resources

Plywood or masonite (any thickness)—4' × 4'

Lath strips (or similar material)—16' long

Model 603 programmable robot (Graymark International, Inc.)

Two steel ¼" washers (Radium-X66 canisters)

Magnet (approximately 1" square × ⅛" thick)

Graph paper (with ¼" squares)

Tape rule

T-square

Pencil

Felt tip marker

Glue

Epoxy cement (optional)

Saw

Hammer

Nails

10. Debug your program so that it works properly.
11. Try using the robot to pick up two canisters from different squares. You may want to challenge other students in a canister-fetching competition.

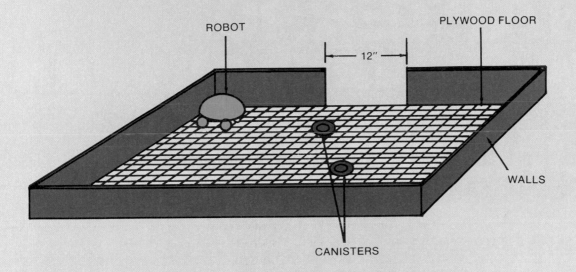

ROBOT

PLYWOOD FLOOR

12"

WALLS

CANISTERS

Technology Connections

1. Robots became practical only after the invention of the computer. Can you name what tasks are performed by the computer inside the 603 robot?
2. More advanced robots are able to sense certain things in their environment. What kinds of senses would make your robot more useful?

Science and Math Concepts

▶ How many TURN LEFT commands are necessary to make the 603 robot turn in a complete circle?

▶ With 360° in a circle, how many degrees does each TURN LEFT command use?

CHAPTER 10

CONSTRUCTION

MAJOR CONCEPTS

After reading this chapter, you will know that:

- Construction refers to producing a structure on a site.
- A construction system combines resources to provide a structure as an output.
- Three subsystems within the construction system are designing, managing, and building.
- Construction sites must be chosen to fit in with the needs of people and the environment.
- A foundation is built to support a structure.
- The usable part of a structure is called the superstructure.
- Structures include bridges, buildings, dams, harbors, roads, towers, and tunnels.

The Romans used the arch to support their bridges, which were called viaducts. (Courtesy of Harvey Binder)

CONSTRUCTION SYSTEMS

Construction refers to producing a structure on a site.

Early people lived in caves or in the brush. They did not have the technology to build structures that would shelter them from the weather or dangerous animals.

The first buildings people constructed were probably simple shelters. Teepees made from animal hides stretched over a wooden frame were used as long ago as 20,000 B.C. These homes were movable. People could take them along as they searched for new sources of food. As people began to settle in villages, they needed more permanent houses. Materials like wood, stone, and mud were used. Later, bricks made from straw and mud were used in construction.

The early Egyptians, Greeks, and Romans were very good builders. The great pyramids in Egypt were built from blocks of limestone 5,000 years ago. The largest pyramid was almost 500 feet tall and is made of over two million blocks of limestone, each weighing more than a ton.

The Romans were skilled engineers. They built cities, roads, and bridges. About 300 B.C. they started building systems called aqueducts for supplying water to their cities. These pipelines, built from stone and cement, brought water from nearby rivers. They also built sewer systems to carry waste from the city of Rome into the Tiber River. One of their greatest contributions to construction technology was the use of the **arch** to hold up buildings.

Construction means building a structure at the place where it will be used. The location is called a **construction site**. Today, about six million people work in the construction industry in the United States. The industry produces over a hundred billion dollars in goods and services in the United States each year.

Even today, people in some parts of the world use natural materials and anything else they can find to construct housing. (Photo by Michael Hacker)

An example of modern construction technology (Courtesy of NY Convention & Visitors Bureau)

(Courtesy of Brendrup Corporation)

RESOURCES FOR CONSTRUCTION TECHNOLOGY

A construction system uses the seven technological resources. If the resources are combined correctly, the result is a usable structure such as a building, bridge, dam, road, or tunnel.

A construction system combines resources to provide a structure as an output.

People

People are needed to design and engineer structures. They are needed to manage the business of construction. Many workers are needed to do the actual building.

The **landowner** decides that there is a need for a structure.

Three subsystems within the construction system are designing, managing, and building.

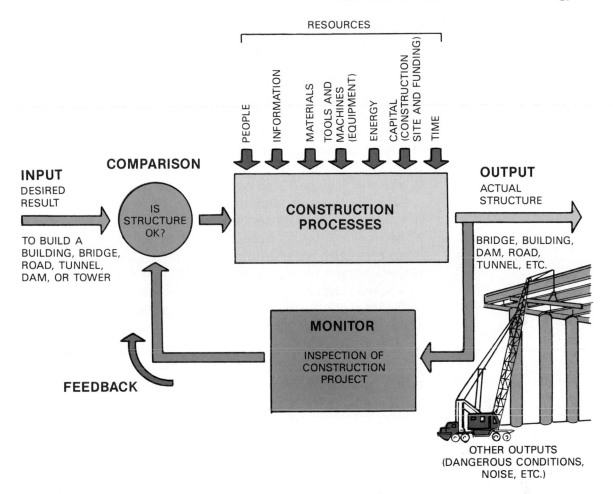

A construction system combines the technological resources to produce a structure on a site.

This could be a home, a housing development, or a shopping center.

Architects design buildings. Their plans show how a structure will be built and where it will be placed on a site. Architects are trained for their work in college. They take courses in mathematics, architectural design, technical and architectural drawing, and art.

Civil engineers work with architects. They help the architects decide if the building can be built as desired. Civil engineers prepare exact drawings and plans for the building framework and foundation. The drawings and plans give information about the size and strength of materials used. They also give details about **utilities** (plumbing, heating, air conditioning, and electrical wiring).

Civil engineers plan bridges, roads, tunnels, dams, and towers. Engineers must go to college. They study mathematics, science, engineering design, technology of materials, and technical drawing. The **structural engineer** plans the building's structure. The structure must be strong enough to support the load it must carry.

General contractors own their own construction companies. They hire workers and oversee part or all of a project. General contractors work closely with everyone on the project.

Estimators work for the contractor. They make an estimate of the project's cost. They use this estimate to prepare a proposal called a **bid**. If the customer accepts the bid, he or she agrees with the cost and **specifications** in the bid.

Project managers make sure construction is carried out properly and meets building codes. They hire and supervise the workers. They try to keep the cost of the project as planned. Some colleges have programs to train construction project managers. Courses are taken in materials and techniques, planning and scheduling, engineering, and accounting.

Tradespeople work on projects from houses to skyscrapers. They may build a swimming pool or a dam. Tradespeople must

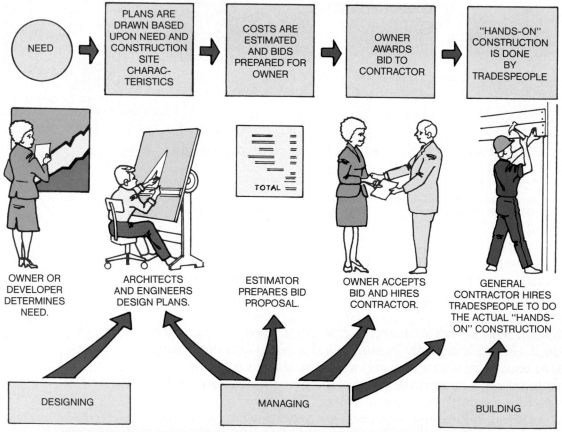

THE THREE SUBSYSTEMS OF CONSTRUCTION (DESIGNING, MANAGING, AND BUILDING) INVOLVE CONTINUOUS COOPERATION AMONG THE OWNER, THE ARCHITECTS AND ENGINEERS, THE CONTRACTOR, AND THE TRADESPEOPLE.

People in the construction industry

Project managers must review construction plans with the architects and engineers before actual construction is begun. (Courtesy of The Turner Corporation, photograph by Michael Sporzarsky)

know how to use the tools and materials of the trade. Tradespeople include carpenters, electricians, plumbers, and masons. Some run heavy equipment such as bulldozers.

Tradespeople may study their trade in high school or at a technical or vocational school. Or they can learn on the job, as apprentices to experienced tradespeople.

Information

In construction, information comes from the people who want the construction done and those who will do it. Information takes the form of plans, bids, and specifications. Specifications include data like the materials to be used, the way the foundation will be built, and even the kind of trees and bushes to be planted around the structure. These are the command inputs to the construction system.

People in construction must be able to make and read mechanical and architectural drawings and blueprints. Tradespeople must have information about building techniques. Engineers must have information about building materials and the loads the structure will support.

Materials

Building materials include concrete, lumber (wood), steel, glass, and brick.

Concrete is made from stone, sand, water, and **cement** (a mixture of limestone and clay). Wet concrete looks and feels like mud. It can be poured into molds to make any shape needed. These molds are called **forms** and are often made out of lumber. Once mixed and poured, concrete sets (gets hard).

Concrete is brittle. To give it more strength, steel rods called reinforcing rods are placed in the forms before the concrete is poured. Sometimes wire screens, called reinforcing mesh, are used. Concrete is used in dams, roadways, tunnels, and build-

This six-building complex uses energy-efficient glass as a primary building material. *(Courtesy of PPG Industries)*

ings—just about every kind of structure.

Lumber is a building material used to provide the framework of homes. Wood is easy to work with and not too expensive. Some composite materials used in building (plywood and particle board) are made from wood. These are strong and their cost is reasonable.

Steel is used for the framework of skyscrapers, bridges, and towers. It is very strong and can be made into cables, beams, and columns.

Glass not only lets the light in but adds great beauty to a structure. Glass can be installed as a single pane. Thermal glass (two or three thicknesses) is used to conserve energy.

Brick is made from clay. The clay is fired (heated) in an oven called a kiln. It becomes very hard. Brick houses are expensive. Labor costs are high because each brick must be set in place by a mason. Brick houses last longer and are more fire-resistant than wood houses.

Tools and Machines

Carpenters, plumbers, and other tradespeople use small hand and electric tools. Construction equipment can be huge, too;

Construction equipment has come a long way since this steam shovel from the early 1900s. *(Courtesy of Perini Corporation)*

A wide variety of power tools and equipment is used to do construction projects. *(Courtesy of The Stanley Works)*

examples of this are cranes and bulldozers. The largest pieces of equipment are used in earth-moving jobs. Special equipment is used for excavating (digging), lifting heavy materials, and building bridges, dams, roads, pipelines, and tunnels.

Robots are being used more and more often in construction. They are useful in dangerous jobs such as working high in the air, below ground, and deep under water.

Energy

Construction systems use energy to operate machines and tools. However, even more energy is used in industries that support the construction industry. Producing materials like concrete, bricks, and steel takes vast amounts of energy. Transporting these materials to building sites also uses energy.

Capital

Construction is expensive. Machines and tools, building materials, and labor are all costly. People who want to build must find money to finance their project. A bank will lend money only if it is fairly certain it will be paid back. A loan for a home is called a **mortgage**. Big projects often use money from both private and government sources.

A loan is paid back over a period of years with interest added to each payment. **Interest** is the fee the bank charges for the loan. If a person borrows $100,000 to build a house, the amount paid back is much more. However, repayment is spread out over many years so the borrower can afford the monthly payments. Home mortgages are usually paid back within fifteen to thirty years.

Land is often the most costly part of construction. In the middle of a city like New York or San Francisco, land could cost as much as $1,000 per square foot. That comes to about $40 million per acre. People who build in big cities must charge high rents for offices and apartments because land costs are so high. Skyscrapers make the best use of expensive land. People who own valuable land usually have an easy time getting a construction loan from a bank. If the loan is not repaid, the bank takes possession of the land.

Time

Construction takes a lot of time. A bridge or tunnel may take years to complete. Houses can be built in a few months.

Modern tools and equipment save time. For example, air-driven staple guns are replacing hammers and nails for fastening shingles to roofs.

New building techniques also reduce construction time. For example, parts of a structure can be **prefabricated** in a factory. Walls, for example, can be built in a factory, then moved to the construction site. Time is saved because the walls can be mass produced.

Modular construction is a technique that is being used more and more often. A module is a basic unit like a room. Modules can be combined to form structures of different shapes and sizes.

SELECTING THE CONSTRUCTION SITE

An important first step in construction planning is choosing a site. This is a decision made by management. Land costs and taxes can vary greatly from one place to another. Often, a few miles make the difference between high and low land costs. The site must be suitable for construction. If it is too hilly, much time and money must be spent on **grading** (leveling) the soil. If the ground is too rocky, it will be hard to dig a foundation.

There are other things to consider, as well. A site for a factory must provide for transportation needs, so goods can be delivered and shipped. Schools should be near the residential area they serve. Banks should be near the city's business district. A housing development should be located near schools and shopping. Bridges must be placed where the conditions are best for a strong foundation.

At the same time, the environment must be preserved. Community needs must be considered. For example, an airport should not be located in the middle of a quiet residential community. If the site is in a historical area, the construction should

The immense construction site for the Miho Dam dwarfs the huge pieces of machinery and equipment below. (Courtesy of Kajima Corporation)

fit in with surrounding buildings. Sometimes, roads or tunnels must be routed around or under historical landmarks to preserve them.

A construction site must be near roads, railroads, or ports so materials and equipment can be delivered. Water and electricity must be available, as well as a way to dispose of wastes. Construction workers should be able to reach the site easily. The best construction site is one that meets all the specifications at the lowest cost.

PREPARING THE CONSTRUCTION SITE

The construction site must be prepared for building. Heavy equipment is used to clear the ground. If there are unwanted buildings on the site, they must be removed. Wrecking balls or explosives are used to demolish buildings. Bulldozers clear trees or brush from an area. Unwanted materials are hauled away by dump trucks.

Before construction starts, the structure must be laid out. A **surveyor** is a person who marks the site to show where the structure will be built. Surveyors use a **transit** to measure and lay out angles. They use an engineer's level to set the elevation (height above ground) of different points.

BUILDING THE FOUNDATION

A **foundation** supports the weight of a **structure**. If you were standing on soft earth, you might sink down. If you stepped on a wide board, your weight would be spread out over a larger area. You wouldn't sink down as far. A foundation spreads the weight of a structure over a larger area of ground so it is well supported. In cold climates, foundations also prevent frost damage to the structure. Foundations are sometimes called **substructures**.

A foundation has three parts. One is the earth on which it rests. The second is the footing, which transfers the structure's weight to the earth. The third is vertical supports which rest on the footing.

If the ground is hard, a **spread** footing is used. It spreads out the weight of the structure, just as your weight is spread over an area as wide as your foot. If the ground is soft, or the site is marshy or under water, **piles** are used. Piles are like stilts. They are driven into the earth until they reach hard ground or rock.

Construction sites must be chosen to fit in with the needs of people and the environment.

Giant shovels remove earth to prepare a site for construction. (Courtesy of GE)

A foundation is built to support a structure.

Piles support the Columbia River Bridge in Portland, Oregon. (Courtesy of Sverdrup Corporation)

A dam is an example of a mass superstructure. (Courtesy of U.S. Department of the Interior, Bureau of Reclamation)

This airport terminal in Riyadh, Saudi Arabia, has a framed superstructure. (Courtesy of The Turner Corporation)

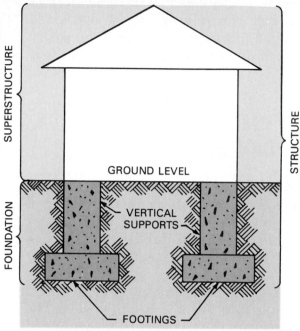

A structure includes a foundation and a superstructure.

This castle is an example of a bearing wall superstructure. (Photo by Michael Hacker)

BUILDING THE SUPERSTRUCTURE

The **superstructure** is the part of a structure that is above the ground (unless the structure is a tunnel or pipeline).

Mass superstructures are made from large masses of materials. They have little or no space inside. Dams and monuments are mass superstructures. They are built from brick, concrete, earth, or stone.

Bearing wall superstructures enclose a space with walls. They are built from brick, concrete, or stone. The castles built in the Middle Ages are bearing wall superstructures. The walls of some of these castles were 20 feet thick or more at the base.

Framed superstructures use a framework to support the building. Today, most buildings are framed superstructures. Lumber is used for framing in most houses. In office and apartment buildings, reinforced concrete and steel are used for framing. Reinforced concrete and steel are stronger, longer-lasting, and more fire-resistant than wood.

The usable part of a structure is called the superstructure.

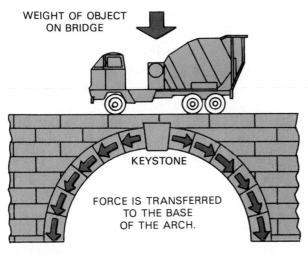

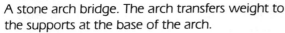

A stone arch bridge. The arch transfers weight to the supports at the base of the arch.

Cantilever bridges extend outwards and are secured at the ends.

TYPES OF STRUCTURES

Bridges, buildings, dams, harbors, roads, towers, and tunnels are different types of structures. Each requires special construction techniques.

Bridges

People have been building bridges since prehistoric times. Bridges that use one beam to cross a distance are called **beam bridges**. These are the simplest kinds of bridges. The strength of a beam bridge depends on how strong the beam is.

The Romans used the arch to support viaducts (bridges) and aqueducts (raised channels that carried water from one place to another). The first **arch bridges** were made of stone. They are now made from concrete or steel because of their strength.

A **cantilever** bridge works like two diving boards facing each other. The sections are firmly attached at their ends. If they do not meet, another section may be added to link them. A cantilever bridge requires a huge force to support each end. **Double cantilever** bridges have been designed to overcome this problem. The two sides of the cantilever section balance each other.

Suspension bridges are used to bridge wide spans. A suspension bridge uses steel cables to hang the deck (roadbed) from towers. Some of the world's most famous bridges are suspension bridges. The Golden Gate Bridge in San Francisco is 4,200 feet long. The George Washington Bridge, which links New Jersey and New York, is 3,500 feet long.

The Severn Bridge in Avon, England, is a suspension bridge, finished in 1966, that took twenty-one years to build. The deck

An early beam bridge

The Severn Bridge spans 3,250 feet. (Courtesy of British Tourist Authority)

was designed so it would not sway in the wind. Deck sections were built in a factory and moved to the bridge site. This kept costs down, since the deck was easier to build in a factory than a hundred feet in the air. The bridge towers rise about 300 feet above the water.

Buildings

There are four kinds of building construction:

1. residential (hotels and housing);
2. commercial (banks, stores, and offices);
3. institutional (schools and hospitals); and
4. industrial (factories).

In the first three kinds of buildings, aesthetic design and beauty are important. In industrial buildings, however, beauty is less important than usefulness. A factory must house many kinds of equipment as cheaply and efficiently as possible.

Land costs for industrial buildings are fairly low compared to land costs for other kinds of buildings. Houses, schools, offices, and hospitals must be located near residential areas. Factories can be built in the country, where land is cheap and noise and pollution do not affect so many people.

The lumber used in building houses is called **dimensional lumber** because it comes in many thicknesses and lengths. Most walls in residences are framed with 8-foot lengths of 2″ × 4″ lumber. These lengths are spaced so the center of each is 16 inches from the center of the next. Insulation, electrical wiring, and plumbing pipes are placed in the framework before the walls are finished. The inside walls are usually made of **plasterboard**. Plasterboard (also known as **Sheetrock**) is sheets of plaster covered with heavy paper. Plasterboard sheets are nailed or glued to the framing.

Outside walls are made from composite or plywood panels. They may be covered with brick veneer or with wood, aluminum, or vinyl **siding**. Siding is attractive and sturdy. Wood siding needs to be painted or stained every few years, but aluminum and vinyl siding need little care. **Insulation** made of fiberglass or plastic foam is installed between the inside and outside walls to conserve energy. Insulation helps maintain inside temperatures and saves on heating and cooling costs.

Most housing construction is done on the site. Sometimes, materials are cut to size in a factory, then assembled on the site. A recent trend is **panelized construction**, in which parts of houses are built in a factory. The walls and roof trusses (framing for the roof) are prefabricated. Complete walls are mass-produced as finished sections that have wiring, plumbing,

Electrical wiring and utilities are installed before the walls are completed. (Photo by Michael Hacker)

windows, and doors. This saves time and money.

Apartment houses and commercial and institutional buildings are framed with steel or reinforced concrete. Beams are the horizontal pieces that support the weight of the floors and walls. Columns are the vertical pieces. Columns transfer the weight from the beams to the foundation. A steel framework is often built elsewhere and moved to the construction site. There it is lifted into place by cranes. Reinforced concrete beams and columns are cast in place at the site. Floors may be made of concrete or steel. The outside walls are usually made of brick or panels of concrete, glass, metal, or plastic.

Tunnels

People might have gotten the idea for tunnels from watching animals burrow. Tunnels under water and through mountains have shortened travel routes since ancient times. The earliest tunnels were dug by the Babylonians about 2000 B.C.

Early tunnels were dug by hand because little machinery was available. The removed earth was hauled away in carts. Workers always feared that the tunnel would cave in around them. In 1818, the **tunneling shield** was invented. This device held the earth up while the tunnel was being dug. The shield

This building has a steel framework. (Photo by Michael Hacker)

The Tacoma Dome

An example of commercial construction is the Tacoma Dome in Tacoma, Washington. The dome is part of a $44 million sports and convention center. The 100,000-square-foot arena seats 26,000 people. It is covered by a 530-foot-diameter wooden dome, the largest in the world.

A dome is a lightweight structure that is very strong. It is like an arch, transferring weight from the top outward and downward to the base. The Tacoma Dome is built of triangular sections. A triangle is a rigid, strong shape.

(Courtesy of Sverdrup Corporation)

In the early 1900s, tunnels were dug by hand. Workers erected wooden arches and supports as the construction progressed. (Courtesy of Perini Corporation)

was pushed along as the work progressed.

Tunnels dug into rock are drilled and blasted by explosives. The opening is supported by steel arches. A new technique uses a concrete mixture called **shotcrete** to spray the walls. Shotcrete prevents water from seeping through the rock.

Tunnels drilled in soft ground may now be dug with machines. These machines have huge rotating cutters as large as 15 feet across. The cutters rotate about five times per minute and push against the earth with a force of nearly a million pounds. As the earth is cut, precast concrete or steel rings are put into place to support the opening.

One of the longest automobile tunnels in the world is the tunnel that connects France and Italy under Mont Blanc in the Alps. The nearly eight-mile-long tunnel saves about a hundred miles of driving. Teams started digging from opposite sides of the mountain and met in 1962, after two years of construction.

Roads

Before ancient Rome, roads were narrow paths used by two-wheeled carts. Roman engineers built over 40,000 miles of roads for the empire's armies to travel. Tunnels and bridges allowed the roads to go in a straight line from one place to another. The Romans even paved their roads, using stones.

Modern road building began in the late 1700s with the ideas of a Scotsman named John Loudon McAdam. McAdam made roads that lasted longer because of good drainage. On a base of hard soil, a stone layer was laid, topped by a layer of tar. McAdam's roads were higher in the center than at the edges, making water flow away from the road. McAdam's name was given to the material that is now used as a surface for many roads, **macadam**. Since the early 1900s, most roads have been built of concrete or macadam.

Before the twentieth century, few roads were paved. Most were made of crushed stone, which worked well for horses and buggies. But as people switched to automobiles, the rubber tires kicked out the stones, ruining the roads. A new type of surface was needed.

Today, roads are built to support heavy loads carried by high-speed vehicles. Safe, well-designed roads allow people to live miles from their work. They have linked our cities and opened up new markets for business.

Road construction begins with choosing the route. When possible, the route stays away from existing structures. Sometimes buildings must be removed to make way for a road, because it would cost too much to go around them.

Next, the ground is smoothed by bulldozers. The soil is

Today's highways are safe for high-speed long distance travel. (Courtesy of New York State Department of Transportation —Clough, Harbour, & Associates)

The Fort McHenry Tunnel

Fort McHenry in Baltimore Harbor is a historic landmark. During the War of 1812, the British bombarded the fort. U.S. soldiers were able to fight off the British force of fifty ships. From an American ship in the harbor, a young attorney, Francis Scott Key, could see that the American flag still waved over the fort. This inspired him to write "The Star Spangled Banner."

Recently, a tunnel was built near the fort to link parts of the interstate highway system. It is hidden, completely out of sight and earshot of the fort. The tunnel has eight lanes, carrying 66,000 vehicles a day. The tunnel took seven years and $750 million to build.

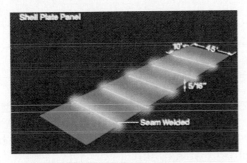

Tube making for the Fort McHenry Tunnel begins with steel panels. The panels are welded together to form a shell plate. Stiffeners are added for strength.

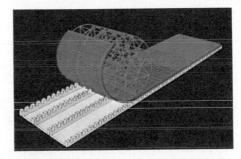

Modules are shaped by wrapping the shell plate around a specially designed reel. More structural pieces and various form plates are added.

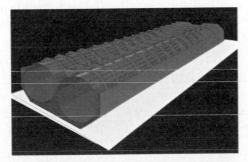

Sixteen modules (eight for each tube) are joined. They form one section of the double-barreled tube. Each tube holds two lanes of roadway.

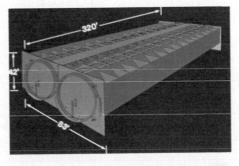

Dam plates seal each end of the tube. Keel concrete is added for strength and rigidity. The section is then launched for a 12-hour tow to the Fort McHenry Tunnel site.

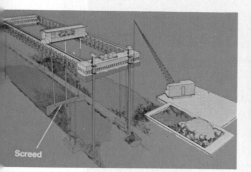

A heavy, plow-like beam from a screed barge dredges along the harbor bottom. This forms the trench that will hold the tunnel.

From a lay barge, the tube section is lowered into the trench. It is then attached to another tunnel segment. Thirty-two tube sections were carefully lowered and connected to form the Fort McHenry Tunnel.

The Fort McHenry Tunnel site

(All photos courtesy of Sverdrup Corporation)

pressed down by heavy rollers. It is then covered with stone, which spreads out the load and provides drainage. The pavement is made of concrete about one foot thick, or from blacktop materials like macadam or asphalt.

Center barriers, good lighting, and traffic control devices are also part of the road-building system.

Other Structures

Structures include bridges, buildings, dams, harbors, roads, towers, and tunnels.

Airports, canals, dams, harbors, pipelines, and towers are other structures that are built on a site. Large construction companies often have different divisions that build different structures. There might be a tunnel division, a pipeline division, and a building division. Smaller companies most often do only one or two kinds of construction.

RENOVATION

Renovation is the process of rebuilding an existing building. Sometimes this is done to change the style of a building. Sometimes it is done because a building needs repair. As the years pass, dust, wind, and water can cause damage. When a structure is renovated, old materials are replaced or renewed. Renovation is often less costly than demolishing a structure and building it all over again.

(Courtesy of Perini Corporation)

(Courtesy of Mardian Construction Company)

(Courtesy of Perini Corporation)

Construction technology
provides us with many
benefits.

(Courtesy of Perini Corporation)

The Statue of Liberty was recently renovated. After 100 years, salt water and air pollution had worn parts of the statue away. The renovated statue was rededicated on July 4, 1986.
(Courtesy of NASA)

SUMMARY

Construction is the building of a structure on a site. Construction systems use the seven technological resources. People engineer, design, manage, and build structures. They use information to carry out these tasks. Building materials like concrete, steel, and wood are used, along with tools and heavy equipment. Energy is needed to run equipment. Capital costs are high because land, material, equipment, and labor are costly. Construction projects take a long time to complete, although new building techniques like prefabrication and modular construction reduce building time.

Construction involves choosing and preparing a site, building a foundation, building a superstructure, installing utilities, and finishing the inside and outside.

Site selection depends on the use of the structure. Commercial buildings are located near business districts. Schools are located in residential areas. The effect of a construction project on the environment and the community should be considered.

Before construction begins, the site must be cleared. Surveyors lay out the structure on the site. The structure must be supported by a foundation, which spreads the structure's weight over a larger area of ground. The superstructure is the usable part of the structure. Mass, bearing wall, and framed superstructures are three types.

Building techniques have been learned through many years of experience. Today, these techniques are used along with a knowledge of materials to build airports, bridges, canals, dams, harbors, pipelines, roads, towers, tunnels, and buildings.

REVIEW QUESTIONS

1. What is the major difference between manufacturing and construction systems?
2. Draw a labeled systems diagram of the construction system.
3. Describe four career opportunities provided by the construction industry.
4. How could you finance the construction of a private home?
5. If you were to choose a site for a movie theater, what are five things you would have to consider?
6. What kinds of superstructures do the following structures have?
   a. the Washington Monument
   b. a tower that supports electrical wires
   c. a skyscraper
   d. a large dam
   e. a castle from the Middle Ages
7. Make a sketch of a suspension bridge.
8. Explain why an arch can support a great amount of weight.
9. Design a tower, using rolls of newspaper as your building material.
10. Name five different types of structures.

KEY WORDS

Arch	Engineer	Macadam	Structure
Architect	Estimator	Mortgage	Superstructure
Cement	Forms	Prefabricate	Surveyor
Concrete	Foundation	Specifications	
Construction	General contractor	Steel	

SEE YOUR TEACHER FOR THE CROSSTECH PUZZLE

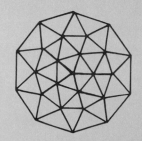

DOME CONSTRUCTION

Setting the Stage

What sort of structure can be built with no internal supports at all? A hint . . . Eskimos have built them for years. The structure we are talking about is, of course, the **dome**. Domed structures are often used for sports stadiums like the Astrodome in Houston, Texas, or for World's Fairs, Expos, or amusement parks.

The weight of a dome is transmitted uniformly from its top outward and downward to its base. As a result, no internal weight-bearing supports are needed. Domes can be made from standardized parts. These parts can be made in a factory and assembled later at the building site. Domes are also fairly light in weight. This means that the foundation for this type of structure can be smaller than conventional foundations.

Your Challenge

Work together with your team to build a small dome-shaped structure that can be used as a greenhouse.

Suggested Resources

Safety glasses
Galvanized steel—22-24 gauge
Round head machine screws—½", 4-40 NC with nuts
Bar folder
Box and pan brake
Notcher
Sheetmetal hole punch—⅛"
Squaring shear
Assorted sheetmetal layout and hand tools

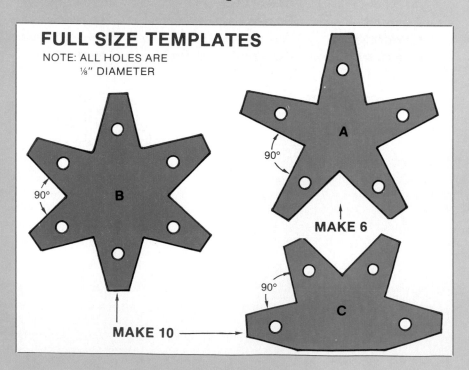

FULL SIZE TEMPLATES
NOTE: ALL HOLES ARE ⅛" DIAMETER

B 90°

A 90° MAKE 6

C 90° MAKE 10

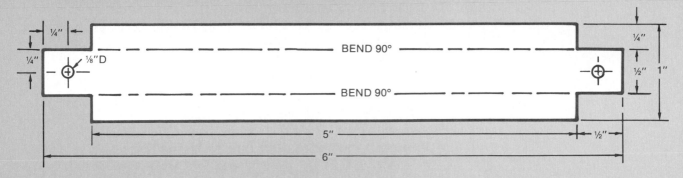

MAKE 35

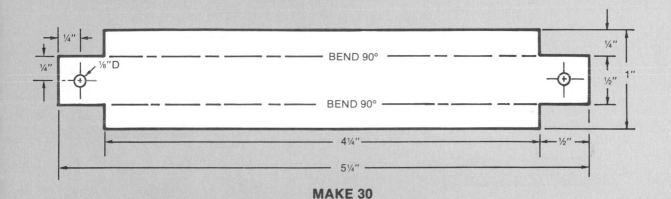

MAKE 30

Procedure

1. Divide up into teams of 3 members each. Be sure to wear safety glasses!
2. Check the list of tools and machines you will need. Find out which members have been instructed by the teacher to use each tool or machine. Check with your teacher BEFORE going any further.
3. Team member #1:
   a. Duplicate the full-size shapes A, B, and C, and use them as templates.
   b. Use a notcher to cut out 6 of shape A, 10 of shape B, 10 of shape C, and 5 pentagons.
   c. Punch ⅛" diameter holes as marked.
4. Team member #2:
   a. Use the squaring shear and notcher to cut out the 6" connecting elements of the dome. Make 35.

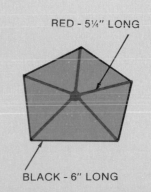

RED - 5¼" LONG

BLACK - 6" LONG

MAKE 5 PENTAGONS

5. Team member #3:
    a. Use the squaring shear and notcher to cut out the 5¼" connecting elements of the dome. Make 30.
6. Team members #2 and #3:
    a. Working together, punch two ⅛" diameter holes as marked on the ends of these elements.
    b. Bend the ¼" strips on the long sides of the connecting elements to 90° angles. Also place a slight bend (approx. 10°) on the ends of these pieces. See detail drawing #1. Check with member #1 before attempting these bends.
7. All team members:
    a. With each member taking one of his/her pieces, assemble one pentagon shape, using shape A as the center and shape B for the outer corners. The 5¼" connecting elements always radiate from the center of the dome.
    b. With each person taking a turn, fasten the connecting elements to the corner shapes using ½" 4-40 round head machine screws and nuts. DO NOT COMPLETELY TIGHTEN THE SCREWS UNTIL THE ENTIRE STRUCTURE IS ASSEMBLED.
    c. Working outward from the completed pentagon, assemble the rest of the structure. Follow detail drawings #2 and #3 carefully.
8. The dome can be covered with plastic and used as a greenhouse.

SLIGHT BEND

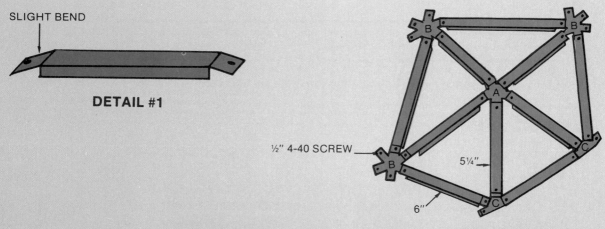

DETAIL #1

½" 4-40 SCREW

5¼"

6"

DETAIL #2

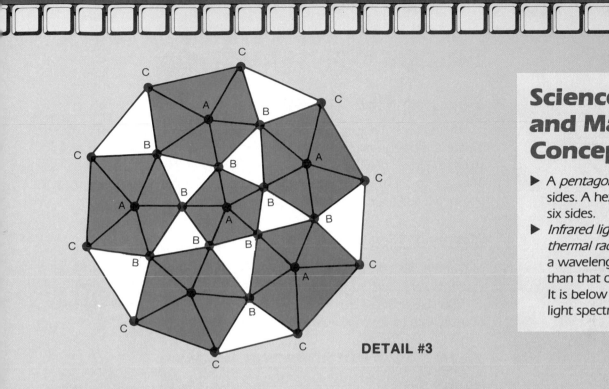

DETAIL #3

Group Processing

Each team member is to complete his/her own rating sheet. Rate yourself from 1 to 10 for each question.

NEVER   SOMETIMES   ALWAYS
1 ....5 10

1. I shared tools and equipment.
2. I took my turn when assembling the dome.
3. I let others take their turn when assembling the dome.
4. I asked for help from other members of the class when I needed it.
5. I helped other class members when they asked for help.
6. I encouraged my teammates by using words like "good job!", "I like the way you did that!", and "Excellent!".

Team members should then get together and discuss their self rating with each other. Make sure you thank each member before you leave class!

Technology Connections

1. A simple dome is not hard to build. It needs no columns or supports to hold it up. Why not?
2. How is the heat from the sun concentrated by a greenhouse? What is the *greenhouse effect?*
3. Why is it possible to use smaller foundations with dome structures?
4. Which two geometric shapes are usually part of the design of a dome? Are there any more?
5. What materials can be used to build a dome? Is an igloo a dome?

BRIDGE CONSTRUCTION

Setting the Stage

If you had to cross a stream without getting your feet wet, building a bridge might be the answer. Logs have been used to cross streams since prehistoric times. But what if the log isn't strong enough to hold your weight? This is the sort of problem that engineers still face when building bridges today.

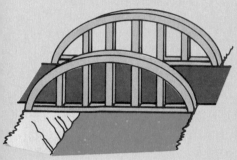

Your Challenge

Design and build a model of a bridge. If desired, small groups of students can work together.

The bridge must be 4" tall and able to span an 8" chasm. It must also be able to hold at least 40 pounds.

Suggested Resources

Safety glasses and
  lab apron
3 pieces of pine—
  ¼" x ¼" x 3'
1 piece of heavy
  cardboard—4" x 9".
  Matting board is good.
1 piece of cardstock—
  8½" x 11". A manila
  file folder works fine.
White glue
Wax paper
Assorted tools and
  machines

Procedure

1. Be sure to wear safety glasses and a lab coat.
2. Make a full-scale drawing of your bridge on graph paper. Do both the front and side views. When you are satisfied with your bridge design, show it to your teacher.
3. Cut the strips of pine to the exact lengths and angles needed for your design. Lay the cut pieces on top of your drawing to check for accuracy.
4. Before gluing the wood pieces in place, cover your drawing with a sheet of wax paper. You can glue the pieces using your drawing as a guide. The wax paper will prevent your wood from sticking to the drawing.
5. Cut small triangles from the cardstock. Use these triangles to reinforce the corners of the bridge. They are known as *gussets.*
6. Give the glued wooden pieces a chance to dry before you start gluing on the gussets.
7. Use the heavy cardboard to make the floor of your bridge. Glue it in place.
8. After it is dry, measure your bridge for the minimum height (4″) and ability to cross an 8″ chasm. Place 40 pounds *on top* of the bridge to test its strength.

Technology Connections

1. *Construction* refers to building a structure on a site. What factors must be considered when choosing a site for a bridge?
2. What type of bridge has its deck supported from above by steel cables?
3. What construction material is made from a mixture of cement, sand, stone, and water?
4. Engineers must calculate all of the stresses (forces) on bridge structures they design. Can you pick out some of the major stress points on your bridge?
5. What can happen to a bridge if it is not engineered properly? Has this ever happened?

Science and Math Concepts

► A *chasm* is a deep cleft or gorge in the earth.
► Concrete has a high *compressive* strength. It resists being compressed or crushed.
► Steel cable has a high *tensile* strength. It is very strong under tension and resists being stretched.

CHAPTER 11

BUILDING A STRUCTURE

MAJOR CONCEPTS

After reading this chapter, you will know that:

- Buildings are constructed in steps. The footing, foundation, floors, walls, and roof are built. Then the utilities and insulation are installed. Finally, the structure is finished.
- The footing is the base of the foundation. It spreads the weight of the structure over a wider area of ground.
- The foundation walls support the whole weight of the structure and transmit it to the footing.
- Walls transmit the load from above to the foundation. They also serve as partitions between rooms.
- The roof protects the house against the weather and prevents heat loss.
- Insulation helps keep the temperature of the house constant.
- Utilities include plumbing, electrical, and heating systems.
- Manufactured houses are built in a factory and taken to the construction site.
- Wind effects must be taken into account in designing and building a skyscraper.

INTRODUCTION

Through many years of experience, people have learned a great deal about construction. Building and management skills and engineering principles are needed in construction technology.

Homes and commercial buildings are the most common structures. In this chapter you will learn how these structures are built.

Buildings are constructed in steps. The footing, foundation, floors, walls, and roof are built. Then the utilities and insulation are installed. Finally, the structure is finished.

HOUSE BUILDING

So you want to build a house! It may sound like a difficult job. But building a house can be separated into a series of steps.

Building even the most beautiful homes involves a series of well-defined steps. (Courtesy of Western Wood Products Association)

PRECONSTRUCTION

Some steps must be taken before construction can start. These are part of the **preconstruction** phase. One of these preconstruction steps is picking the right location for the house.

Picking the Location

Who decides where a house will be built? Most often, it's the builder. But if a house is custom-built (built for the person who will live in it), the owner helps decide, along with the builder and the architect.

How does a builder decide where to build a house? The cost of the lot is an important factor. The cost of the land will depend on how desirable the location is. If the land is near a famous ski resort or has a beautiful view or is on a lake or river, it may be very costly.

Utilities and roads are another factor. Are utilities such as sewer, water, and electric service readily available? Does a road provide access to the lot? If not, a new road will have to be built, and that will add to the cost of the house.

How the house will be placed on the lot is also important. During recent years, energy costs have risen greatly. For this reason, builders try to use the sun for heating the house in winter. In the Northern Hemisphere, the sun follows a southerly path across the sky. Thus, the wall with the most window glass is placed to face south so sunshine can help with winter heating. Builders also try to use broadleaved trees on the lot for summer shade. In the winter, when the leaves fall, the sun shines on the house and helps to heat it.

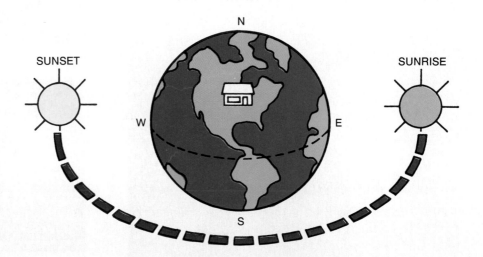

The sun is closest to the earth at the equator. A house built in the northern hemisphere would have large windows facing south to take advantage of the heat of the sun.

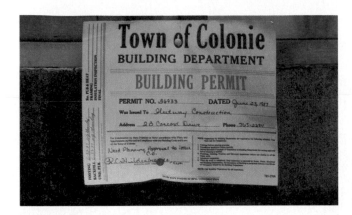

The building permit must be displayed during construction. *(Photo by Michael Hacker)*

Building Permits and Codes

Another preconstruction step is getting necessary **building permits**. A building permit allows the builder to begin work. Before a permit is issued, the house plans must be approved by officials in a county or community building department.

Each city, town, and county has its own building department. It has its own **building codes**, a set of construction guidelines that ensure buildings are safe and well built. For example, a building code might tell how high windows must be above the floor, or the sizes of pipes to use in plumbing.

The building department generally sends **building inspectors** to check different steps in construction as they are completed. At each step, an inspector must look at the work to make sure it meets the codes. After the building is completed, the building department issues a **Certificate of Occupancy (CO)**. The CO means that the building has passed all inspections and is ready to be occupied.

CONSTRUCTING THE FOOTING AND FOUNDATION

All structures have some kind of a foundation. House foundations have two parts. They are the **footing** and the **foundation wall**.

The Footing

The footing for most houses is made of concrete. It is a base for the foundation wall. The **spread footing** distributes the weight of a building over a wider area of the ground. The **frost line**

The ground under the leaning Tower of Pisa settled unevenly. This uneven settling caused the tower to lean. The tower is 191 feet tall. It continues to tilt at the rate of one inch every eight years. The top is about 16 feet out of plumb (off exact vertical). *(Courtesy of Italian Government Tourist Agency)*

The footing is the base of the foundation. It spreads the weight of the structure over a wider area of ground.

The footing is dug to a depth below the frost line.
(Courtesy of American Wood Preservers Bureau)

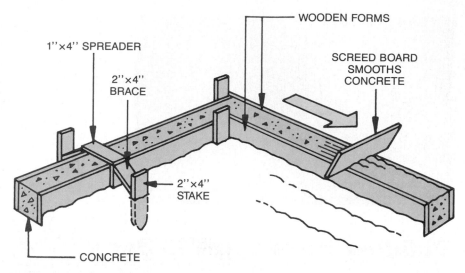

1"×4" SPREADER

2"×4" BRACE

WOODEN FORMS

SCREED BOARD SMOOTHS CONCRETE

2"×4" STAKE

CONCRETE

Wooden boards contain the concrete as it is placed.

determines how deep the footing must be. The frost line is the depth to which the ground freezes in winter. In colder climates, such as in Maine, the frost line could be as much as 7 feet below the surface of the ground (below grade). In warmer climates, such as in southern California, the frost line might be only an inch or two below grade.

The footing must begin below the frost line because when the water in the ground freezes, it expands. The movement of the ground could cause the footing to move or crack. When the footing rests on ground below the frost line, this is less likely to happen.

For the footing, workers first dig a trench where the foundation wall will be built. The width of the trench is about twice as wide as the foundation wall. Long boards of 2 x 8 inch lumber are placed along the sides of the trench to keep it from filling with dirt. The trench is now a board-lined form for the concrete that will become the footing. The board lining is braced with wood while the concrete is being poured. When the concrete cures (becomes hard), the boards are removed.

The Foundation Wall

Next comes the foundation wall. It is built on top of the footing and supports the weight of the house. The foundation wall is most often made of concrete blocks. These blocks are about 8 x 8 x 16 inches. They have hollow cores to reduce their weight. Sometimes the wall is made from concrete poured into forms. The foundation wall can also be made

The foundation walls support the whole weight of the structure and transmit it to the footing.

A concrete block foundation.
(Courtesy of Michael Hacker)

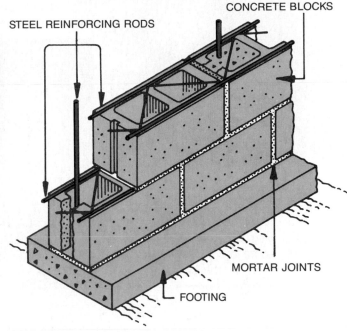

Concrete is strong under compression, but weak under tension. Steel reinforcing rods are used to give the foundation more tensile strength.

from lumber that is pressure treated to keep it from rotting. Wooden foundations are becoming more popular because they provide for a dry basement. The basement can then be used as a living space.

Concrete block foundations are laid by a **mason**. A mason is a worker who builds with concrete, concrete block, stone, and brick. Concrete blocks are attached to the footing and to each other with **mortar**. Mortar is a mixture of cement, lime, sand, and water. It acts like a glue, bonding the concrete blocks to the footing and to each other.

Steel **reinforcing rods** may be used to anchor the foundation walls to the footing. These long steel rods are placed into the footing and mortared in place in the middle of the block.

Horizontal parts of the foundation must be **level** (exactly horizontal) and vertical parts must be **plumb** (exactly vertical). If the foundation is not level and plumb, the house built on top of it will be crooked.

If a house is to have a basement with an eight-foot ceiling, the foundation walls are built 12 blocks high. Since the blocks are each 8 inches high, a 12-block-high wall will be about eight feet tall. In a house without a basement, the wall can be lower. This will provide for a **crawl space** under the house. A crawl space gives only enough room to install and service utilities like heating and plumbing.

The foundation wall must be constructed so that it is perfectly level. (Courtesy of Portland Cement Association)

Mason checking plumbness with a level held vertically as he lays the first course of block on the footing. (Courtesy of Portland Cement Association)

Slab foundations, sometimes referred to as thickened slabs, are suited to the warmer climates where the frost line is not far below grade. These foundations are made from a large slab of concrete. They consist of a shallow footing poured together with the slab. Slab foundations provide a very large area over which the weight of the house may be spread. The bottom of the footing should be at least one foot below the natural grade line and be supported on solid ground. Wire mesh and sometimes reinforcing rods are put over the slab area before the concrete is placed. These are used to help keep the slab from cracking when the concrete **cures** or hardens. Anchor bolts are inserted in the foundation when the concrete is placed. The bottom plate of the outside walls is anchored to the foundation using anchor bolts. Plumbing, heating, and air conditioning

Combined slab and foundation. The gravel fill should be of a size that will be retained on a 1-inch-mesh screen.

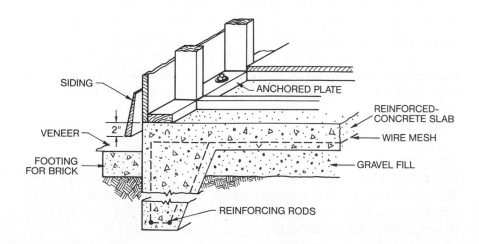

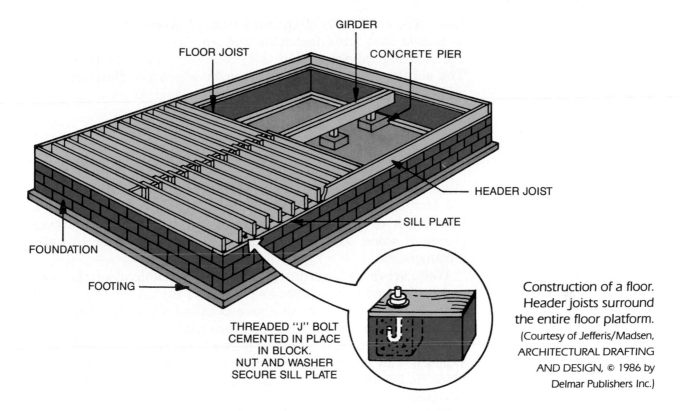

GIRDER

FLOOR JOIST

CONCRETE PIER

HEADER JOIST

SILL PLATE

FOUNDATION

FOOTING

THREADED ''J'' BOLT
CEMENTED IN PLACE
IN BLOCK.
NUT AND WASHER
SECURE SILL PLATE

Construction of a floor.
Header joists surround
the entire floor platform.
(Courtesy of Jefferis/Madsen,
ARCHITECTURAL DRAFTING
AND DESIGN, © 1986 by
Delmar Publishers Inc.)

ducts are installed under the slab before it is placed. Flooring materials like tile and carpet are laid directly on the concrete slab.

BUILDING THE FLOOR

The floor is built on top of the foundation. The floor frame is built from long boards called **floor joists**. Floor joists are usually spaced 16 inches on center. That is, the center of one joist is 16 inches from the center of the next joist. Floor joists are made of lumber that is 2 inches thick and from 6 to 12 inches wide. The length of the boards is between 10 and 16 feet. The boards are lined up on edge across the foundation.

Often, the foundation is more than 16 feet wide. The builder could buy longer boards, but these are costly. Instead, a strong wooden or steel girder may be placed down the middle of the floor, supporting joist sections on either side. The girder is supported from below by a row of piers or columns.

Since the foundation is concrete, the wooden joists cannot be nailed directly to it. Instead, bolts are placed at the edges of the concrete foundation. A wooden **sill plate** is attached to the bolts and the joists are nailed to the sill plate. The sill plate is a piece of lumber, approximately 2 inches thick.

After the joists have been nailed on, the **subfloor** is nailed to

Plywood subfloor. (Courtesy of Michael Hacker)

them. The subfloor is often made from plywood. Plywood comes in panels that are 4 feet wide and approximately 8 feet long. For flooring, plywood that is ½ inch or ⅝ inch thick is used. The subfloor provides the surface to which the finished floor will be attached.

FRAMING THE WALLS

Walls are generally built after the floor is finished. Most houses are framed superstructures. That is, the basic building is a framework of many parts. **Framing** the walls means cutting pieces of wood to size and fastening them together to form a framework.

Walls serve two purposes. They carry the load of the roof and ceiling, and they serve as partitions for the rooms. A wall that supports weight from above is called a **load-bearing** wall. Although walls are vertical, they are constructed horizontally. They are laid out and nailed together lying flat on the subfloor. When a wall is complete, with door and window openings in place, it is raised to its final position. Only then is it nailed into place.

The vertical parts of the wall are called **studs**. These are normally made from 2 x 4-inch lumber and are bought pre-cut. A single bottom plate and a double top plate are used along with the pre-cut studs to frame the wall section. When the wall is lifted into place it is approximately 8 feet tall. **Jack studs** are shorter studs that are used above and below windows and above doors.

The top and bottom of the wall are made from horizontal pieces of lumber called the **top plate** and the **bottom plate**. The top plate of the wall is made from a double layer of 2 x 4s; the bottom plate of the wall is made from a single layer of 2 x 4s.

When a wall is built, the studs are cut first. They are laid on edge on the subfloor between the top and bottom plates. They are then fastened to the plates with nails. If a partition (inside wall) will connect to an outside wall, extra studs are used to provide more surfaces for nailing. At corners, **corner posts** are used. They provide an inside and an outside surface to which wall covering can be nailed. Bracing is sometimes added in the corners to keep the wall from racking (moving out of plumb).

When windows and doors are framed, a strong piece of wood called a **header** is nailed across the top of the window or door opening. The header carries the weight from above. It transmits the load to the studs below it. **Trimmers** are short studs that support the header. They are attached to the studs along the window opening.

Walls transmit the load from above to the foundation. They also serve as partitions between rooms.

The wall is built horizontally.
(Courtesy of Mark Huth)

Carpenter using an automatic nailer to frame walls.
(Courtesy of Paslode Corporation, an ITW Company)

After completion, the wall is raised to the vertical position. (Courtesy of Mark Huth)

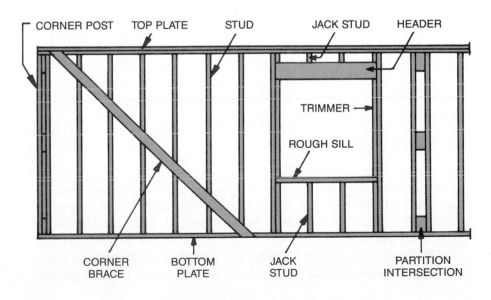

CORNER POST   TOP PLATE   STUD   JACK STUD   HEADER

TRIMMER

ROUGH SILL

CORNER BRACE   BOTTOM PLATE   JACK STUD   PARTITION INTERSECTION

Typical framing for an exterior wall (Courtesy of Lewis, CARPENTRY, © 1984 by Delmar Publishers Inc.)

Spacing Between Studs

Building codes specify how studs are to be spaced. The spacing between the studs is governed by the ability of the lumber to support the load above it. When 2 x 4-inch studs are used, they are usually installed 16 inches on center. When 2 x 6-inch studs are used, they are spaced farther apart, 24 inches on center.

Since the 2 x 6-inch studs are spaced farther apart, fewer of them are needed in a wall. In a 48-inch-wide wall section, only three 2 x 6s would be needed.

Four 2 x 4s would be needed for the same wall.

The volume of wood used is about the same in either case, but there is an advantage in using 2 x 6s. The 2 x 6s make a wall that is more energy efficient. Studs conduct heat from the inside of the house to the outside. Fewer studs mean less heat loss in winter. Also, there is more room for insulation when 2 x 6s are used. Only 3½ inches of insulation will fit in a wall of 2 x 4s. A wall of 2 x 6s can hold 6 inches of insulation.

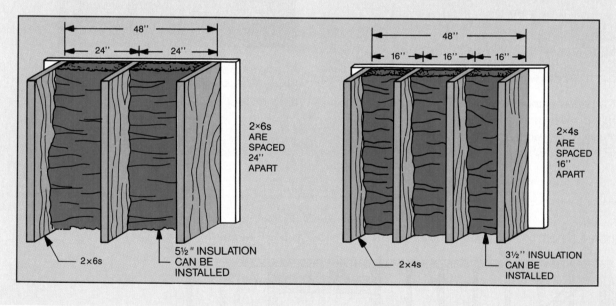

SHEATHING

After the wall has been framed, it is covered with **wall sheathing**. Wall sheathing can be plywood, particle board, wooden planks, or rigid foam board. Most often, 4 x 8-foot sheets of sheathing are used.

Wall sheathing is used to make the frame of the house stronger. It also provides a surface on which outside wall coverings like

This house uses a combination of plywood and rigid foam board sheathing. (Courtesy of Clara Littlejohn)

wood, vinyl siding, or brick veneer can be fastened. Sheathing closes in the building and protects it from the weather.

During framing, the carpenter prepares for sheathing by placing studs carefully. Sometimes the long studs bow up toward the center. The carpenter sights along the length of the stud to see which edge bows up. This is called a **crown**. The carpenter will place the studs so all the crowns face toward the outside of the house. That way, the entire wall will bow out from one corner to the next, instead of bowing in and out, in and out. It is much easier to put on sheathing and interior finish when the studs bow only in one direction.

Sheathing may be nailed to the studs before the wall section is raised and nailed in place. It is generally nailed on over the whole wall, including the window and door openings. After a wall has been sheathed, the carpenter saws out the sheathing that covers the openings. This may seem wasteful. However, it is a fast way to do the job and saves on the cost of labor. Pieces of sheathing that are cut from large openings can sometimes be used to cover other areas of the wall.

A laser beam can provide a perfectly horizontal line from which measurements may be made. (Courtesy of Spectra-Physics)

ROOF CONSTRUCTION

The roof protects the house against the weather. It prevents heat from escaping in cold weather. The roof also affects the way the house looks. In a single-story house, the roof provides the ceiling above the first floor. In houses with more than one story, ceilings are built above lower stories by placing joists on top of the top plate of the walls. The ceiling is nailed to the bottom of the joists and the subfloor is nailed to the top.

The most common kind of roof is a gable roof. This is a roof

The roof protects the house against the weather and prevents heat loss.

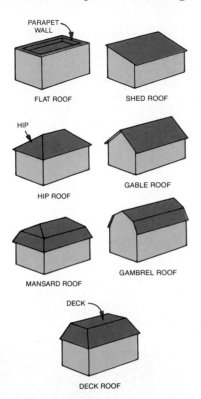

Principal types of roofs.

with an "A" shape. The roof slopes off in two directions from a peak. The climate determines how steep the slope or **pitch** of a roof must be. In very cold climates with heavy snowfall, the pitch will be very steep. Snow is more likely to slide off the roof instead of piling up, melting, and leaking into the house.

Framing the Roof

In the past most roofs were framed. To frame a roof, joists are installed across the top plates of the walls. The joists are nailed to the top plates directly above the wall studs. Then roof **rafters** are installed. One end of the rafter is nailed to a joist. The other is raised and attached to a ridge board that forms the peak of the roof. The ridge board acts as the central support for the ridge rafters. It runs the length of the roof. After the roof has been framed, plywood sheathing is nailed over it. This is called **roof decking**. The last step is to cover the decking with some kind of weatherproof material.

Roof Trusses

Roof construction is easier than it used to be. Today, carpenters do not have to measure, saw, and then nail every board into place. Instead, most of a roof is prefabricated. It is built elsewhere, in the form of big wooden triangles called **roof trusses**.

Roof trusses are made in a factory and trucked to the construction site. The trusses are hung upside down across the

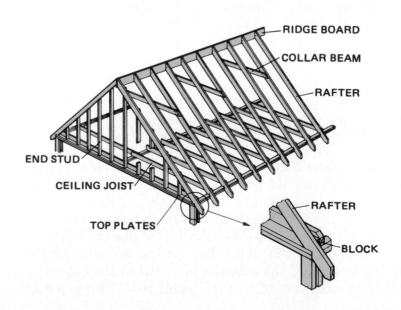

Conventional method of framing a roof. (Courtesy of USDA Forest Service, Forest Products Laboratory)

Earthquakes and No-Fault Houses

The earth's crust is like the loose peel of an orange. Big plates of it move slowly and constantly across the surface of our planet. At the center of the earth is a core of molten rock. When the molten core moves, cracks are created in the earth's crust. These cracks are called **faults**. They occur along areas called **fault lines**. Sudden shifts in the plates along these fault lines can cause earthquakes. Structures built on a fault line might be subjected to sudden stress.

In 1964, an earthquake in Alaska caused many deaths and much destruction. Homes and buildings were shaken to pieces.

A team of investigators went to Alaska to see how the damage had happened. They studied the houses that were destroyed. They found that most of the houses broke apart where the different pieces of the frame were nailed together.

Couldn't houses be designed to withstand an earthquake? Research was done on this problem for about ten years. The breakthrough came in the late 1970s. The answer was the Truss-Frame System (TFS).

The TFS makes one structural unit out of a roof truss, two wall studs, and a floor truss. Special strong metal fasteners with sharp teeth hold the wooden parts together. The TFS units are put into place and sheathed. When sheathing is attached, these parts make a building that is stronger than most framed structures.

Truss-Frame Systems reduce the time needed to build a house by up to half. Because of lower costs for labor, the selling price is as much as 10-25 percent lower. The TFS also helps to conserve forest resources. A TFS house uses 30 percent less lumber because framing is done with 2 x 4s spaced 24 inches on center.

Roger Tuomi is the name of the man who designed the TFS. He took out a public patent on his design. This means that anyone can use it. In the last five years, builders in 35 states have used the Truss-Frame System. The TFS shows clearly how careful study and creative design can improve technological processes.

(Photos courtesy of Forest Products Lab)

width of the house (like a V). They are placed on the top plates of two walls. Then a team of carpenters (or a small crane) swings them upright. Once in place, the trusses are nailed to the top plate.

Roof trusses are carefully designed and built. Because they can be so precisely designed, they can be built of thinner lumber than roofs that are framed by hand. The cost of trusses for a roof is about the same as the cost of wood for a framed roof. But the labor needed is a lot less. A framed roof takes 2 or 3 days to construct, while a roof made of trusses takes 2 or 3 hours.

Roofing

When the roof has been framed and roof decking nailed on, **roofing** material of some kind is applied. Roofing refers to covering the roof with weatherproof material. Roofing protects the decking from rotting. It is applied soon after the decking is in place to prevent rain and snow from getting into the house.

Roofing material is sold in **squares**. A square of roofing will cover 100 square feet of roof surface. Asphalt, fiberglass, or wooden shingles are most often used as roofing materials.

Before shingling the roof, roofers cover it with paper that has been soaked with asphalt. This material is called **asphalt felt**. It serves as an **underlayment** for the shingles. Asphalt is the same material that is used to pave roads. It is a tar-like

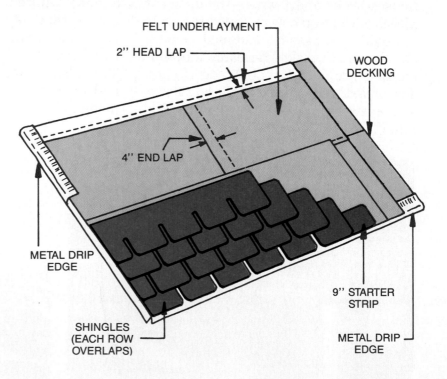

Asphalt shingles are installed in strips.

substance that is waterproof. Asphalt felt is stapled to the decking in horizontal rows. Each row (called a **course**) overlaps the course next to it by 2 inches.

Asphalt Shingles

Asphalt shingles go on over the underlayment. Asphalt shingles make a good roofing material. The shingles are covered with granules of slate, granite, or other minerals, and they come in several colors. The granules make the roof look good and protect the shingles from damage. They reflect the sun's heat, which could soften the shingles. Dark-colored roofs absorb more heat and raise the temperature inside the house. Light-colored roofs reflect more heat and keep the house cooler. Asphalt shingles are nailed or stapled in place. Each course of shingles is put on overlapping the one below it. The overlap helps protect against the weather.

Wooden Shingles and Shakes

Wooden shingles have been used since Roman times. The Romans used oak to make their shingles. Wooden shingles were used throughout Europe until around A.D. 1600 when there was a shortage of wood.

Wooden shingles are sawed from a log. Shingles that are split from a log are called **shakes**. Wooden shingles and shakes are made from Western red cedar, cypress, and redwood trees. These woods resist rot because of their natural oils. The trees from which they come grow slowly. Because of this, the wood has a tight grain. It does not expand much when the wood is soaked with water. This makes the shingle or shake less likely to crack and split.

When wooden or shake shingles are to be used on the roof,

Hand-splitting shakes using a mallet and a froe. (Courtesy of Red Cedar Shingle and Shake Bureau)

Roof with wooden shingles. (Courtesy of Red Cedar Shingle and Shake Bureau)

the sheathing material cannot be a solid material such as ply-wood. The wooden shingles expand or shrink according to the weather conditions. If they are laid over a solid decking material they lose their ability to expand or shrink. The decking material is usually made made from 1 x 6-inch material, spaced 1 inch apart on the rafters. No underlayment is used on the decking before the shingles are installed. No underlayment is used. Underlayment would trap water between itself and the wood and the shingles and shakes would remain wet and rot.

INSULATING THE HOUSE

Insulation helps keep the temperature of the house constant.

Insulation is material that does not conduct heat well. It is usually placed within the wall, between the inside and outside surfaces of the house. The insulation slows the movement of heat through the walls. Because of this, heat escapes more slowly to the outside on cold days. It enters the house more slowly on hot days. It costs less to heat the house in winter or cool it in summer. Insulation helps keep the house temperature constant.

Some materials are better insulators than others. Fiberglass and some kinds of plastic are used for insulation. Fiberglass comes in **blankets** that are 3½, 5½, or 9 inches thick. The blankets are in rolls 30 to 80 feet long with a waterproof backing. This can be waterproof paper, aluminum foil, or plastic sheeting. The rolls are cut into shorter **batts**. Insulation is stapled on walls or laid between ceiling joists, with the paper or foil facing the inside of the house. Fiberglass insulation is also produced as loose fibers. It is blown into walls through drilled holes, after the walls are finished.

Insulation is also made from plastics like polyurethane. A gas is mixed with the plastic while it is being manufactured. The gas makes the plastic foam like shaving cream. The foam

Fiberglass insulation installed between wall studs and roof rafters in a garage.
(Courtesy of Clara Littlejohn)

hardens and is made into boards that are 4 feet wide by 8 feet long and 1½ inches thick. The insulation board is covered with metal foil on one or both sides. The boards are fastened to the studs with special fasteners that have wide heads.

The waterproof material used over insulation acts as a **vapor barrier**. It is placed there to prevent **condensation**. To understand why, think about what happens to your bathroom mirror after you shower. Warm air can carry more moisture than cool air. When warm, moist air cools (as when it touches a cold surface like a mirror) it condenses. That is, droplets of water form.

If this were to happen on the inside of a wall, the wood would get wet and might rot. The vapor barrier keeps the moisture inside from reaching the cold surfaces near the outside wall. It prevents condensation.

How well a material insulates is indicated by a number called its **R value**. The better the insulator, the higher the R value. For example, fiberglass batts that are 3½ inches thick have an R value of 11. Those that are 6 inches thick have an R value of 16.

FINISHING THE HOUSE

When the framing, sheathing, and roofing are done, the inside and outside of the house can be finished. **Exterior finishing** means applying material like siding to the outside walls of the house. It can also mean painting, or putting on shingles or shakes. **Interior finishing** means finishing the inside walls and ceilings.

Exterior Finishing

Exterior finishing makes the outside of a house more weatherproof. It also makes for a better appearance. Wood siding is

Wooden shingles are often used as siding. (Courtesy of Red Cedar Shingle and Shake Bureau)

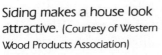

Siding makes a house look attractive. (Courtesy of Western Wood Products Association)

Plywood paneling has surfaces made from hardwood veneers. Expensive hardwood grain patterns are sometimes photographically simulated. Paneling is used to beautify the inside walls of a home. (Courtesy of American Plywood Association)

one outside finish that is often used. Siding is made from wooden boards that are nailed horizontally or vertically to the sheathing. A form of siding called **clapboard** is thicker on one edge than on the other. Clapboard is nailed on so each board overlaps the top of the one below.

Wooden siding rots unless it is protected. Some kind of coating must be applied to the wood. Sometimes, an oil-based stain is used. More often, siding is painted.

Shingles and shakes are also used as siding. These are very much like the materials used in roofing. Generally, they come in the form of panels. Several shingles or shakes are glued to a piece of plywood. The plywood panel is nailed to the sheathing. Using these panels is faster and easier than nailing shingles and shakes on one by one.

Many homes today have vinyl siding. Vinyl siding looks like wood, but it is made of plastic. It never needs painting and will not rot.

Other exterior finishes are plywood, aluminum siding, brick veneer, and stucco. When brick or stone veneer sidings are to be used, the footing of the outside walls needs to be extended by at least 5 inches in width (see figure on page 308). This gives the bricks or stone a good foundation for support. Sandstone and limestone are the most commonly used stone veneers. The mortar used for installing veneer siding is made of cement, hydrated lime, and fine sand.

Interior Finishing

Interior finishing is often called **drywall** construction. The inside walls and ceilings are finished with gypsum wallboard (also known as plasterboard or sheetrock). Finishing includes taping the joints (cracks between boards) and smoothing the wall, then painting, paneling, or wallpapering.

Gypsum wallboard is made from plaster that is sandwiched between two layers of paper. It comes in 4 x 8 foot panels. The wallboard is fastened to the studs with special drywall nails or screws. The fasteners are hammered in so their heads lie slightly below the surface of the wallboard. This forms a shallow dimple in the wallboard. **Joint compound** (a plaster-like substance) is then applied to the dimple, filling it up and covering the fastener head.

The joints between the panels of wallboard must be filled to make a smooth surface. This is done by taping them. The first step is to apply joint compound to the crack. Then a piece of paper or fiberglass tape is applied. The joint compound holds it in place. More joint compound is added on top. When the joint compound dries hard, it is sanded smooth.

Paint

Paint is the finish most often used to cover wallboard. Paints can be oil-based or water-based. Oil-based paints last longer, but they are smelly to use. They are also harder to clean up. Turpentine or mineral spirits must be used to clean up or thin oil-based paints.

Water-based (latex) paints are thinned with water. While they are wet, water-based paints can be cleaned up with water.

Paint can be purchased as **flat**, **semigloss**, or **gloss**. Gloss is a paint's light-reflecting ability. Flat paints have no shine. They are generally used for living rooms and bedrooms. Semigloss and gloss paints are easier to keep clean than flat paints. They can be scrubbed clean without affecting the paint. Semigloss and gloss paints are used in kitchens and bathrooms, where walls must often be wiped down.

Paints have two main ingredients. The **vehicle** is the liquid part of the paint that makes it possible to brush or spray on. **Pigments** are particles that are mixed into the vehicle to give a paint its color. Chemicals and minerals are used to make pigments. Two white pigments are titanium dioxide or lead white. Iron minerals make ochre (yellow), sienna (brown), and iron oxide (red). Lampblack makes black paint.

New technologically advanced latex paints are easy to apply. They are easy to clean and last a long time. (Courtesy of PPG Industries Inc.)

INSTALLING UTILITIES

Before the inside walls are finished, parts of the plumbing and heating systems and the electrical wiring are installed. The major portion of these systems is hidden in ceilings, floors, and walls.

Utilities include plumbing, electrical, and heating systems.

Plumbing fixtures are fed by pipes installed behind the walls. (Courtesy of Kohler Company)

PLUMBING

Plumbing in the home includes the hot water and cold water supplies and drainage. These three systems are separate from each other. The main water supply into the house feeds both the cold and hot water systems. The fresh water coming into the house is kept separate from the waste water that leaves the house. Fresh water and waste water are carried in different pipes and never allowed to mix. Fresh water comes from a well drilled for the house or from a community reservoir. Reservoir water passes through treatment plants and is carried through underground pipes to the home.

The water in the home moves through pipes under pressure. Cold water is carried directly to sinks, showers, tubs, toilets, washing machines, and outside faucets. Cold water also goes to a **hot water heater**. Hot water heaters burn oil or gas or use electricity to heat the water. Once the water is heated, it circulates through a separate system of pipes. Some of the hot water is piped directly to **faucets**. This is known as **domestic hot water**. Often, faucets mix the cold and hot water.

Water pipes in the home are generally made from one of two materials, copper or polyvinyl chloride (PVC) plastic. Copper does not rust and has a smooth surface that lets water flow easily. It can be easily bent and joined.

To cut copper pipe, a **tubing cutter** is used. Copper pipes are joined with copper **fittings**. Fittings have many forms. **Couplings** are fittings that join two pipes. **Tees** provide a way to

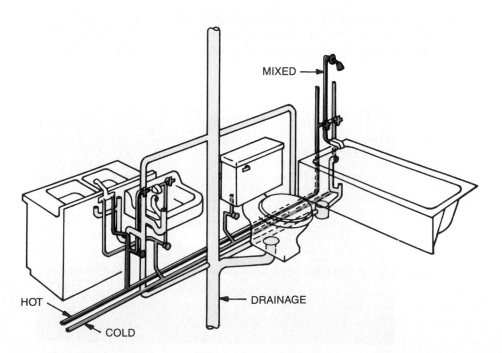

Plumbing system in a bathroom

join three pipes. **Elbows** make it possible to join pipes at 45 or 90 degree angles. With **unions**, the flow from one pipe into another can be stopped.

Copper fittings are usually **soldered** onto copper pipe. Solder is a metal alloy of tin and lead. It melts at about 450° Fahrenheit. **Soldering flux** is first applied to the joint. The flux keeps the copper from oxidizing when it is heated. A propane torch is used to heat the pipe to a temperature that will melt the solder and make it flow. The solder fills the space between the pipes, making a waterproof joint. **Compression fittings** are also used to join pipe. These fittings use a collar that can be tightened around the pipe to make a watertight connection.

Today, PVC pipe is being used more and more. PVC is cheaper than copper. It will never corrode. PVC pipe is joined using a chemical bonding cement or with compression fittings.

Drainage systems sometimes use cast iron pipe. Cast iron pipe is very strong and also resists corrosion.

HEATING SYSTEMS

Most heating systems use oil, natural gas, or electricity to heat a house. Some homes today have coal- or wood-burning stoves or solar heaters. Most systems are based on a furnace that warms air or water and circulates it to the areas to be heated. In a forced-air system, oil or gas is burned. The heat causes steel fins on a heat exchanger to get hot. Fans blow air over the heat exchanger through ducts (sheet metal or plastic pathways). The ducts carry the warm air to rooms.

Some furnaces heat water in a **boiler** to 150-180° Fahrenheit. Hot water is then pumped through pipes throughout the house to radiators in all the rooms. The water-heated radiators heat the air around them. The water then goes back to the boiler for reheating.

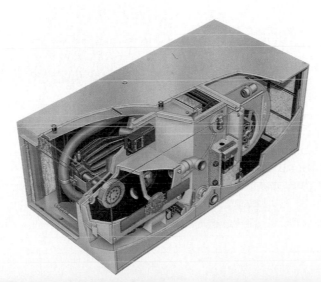

Cutaway view of a forced-air furnace (Courtesy of Lennox Industries, Inc.)

ELECTRICAL SYSTEMS

*National Electrical Code®
and NEC® are registered
trademarks of the National
Fire Protection Association
Inc., Quincy, MA 02269.*

The **National Electrical Code® (NEC)®** sets standards for the safe installation of electrical systems. Most building codes require builders to meet NEC standards.

Electrical service is supplied to the home by power companies. Generally, these companies provide 120-volt and 240-volt service. **Voltage** is a measure of the force with which electric

Remodeling

Remodeling is changing an existing house to improve or enlarge it. Floor coverings or roofs may need to be redone. Walls may need to be repainted. Plumbing or wiring may need to be replaced. Sometimes, more rooms are needed such as a family or bedroom. Garages can be converted into dens. The size of a room can be increased by moving out a wall. Some homeowners remodel to increase the value of their home for resale purposes.

Conservation of energy plays a large role in remodeling. Insulated siding can be added to lower fuel requirements for a house. Solar devices such as solar screens can be added to existing windows, and solar hot water systems can be attached to the roof. Insulation can be blown or laid in attics.

Remodeling can be expensive to the homeowner; however, the end product is worth it. More room for the family to live and entertain is important. Energy-saving devices save money for the family. Energy is conserved when fewer demands are made by energy-saving devices. A structure pleasing to the eye brings great satisfaction to the owner. It also increases the value of a house if the owner should decide to sell the house.

Converting a garage into a family room increases the living area and adds to the value of a structure. Storm windows are installed to save energy. (Photo by Margaret Rutherford)

current is pushed through wires. The 120-volt service powers lighting and most appliances. The 240-volt service is used for stoves and appliances such as air conditioners that use a lot of electric current.

The electric service comes into a house by way of service-entrance equipment. This includes a **watt-hour meter**, a **main disconnect** switch, and the **electrical panel**.

The watt-hour meter measures the amount of electrical energy used in the house. Once every month or two, the power company sends someone out to read the meter. The company then sends a bill for electricity used during that period.

The main disconnect switch can shut off all the power coming into the house. It can be used in an emergency such as an electrical fire.

The electrical panel is used to send electricity to the different branch circuits in the house. The branch circuits supply power to different areas of the house. One might serve only the kitchen, while another sends electricity to a bedroom and nearby hallway. Each branch circuit has its own **circuit breaker** in the electrical panel. Circuit breakers have replaced **fuses** in most houses. Circuit breakers control the amount of current that can safely pass through household wiring. In a short circuit, current suddenly increases. This causes the breaker to trip, shutting off the current. Once the short circuit is corrected, the breaker can be reset.

Electricity is distributed from the power company to the home through overhead transmission wires. These must be repaired after damage from wind and rain storms. (Courtesy of Southern California Edison)

Series and Parallel Circuits

Electrical devices are wired in **series** or in **parallel** circuits. A series circuit provides only one path for current to follow. If anything affects the path, electricity stops flowing. Some Christmas tree lights are wired in series. If one bulb is removed or burned out, the entire string goes out. Circuit breakers and fuses are connected in series with their circuits. In series cir-

When several businesses share a building, separate watt-hour meters are installed for each. (Courtesy of Southern California Edison)

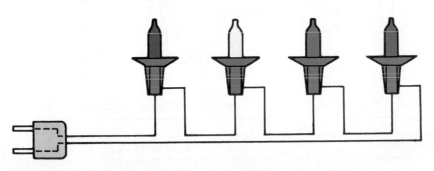

A series circuit has only one path for current flow.

cuits, the voltage is divided among all the electrical components.
A parallel circuit has more than one path for current flow.
Outlets are wired in parallel. When it is plugged in, each appliance receives its own source of voltage. Several appliances can

Grounding Electrical Equipment

All metal electrical equipment is grounded to protect people against electric shock. Electric drills, for example, have metal casings. One of the electrical wires carries a voltage of 120 volts to the motor inside the drill. This is called the **hot** wire. Imagine what would happen if the insulation on the hot wire in the drill became frayed. The hot wire would touch the metal case.

Since metal conducts electricity, the case would have 120 volts applied to it. The person using the drill would then also have 120 volts applied to him or her. If that person were standing on the ground, electricity would flow from the

drill through the person to the ground. The result would be a shock that could cause injury or death.

Electricity takes the path of least resistance. A person is not a very good conductor of electricity. A metal wire is a good conductor. If electricity can flow through a grounding wire or through a person, it will flow through the wire. The round prong on electrical plugs carries the ground wire. It should never be cut off. The other end of the ground wire is connected to the metal casing of the drill. When it is plugged into an electrical outlet, the ground wire provides an electrical path to the earth.

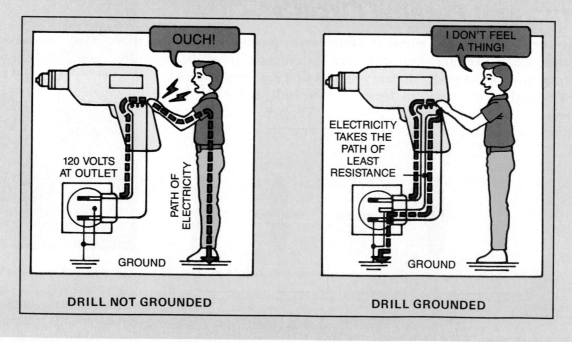

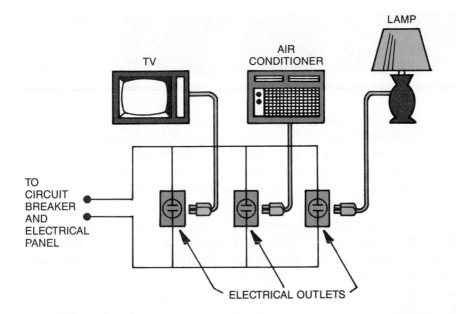

A parallel circuit has more than one path for current flow.

be plugged in to the same outlet. If one is unplugged, the others will still receive electricity.

Electrical wire is covered with heavy insulation. The insulation keeps the wires from touching one another. When wires touch each other, it is called a short circuit.

Almost all the cable used in homes today has an extra wire within it. This extra wire is used to connect all the metal outlet boxes. In this way, the outlet boxes are **grounded**. That is, the end of the extra wire is connected directly to the earth. When electrical equipment is plugged into the grounded outlet box, it too is grounded. Grounding protects against electric shock.

Today many builders use plastic boxes for electrical outlets and switches. Plastic boxes reduce the chance of an electrical short circuit.

MANUFACTURED HOUSING

In the United States, most houses are framed out on site. A few parts such as trusses are manufactured in factories and trucked to the site. In some countries such as Japan and Sweden, there is a trend toward **manufactured housing**. In Japan, 15 percent of new homes are built in factories. In Sweden, more than 90 percent of new homes are built in factories.

These homes are not built **stick-by-stick** on site. They are turned out in factories that work much like automobile plants. Walls are framed, sheathed, and insulated on assembly lines. Windows, plumbing, electrical wiring, and even kitchen and

Manufactured houses are built in a factory and taken to the construction site.

Landscaping

After construction of the house has been completed, the area around the structure is landscaped. The designing and completion of landscaping can be done by the contractor, an architect, or, in some cases, the homeowner. Landscaping includes installing driveways and sidewalks, leveling the yard, and planting grass, trees, and shrubs.

Landscaping improves the appearance of a structure, holds the soil in place, and provides a path for walking or driving up to the house. The type of landscaping depends on the size of the yard, type of soil, climate, and zoning laws. The owner's income level and personal preferences also influence the amount and type of landscaping of a residence.

The environment is considered when landscaping. Conservation (taking care and preserving) of our natural resources determines the materials and plants used. Environmentally conscious individuals design and then thoroughly prepare the soil around a house. They plan the arrangement of patios, decks, sidewalks, and driveways. Native plants requiring minimal upkeep are planted. Watering systems and methods are used to conserve water. Mulch is used around trees and plants to hold moisture in the ground. A program of proper maintenance of lawns and shrubs is followed.

Xeroscaping is landscaping an area of a yard so that it requires very little maintenance. In areas where there is little rainfall, a variety of rocks, native trees, plants and shrubs are used. Areas are paved, and rocks and gravel are placed to achieve a low-maintenance landscape.

When a homeowner must move and sell a house, a well-landscaped house helps sell the house. Many prospective buyers remember a house by the first impression they get. Everyone likes to have a beautiful well-landscaped yard which requires little maintenance.

Installation of electronically controlled lawn sprinkling systems allows for watering of the lawn at times allowed by city ordinances. Watering at certain times of the day conserves the water supply. (Photo by Margaret Rutherford)

A front-end loader is used to pack part of a retaining wall which will support soil. (Photo by Margaret Rutherford)

Assembling manufactured houses in a factory (Courtesy of Cardinal Industries, Inc.)

Installation of a manufactured house (Courtesy of Cardinal Industries, Inc.)

A finished module ready for transport (Courtesy of Cardinal Industries, Inc.)

bathroom cabinets are installed. Interior finishing might be completed. The entire house can be built and delivered to the site. All that must be done then is to put the house on its foundation and connect the utilities.

Manufactured houses are built in modules (standard size sections) of about 12 x 20 feet. A module can be one room or several. The modules are put together at the site to create the completed house.

There is some manufactured housing in the United States. You may have seen motel rooms, restaurants, and diners that are prefabricated and then moved to the site where they are used. This kind of construction saves greatly on labor costs.

Steel and reinforced concrete are used on commercial structures like the IBM building. (Courtesy of Turner Construction Company)

COMMERCIAL STRUCTURES

Commercial structures are buildings that are used for banks, stores, and offices. They usually have many tenants, and are therefore much larger than most homes. Like houses, commercial structures have footings and foundations. Their footings and foundations are made from reinforced concrete. The concrete must be very strong to support the weight of a large building.

Like most homes, commercial buildings are often framed. However, steel and concrete are used instead of wood. Steel **beams** are like floor joists. They are horizontal, and support the floors and the walls. Vertical **columns** made from concrete or steel beams are like the wall studs. They transfer the load on the beams to the ground. The columns on lower floors support

Installing steel beams and columns (Courtesy of Turner Construction Company)

more weight than those on upper floors, so the lower columns must be very strong.

The Effect of Wind on Tall Buildings

Wind effects must be taken into account in designing and building a skyscraper.

Wind is often stronger at the top of skyscrapers than it is on the ground. Not only is the wind stronger at these heights, but the taller the building, the greater the wind effect. A tall building is like a long lever connected to a pivot in the ground. If you apply a small force on one end of a long lever you can exert a large force at the other. A pry bar used to remove nails or lift something heavy is a good example. When wind blows against the top of a tall building, the building sways. This is called **drift**. Drift is the distance the building moves from the vertical center.

In designing a tall building, much thought must be given to the effect of wind (the **wind load**) as it blows against the building. The wind load of a building increases as the square of the building height. (Remember that the square of any number is that number times itself.) A building that is 20 feet tall is twice as high as one that is 10 feet tall; its wind load, therefore, will be four times that of the 10-foot-high building.

Two of the tallest buildings in the world are the World Trade Center towers in New York. These buildings are 1,350 feet high (110 stories). They must be able to withstand about 4,000 times the wind load of a 20-foot house. In a strong wind, the building may drift three feet from center. Can you imagine how a person standing on one of the top floors feels when that happens! In a strong wind, a large force is exerted on the foundation. The foundation must be very strong to counter the wind's force. The foundation of the World Trade Center buildings rests in bedrock, 70 feet below the ground.

When engineers plan buildings like these towers, they must first find out what winds are like at the building site. They generally study wind records from the past 50 years. The strongest wind that has occurred during the last 50 years is called a **50-year wind**. Buildings are designed to withstand the force of a 50-year wind. That means that the building materials and design are chosen so the building will not be damaged by the strongest wind of a 50-year period.

Why not design a building that will withstand 100-year winds (the strongest wind in a 100-year period)? The reason is cost. It would probably cost a lot more to design such a building than to repair damage caused by a 100-year wind.

Generally, cost/benefit trade-offs are made in designing buildings. Costs need to be kept as low as possible while still providing safety for people who will use the building.

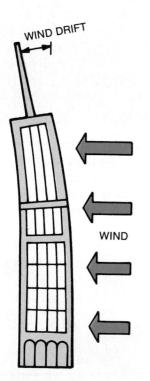

The towers of the World Trade Center drift 3 feet in high wind, and up to 7 feet during a hurricane.

Stiffening the Building

Buildings are designed to be stiff. This keeps drift as small as possible. To stiffen a building, builders use materials that do not bend easily. Such materials are concrete and specially constructed steel shapes.

If the outer walls of a skyscraper are stiff, the entire building acts like a huge hollow tube sticking out of the ground. The entire building, not just the inner core, resists bending.

One way of making the outside of a building stiff is to use concrete panels on the exterior. Another way is to build steel trusses into the building framework.

SUMMARY

Building and management skills and engineering principles are needed in modern construction technology. Home construction involves building the footing, foundation, floors, walls, and roof. It involves installing utilities and insulation and finishing the structure on the outside and the inside.

The footing is generally made from concrete. It acts as the base of the foundation and spreads the weight of the building over a wider area. The foundation supports the weight of the structure. It transmits that weight to the footing.

Walls are framed using 2 x 4-inch or 2 x 6-inch lumber. Walls transmit the load from the floors above them to the foundation. They also serve as partitions between rooms.

Sheathing covers the exterior walls. It makes the structure stronger. Sheathing closes in the building and protects it against the weather. It also provides a surface on which to attach outside wall coverings such as siding, shakes, or shingles.

The roof protects the house against wind, rain, and snow. It prevents heat from escaping in cold weather and makes the house more attractive. In the past, most roofs were framed. Today, roofs are made from factory-built trusses. Trusses are carefully designed. Because of the precision of their design, they can be built from thinner lumber than framed roofs.

Roofing materials such as asphalt shingles, wooden shingles, and shakes are used to cover the roof. They also add to the appearance of the house.

Insulation helps to keep the inside of the house at the desired temperature. It prevents heat from entering in the summer or escaping in the winter. Insulation can be made from fiberglass in the form of loose fibers or in blankets. Sheets of polyurethane foam are also used as insulation.

The outside of the house is finished with siding of wood or vinyl. Shingles and shakes are also used in finishing outside

The Norwest Corporation headquarters in Minneapolis is designed as a concrete tube. The 950-foot high building uses high-strength concrete that costs half as much as steel. (Courtesy of Kenneth Champlin of Cesar Pelli and Associates)

Giant trusses stiffen the John
Hancock Center in Chicago.
(Courtesy of John Hancock Center)

walls. The inside of the house is finished with gypsum wallboard. Cracks between sheets of wallboard are taped and smoothed with joint compound. Paint, wallpaper, or paneling is used to cover the wallboard.

Utilities include the plumbing, heating, and electrical systems. Plumbing systems include hot and cold water supplies and drainage. The drainage system carries waste water. Waste water is not allowed to mix with the water in the fresh water systems. Plumbing pipes are made from copper, plastic, or cast iron. Pipes are joined together with solder, cement, or fittings.

Furnaces used in heating use oil, natural gas, or electricity to provide heat. A furnace warms air or water and circulates it to heat rooms in the house.

The electrical system carries electricity from the electrical panel, to circuit breakers, and then to branch circuits throughout the house. Electrical outlets in the home are connected in parallel. If one appliance is unplugged, the others with keep working. All electrical equipment with metal cases should be grounded to guard against electrical shock.

Some buildings are manufactured in a factory. These structures are made from standard size modules. They are moved from the factory to the site and put together there. Manufactured housing saves on labor costs.

Commercial buildings such as banks, stores, and offices also require footings and foundations. Since these buildings are often quite tall, framing materials are steel and concrete rather than wood.

Tall buildings must be built to withstand strong winds. The outsides of these buildings are stiffened with carefully chosen materials. Their foundations are generally quite deep.

(Courtesy of Holiday Corporation)

REVIEW QUESTIONS

1. List three factors to consider when choosing a lot on which to build a house.
2. How are the footing and the foundation wall alike? How are they different?
3. Why are slab foundations well suited to warmer climates?
4. What are two purposes served by the walls in a house?
5. Sketch a section of framed wall that includes one window opening. Include and label the studs, top and bottom plates, headers, trimmers, and jack studs.
6. Why is sheathing nailed over the entire wall, including windows and doors, when it is installed?
7. Why is a trussed roof faster to build than a framed roof?
8. Think about a house you might design for yourself. What kind of roofing material would you use?
9. How does insulation increase comfort and cut down on cost?
10. What purpose does the vapor barrier on the outside of insulation serve?
11. Why are there separate systems for fresh water and waste water?
12. Explain how a home heating system works. Use a simple system diagram as part of your explanation.
13. Are circuit breakers connected in series or in parallel with the electrical outlets in a room? Explain your answer.
14. How does grounding electrical equipment guard against electrical shock?
15. What are some of the differences between commercial buildings and houses?
16. Why does wind affect tall buildings to a greater degree than it affects short buildings?

KEY WORDS

Asphalt	Frost line	*National*	Stud
Bottom plate	Girder	*Electrical Code*	Slab foundation
Building permit	Header	Pitch	Subfloor
Circuit breaker	Insulation	Plumb	Top plate
Floor joist	Manufactured	Plumbing	Truss
Footing	housing	Rafter	Vapor barrier
Foundation wall	Mason	Sheathing	Wind load
Framing	Mortar	Sill plate	

**SEE YOUR TEACHER FOR
THE CROSSTECH PUZZLE**

PREFAB PLAYHOUSE

Setting the Stage

He tore off the last wall, revealing rotted 2 × 4s. The house was so old that the foundation had settled into the ground in places, throwing the whole superstructure askew. The project in the next weeks will be to calculate the amount of wood needed to replace the frame, order it from the lumberyard, and replace the old framing boards.

Your Challenge

Design and construct a model prefabricated playhouse to be sold to the school or someone in your community. Use a reference book on residential construction to help you. (You may want to check with your customers for placement of windows, doors, and paint.)

Procedure

1. Divide your work crews into six teams (four wall teams and two roof teams).
2. Draw a framing layout for each wall and roof section. Studs and rafters will be 8" on center. Walls will be 4' × 4'. Roof pitch and length will be determined by the two roof teams. Draw a door or window in each wall section. Use the carpentry book for information on the correct layout of studs and rafters.

Walls

1. Determine the correct nail size to use for each nailing process. Attach the studs to the top and bottom plate of the walls, using two nails for each end of the stud.
2. Lay 4' × 4' covering on each wall section and trace the openings for doors and/or windows.
3. The teacher will help you cut each opening.
4. Nail each wall covering in place.
5. Determine how each wall section will be fastened to the other wall sections. Precut the corner pieces.

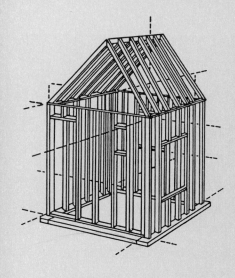

Suggested Resources

23 boards for framing—1" × 2" × 12'

2 boards for base—2" × 4" × 8'

1 board for ridge board—1" × 3" × 8'

2 lbs. cement coated nails

½ lb. common nails (assorted sizes)

3—4' × 8' sheets of homosote, ¼" plywood, or masonite

Rafter assembly jig

Reference books on modern carpentry

Roof

1. Using the reference book, lay out a rafter pattern with the correct angle for the ridge board and bird's mouth. Cut the rest of the rafters using this pattern.
2. Place each rafter in a rafter assembly jig provided by your teacher. This jig will hold all rafters for one side of your roof in place. Nail a 1" × 3" ridge board to each set of rafters. Nail a top plate in the bird's mouth.
3. Turn the roof section over and nail the covering material in place.

Delivery and Assembly

1. Draw a set of directions for assembly.
2. Assemble the walls at the site.
3. Nail the roof section in place from the inside of the building through the top plate at the bird's mouth. Then nail the two ridge boards together.

Technology Connections

1. You need to supply the purchaser with a snow-load specification for the roof you designed. You will find this information and charts in the reference book you used.
2. Describe some ways of making your roof stronger.
3. What are the advantages and disadvantages of on-site construction versus prefabricated construction?
4. Why are studs usually placed 16" or 24" on center for framing?

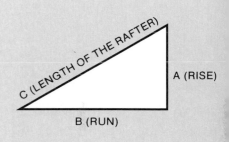

Science and Math Concepts

► The length of a roof rafter is determined by using the following formula:

$$C = \sqrt{A^2 + B^2}$$

► A roof that rises 4" per foot of run will have a 4 in 12 slope.

INSTALLING ELECTRICAL SYSTEMS

Setting the Stage

Electrical systems are installed after the frame of the building has been constructed, but before the interior walls have been installed. Electrical systems are composed of several different circuits, each with different purposes, and located in different parts of the structure. All of the circuits must be connected to the service panel.

Your Challenge

Install an electrical circuit in which a light fixture is controlled by a switch. You will be working in groups for this activity. Each group will wire a circuit in one panel of the wall frame.

Procedure

1. Assemble the wall frame(s).
2. Mount the rectangular and octagonal outlet boxes as shown in the drawing.

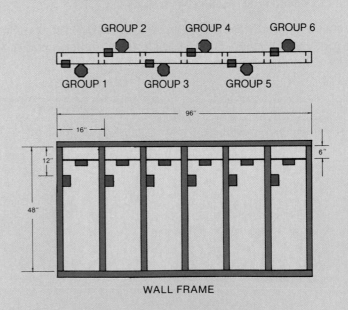

WALL FRAME

3. Cut 36" of Romex and attach the plug to one end.
4. Measure and cut the amount of Romex needed to connect the two boxes. Allow approximately 8" in each box to make connections.
5. Install the opposite end of the plug wire in the octagon box, allowing approximately 8" to make connections.

Suggested Resources

Per Group:

Romex with ground—size 14-2

One steel rectangular outlet box with internal wire clamps

One steel octagon outlet box with internal wire clamps

One SPST light switch

One porcelain ceiling lamp socket

One single switch plate or cover

One box hanger for 16" centers

Three red wire nuts

Three grounding clips

One light bulb

One heavy duty three-prong plug for solid cable

Wall frame (one per six groups)

Per Class:

Two lengths of 2" × 4" construction grade lumber—8' long

Seven lengths of 2" × 4" construction grade lumber—4' long

Twelve common nails—size 16d

6. Install the cable to connect the boxes. Clamp all wires with the internal wire clamps.
7. Use a cable stripper to remove about ¾" of the sheathing (outside insulation) of the cable from the clamps to the ends of all wires. Be careful not to disturb the colored insulation.
8. Attach the ground (bare) wires to the outlet boxes with grounding clips.
9. Following the circuit diagram, connect the wires in the octagon outlet box with wire nuts.
10. Using needle nose pliers, form a partial circle with both stripped ends of the wires in the rectangular outlet box. Place the wires around the terminals of the switch so that the wire points in a clockwise direction. Tighten the terminal screws on the switch. No bare wire should be showing.
11. Test your circuit with a circuit tester, then ask your teacher to check your work. All grounds must be connected, and no bare wires should touch.
12. Attach the switch and light socket to the outlet boxes with the screws provided. Bend the wires in a "Z" shape as you push them into the boxes. Screw the switch plate to the front of the switch box. Put a light bulb in the socket.
13. Under the supervision of your teacher, plug your circuit into an electrical outlet and turn the light on and off.

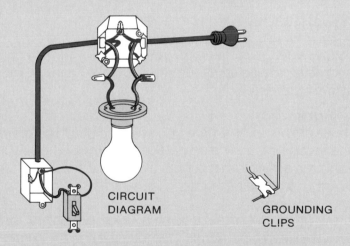

CIRCUIT DIAGRAM

GROUNDING CLIPS

Technology Connections

1. An electrical circuit in a structure is made up of several devices which have different purposes. What is the purpose of a duplex outlet receptacle? A switch? A light fixture outlet?
2. Many of the things in our homes work by electricity. How would your life be changed without electricity in your home?
3. What happens when someone tries to use more electricity in a structure than the electrical system was designed to provide?

Science and Math Concepts

▶ A *watt* is the unit of measurement that tells us how much electrical power is being used. To calculate watts, multiply volts × amps.

▶ Kilowatt hours (KWH) are how electricity is metered (sold). A *kilowatt hour* is 1000 watts used for one hour.

LASER CONSTRUCTION

Setting the Stage

There are many applications of lasers in the construction industry. A laser's most valuable asset is its ability to be directed anywhere, including over long distances. A helium-neon laser is used because its power is low enough to be safe, yet the beam is easily seen. A helium-neon (HeNe) laser is used to align underground pipes by projecting the beam in a straight line. The laser can also be used to level things such as floors, ceilings, and walls.

Your Challenge

Demonstrate the application of the laser in the construction industry:

1. Using six height adjustment jigs, align two sections of plastic drain pipe with a laser. The pipe must be laid with a 1-degree pitch (⅛" per ft.).
2. Lay three courses (layers) of bricks, using clay for the mortar, aligning the bricks with a laser beam.

Procedure

CAUTION: Follow safety directions given to you by your teacher, and never look directly into a laser light beam or into its direct reflection.

Drain Pipe Alignment

1. Place the laser at the point where you want to start the drain line. Lay one section of drain pipe on the jigs provided by your teacher. Using the acrylic target and a ruler, adjust the height of the laser or the jigs so that the laser is directed at the center of the drain pipe entrance.
2. Now align the other end of the drain pipe, placing a black target in back of the drain pipe. Remember the pipe has a 1-degree pitch, so the beam projected on the target will be 1¼" above the center of the drain pipe. The first piece of pipe now has a 1-degree pitch. (Figure 1)
3. Change the laser and align the beam to hit the center of the acrylic target at the entrance to the drain pipe and at the end of the first section of drain pipe. The pipe should still have a 1-degree pitch. (Figure 2)
4. Add as many sections of drain pipe as needed. Each time a new section is added, the end section must be aligned so that the laser beam hits the center of the drain pipe. (Figure 3)

Suggested Resources

Helium-neon laser
Black 4" × 4" target
Height adjustment jigs
Acrylic target — ⅛" × 4" × 4"
2 — 4" plastic drain pipes and couplings
Play-dough or plasticene clay
40 scaled wood blocks — 8" × 8" × 16" (3/32 = 1")
Level — 4-foot

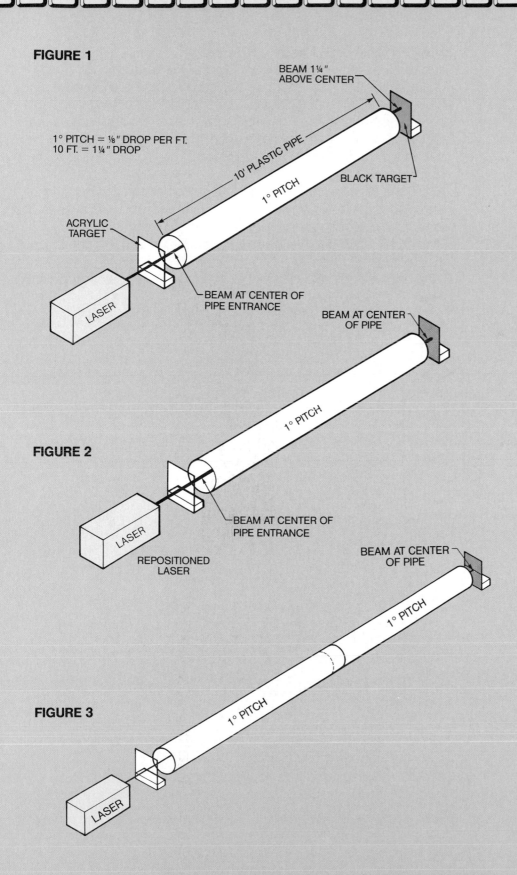

FIGURE 1

BEAM 1¼" ABOVE CENTER

1° PITCH = ⅛" DROP PER FT.
10 FT. = 1¼" DROP

10' PLASTIC PIPE

1° PITCH

BLACK TARGET

ACRYLIC TARGET

BEAM AT CENTER OF PIPE ENTRANCE

LASER

BEAM AT CENTER OF PIPE

FIGURE 2

1° PITCH

BEAM AT CENTER OF PIPE ENTRANCE

LASER

REPOSITIONED LASER

BEAM AT CENTER OF PIPE

1° PITCH

1° PITCH

FIGURE 3

LASER

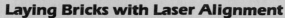

Laying Bricks with Laser Alignment

1. Make two small jigs by mounting a piece of acrylic on a small piece of wood. The height of the acrylic surface should be 2½ times the height of the bricks you are laying. Scratch a horizontal reference line one layer of bricks plus the mortar above the base of the jig. Scratch another reference line one layer plus the mortar above the last line. (Figure 4) Place the jigs at each end of the last course of bricks.
2. Place the laser in line with the bricks so that the beam projects through the acrylic at the highest reference line. The laser is now aligned for the next course of bricks. (Figure 5)
3. As you lay each brick, align the top of the brick using the lower reference line on the acrylic jig. (Figure 6)
4. After laying each course of bricks, reposition the laser and repeat steps 2 through 4.

FIGURE 4

FIGURE 5

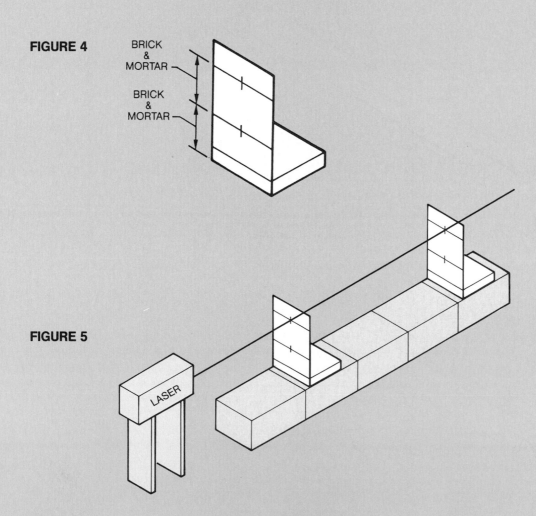

BRICK & MORTAR

BRICK & MORTAR

LASER

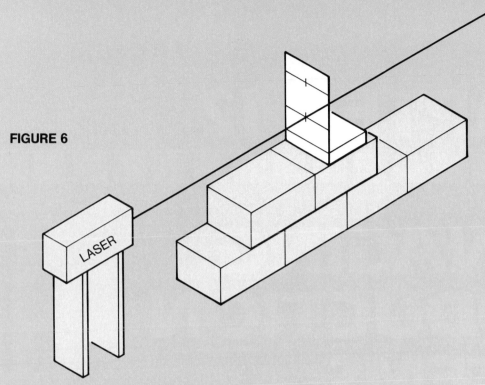

FIGURE 6

Technology Connections

1. Using a 4-foot level, tape measures, and chalk lines, try accomplishing the same tasks you have just accomplished using the laser.
2. Could you have the laser turn a corner by using a mirror?
3. List the operations that have to be accomplished before a foundation wall is built and aligned with a laser.
4. Why are alignment and leveling important in the building of a structure?

Science and Math Concepts

▶ The angle of incidence is equal to the angle of reflection.
▶ The incident ray and the reflected ray lie in the same plane.

341

CHAPTER 12

MANAGING PRODUCTION SYSTEMS

MAJOR CONCEPTS

After reading this chapter, you will know that:

- A company's management must coordinate the work of different departments to make the best use of resources.
- Architects design a building's shape and choose materials for it.
- Engineers design a building's structure and its major systems.
- A general contractor directs the work of many different people on a building project.
- A company's marketing department decides what market the company will make products for, what features those products will have, and how they are to be sold.
- A company that makes a product should provide service and technical information about the product after it has been sold.
- Whether a company survives and does well depends on its financial management.
- Managing includes planning, organizing, leading, and controlling.

MANAGING PRODUCTION SYSTEMS

It is not enough to manufacture a good product or construct a good building. The success of either kind of project depends to a large degree on how well it is managed. It is important to work within a schedule, within a budget, and safely. It is also important to deliver a product in good condition, and to be able to fix it if it breaks down later.

Directing the use of the seven resources in manufacturing or construction is the job of a company's **management**. Management also decides what products to make, and how to interest people in buying the products.

The ways manufacturing and construction projects are managed are very much alike. Specific management jobs, though, are quite different, because of the differences between the two kinds of projects. In this chapter, managing each of these systems is covered separately.

A company's management must coordinate the work of different departments to make the best use of resources.

WHO MANAGES A CONSTRUCTION PROJECT?

Architects and Engineers

You may remember from Chapter 10 that structures are designed by **architects**. Architects work directly for the **owner** of the building. Architects choose the shape and form of the building and the materials from which it is built. They are responsible for the many thousands of details of the building design.

Architects also look at how the building will affect the buildings around it and how it might be affected by new buildings built after it is finished. For example, will the building cast a large shadow on nearby buildings? In most large cities, building codes do not permit a building to be built if it will block the view of the sky from nearby buildings. Architects deal with this kind of problem by making buildings smaller at the top than at the bottom. This design gives more light to surrounding buildings.

The job of **engineers** is to make sure that the building is structurally sound. They choose the size of each column and beam and make sure it will carry the load of the building and its contents. Engineers often use computer aided design (CAD) to do this kind of work.

Architects design a building's shape and choose materials for it.

Plans and drawings are being prepared for a new building in this architect and engineers' office. (Courtesy of The Turner Corporation, photograph by Michael Sporzansky)

Specialists help architects and engineers in highly specialized areas such as this telephone and communication cabling installation.
(Photo by Robert Barden)

Engineers also design the major systems within the bulding. These systems include the electrical system and the heating, ventilating and air conditioning (HVAC) system. They also include the fire detection, telephone, and plumbing systems. As the building goes up, both engineers and architects visit the site often to check the work. They must make sure the job is going according to plan.

Specialists are often hired to design some of the systems in a building. These specialists work with the owner, architect, and engineer. Specialists work on security systems, fire detection and prevention systems, and communication systems. Specialists might design these systems, but the architect and engineer are still responsible for them.

Contractors

Once a building has been designed, it must be built. Many different jobs must be coordinated even on fairly small projects. Very small projects may be managed by the owner. If a job is more complex, however, the owner usually hires a manager. A **general contractor** is a person or company who takes the overall responsibility for a construction project. The contractor must do the many jobs of management. People must be hired to work on the building. Work must be scheduled so the many jobs are done in the right order. Materials must be purchased. Delivery must be scheduled near the time they are to be used.

The written agreement between the owner and the general contractor is called a **contract**. It states what the contractor will do and how much the owner will pay. The contract is often very long and includes the architect's and engineer's drawings. The contract tells in detail what will be done, when it will be done, and who will do it. It also usually tells who is responsible if there is an accident, and who must get the building permits. There may also be penalties that will come out of the contractor's pay if the job is not finished on time.

The general contractor can have its own employees work on the job. Or it can hire other companies, called **subcontractors**, to do some or even most of the work. On a large construction project, there may be dozens of subcontractors, each working on a part of the building. These may include plumbing, carpentry, and masonry companies. General contractors often use both their own workers and subcontractors. They have their own contracts with their subcontractors. These are called **subcontracts**.

Again, these subcontracts are very long and detailed. They spell out every aspect of a job and tell who will do what, so two workers don't end up doing the same job, but all jobs are assigned to somebody. If anything is left out that must be done (or changes are made that mean more work or materials are needed), the subcontractor will charge extra. These charges are called **contract extras**. If the job is poorly managed, or the owner keeps asking for changes, the price of the project may be driven up. These additional costs are often called **cost overruns**.

Project Managers

On a very large project, a separate company, called a **project manager**, may be used. Project managers oversee the contracts, scheduling, material deliveries, and overall progress of the job. The general contractor is still responsible for much of the contruction, but not for managing all the subcontractors. The project manager works directly for the owner, and not for the contractor. This is often necessary on very large projects such as skyscrapers. They are so complex that special skills are needed to manage them.

One job of the project manager or the general contractor is arranging the work of subcontractors so work progresses smoothly. The work of one subcontractor should not interfere with the work of another. For example, water pipes must not block electrical boxes or heating vents. Before work starts, meet-

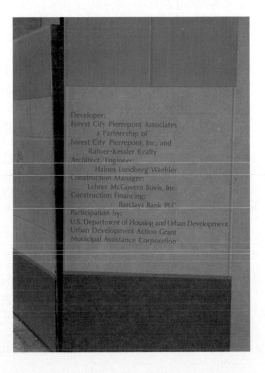

This sign posted at a construction site lists some of the companies and agencies that are involved in the planning, financing, and managing of the project. (Photo by Robert Barden)

ings are held with all of the subcontractors present. They mark on a master drawing where they plan to put their systems. They work out plans in areas where there may be problems so that systems will not interfere with each other. This process is called **coordination**.

In some parts of the country, all construction workers are represented by **unions**. These are labor organizations that work with companies to set pay and working conditions for their members. Each union claims a carefully described part of the work, called a **jurisdiction**, for its members.

On a job with union workers, care is taken to choose the correct trade for each job. Carpenters, for example, may not do electrical work. In some areas of construction, it may not be clear which union workers should do the work. This can cause problems with the unions. A manager's skill in getting union workers to agree on a solution is often important in getting a job done quickly and well.

SCHEDULING AND PROJECT TRACKING

Scheduling is a big part of the general contractor's or project manager's job. Different jobs must be done in the right order for safety and to make sure that systems already in place are not damaged by later work. For example, a floor must be structurally sound and properly prepared before finish work can be started. Electrical wiring cannot be done until walls are framed.

With so many tasks and workers on a single job site, special management tools are needed to set a schedule and stay on it. One of these tools is a **Gantt chart**. A Gantt chart is a kind of bar graph that shows when a particular kind of work is to start and when it is to be finished. The chart shows where one job must wait to start until another is done. The impact of changes in schedule can be seen on the chart. The number of work hours is also shown on the Gantt chart. The chart is updated often to show actual start and finish dates, and how changes will affect the project. Gantt charts are used in managing both construction and manufacturing systems.

Meetings, called **project meetings**, are held regularly as work goes on. The owner, architect, engineer, project manager, general contractor, and some of the specialists meet to talk about the work. Written notes called **minutes** record everything important that happens at the meeting. Copies of the minutes are sent to everyone who attended the meeting after it is over. Any

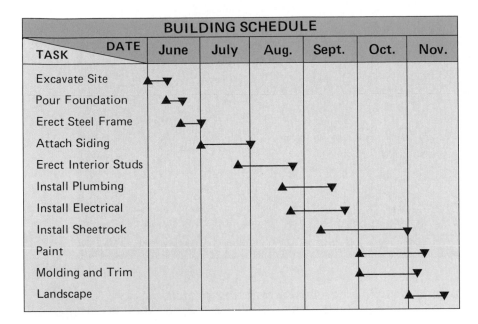

The Gantt Chart is used to help managers schedule and monitor a project.

problem that cannot be solved during the meeting is called an **action item**. Action items are recorded in the minutes. Work done on each action item is reported at the next meeting. In this way, people can present problems quickly and they can be handled by everyone concerned. Project meetings are usually held once a week or once every other week.

PERMITS AND APPROVALS

Building and fire departments must approve and inspect construction projects. Before, during, and after construction, many different checks must be carried out. **Permits** and approvals are necessary to protect both the workers and the people who will pass by or work near the construction site. They also protect the health and safety of people who will later occupy the building.

Before construction begins, a building permit must be issued. To get a building permit, plans and drawings of the building must be submitted to the local government agency that issues permits. The builder must also have the approval of the planning and **zoning boards**.

A community's zoning is its master plan for how land is to be used. For example, in one area, only homes may be built, while another area is for factories and yet another for stores. Zoning also involves looking at how new construction will affect the community. Will there be enough schools, roads, fire protection, parking spaces, and so on? Sometimes a builder must agree to build new roads or donate land for a school to get a

These are some of the permits required to be posted at a construction site. (Photo by Robert Barden)

Special structures sometimes have to be made to protect the public from falling tools and debris. (Photo by Robert Barden)

zoning board to agree to a building project.

For commercial buildings, a **life safety plan** must also be prepared. The plan tells how stairways, exit doors from all areas, and other features of the building will protect people if there is a fire or other kind of emergency.

Permits for jobs at the site may have to be obtained as work progresses. For example, if the site is next to a sidewalk, the builder may have to close it off to protect pedestrians. A permit must be obtained to do this. The builder may be required to build a walkway with a roof so people can get by the site safely. This will protect passersby in case tools or building materials are dropped. If a crane is needed to lift large parts or equipment into place, a permit must be obtained. If the crane is parked in the street it will block traffic. Yet another permit must then be obtained to close the street off. Permits must be obtained to dig up the street near the building to hook up electrical, water, sewer, and gas services.

When the building is almost finished, the major systems of the building are tested to make sure they were installed properly. Elevators must be tested and approved before they can be used. The fire department may send someone to watch the fire detection or fire suppression systems being tested. A fire suppression system might be a sprinkler system such as those used in offices and living areas. Other types of systems are often used to fight fires in computer and electrical areas.

Not all building systems have to be tested by city officials. The building owner will have them tested to be sure that all systems are working. After all systems are checked and approved, and the building is finished, one step remains. The local building department must issue a **Certificate of Occupancy (CO)**. The building may not be occupied until the CO has been issued.

Some of the new major systems that have to be tested in a new building. (Photo by Robert Barden)

BUILDING MAINTENANCE

After the building has been completed, the owner has new management jobs to do. If the building will be rented, it must be advertised or a rental agent must be hired. It is important to fill the building with renters as soon as possible, so there is money coming in. The owner must make payments on construction loans or a mortgage. If the building or a part of it sits empty, the owner must still pay the mortgage even though there is no rental income.

The building must also be maintained. All the systems must be kept working properly. Regular inspections (fire, elevator, health) required by law must be done. The building must be kept in a clean, safe, and neat condition to attract new renters and keep present ones happy. If the owner's company occupies the building, the building must be maintained for the company's workers.

MANAGING MANUFACTURING SYSTEMS

Managing manufacturing systems is a big job. It involves coming up with new products to make and sell. It involves developing and manufacturing these products at the lowest cost, selling them, and servicing them. While each of these tasks is handled by specialists, the overall job must be managed carefully by a person or a team of people. This can be a general manager, a management team, or a company president.

Marketing

Market research, research and development, and making the prototype have all been discussed in Chapter 9. It is the job of the marketing department to decide what features a product should have. To do this, they must decide who the potential customers are. This is called the **market**. They must then decide what products to make. Some companies have the strategy of making the same product as other companies, but making it better or more cheaply, or doing a better job of advertising. Other companies analyze the market and look for products that people need that no other company is making. This is a **market gap analysis**.

The marketing department also tries to find out how much the product can cost and still sell well. Based on these data, the marketing department makes an estimate of how many of one sort of product will be bought by people in a year (the **total market**). They also estimate what part of the public will buy their particular product rather than one made by another company. This is called the **market share**.

The total market times the market share is the company's potential for sales. If this is a large enough number, it is worthwhile to develop the product. Product development is often done in an area of the company called Research and Development (R&D).

A company's marketing department decides what market the company will make products for, what features those products will have, and how they are to be sold.

Research and Development (R&D)

Research is the search for new materials, processes, and methods that can be sold or used by a company. Research is done in fields that might turn up helpful discoveries. But it is usually not directed at a specific product.

Development is the use of these new discoveries together with already known methods of solving a problem. Development is most often directed at a specific product or group of products.

Development works on producing a **prototype**. A prototype is a test version of the product. It is used to find out how

Research is the search for new materials, processes, and techniques. (Courtesy of Cetus Corporation)

Models and prototypes are built so that a product can be tested before it can be manufactured. (Courtesy of General Motors Design)

people are likely to feel about the product. It is also used to find out how hard it will be to manufacture the product. After the prototype has been made, it is test-marketed. The prototype is shown to or tried by potential customers to get their reaction to it. This feedback is then used to improve the product before it is put on the market to be sold.

Production

The product may be changed to make it easier to manufacture and to add features that test marketing showed were needed. This step is called **production engineering** or **productizing**. After a product is productized, it can be put into production.

During production, quality is checked constantly to make sure it stays high. **Quality control**, or QC, is the checking of quality throughout production. Materials that will be used in production are checked. The product is checked at each step of manufacture. The final product is then checked before it leaves the plant. The reputation of a company for high-quality products can be traced back to quality control.

Management must also make sure that the manufacturing plant is safe and that laws and regulations are being followed. The Occupational Safety and Health Administration **(OSHA)** has set down rules for safety on the job. These rules must be followed carefully or a company can be fined or even closed down.

The Environmental Protection Agency **(EPA)** is another agency that keeps an eye on manufacturers. EPA rules prevent manufacturers from polluting the water and air with manufacturing byproducts. Rules cover the kind and amount of substances that come from smokestacks. They list substances that

Quality control inspections at several points in the manufacturing process ensure a high-quality product. (Courtesy of Grumman Corporation)

can and cannot be dumped down a sink drain. They describe the steps to take to store or get rid of toxic wastes.

As in construction, some factories are unionized. Union contracts set pay and work rules for plant workers. Management must negotiate a contract with the union. Management must plan jobs to use the right class of worker for each job.

Servicing

A manufacturer must have a plan to take care of products that need maintenance or that have broken after they were sold. Most products now come with a warranty. It gives the terms under which a company will repair or replace a defective product. Most often, there is a time period during which repair or replacement may be made at little or no cost to the buyer. This can be months or years. After the warranty period, the product becomes either a **throwaway** or a repairable product. If it is a throwaway product, a person must buy a new one—there is no way to fix the old one. Throwaways are usually small and inexpensive.

If the product can be repaired and put back into service, the company must have a repair plan of some kind. Sometimes the buyer has to mail the product back. The company must have a repair department that can provide cost-effective, rapid

A company that makes a product should provide service and technical information about the product after it has been sold.

repairs. This requires workers who range in skill from entry level to highly skilled, depending on the products that are to be serviced.

Another way to handle repair and maintenance is to have another company do the work. The dealer or store owner who sold the product may take care of it. Not all dealers have a repair department for this kind of work.

Authorized repair service like this form part of a company's servicing plan. (Photo by Robert Barden)

SELLING THE PRODUCT

The marketing department must make a plan for selling the product. The sales department puts this plan to work. How a company sells a product depends on the kind of product it is trying to sell.

In **direct sales**, company salespeople sell directly to customers. If customers are spread all over the country, the company may have many different sales offices. The size of a company's sales in an area must be large enough to justify opening an office there.

Sometimes a company does not have enough sales in an area to warrant opening an office. Instead, it may hire a **sales representative** or "rep" organization. Sales reps often sell the products of many companies. They sell products that are similar but do not compete with each other. When a sales representative takes an order, an order is then placed directly with the factory. The manufacturer delivers the product to the customer. The customer pays the manufacturer. After the sale, the manufacturer pays the sales representative a **commission**. This is a percentage of the sale price. The sales rep may have to wait a long time before being paid for the sale.

Dealers sell products to people by taking orders for them and then placing orders with the manufacturer. The manufacturer then ships the products to the dealer. The dealer sees that the customer gets the order, and takes payment for it. The dealer charges the customer more than the dealer is charged by the factory. The dealer also keeps a small amount of the products on hand to sell directly to people.

Retail stores are the kind that you are probably most familiar with. Retail stores buy products from manufacturers in large quantities. They then sell them to people who walk into the store. A grocery store is an example of this. Retail stores make money because they sell products to the public at a higher price than they buy them for.

Companies that sell large amounts of products often use **discount distributors**. Distributors buy very large quantities of products from the manufacturer at a low price. They are stored

Distributors like this buy products in large quantities from manufacturers and sell them to the public at showroom and warehouse buildings. (Photo by Robert Barden)

in a warehouse and then sold to customers at a higher price. Distributors sometimes use catalogs or mail order advertising to sell the products. Some have showrooms where people can get a good look at the products before they buy.

FINANCING THE MANUFACTURING SYSTEM

Whether a company survives and does well depends on its financial management.

Both the products a company makes and how well they sell are very important. But a company's survival depends on its **financial management**. Financial management is the job of managing a company's expenditures. Planning ahead and being careful about the way company money is spent are both important in keeping a company healthy and growing.

Before a business of any size is started, a **business plan** must be prepared. The plan states the goals of the business, the methods that will be used to reach them, and the amount of money needed to start the business and keep it going. One of the most important parts of a business plan is the **cash flow analysis**. The cash flow analysis predicts how much money will have to be spent each week or each month. It also states how much income is likely to come in during that same period. If more income comes in than money goes out in the period of time, the business is said to be operating at a **profit**. If the

SPREAD SHEET: SIX MONTH CASH FLOW						
	JAN	FEB	MAR	APR	MAY	JUNE
INCOME, DOLLARS	2400	3000	4500	4000	5000	5500
EXPENSES						
Rent	850	850	850	850	850	850
Telephone	116	173	164	175	204	227
Salaries	575	1270	2350	2350	2525	2610
Materials	255	478	763	652	940	985
Shipping	18	22	35	25	38	43
Insurance	125	125	125	125	125	125
TOTAL	1939	2918	4287	4177	4682	4840
INCOME−EXPENSES	461	82	213	−177	318	660
CASH TO START 4000						
CASH IN BANK	4461	4543	4756	4579	4897	5557

A spreadsheet shows the cash flow of a business. If an expense or income item changes, the effect of the change on the whole business can be seen quickly.

expenses are more than the income, the business is operating at a *loss*.

Most *start-ups*, or new businesses, are expected to run at a loss for some time while they develop their products and attract regular customers. During this time, there is little income. The company must start out with enough money to pay bills while it is in this start-up phase. The money can come from the personal savings of the people who are starting the business, or from a loan. It can also come from a *venture capitalist*. This is a person who supplies money to a new or growing company. In return, the venture capitalist gets part ownership in the company.

Another way for a company to raise money is to sell shares of stock to the public. A share of stock is a part ownership in the company. When people buy stock in a company, they become *shareholders*. A company that makes a profit may give some of the profit to shareholders. If the company does well, the price of its stock may rise. Shareholders can then make money if they sell their stock. If a company does poorly, its stock price may go down. Shareholders could lose some or all of the money they have invested. The sale of stock is regulated by the Securities and Exchange Commission (SEC).

To keep cash needs low, a company tries to get its development work over with as quickly as possible. In this way, it can start selling its products and start earning money more quickly. Managers try to make sure manufacturing is done as quickly as possible for the same reason. They try to have all the materials necessary to make a product at the plant just before they are needed. (See "Just-In-Time Manufacturing" in Chapter 9.)

To schedule manufacturing, managers use the *PERT chart*. PERT stands for *Program Evaluation Review Technique*. It was first used by the U.S. Navy during the Polaris missile and submarine project. This was the most complex manufacturing project undertaken to that time.

The PERT chart is a powerful scheduling tool. It lists each step necessary to complete a project. It shows the order of the steps that are to be taken. The time needed to complete each step is also shown. The effect of a late completion date on the rest of the schedule can be quickly seen on the PERT chart. Using the PERT chart, a manager can keep careful track of what is happening and move resources to the most important jobs to stay on schedule.

A company usually has to pay suppliers before it gets its payment for the products it will make. Keeping the smallest possible inventory (stock) for the shortest possible time is important. In this way, cash needs will be kept as low as possible.

One way to measure inventory is how many times it is

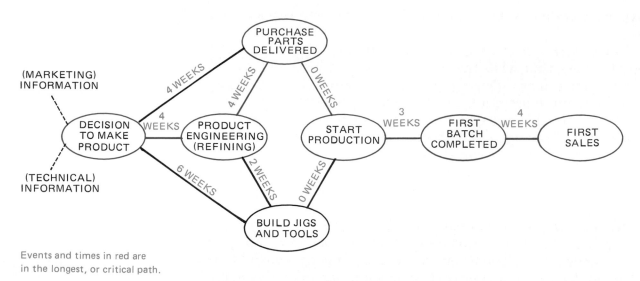

PURCHASE
PARTS
DELIVERED

4 WEEKS

4 WEEKS

0 WEEKS

(MARKETING)
INFORMATION

DECISION
TO MAKE
PRODUCT

4
WEEKS

PRODUCT
ENGINEERING
(REFINING)

START
PRODUCTION

3
WEEKS

FIRST
BATCH
COMPLETED

4
WEEKS

FIRST
SALES

(TECHNICAL)
INFORMATION

6 WEEKS

2 WEEKS

0 WEEKS

BUILD JIGS
AND TOOLS

Events and times in red are
in the longest, or critical path.

PERT charts are another management tool that helps in scheduling and monitoring large, complex projects.

completely used up in one year. This is called inventory turn. A company that can manufacture a product and sell all its inventory in sixty days has a turn of about 6 times per year. (That is, 365 days divided by 60 days.)

COMMON ELEMENTS OF MANAGEMENT

Managing includes planning, organizing, leading, and controlling.

While the tasks of construction managers are different from the tasks of production managers, there are some basic tasks that all managers do. Managing includes planning, organizing, leading, and controlling.

In construction, building design and making the financial arrangements are examples of planning. Deciding who the general contractor will be and who each of the subcontractors will be are examples of organizing. Promoting safety and good work habits and quickly resolving disputes are examples of leadership by the project manager. Progress meetings are one way of controlling the project.

In manufacturing, market research and R&D are two examples of planning. Making sure the right people, parts, and machines are in the right place at the right time are examples of organizing. Selecting the correct market to be in and making everyone interested in high quality are two examples of leadership. Quality control, the use of PERT charts, and monitoring product sales are three examples of controlling a manufacturing system.

SUMMARY

The success of a manufacturing or construction project depends largely on how well it is managed. The coordination and careful use of the seven resources of the production system are part of the job of a company's management. Management must coordinate the jobs of different departments in the company to make the best use of resources.

Architects design a building's shape and choose basic materials for it. Engineers design the building's structure and its major systems. Specialists in different fields help design other systems such as security and fire protection.

A general contractor directs the work of many different people on a construction job. General contractors hire subcontractors to do different parts of the work. On very large jobs, separate companies called project managers are hired to oversee contracts and coordinate the many jobs.

Scheduling large building jobs often requires the use of the Gantt chart. The Gantt chart is a kind of bar graph that shows the start and completion dates for different parts of the construction job. Progress is reviewed at regular project meetings.

Permits and approvals are necessary before building begins, during building, and at completion. Some of these permits are zoning approval, a building permit, permits to close sidewalks and streets, and permits to dig up streets. When construction is finished, and the building and its safety systems have been inspected, a Certificate of Occupancy is issued.

A company's marketing department decides what market the company will develop products for, what features they should have, and how to go about selling them. The marketing department also tries to set a price for the product at which the product will sell and the company will make money.

Research is the search for new materials, processes, and methods that may be useful to a company. Development is the application of these discoveries along with previously known methods to a product. Quality control is the monitoring of quality as the product is being made.

A company that makes a product must develop a way to support the product after sale. This support is called servicing.

A company may use one or more methods of selling its products. These include direct sales, using sales representatives, selling through dealers, and selling through distributors.

Sound planning and careful control of the company's finances are both necessary if a company is to survive and grow. Planning a future business requires a business plan. Cash is important in starting a new business or in expanding an already existing one. A company can get money from the savings of the people who started it, or from a loan, or from venture capitalists. It can also raise money by selling stock.

To keep a company's cash needs to a minimum, products must be brought to the market as quickly as possible. It is important to make products as quickly as possible while keeping quality high, and to keep inventories as low as possible. PERT charts help achieve this goal.

Four common elements of all good mangement are planning, organizing, leadership, and control.

(Courtesy of Turner Construction Company)

(Courtesy of Corning Glass Works)

REVIEW QUESTIONS

1. What part does management play in a production system?
2. What do architects do on a construction project? What do engineers do?
3. List at least three tasks assigned to the general contractor.
4. What are subcontractors?
5. Why must a contract between the general contractor and the owner be so long?
6. How is the job of a project manager different from that of a general contractor?
7. What is coordination between subcontractors on a construction job? Why is it important to getting the best quality work done, and the job finished on schedule?
8. How does a Gantt chart help in keeping a construction project on schedule?
9. What are the four basic tasks that all managers do?
10. What is the difference between marketing and sales?
11. How are research and development different?
12. Is quality control in the manufacturing stage important to the jobs of marketing and sales? Explain your answer.
13. Name four ways a manufacturer might sell products.
14. What three things should be included in a business plan?
15. Draw a PERT chart for making hot cocoa, from the purchase of ingredients through cleaning up afterward.
16. If it takes 90 days for a company to produce and sell a product, what is the approximate turn on the product?

KEY WORDS

Action item	Direct sales	Overruns	Research and
Architect	Distributor	Owner	development
Business plan	Engineer	Permits	Sales
Cash flow analysis	EPA	PERT chart	representative
Certificate of	Gantt chart	Productizing	Shareholder
occupancy	General	Profit	Subcontractor
Commission	contractor	Project	Throwaway
Contract	Loss	manager	Union
Coordination	Marketing	Prototype	Venture capitalist
Dealer	OSHA	Quality control	Zoning

SEE YOUR TEACHER FOR THE CROSSTECH PUZZLE

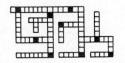

ONE, IF BY LAND . . .

Setting the Stage

The manufacturing industry usually doesn't put a new product on the market "overnight." It can take many years of planning, research and development, production, and marketing to establish a new company or introduce a new product. There are seven resources of technology: people, information, materials, tools and machines, energy, capital, and time. These resources play an important role in the decisions that industry must make. If a wrong decision is made, it can be a *very* expensive mistake.

Your Challenge

Organize and establish a company that will manufacture lanterns using an assembly line to make the manufacturing process more efficient.

Procedure

1. Elect the executive board (president, vice president, secretary, and treasurer) of the new company known as *Lanterns, Inc.* The foreperson, safety supervisor, advertising and publicity staff, and other workers will later be "hired" by the board.
2. Determine the responsibilities of each executive board member.
3. Develop as a group a list of what resources are probably needed to start *Lanterns, Inc.* This list should include people, information, materials, tools and machines, energy, capital, and time.
4. Using the chalkboard or large sheet of paper and 3" × 5" cards, develop a flowchart of the *steps* in making a lantern.
5. Using the preceding step as a guide, develop another flowchart of the *assembly line* needed to efficiently mass-produce the lanterns. This chart should include the machines, tables, tools, work stations, quality control checkpoints, etc. needed.
6. Everyone in the class should contribute to the design and fabrication of any jigs and fixtures needed for the assembly line. Accuracy is especially important at this stage.
7. The executive board of *Lanterns, Inc.* should interview "prospective employees" for the company's job openings. A standardized job application should be completed by each applicant.

Suggested Resources

Safety glasses and lab aprons
Heavy gage tin plate
Steel or brass rod—3/16" in diameter
Copper tubing—3/4" in diameter
Spot welder
Propane soldering torch
Solder and flux
Squaring shear
Notcher
Bar-folder
Box and pan brake
Slip-form rolls
Variable speed drill
Drill bits

8. The assembly line positions should be rotated periodically. When people switch jobs in the assembly line, they may have to be "retrained" for their new positions.

9. The safety supervisor's responsibility includes making sure students wear safety glasses and any other protective equipment during the manufacturing process. The safety supervisor also helps to ensure that all workers are following the safety instructions described by the teacher.

Note: Refer to the drawings for the following steps.

10. Using the squaring shear, cut 3 ¾" × 13 ½" pieces of heavy gage tin plate for the body of each lantern.

11. Use the notcher to cut out the corners and the 90° "V" cuts on the edges of the body.

12. The bar-folder is now used to bend the ¼" hems to the *inside* of the finished lantern.

13. The ⅜" laps are bent on the bar-folder to a 90° angle in the same direction as the ¼" hems were bent.

14. Complete the bending of the lantern body using the box and pan brake. Be careful not to crush any of the laps during this step.

15. The 1" × 6" corner posts (two for each lantern) are cut from heavy gage tin plate with the squaring shear. One-quarter inch of *one* long edge of each corner post is folded over into a hem on the bar-folder. The bar-folder is also used to make the final bend, a ⅜", 90° bend, in the long direction.

16. The corner posts can now be spot welded to the lantern body. *Be absolutely sure all of the lantern angles are exactly 90° before welding.*

17. Using a template, trace the shape of the lantern top onto tin plate. Cut out the top using tin snips, aviation snips, or the notcher. Make sure there are no sharp burrs on the edges of the lantern top. File or sand as necessary. Scribe the bending lines onto the layout of the lantern tops.

18. Bend the lantern tops to a pyramid shape using a box and pan brake. Clamp and spot weld the tops together. Slightly bend the lower "rounded" part of the lantern top so it fits firmly on the lantern body.

19. Make sure the completed top fits properly on the lantern body. Weld it in place.

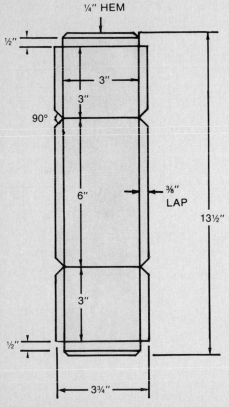

LANTERN BODY LAYOUT

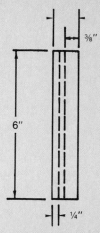

CORNER POST LAYOUT
(MAKE 2)

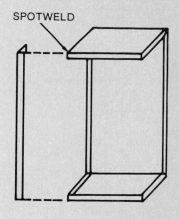

SPOTWELD

20. Drill two ¼" holes 1" down from the point of the top. These holes should be made on opposing sides of the "pyramid" shape. The handle ring will be inserted through these holes.
21. To make the handle ring for the lantern, cut a 9" long piece of steel or brass rod with a hacksaw. File both ends round.
22. Use the slip-form rolls to bend the rod into a circle. Insert the completed handle ring through the ¼" holes drilled in the lantern top.
23. Cut ¼" × 4" strips of tin plate for the "X" designs used in the lantern windows. A total of eight ¼" × 4" strips are needed per lantern. Spot weld these strips into an "X" maintaining a 90° angle at the intersection. Four X's are needed for each lantern. Weld these to the inside of the lantern.
24. To make the candle holder, cut a 1" long piece of ¾" diameter copper tubing with a tubing cutter. Remove any burrs, shine on the buffing wheel, and open-flame solder this piece to the center of the bottom of the lantern. Wash off the excess soldering flux.

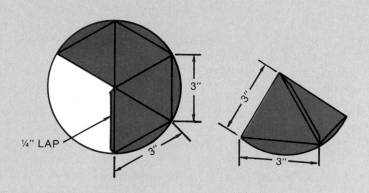

LANTERN TOP LAYOUT

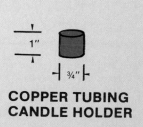

COPPER TUBING CANDLE HOLDER

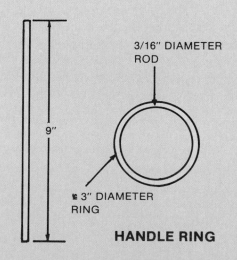

HANDLE RING

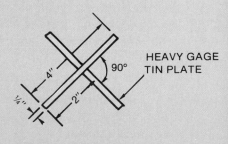

WINDOW CROSSES
(MAKE 8)

Technology Connections

1. Why is it important to make a *prototype,* or "original" working model, of the project being mass-produced before going into full production on the assembly line?
2. Why is accuracy important when manufacturing most products?
3. What is the purpose of quality control checkpoints?
4. How do mass production techniques differ from the craftsman techniques?
5. Why is advertising so important to the manufacturing industry? Make a list of the different ways manufacturers can advertise a product.
6. Match the advertising slogans:

   1. Soup is good food!   Allstate Insurance   _____
   2. 99 and 44/100% pure!   New York City   _____
   3. The wings of man   Campbell's Soup   _____
   4. When it rains, it pours!   General Electric   _____
   5. We bring good things to life! U.S. Army   _____
   6. You're in good hands . . . Greyhound Bus   _____
   7. Over 30 billion sold!   Eastern Airlines   _____
   8. Be all that you can be!   Ivory Soap   _____
   9. The Big Apple   McDonald's   _____
   10. Leave the driving to us!   Morton Salt   _____

Science and Math Concepts

▶ A spot welder fastens metal by passing electricity through it. The heat needed to melt the metal is caused by *resistance* to the flow of electricity.

Equipment and Supplies

(This activity can be carried out by using any one or a combination of the following materials — wood, metal or plastic.)

Standard lab equipment, including either hand or power tools to cut stock to length and drill holes in the selected materials

(Optional) equipment for testing of geometric shapes)

Standard drill press

Bathroom scales

Lengths of stock

    Wood — may be as small as popsicle sticks or as large as wood lath

    or

    Metal — approximately 26-gauge, in ½" strips for small structures or thin wall electrical conduit for large structures

    or

    Plastic — ⅛" sheet acrylic in ½" strips for small structures, or ½" plastic water pipe for large structures

Fasteners — Small bolts or other fastening devices to attach the ends of the components together

Miscellaneous materials to construct jigs and fixtures used in the manufacturing of the components

PRODUCTION COMPANY

Objectives

When you have finished this activity, you should be able to:

■ List three geometric shapes and list two advantages and two disadvantages of each.

■ Set up a manufacturing company to design, test, and manufacture components to be used in a construction company.

■ Establish a construction company which will use the components manufactured in the class to build structures.

■ Distinguish between manufacturing and construction industries and list ten items produced by each.

■ Better understand the importance of each individual's work in order for an organization to be successful.

Concepts and Information

As we look around, we see a large variety of objects that have been constructed from a variety of materials. We also find an infinite number of sizes and shapes in our surroundings. Upon more careful study, notice that all of these shapes are made up of curved or straight lines, which are parts of circles, rectangles, or triangles. During this activity, you will learn more about those geometric figures that are made up of straight components. These shapes are used to construct a

EXAMPLES OF STRAIGHT-SIDED GEOMETRIC FIGURES

TRIANGLES (THREE-SIDED FIGURES)

RIGHT   ISOSCELES   EQUILATERAL

QUADRILATERALS (FOUR-SIDED FIGURES)

variety of structures, such as roof and floor trusses, bridges, geodesic domes, and towers. Also, you will have the opportunity to be part of a manufacturing or construction company that performs the design, fabrication, and construction of a structure.

(Courtesy of Marriott Corporation)

Whatever a production company decides to manufacture or construct, it must meet certain standards of quality and still make the product within the price range of the customer. In the production of large structures, one of the major concerns is to be able to build the structure with the least amount of materials. As larger-sized items are produced, the factors of material costs, weight, and ease of production all play a part in how efficient the end product will be. Therefore, engineers design items that will have adequate strength but use a minimum amount of materials. This can be seen in the framing of homes, construction of bridges, electrical transmission towers, and automobiles.

Often the product made by one company is used as an input for another company. For example: a logging company harvests trees, which are the output of the landowner but are the input for the logging company. The logs are then sold to a sawmill (output of the logging company, input for the sawmill), which in turn manufactures lumber (output of the sawmill, input for the construction company). The lumber is sold to a construction company, which constructs homes that are sold to the homeowner.

Sometimes companies are organized into various divisions. Each division produces a service or part that will be used by another division of the same company.

Activity

In the following activity, your class will set up a production company with a design and engineering division, a manufacturing division, and a construction division. The design phase of the entire project will be the responsibility of the design and engineering division. This division will prepare the specifications and drawings for the components to be made by the manufacturing division. The construction division will then use these components to construct various structures. By working together, the company will make a profit so it can remain in business.

Procedures

1. With two or three other students, design a variety of straight-sided geometric shapes using provided materials, such as popsicle sticks and fasteners.
2. Test the geometric shapes with a drill press and a bathroom scale, or other material-testing apparatus to determine the strength of each shape. Choose the shape you'd like to use for your structures.

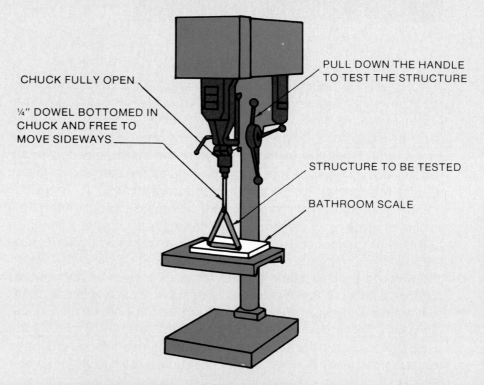

CHUCK FULLY OPEN

¼" DOWEL BOTTOMED IN CHUCK AND FREE TO MOVE SIDEWAYS

PULL DOWN THE HANDLE TO TEST THE STRUCTURE

STRUCTURE TO BE TESTED

BATHROOM SCALE

CAUTION: MAKE SURE DRILL PRESS IS UNPLUGGED! DO NOT APPLY MORE THAN 50 LB. BE CAREFUL TO AVOID SPLINTERS SHOULD THE STRUCTURE BREAK DURING THE TEST. GOGGLES SHOULD BE WORN DURING THE TEST.

3. Divide the class into design teams of three to five members each. Design and sketch a minimum of four structures that can be constructed from geometric shapes fastened at the ends to each other.
4. As a class activity, select one, two, or three structures to be built. Each structure should be built from multiples of the same geometric shape.
5. Set up a company with three divisions: a design and engineering division, a manufacturing division, and a construction division. Select a vice president of each division, a company president, and other company and division officials as is necessary to carry out needed business and make company and division decisions.

One suggested format for the company is as follows:

Component Production Company:
Company President
Vice President of Engineering and Design
Vice President of Manufacturing
Vice President of Construction
Manager of Personnel Dept.
Financial Manager
Manager of Materials Dept.
Tool and Machine Supervisor

(Courtesy of Montana Power Company)

6. Build a prototype or small model of the structure to make sure the components will work properly.
7. Design and make detailed drawings and specifications of the components to be produced.
8. Under the direction of the financial manager, determine how to obtain capital to purchase the materials needed to build the components.
9. Design and build jigs and fixtures to be used in the manufacture of the components.
10. Set up a production line so the components will move from one station to the next with the least amount of wasted time and motion so the line is efficient.

(Courtesy of Montana Power Company)

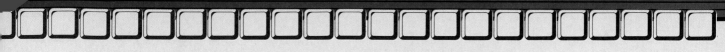

11. Establish quality control devices that will ensure a quality product. The product must meet the specifications originally agreed on at the beginning of the production run.
12. Operate a trial run to make sure all jigs, fixtures, and materials are in the proper working order to assure a smooth run.
13. Complete the production run.
14. Stockpile the components with proper identification. Deliver to the construction division for assembly.
15. Write detailed instructions on how to assemble the components into desired structures.
16. Construct the structures and inspect during construction to make sure each structure meets original design specifications.

Review Questions

1. List the seven resources that are required by any production company in order for it to be successful.
2. List several inputs of the engineering and design division of your company. Do the same for your manufacturing division and your construction division.
3. What is the processing phase of the manufacturing and construction divisions?
4. List the outputs of the manufacturing and construction divisions of your company.
5. Determine those activities that provide feedback for your company.
6. Discuss what could happen to a company if any one of the employees did not do the best possible job.
7. Make suggestions on how the manufacturing division of your company could have produced the components more efficiently.
8. Make suggestions on how the workers in the construction division may have been able to do their jobs more efficiently.
9. Study your surroundings and list at least ten different items that are built in such a way that a triangle is used in the design to add strength and stability to the device or structure.
10. List the major differences between a constructed item and one that is manufactured.

CAREER PAGE

CAREERS IN PRODUCTION

Production technology includes construction and manufacturing. Workers in the construction trades build, repair, and modernize homes and other kinds of buildings. They also work on a variety of other projects, including airports, mass transportation systems, roads, recreation facilities, and power plants. Most manufacturing workers work in manufacturing plants, although some jobs involve sales and considerable travel.

OCCUPATION	FORMAL EDUCATION OR TRAINING	SKILLS NEEDED	EMPLOYMENT OPPORTUNITIES
ARCHITECT—Plans and designs attractive, functional, safe, and economical buildings.	College degree (bachelor's degree in architecture) as well as three years of experience in an architect's office.	Engineering design and managerial skills. Knowledge of building materials and modeling techniques.	Above average. Rapid growth in construction of non-residential structures will increase the demand.
JOURNEYMAN—A member of the building trades, such as:	On-the-job training; two- to four-year apprenticeship programs. A high school education including courses in basic mathematics, applied science, electricity and electronics, mechanical drawing, and construction technology.	Sketching; reading drawings; must layout, measure, cut, shape, and fasten materials; use hand and power tools safely. Must know about building codes and regulations.	Average. As the population grows, more journeymen will be needed to help build and maintain structures.
Carpenter—Builds framework, frames the roof and interior partitions.			
Concrete mason—Places and finishes concrete.			
Electrician—Installs, assembles, and maintains electrical systems.			
Plumber—Installs and maintains water and heating systems.			
Roofer—Installs and repairs roofs.			
MANAGER AND ADMINISTRATOR—Plans, organizes, directs, and controls an organization's major functions.	College degree and management training. Top managers often have a master's degree in business administration.	Determination; self confidence, high motivation; strong decision-making, organizational, and interpersonal skills.	Opportunities will increase faster than the average occupations as business operations become more complex.
MANUFACTURING SALESPERSON—Most manufacturers employ sales people who market products to consumers in other businesses.	For technical products, college degrees in scientific or technical fields. For nontechnical products, college degrees in liberal arts or business administration.	A pleasant personality and appearance, and the ability to get along well with people are important.	Lower than average. Many large firms and chain stores buy direct from manufacturers, but this is a large occupational field with many yearly openings.

Data from *Occupational Outlook Handbook, 1986-87*, U.S. Department of Labor.

SECTION

4

(Courtesy of Amoco Corporation)

ENERGY, POWER, AND TRANSPORTATION

CHAPTER 13

ENERGY

MAJOR CONCEPTS

After reading this chapter, you will know that:

- Work done on an object is equal to the distance it moves multiplied by the force used in the direction of the motion.
- Energy is the ability to do work. It is the source of the force that is needed to do work.
- Kinetic energy is the energy of a moving object. Potential energy is the energy an object has because of its position, shape, or other feature.
- Potential energy can be changed into kinetic energy and kinetic energy can be changed into potential energy.
- The principle of conservation of energy states that energy cannot be created or destroyed, but it can be changed from one form to another.
- Energy sources are limited, unlimited, or renewable.
- Most of the energy used in the United States today comes from limited energy sources.

INTRODUCTION

Energy is one of the seven resources of technology. In fact, changes in technology throughout history have depended in large part on this resource. For many thousands of years, energy came from human and animal muscle. Later, people learned to use moving wind and water for energy. Mills that ground grain into flour used the energy of falling water in a waterfall or rushing water in a stream or river. Pumps that were run by wind were put in places where the wind always blew.

During the Industrial Revolution, energy technology changed. Coal and oil provided new energy sources for factories as machines became a more and more important part of manufacturing. Glass factories were built near sources of natural gas. Steel mills were built near coal mines. As with wind and water, users of large amounts of energy were often located close to its source.

The new industries of today do not need as much energy as older heavy industries. For example, factories that make electronics equipment do not need as much energy as steel mills. Also, many of today's factories use electricity only. They do not need to be near an energy source. Electricity can be used far from power plants where it is generated.

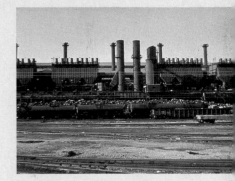

Industries often grew near the source of energy needed to make them run. Steel mills are often located near coal and iron deposits. (Courtesy of American Iron and Steel Institute)

WORK AND ENERGY

Work

You probably think that doing two pages of math homework or writing a report is work. Reading this chapter in one night would be really hard work. In science, though, none of this is work. In science, the word *work* has a different—and very exact—meaning.

Work is done when a force pushes or pulls on an object, causing the object to move. The amount of work done is equal to the distance the object moves multiplied by the force in the direction of movement. Work can be measured in foot-pounds.

Work done on an object is equal to the distance it moves multiplied by the force used in the direction of the motion.

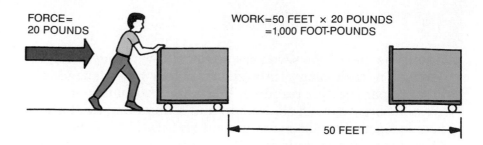

Work is done only when a force moves an object over a distance.

Think about this: Two boys pull on ropes hitched to the opposite ends of a cart for an hour. The boys are equally strong. Since neither is stronger, the cart does not move. Has work been done? No, because even though the boys have exerted a great deal of force on the cart, it did not move.

Energy

Energy is the ability to do work. It is the source of the force used to do work. More energy is needed to do a large amount of work than to do a small amount of work. Energy can have many forms. Much of today's technology concerns changing energy from one form into another in which it can do useful work.

Kinetic energy is the energy an object has because of its motion. A stone falling into a pond has kinetic energy. When it hits the water, it will splash some of the water out of the pond. The splashed drops of water then have kinetic energy. A bullet fired from a gun has kinetic energy. A moving bicycle has kinetic energy. The amount of kinetic energy an object has depends on its weight and how fast it is going. For example, a car traveling at 60 miles an hour has far more kinetic energy than a bike moving along at 5 miles an hour.

Potential energy is energy that is stored in an object because of its position, shape, or some other feature. The string of a bow that is pulled back, ready to send an arrow into a target,

Energy is the ability to do work. It is the source of the force that is needed to do work.

Kinetic energy is the energy of a moving object. Potential energy is the energy an object has because of its position, shape, or other feature.

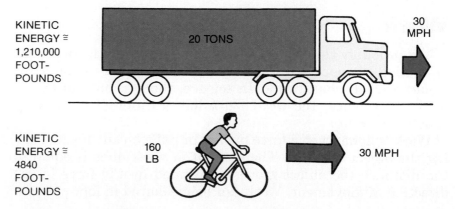

If two objects are moving at the same speed, the larger object has more kinetic energy.

POTENTIAL ENERGY
STORED IN SPRING

POTENTIAL ENERGY
STORED IN
MOLECULES
OF WOOD

POTENTIAL ENERGY
STORED IN POSITION
ABOVE FLOOR

Potential energy is energy that is stored in an object due to its position, shape, or other feature.

has potential energy. It was put there by the person who pulled back the bowstring. A rock held over mud has potential energy. It was put there by the person who lifted the rock up. When the rock is dropped, it will do work by pushing the mud aside as it sinks. Potential energy can be stored in other ways. It is stored in the gasoline used to fuel a car. It is stored in a magnet that can be used to pick up a nail.

Potential energy can be changed into kinetic energy. When a person lets go of the string of a bow, the potential energy changes to the kinetic energy of the moving string and the flying arrow. For an object to have potential energy, kinetic energy must have been used to change it. It must have been lifted or stretched or changed in some other way.

Energy can be changed in yet another way. It can be changed from one form to another. The energy stored in gasoline is stored in the form of chemical energy. When gasoline is burned in an engine, it is changed to light and thermal (heat) energy. The engine changes the heat energy into mechanical energy. Changing energy from one form to another is a major job of technology. An important principle of science is that of the

Potential energy can be changed into kinetic energy and kinetic energy can be changed into potential energy.

The gravitational kinetic energy of the falling water is being converted to electrical energy. Conversion of energy from one form to another is one of technology's most important tasks.
(Courtesy of United States Department of Energy)

conservation of energy. This principle states that energy cannot be created or destroyed, but that it can be changed from one form to another.

Energy in Our Modern Society

The principle of conservation of energy states that energy cannot be created or destroyed, but it can be changed from one form to another.

Our society uses a large amount of energy each day. We use energy to light our homes at night. We use it to heat our homes when it is cold and cool them when it is hot. We use energy to get to and from school and work. We use energy when we pick up the telephone to call our friends. Large amounts of energy are needed to construct new buildings and manufacture products. Energy is needed to run equipment on farms, making them more productive.

Energy in the United States

The total amount of energy used in this country each year is about 80 **quads**. A quad is one quadrillion (1,000,000,000,000,000) Btus. Btu stands for British thermal unit. It is the amount of energy needed to raise the temperature of one pound of water by one degree Fahrenheit. A quad equals the energy given off by burning about 20 gallons of gasoline every day for a year.

The pie chart on the left shows how much energy comes from different sources in the United States each year. The pie chart on the right shows how that energy is used.

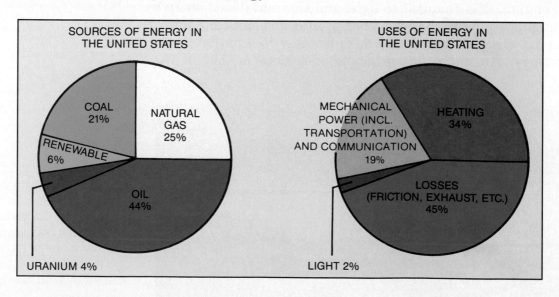

SOURCES OF ENERGY IN THE UNITED STATES

COAL 21%
NATURAL GAS 25%
RENEWABLE 6%
OIL 44%
URANIUM 4%

USES OF ENERGY IN THE UNITED STATES

MECHANICAL POWER (INCL. TRANSPORTATION) AND COMMUNICATION 19%
HEATING 34%
LOSSES (FRICTION, EXHAUST, ETC.) 45%
LIGHT 2%

TYPES OF ENERGY SOURCES

Limited	Unlimited	Renewable
Coal	Solar	Wood
Oil	Wind	Biomass Gasification
Natural Gas	Gravitational	Biomass Fermentation
Uranium	Tidal	Animal Power
	Geothermal	Human Muscle Power
	Fusion	

The energy used in this country comes from many sources. It is used in many ways. The technological tools that people have made to solve problems require energy. People must develop new ways to supply more energy.

Energy sources can be described as **limited**, **unlimited**, or **renewable**. Limited energy souces are those of which we have a fixed supply, such as oil. They are sources that we will run out of if we continue to use them. Unlimited resources, such as the sun, are energy sources that we have more of than we can ever use. Renewable energy sources, such as wood, are those that can be replaced as they are used. These sources must be managed carefully so that we do not use more than we can replace.

Energy sources are limited, unlimited, or renewable.

LIMITED ENERGY SOURCES

As you can see from the pie chart of energy sources, most of the energy used by the United States today comes from limited energy sources. It takes a long time for nature to make these energy sources. As we use them up, there is no hope that more will become available. It takes millions of years for coal, oil, and natural gas to be created. At our present rate of use, it is estimated that we have only a few hundred years' supply of oil and natural gas, and 1,000 years' supply of coal left. The rate of use is likely to rise and keep on rising, but new energy reserves are also being discovered.

Most of the energy used in the United States today comes from limited energy sources.

Fossil Fuels

Oil, natural gas, and coal are all called **fossil fuels**. This is because they come from the remains of plants and animals that lived millions of years ago. After the plants and animals died, their bodies did not rot completely away because they were covered by fallen trees, leaves, and mud. Additional layers of soil material, along with movements of the earth, buried the plant and animal remains deeply. There, the great pressure changed them into oil, gas, or coal over millions of years.

Molecules are two or more atoms joined together by a chemical bond. The molecules in fossil fuels are held together with high-energy bonds. When fossil fuels are burned, the molecules break down into simpler molecules. As they break down, they release much of the energy in the high-energy bonds. This is the energy that we get from fossil fuels. The changes that take place during the burning of the fuels are called **chemical changes**. A chemical change means that the chemical structure of the fuel has changed. Energy from the burning of fuel is sometimes called **chemical energy**.

The more energy released, the better the fuel is. The bonds in gasoline, which is made from oil, release a great deal of energy when the gasoline burns. That is why gasoline is so widely used as a fuel.

Coal was one of the first fossil fuels to be used widely during the Industrial Revolution. Coal can be mined from the surface of the land by **strip mining**. Very large holes are dug into the ground and the coal is removed. This ruins the land, leaving holes and causing erosion. In most places today, strip miners must fill in the hole when mining is finished. They must restore the land by planting trees and grass.

Coal found deep below ground has different forms at different depths. To reach deep coal, miners have to tunnel into the earth, dig the coal out, and transport it back to the surface. Coal mining can be dangerous. There may be cave-ins, gas in the mines, and health problems from breathing coal dust every

Coal is transported in large quantities, by barges, trucks, or trains. (Photo by Jeremy Plant)

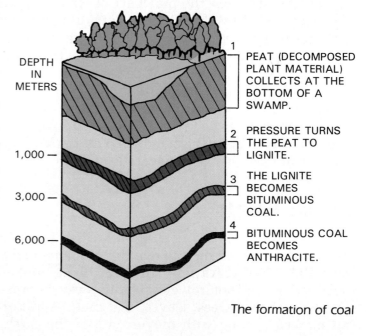

DEPTH IN METERS

1,000 —
3,000 —
6,000 —

1 PEAT (DECOMPOSED PLANT MATERIAL) COLLECTS AT THE BOTTOM OF A SWAMP.

2 PRESSURE TURNS THE PEAT TO LIGNITE.

3 THE LIGNITE BECOMES BITUMINOUS COAL.

4 BITUMINOUS COAL BECOMES ANTHRACITE.

The formation of coal

day for many years. Modern equipment and safety standards are helping to make mining safer.

In the early part of this century, coal was widely used to heat homes. Coal was stored in a coal bin in a basement or outside the house. It was then burned in a stove or central heater to provide warmth. Coal has since been replaced by oil, gas, and electricity for home heating. It is still burned to provide heat for industrial processes such as steelmaking.

Coal is the limited energy source of which we have the most, but there are problems with its use. Coal must be moved in large quantities by train, barge, or truck to its destination. Another problem is that burning coal produces sulfur dioxide. This is an air pollutant. Engineers are working to solve these problems so that more coal can be used.

Technology in the Coal Mines

Technology has made coal mining faster and safer. Coal that is near the surface of the ground is strip-mined. In strip mining, large earth movers, shovels, and trucks are used to dig the coal and put it in waiting railroad cars. In this country, strip mines must be reclaimed when mining is finished. That is, the holes left by coal removal must be filled in and trees and plants replaced.

In underground mines, two shafts are dug. One is used to move workers to and from the coal seam. The second is used to lift coal to the surface. Large machines called continuous miners and longwall miners are used to loosen coal from the wall of the mine. The coal is then carried to waiting trucks or carts. These machines are used together with other machines that hold up the mine roof while mining continues.

This heavy shovel and truck are being used for strip mining. (Courtesy of United States Department of Energy)

Longwall miners are used in underground coal mines. (Courtesy of United States Department of Energy)

One new way of transporting coal is by pipelines. Coal is crushed and mixed with water to form a slurry. The slurry can be pumped through pipes. Ways are also being found to make coal burn more cleanly. Pollutants can be removed by cleaning the coal carefully before it is burned. They can also be removed while the coal is burning. After the coal has burned, smoke can be cleaned by devices called scrubbers. Scrubbers are installed in smokestacks. Because of advances in these areas, coal will once again become an important energy source in this country.

Oil, or "black gold," is the energy source we depend on the most. About half of the energy we use comes from oil. The remaining supply of oil is much smaller than that of coal. Oil is used much more than coal because it is more easily taken from the ground, stored, and transported. It can also be made into many other useful fuels. Some of these fuels are home heating oil, diesel fuel, gasoline, and jet fuel.

Oil is in such demand that oil wells are drilled wherever there is oil in the ground. Wells are even dug in areas with harsh climates, such as the northern coast of Alaska. They are also drilled in the ocean floor.

Natural gas is used for home heating and cooking. It is also used as a fuel in the glass industry. Huge gas-fired furnaces melt glass in large quantities. Gas is also used by other manufacturing industries.

Oil is extracted from the ground by wells such as this . . . (Courtesy of United States Department of Energy)

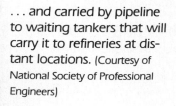
. . . and carried by pipeline to waiting tankers that will carry it to refineries at distant locations. (Courtesy of National Society of Professional Engineers)

The High Technology Search for Oil

Oil and gas form only where there is the right combination of rock types and structures. People who look for oil search for this combination. In their search, they use sensitive tools. These include magnetometers, seismographs, and gravimeters.

Magnetometers are used to sense magnetic fields. Rocks that are near oil fields are generally not magnetic.

Seismographs measure vibrations in the earth created by setting off a small explosive just beneath the surface. Oil explorers look at the time it takes for vibrations to travel to underground rock layers and then bounce off. They look at the strength of the vibrations.

They use this information to make a kind of picture of rock layers deep under the ground.

A gravimeter measures gravity. Rock formations underground will change the gravimeter's readings. Geologists use this as another tool in mapping underground rocks.

Photographs taken from satellites are also used to find land formations that are likely to yield oil. Computers are used to enhance these photographs, often by showing different kinds of terrain in different colors.

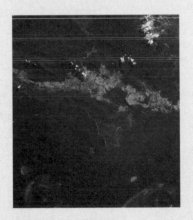

A satellite image (Courtesy of Litton Industries, Inc.)

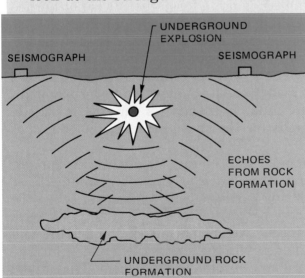

Diagram of seismograph in use

People go to great trouble to extract oil from the earth. For example, this offshore rig is drilling for oil under the seabed. (Courtesy of DuPont Company)

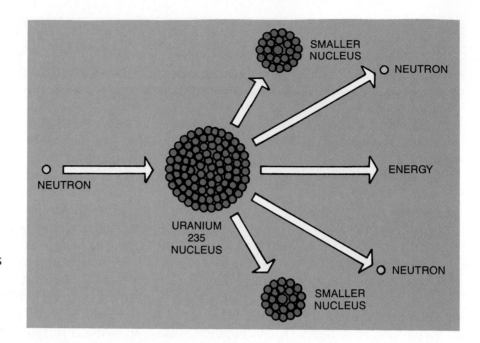

When a large atomic nucleus is split, a very small amount of its matter is converted to an enormous amount of energy.

The atomic bomb produces incredible amounts of energy from nuclear fission. (Courtesy of Los Alamos National Laboratory)

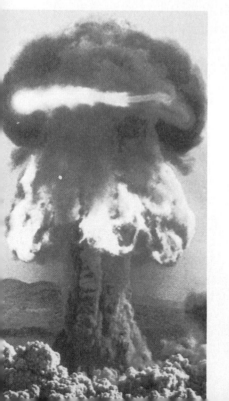

Nuclear Fuels

Uranium is another important limited energy source. Unlike oil, gas, and coal, uranium is not a fossil fuel. It is not burned to obtain energy. Uranium is a **nuclear**, or **atomic** fuel.

The great scientist Albert Einstein was the first to understand that energy can be changed into matter and matter can be changed into energy. His formula, $E = mc^2$, shows that a tiny amount of matter can be changed into a huge amount of energy. (In the formula, E stands for energy, m stands for matter, and c stands for the speed of light, 186,000 miles per second.)

Matter can be changed into energy in **nuclear fission**. In nuclear fission, a large atom such as that of uranium-235 is bombarded (hit) with tiny particles called **neutrons**. When the nucleus (the atom's core of protons and neutrons) is hit by a neutron, it splits. It forms two smaller nuclei and lets off neutrons. It also gives off energy in the form of heat and light. The new neutrons bombard more atoms around them. They make these atoms split, giving off more energy and more neutrons. In this way, a chain reaction is set off. Huge amounts of energy can be produced, causing an explosion. This is what happens when a nuclear bomb explodes. Nuclear energy can also be controlled by controlling the amount of neutrons. This is what happens in a nuclear power plant.

A small amount of atomic fuel can produce a huge amount of energy. However, there are risks with nuclear power that fossil fuels do not have. The fuel and the waste products from a nuclear

The energy released by nuclear fission is harnessed to generate electricity in this nuclear power plant. (Courtesy of United States Department of Energy)

power plant give off high-energy particles (called **radiation**). Radiation can cause burns and sickness. It can kill people if it reaches very high levels. Safety precautions must be taken to make sure that people are not exposed to radiation. Care must also be taken to prevent radioactive gases from escaping into the air from a nuclear power plant.

Another major problem with nuclear energy is that spent (used up) fuel remains radioactive for thousands of years. Presently these wastes are stored in buried blocks of concrete or naturally occurring salt formations. No one has yet found a completely safe way to store radioactive waste. Despite these problems, throughout the world there are hundreds of power plants, ships, and research facilities that use nuclear energy.

UNLIMITED ENERGY SOURCES

Unlimited energy sources are those that are so abundant or replenish themselves so quickly that we will never run out of them. For example, solar energy is unlimited, although the sun will burn out in a few billion years. It is a good idea to use unlimited energy sources like the sun. But it can be difficult to find ways to harness these sources. Still, the effort is worthwhile, since we know that in time we will run out of limited sources such as oil and gas.

Solar Energy

Every fifteen minutes, the sun provides enough energy to meet the world's needs for one whole year. We depend on solar energy for the heat and light necessary to support life on earth.

An aerial view of a solar electricity-generating plant. (Courtesy of Southern California Edison)

Other forms of unlimited energy come from the sun. For example, the sun heats the air, causing large air movements that provide **wind energy**.

The sun's energy can be used by people in many ways. In **active solar** systems, the sun's heat is used directly for a heating job. For example, solar collectors are placed on the roof of a house to heat water. In some solar collectors, mirrors called **parabolic reflectors** focus the light from the sun at one spot. This increases the temperature at that spot. In large installations, many such mirrors can make a very large reflector that can generate very high temperatures at one spot. The heat collected can be used to boil water, creating steam, which is used to turn a turbine. The turbine can be used to generate electricity.

Passive solar designs for houses use the sun for heating. Windows, walls, and doors are carefully placed so the sun can be used for heating. Home builders try to use passive solar design in some way, as described in Chapter 11.

Solar cells, or **photocells** (short for photovoltaic cells) turn light into electricity. Many of them together can generate enough electricity to do useful work. Solar cells are used in remote

NASA is developing this Power Extension Package (PEP). It will use a large array of solar cells to convert sunlight into electrical energy. Most satellites and other space vehicles use solar cells in one way or another. (Courtesy of NASA)

Many buildings built today incorporate both active and passive solar energy. (Courtesy of General Electric Company)

The Solar Challenger's only power source was sunshine. About 16,000 solar cells changed the sun's rays into electricity to power the plane's motor. (Courtesy of DuPont Company)

areas that are not served by power lines. They can be used to charge batteries that run radio relay stations, radio telephones, and other electrical devices. Solar cells are used on most satellites and space vehicles. They provide power directly, or charge on-board batteries. One possible space project that has received some attention is a solar-power satellite. It would collect the sun's energy in solar cells. Then it would send this energy to the earth using a microwave beam.

Wind Energy

Wind is air that moves because of the sun's unequal heating of the earth's surface, which heats the air above it. Wind has been used as an energy source for hundreds of years. Machines that harness the wind have been used to pump water, grind grain, and move ships across the water. Today the wind is used to generate electricity.

Until the steam engine was invented, ships used the wind as their major source of energy. Sailing ships opened up new parts of the world to exploration and trade. In some places, such as the Far East, wind-powered boats are still widely used. Today, sailboats are used mostly for recreation in this country.

Wind-powered generators cannot make electricity when the wind isn't blowing or is blowing below a certain speed. Because of this, they are useful only in those places where the wind blows briskly most of the time. Large wind-powered generators are noisy. They can also interfere with television signals. For these reasons, they are located away from residential areas.

Research is being done to find new ways to use wind power. Two novel wind-powered ships are illustrated in Chapters 8 and 15. Other new uses are windmills that make electricity in very low winds, and diesel-powered freighters that get some of their power from sails.

The Darrieus windmill looks like an eggbeater. Wind blowing from any direction makes the blades turn. (Courtesy of United States Department of Energy)

Gravitational Energy

Long ago, water wheels provided power for grinding grain into flour. Now the power of falling water is used to turn today's version of the water wheel, the **turbine**. Turbines are connected to generators that produce electricity. In some places, dams have been built to produce power from falling water. This way of producing energy is called **hydroelectricity**. Gravity also causes tides, resulting in large movements of water in oceans and rivers. **Tidal energy** is being used experimentally to make electricity.

Energy from falling water can generate enough electricity to supply the needs of entire cities. (Courtesy of Kajima Corporation)

BASIN

PENSTOCK

TURBINE GENERATOR

TAILRACE

Water falling through a penstock turns the blades of a turbine. The turbine is connected to a generator, which produces electricity.

Geothermal Energy

The earth's center is a hot molten core. Heat from this core moves slowly out toward the planet's surface. About three miles below the surface of the earth, the temperature is around 600° Fahrenheit. When this heat reaches groundwater in the crust, it heats it to high temperatures. Geysers like "Old Faithful" at Yellowstone National Park result from steam and hot water escaping upward through cracks in the earth's surface. It is possible to use this steam to turn turbines and generate electricity.

Only a very small part of our energy now comes from geothermal sources. New technologies could turn geothermal energy into an important energy source in years to come.

This geothermal electric power plant generates 900 million watts. (Courtesy of Pacific Gas and Electric)

Fusion

Fusion is another way of changing matter into energy. In fusion, the nuclei of two atoms are forced together. The result is a new nucleus and the release of a huge amount of energy. Energy is needed to force the nuclei together, but under the right conditions more energy is given off than is used. To force the nuclei together in a fusion or hydrogen bomb, an atomic bomb is used. The fusion of two atoms requires a temperature of over 100 million degrees Fahrenheit.

It is hoped that someday fusion will provide a way to generate electricity. Fusion power plants will use deuterium and tritium as fuel. These are found in sea water. The waste products of fusion are not radioactive and the process would not cause pollution. Many people think that fusion plants will provide most of our electricity in the future. Fusion will replace coal or oil in generating plants. A successful fusion power plant has not yet been built, but research goes on.

The researchers at this Tokamak fusion reactor at Princeton Plasma Physics Lab are trying to make controlled fusion power a reality in our lifetime. (Courtesy of United States Department of Energy)

RENEWABLE ENERGY SOURCES

Renewable energy sources are those that can be replenished rapidly. With careful planning, they could be limitless. If they are not replenished, they will be used up and are then considered to be limited.

In China, human power is an important source of energy. Bicycles outnumber private automobiles by a million to one. (UN photo 152.7 15/John Isaac)

Human and Animal Muscle Power

The first source of energy people used was muscle power, first human, and then animal. At first, human muscle power could only be used for small tasks. When people learned to work together, large jobs could be done using human power.

Later, people learned how to use animal muscle for the power they needed. They harnessed oxen, donkeys, and other animals to machines. The machines could plow the land, pump water, and do other jobs. In Egypt, Greece, Rome, and Mexico, there are large stone buildings that were built thousands of years ago. They were built using human and animal power for hauling, lifting, and placing huge building blocks. In some parts of the world, human and animal power are still important sources of energy.

Biomass

Biomass is vegetation and animal wastes. Biomass can serve as a major source of renewable energy. Three basic biomass processes are used to produce energy. The first is **direct combustion** (burning) of waste products. Burning wood is a biomass process. In some parts of the world there is not much wood. In these places, dried animal wastes are gathered and burned to provide heat.

The second way to process biomass is **gasification**. Methane gas is produced as the biomass rots. It is collected and stored to be used as a fuel.

The third process is **fermentation**. Fermentation uses microorganisms to turn biomass such as grain into alcohol and carbon dioxide gas. The alcohol can be stored and used as a fuel or it can be added to other fuels to make them last longer. An example of this is **gasohol**, a mixture of gasoline and alcohol.

Wood

Wood is a form of biomass. The burning of wood was the major way energy was produced until the Middle Ages. A cord of wood (a stack 4 ft. x 4 ft. x 8 ft.) can provide the same amount of heat as about 200 gallons of oil. Some woods are better than others for heating. Hardwoods contain more heat energy per cord than softwoods. Oak is a very good wood to use for firewood. Around A.D. 1600, a shortage of firewood developed. Great forests were used up as people burned wood without thinking about what would happen when all the trees were gone. In some parts of this country, heating with wood has become more popular in recent years. People use wood stoves to help heat their houses when oil prices climb.

Wood is renewable. But forests must be carefully managed. Once trees are cut in an area, it is replanted quickly. Managers look after the young forest to make sure weeds, diseases, and insect pests do not slow growth or kill the trees.

SUMMARY

Work is done only when a force moves an object. The amount of work equals the distance the object moves multiplied by the force in the direction of the motion. Energy is the ability to do work. It is the source of the force needed to do work.

Kinetic energy is energy in motion. The amount of kinetic energy that an object has depends on the object's weight and speed. Potential energy is energy stored in an object due to its position, shape, or other features. Potential energy can be changed into kinetic energy, and vice versa.

The principle of conservation of energy states that energy cannot be created or destroyed, but it can be changed from one form to another. Thus, chemical energy stored in fuel oil can be changed into thermal (heat) energy. Thermal energy can boil water to make mechanical energy in the form of steam pressure. Steam pressure can turn a turbine to drive a generator to make electrical energy.

Energy sources can be limited, unlimited, or renewable. Most of the energy used in the United States comes from limited energy sources. The major limited energy sources are fossil fuels and nuclear fuels used in nuclear fission reactors.

Fossil fuels such as oil, natural gas, and coal were formed many millions of years ago. They come from heat and pressure on the buried remains plants and animals. Because the process of making these fuels takes so long and we are using them at such a rapid rate, we could run out of these energy sources.

In fossil fuels, energy is stored in the high-energy bonds that hold molecules together. When fuel is burned, these molecules break down into simpler molecules, releasing some of the energy stored in the high-energy bonds. The more energy released, the better the fuel.

Reserves of coal are larger than those of any other fossil fuel. Problems of using coal include mining, transportation, and the pollution it creates when burned. Work is being done to solve these problems.

About half the energy we use comes from oil. Oil is refined to form other fuels. These fuels include home heating oil, diesel fuel, gasoline, and jet fuel. Natural gas is used for home heating and cooking.

Nuclear fuels give up energy when small amounts of matter are converted to huge amounts of energy through nuclear fission. Fission occurs when an atomic nucleus is split into smaller nuclei, neutrons, and energy. Strict safety precautions must be used in handling fuel and waste products, and during the operation of nuclear plants, so people are not exposed to radiation.

Solar energy can be used in buildings to heat water or living spaces through active or passive solar systems. Solar cells change the sun's light directly into electricity. They are used in remote locations and in space vehicles.

Wind energy has long been used in transportation and agricultural systems. It is now being used to generate electricity. Gravitational energy is harnessed when water flowing over a dam runs a generator or a grinding wheel. The earth's geothermal power has been tapped to generate electricity. Atomic fusion is a promising unlimited source of energy. Fusion may one day produce large amounts of energy from materials found in sea water.

Renewable energy sources must be managed properly so that we do not use more than is produced. Renewable sources include human and animal muscle power and biomass processes. Biomass processes are direct combustion, gasification, and fermentation.

(Courtesy of United States Department of Energy)

REVIEW QUESTIONS

1. A girl pushes on a bicycle with 10 pounds of force, moving it 100 feet. How much work has she done?
2. A boy pushes on a car with 25 pounds of force, but does not move it. How much work has he done?
3. While playing pinball, a boy draws back the spring-loaded shooter to put a ball into play. At what point does the shooter have potential energy? At what point does it have kinetic energy? At what point does the ball have kinetic energy?
4. Will the energy generated by falling water in a hydroelectric plant be more, less, or the same as the gravitational energy stored in the water that falls (assuming there are no losses in the generator)? Explain your answer.
5. Is solar energy really unlimited? Why do we call it an unlimited energy source?
6. How is energy stored in a fossil fuel?
7. Name three fossil fuels.
8. Why are researchers trying so hard to solve the problems of using coal for energy?
9. How is nuclear fission different from nuclear fusion? Why is fission considered an limited energy source while fusion is considered an unlimited energy source?
10. Why would a solar-powered car be an impractical means of transportation?
11. Is wood used for home heating in your area? Why or why not?

KEY WORDS

Active solar	Fission	Kinetic energy	Quad
Biomass	Fossil fuel	Nuclear fuel	Radiation
Conservation of energy	Fusion	Parabolic reflector	Solar cell
Energy	Gasohol	Passive solar	Work
Fermentation	Gasification	Potential energy	
	Hydroelectricity		

SEE YOUR TEACHER FOR THE CROSSTECH PUZZLE

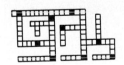

HOT DOG!

Setting the Stage

The NASA training plan was simple. They took us by helicopter to the middle of the desert and waited to see if we would make it back. We were given mirrored thermal blankets, some water, a knife, a first-aid kit, and a radio transmitter. We were only to use the radio in an emergency. No matches, no food, and no wood!

We had no trouble catching small animals, but not one of us wanted to eat the meat raw. Now we had to find a way to make our catch edible.

Your Challenge

Construct a device that can cook a hot dog using solar energy.

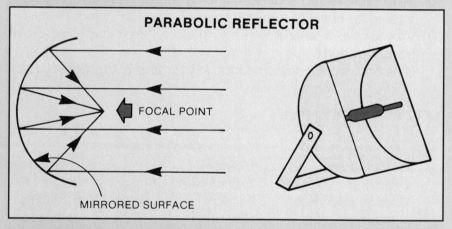

PARABOLIC REFLECTOR

FOCAL POINT

MIRRORED SURFACE

A parabolic reflector takes the parallel rays of the sun and reflects them back through a single point called the focus, or focal point.

Procedure

1. Be sure to wear safety glasses and a lab coat.
2. If you have not been told how to use any tool or machine that you need to use, check with your teacher BEFORE going any further.
3. Lay out a parabola with a 6" focal length on a large sheet of graph paper. The handout from your teacher will show you how to do this. Mark the *focal point* and complete the layout. Cut out the parabola with scissors and use it as a template.

Suggested Resources

Safety glasses and lab apron
Tin plate — 26 gauge, 22¼" × 12"
Pine — ¾" × 8" × 40"
Band iron — ⅛" × ¾" × 32"
Steel rod — ⅛" × 14"
Galvanized steel — 22 gauge, 1" × 5"
12 round head wood screws — ⅝" #4
2 round head machine screws — 1¼", ¼" #20
2 wing nuts — ¼" #20
Mirrored mylar
Spray adhesive
Finishing supplies
Jig or band saw
Drill press and drills
Diacro bender
Bar folder and box and pan brake
Sheetmetal hole punch — ⅛"
Squaring shear
Hack saw
File
Belt sander

4. Trace the parabola onto ¾" pine and carefully cut it out with a band saw. You will need two wood pieces for the cooker.
5. Smooth and trim the edges of the pine to final size using a belt sander. *The edge with the parabolic curve must be very accurate.*
6. Drill a ³⁄₁₆" diameter hole in the focal point and a ¼" hole for the stand in each piece.
7. Sand, stain, and finish the wood.
8. Cut a piece of tin plate about 22¼" × 12". Bend a ½" hem on the two shorter ends.
9. Locate five holes ⅜" in from the edge and equally spaced along the two long edges of the tin plate. Punch or drill ⅛" holes at these ten points.
10. Cut a piece of mirrored mylar 24" × 14". Using spray adhesive, cement the mylar to the tin plate on the side opposite the hems. Trim to size with scissors.

11. Fasten the tin plate to the wood pieces using screws. Start in the center and work your way toward the ends. Two students helping each other will make this step much easier.
12. Cut the 32" long cooker stand from the ⅛" × ¾" band iron. Drill ¼" diameter holes ¾" in from both ends. Bend to shape with a diacro bender.
13. Clean, prime, and paint the cooker stand.
14. Attach the stand to the cooker with 1¼" machine screws and wing nuts.
15. Cut a piece of galvanized sheetmetal 1" × 5" for the focusing sight. Mark the bending lines 1" in on both ends. Lay out and punch the three ⅛" holes.
16. Using wood screws, fasten the focusing sight parallel to the center line of the cooker.
17. Cut a 14" length of ⅛" steel rod. File one end to a rounded point. Bend 1½" of the opposite end to 90 degrees.

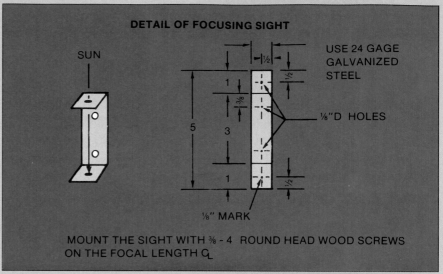

DETAIL OF FOCUSING SIGHT

SUN

USE 24 GAGE
GALVANIZED
STEEL

5

1

3/8

3

1

1/2

1/2

1/2

1/8"D HOLES

1/8" MARK

MOUNT THE SIGHT WITH 3/8 - 4 ROUND HEAD WOOD SCREWS
ON THE FOCAL LENGTH C_L

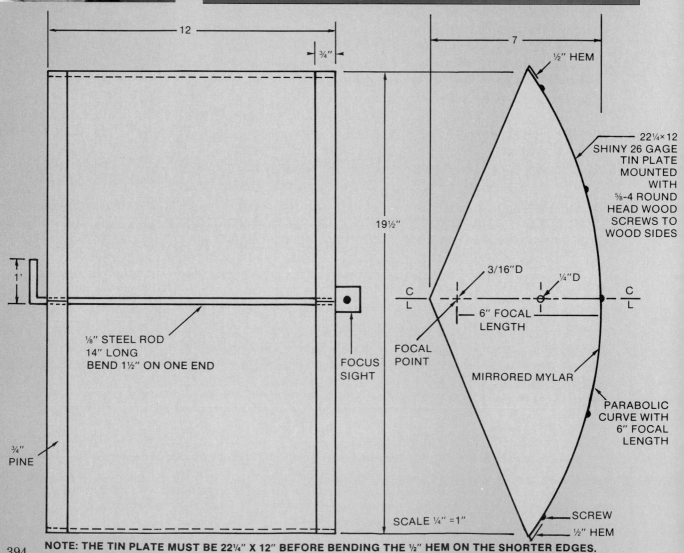

12

3/4"

7

1/2" HEM

19½"

22¼×12
SHINY 26 GAGE
TIN PLATE
MOUNTED
WITH
5/8-4 ROUND
HEAD WOOD
SCREWS TO
WOOD SIDES

1'

3/16"D

1/4"D

C
L

C
L

6" FOCAL
LENGTH

1/8" STEEL ROD
14" LONG
BEND 1½" ON ONE END

FOCUS
SIGHT

FOCAL
POINT

MIRRORED MYLAR

PARABOLIC
CURVE WITH
6" FOCAL
LENGTH

3/4"
PINE

SCREW

1/2" HEM

SCALE ¼" = 1"

394 **NOTE: THE TIN PLATE MUST BE 22¼" X 12" BEFORE BENDING THE ½" HEM ON THE SHORTER EDGES.**

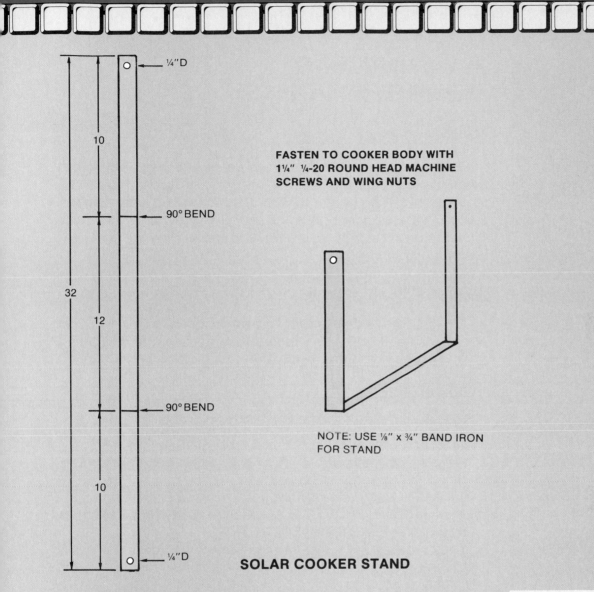

FASTEN TO COOKER BODY WITH 1¼" ¼-20 ROUND HEAD MACHINE SCREWS AND WING NUTS

¼"D

10

90° BEND

32

12

90° BEND

10

¼"D

NOTE: USE ⅛" x ¾" BAND IRON FOR STAND

SOLAR COOKER STAND

Technology Connections

1. What are some advantages of using solar energy? What are some disadvantages?
2. How is the heat from the sun concentrated by the solar cooker? Why must the parabolic reflector be as smooth and reflective as possible?
3. White objects (like marshmallows) do not cook very well on the cooker. Why not?
4. What effect would increasing the size of the reflector have on the time it takes to cook a hot dog? Why?

Science and Math Concepts

▶ The *focal point* is the point to which a lens or mirror converges parallel rays of light.
▶ A *parabolic reflector* is a type of concave mirror that focuses incoming parallel rays of sunlight to a focal point.

A PENNY FOR YOUR THOUGHTS!

Setting the Stage

Energy that is stored is known as *potential energy.* A stretched rubber band has enough potential energy to fly through the air for some distance. A boulder at the top of a hill also has great potential energy. As the boulder rolls down the hill or the rubber band flies through the air, the potential energy becomes *kinetic energy.* Kinetic energy is energy in motion.

Your Challenge

Design a device that can toss a penny into a 2' diameter target placed 15' away. Use only the resources listed below. The device must sit on the ground and have some sort of trigger mechanism.

Procedure

NOTE—Read the entire procedure before you begin.

1. Be sure to wear safety glasses and a lab coat.
2. Make a sketch and plan of your device before beginning to build it.
3. Computer aided drawing (CAD) is recommended after the first sketch is made. If CAD is not available, a full-scale drawing on graph paper is usually helpful.
4. If you have not been told how to use any tool or machine that you need to use, check with your teacher BEFORE going any further.
5. Carefully cut, bend, and assemble your penny-toss device.
6. Be careful! Resources are limited, so use the ones you have wisely.
7. Remember—hot glue is HOT!
8. You may be judged on originality, neatness, and construction techniques as well as accuracy.
9. A competition for the greatest throwing distance may also be held—67'3" is the record so far!

Suggested Resources

Safety glasses and lab apron

3 pieces of any hardwood—¼" × ¼" × 3'

1 piece of sheetmetal—6" × 9" (22–24 gauge)

1 piece of string—3' long

3 paper clips

Rubber bands

Unlimited use of fasteners (nails, screws, rivets, etc.) and shop tools and machines (saws, hammers, files, drills, etc.)

Hot glue gun and glue sticks

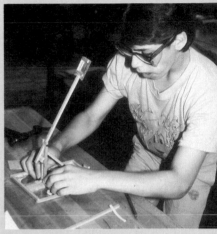

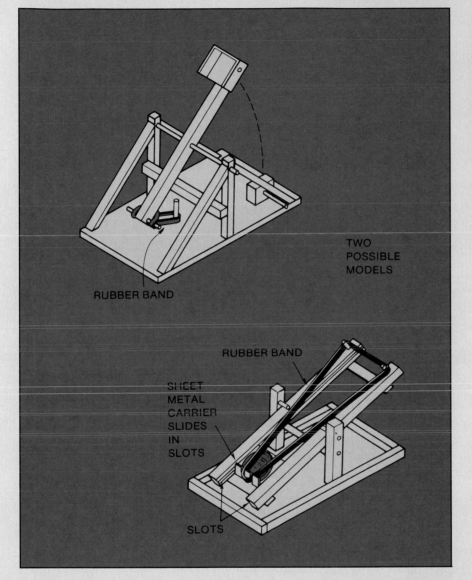

TWO
POSSIBLE
MODELS

RUBBER BAND

RUBBER BAND

SHEET
METAL
CARRIER
SLIDES
IN
SLOTS

SLOTS

Technology Connections

1. Solving technological problems requires skill in using all seven resources. These resources are people, information, materials, tools and machines, energy, capital, and time.
2. Where did your penny-toss device get its energy?
3. What types of devices were used in the middle ages to throw or shoot stones or arrows?
4. What do you think would happen to the throw distance, or range, of the penny-toss device if you used something heavier than a penny?
5. What can you do to increase the range of the penny-toss device?
6. Why does the penny continue to fly after it has left the penny-toss device?

Science and Math Concepts

▶ *Potential energy* can be defined as stored energy or energy that an object has because of its position or condition.
▶ *Kinetic energy* can be defined as energy that matter has because of its motion.
▶ Newton's first law of motion: If an object is at rest, it tends to stay at rest. If it is moving, it tends to keep on moving at the same speed and in the same direction. This is known as *inertia*.

MUSCLE POWER

Setting the Stage

Through our muscles, our bodies have potential and kinetic energy. In this activity you are going to convert some of the stored or potential energy of your muscles into kinetic energy by pedalling a bicycle. Now this seems easy, but let's make it a bit more challenging. Let's test how much muscle power you have by then converting this kinetic energy into electrical energy via a generator! Who can produce the most electricity?

Your Challenge

Using the bicycle/generator set-up provided by your instructor, find out just how much power in the form of electrical output you can produce.

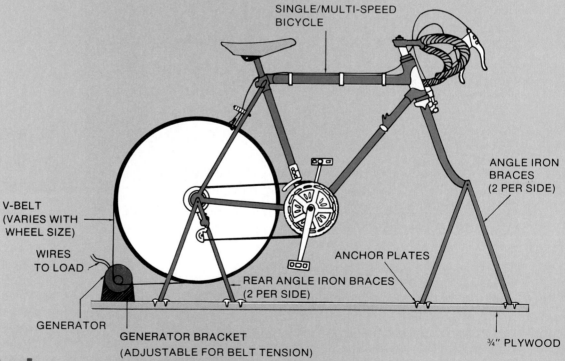

Suggested Resources

Bicycle/generator set-up
Voltmeter (if not built in)
Ammeter (if not built in)
Lights and switches
Lots of muscle power!

Procedure

1. Check the bicycle and make sure it is attached securely to the frame.
2. Check the tension and placement of the belt on the bicycle rim and generator.

3. Make sure all switches to the lights are turned off.
4. Taking turns, each student will mount the bicycle.
5. Begin pedaling and maintain a steady speed.
6. Turn on light number 1, and note the resistance to your pedaling. The light should light up. (Be sure that no one touches any exposed wires or terminals)
7. Have your instructor or another student quickly measure and record your voltage and current output.
8. Keep on pedaling and turn on light number 2. The second light should light up.
9. Have your instructor or another student measure and record your voltage and current. See how bright you can get the lights! Pedal faster!
10. If you still have some energy left, turn on light number 3 and see how bright you can get them all to light. Also take readings of voltage and current at this time.

LAYOUT OF LOAD/TEST BOARD

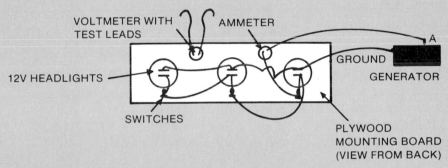

NOTE: Use 12v generator available from local salvage yard. There are different types of generators. Consult your local service center for particular wiring information pertaining to your unit. Lights are wired with switch controls for each to increase load. Plywood mounting board may be attached to ¾" base.

Technology Connections

1. Why did the pedaling get harder after each light was turned on?
2. If a multi-speed bicycle is used what is the effect of gearing on the output of the generator?
3. What would be the mechanical advantage of this system? *Hint:* Measure the circumference of the bicycle wheel and generator pulley. What would happen if we were to change the circumference of either?
4. Who produced the highest voltage and current readings, or the brightest lights? Was he or she the biggest person in class? Do you think that size makes a difference?

Science and Math Concepts

▶ Your muscles have potential (stored) energy which can be converted into kinetic (motion) energy.
▶ Power transmission took place via a belt driven system.
▶ The generator (mechanical energy) produced electrical output that was created by your energy input (human muscle power).
▶ You produced work because the force of your leg muscles moved the pedals of the bicycle.

CHAPTER 14

POWER

MAJOR CONCEPTS

After reading this chapter, you will know that:

- Power is the amount of work done during a given period of time.
- An engine is a machine that uses energy to create mechanical force and motion.
- A transmission is a device that transmits force from one place to another or changes its direction.
- Modern engines change the energy stored in fuel to mechanical force and motion.
- Both external and internal combustion engines change the potential energy stored in a fuel into heat. The heat expands a gas, which moves a piston.
- Newton's third law of motion states that for every action, there is an equal and opposite reaction.
- A generator changes rotary motion into electrical energy.
- An electric motor changes electrical energy into rotary motion.

WHAT IS POWER?

Chapter 13 discussed sources of energy. In industry and in the home, these sources of energy are used to perform work. The machines that use energy sources to do work are called **power systems**. Power systems are found in automobiles, jet airplanes, and the tape drive of a cassette recorder.

In Chapter 13, the words *work* and *energy* were defined. You will remember that both words have precise scientific meanings. The word **power** also has a precise meaning. Power is the amount of work done during a given period of time. If a certain amount of work is done in ten hours, then ten times the power is used to do the same work in one hour. Power measures how quickly work is done.

Power is measured in **horsepower**. One horsepower is equal to 550 foot-pounds per second. It is also equal to 33,000 foot-pounds per minute. Another measure of power is the **watt**. Watts are units of measurement in the metric system, which uses meters rather than feet to measure length. One horsepower is equal to 746 watts.

Power is the amount of work done during a given period of time.

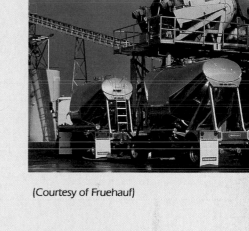

(Courtesy of Fruehauf)

Power is needed to light our cities, to provide us with transportation, to cook our food, and to build buildings. (Courtesy of Perini Corporation)

(Courtesy of New York Power Authority)

Power systems come in many shapes and sizes, and perform many different kinds of jobs. (Courtesy of Lockheed-California Company)

POWER SYSTEMS

An engine is a machine that uses energy to create mechanical force and motion.

Power systems generally have two major parts: an **engine** and a **transmission**. An engine is a machine that uses energy to create mechanical force and motion. Engines are found in automobiles, trucks, jet aircraft, and home appliances. The atomic reactor on a nuclear submarine is an engine.

A transmission, or drive, is a device that transfers force from one place to another or changes its direction. A transmission may also change the force in other ways. It can increase the force, decrease it, or divide it into smaller parts. An automobile has a transmission. Belts and pulleys are transmissions, as are chains and gears. A transmission is chosen to meet the needs of an engine used for a specific job.

A transmission is a device that transmits force from one place to another or changes its direction.

Simple engines were used by people as long ago as 600 B.C. These engines used the energy of animals and the wind. They did jobs such as pumping water, grinding grain, and lifting loads. Later, the energy of running water was used to grind grain and saw logs.

Simple engines such as these must be located near their energy source. An engine that uses the energy of running water has to be near a river or stream. An engine that uses wind has to be located in a windy place. This is a disadvantage. Another disadvantage is that these engines depend on energy that may not always be available.

While they are still in use in some places, these simple engines have generally been replaced by other kinds of engines. Today, engines use the energy in fuels instead of wind or running water. They change the energy stored in fuels into mechanical force and motion. Most of these fuels are portable. They can be moved from place to place. They also contain a great deal of energy. When a portable fuel is used, an engine can go where it is needed.

ENGINES

Engines can do many different jobs. They supply the electricity to light homes. They power automobiles and planes. They carry rockets into space. There are many different kinds of engines, using many different kinds of fuels. Some of these engines are: **external** and **internal combustion engines**, **reaction engines**, **electric motors**, and **nuclear reactors**.

External Combustion Engines

In an external combustion engine, the fuel is burned in one chamber (section of the engine). This heats a liquid or gas in

Wind and running water were the earliest sources of energy for engines.

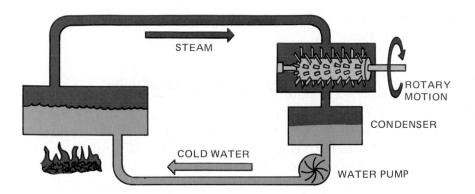

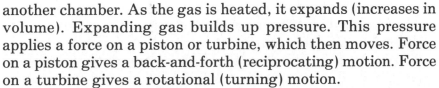

In a steam turbine engine, the force of the expanding steam is converted into rotary motion by the turbine. (Courtesy of New York Power Authority)

Modern engines change the energy stored in fuel to mechanical force and motion.

another chamber. As the gas is heated, it expands (increases in volume). Expanding gas builds up pressure. This pressure applies a force on a piston or turbine, which then moves. Force on a piston gives a back-and-forth (reciprocating) motion. Force on a turbine gives a rotational (turning) motion.

The steam engine is an early example of an external combustion engine. You will find a diagram of a steam engine in Chapter 15. In the steam engine, a fuel such as wood or coal is burned, heating water. The water boils, turning into steam. The steam expands, pushing on a piston. The piston is driven forward, then back. The motion of the piston depends on the position of a slide valve. A flywheel and connecting rod are used to change the movement of the piston into rotary motion. The flywheel builds up **momentum**. That is, once it begins moving, it keeps on turning. This smooths out the rotary motion.

During the Industrial Revolution, steam engines were used to run machines in factories. They were also used to move trains and boats. In a factory, the flywheel of the steam engine was connected by canvas belts to a shaft that ran the length of the factory, high overhead. Where power was needed, a wheel was mounted on the shaft. A canvas belt was put on the wheel. On the factory floor, the machine that had to be run also had a wheel. The other end of the canvas belt was placed on the machine's wheel. The canvas belt was left loose. When the shaft near the roof was turning, the motion was not transmitted to the wheel as long as the canvas belt was loose. When power was needed, the machine operator pulled on a rope connected to an **idler wheel**. This would press on the canvas belt, tightening it. The belt would then turn the shaft of the machine.

In this way, one steam engine could power a large number of different machines. Each machine operator controlled the power going to his or her machine. The canvas belt, overhead shaft, and idler wheels were the transmission, or drive, for the power system.

In railroad locomotives powered by steam engines, the drive wheels of the locomotive are connected to steam pistons. In

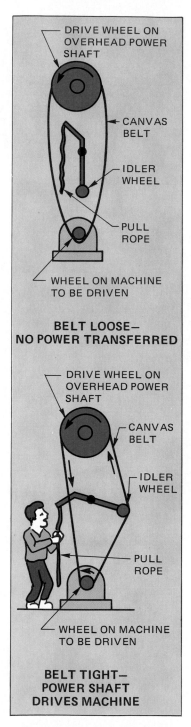

DRIVE WHEEL ON OVERHEAD POWER SHAFT

CANVAS BELT

IDLER WHEEL

PULL ROPE

WHEEL ON MACHINE TO BE DRIVEN

BELT LOOSE— NO POWER TRANSFERRED

DRIVE WHEEL ON OVERHEAD POWER SHAFT

CANVAS BELT

IDLER WHEEL

PULL ROPE

WHEEL ON MACHINE TO BE DRIVEN

BELT TIGHT— POWER SHAFT DRIVES MACHINE

The machine operator in this old factory would turn his machine on by pulling on a rope connected to an idler wheel, tightening the canvas rope.

steamships, the flywheel of the engine is connected to the ship's propeller.

Internal Combustion Engines

In 1876, the first successful internal combustion engine was invented in Germany by Nicolas Otto. It was successful because it was very small. It was also much more efficient than the steam engines of the time. In the internal combustion engine, fuel is burned in a closed chamber. This is the combustion chamber. The burning fuel becomes an expanding gas. As in a steam engine, the gas pushes a piston. The piston is connected by a rod to a crankshaft. The crankshaft changes the piston's reciprocating motion into rotary motion.

The internal combustion engine has come into widespread use. It is used in nearly all cars and trucks. It is also used in some airplanes, many railroad locomotives, and ships. Small

Everywhere we look, there are internal combustion engines.

(Courtesy of American Motors Corporation)

(Courtesy of American Motors Corporation)

(Courtesy of American Motors Corporation)

(Courtesy of Fruehauf)

engines are used in lawn mowers and go-carts. They are used in portable generators, leaf blowers, snow throwers, and outboard engines.

In both internal and external combustion engines, the energy that is used is the energy stored in the molecular bonds of the fuel. When the fuel is burned, the energy is released in the form of heat. The heat expands a gas, causing the piston to move. When the piston or its flywheel makes an object (the **load**) move, work is done. In this way, the engine delivers power.

The two kinds of engines are different in several ways. In an external combustion engine, the fuel is separate from the gas that expands. In the steam engine, the fuel could be wood or coal and the gas is steam from water. Both must be present for a steam engine to work. In the internal combustion engine, the fuel is also the expanding gas. Only the fuel is needed. The fuel used in an internal combustion engine must therefore burn quickly. It must form a gas that expands rapidly, pushing hard on the piston. The fuel used in an external combustion engine burns more slowly. It must only release enough heat to make the water boil.

Another kind of internal combustion engine is the **diesel** engine. It works like the gasoline engine, except that no spark plug is needed to ignite the fuel and air. In a diesel engine, air is compressed by a piston. As air is compressed by the piston, it gets hotter. When the air is very hot, diesel fuel is sprayed into the cylinder. The heated air is hot enough to make the fuel catch fire without a spark. This makes the diesel engine much simpler than a gasoline engine. Diesel engines are used in large trucks, locomotives, and ships. They are known for their low maintenance and long life. On the other hand, they do not have the quick response of gasoline engines.

Both external and internal combustion engines change the potential energy stored in a fuel into heat. The heat expands a gas, which moves a piston.

Diesel engines do not require spark plugs to operate. They provide long life with low maintenance.
(Courtesy of Ford Motor Company)

Energy Conversion in an Automobile Engine

Automobiles use the internal combustion engine. In an automobile engine, gasoline is burned to produce heat. The heat is then changed to mechanical energy. Since there are four steps in this change from heat to mechanical energy, it is called a four-stroke cycle.

During step one (the intake stroke), the piston moves downward. This creates suction. It pulls a mixture of gas and air into the cylinder through an open intake valve.

During step two (the compression stroke), the piston moves up and compresses the fuel. When the piston reaches the top, the spark plug fires. This ignites (starts the burning of) the gas-air fuel mixture. The heat from the explosion makes the gases expand. The expanding gases press on the piston, pushing it down. This third step is called the power stroke. During step four, the piston moves back up. The exhaust valve opens. The burned gases are forced out. The cycle begins again.

Gasoline is a source of potential energy. It burns, and the energy becomes heat energy. The heat energy makes the engine parts move. The moving parts then have kinetic energy.

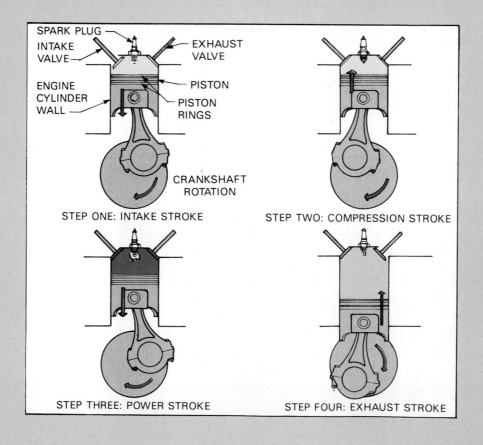

SPARK PLUG
INTAKE VALVE
EXHAUST VALVE
ENGINE CYLINDER WALL
PISTON
PISTON RINGS
CRANKSHAFT ROTATION

STEP ONE: INTAKE STROKE

STEP TWO: COMPRESSION STROKE

STEP THREE: POWER STROKE

STEP FOUR: EXHAUST STROKE

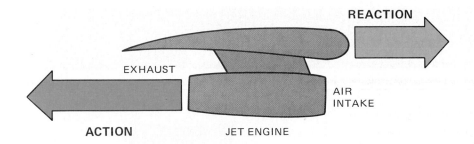

REACTION

EXHAUST

AIR INTAKE

ACTION

JET ENGINE

A jet engine is a good example of Newton's Third Law.

Reaction Engines

Newton's third law explains why reaction engines work. It states that for every action, there is an equal and opposite reaction. You can demonstrate this law for yourself. Lean against a wall and push against it with both hands. The action of pushing against the wall (action) pushes you away from the wall (reaction). **Jet engines** and **rocket engines** are reaction engines. Diagrams of both kinds of engines are shown in Chapter 15.

In a jet engine, air is pushed into a combustion engine by a compressor. There, jet fuel is sprayed into the chamber and mixed with the air. The mixture catches fire and burns rapidly. The burning fuel expands, rushing out the exhaust nozzle. The

Newton's third law of motion states that for every action, there is an equal and opposite reaction.

Rockets do not need outside air to operate. This rocket is launched underwater from a submarine. (Courtesy of Lockheed Horizons)

Jet engines have come into widespread use because they provide large amounts of power and are very reliable. (Courtesy of Boeing Corporation)

The nuclear reactor aboard this submarine supplies all of its power needs, including propulsion and electricity. (Courtesy of Lockheed Horizons)

How Power Plants Make Electricity

Many different kinds of electric power plants are in use today. All use some form of energy to turn the shaft of a generator. A generator changes mechanical rotary motion into electrical energy.

In a generator, a cylinder called a **rotor** spins within a non-moving housing called a **stator**. The rotor has large permanent magnets attached to it. The stator has coils of wire, called windings or **poles**, spaced evenly near the rotor. As the rotor turns, the moving magnets repeatedly change the magnetic field around each of the poles on the stator. As the magnetic field changes around any piece of wire, a voltage is generated. In the generator, the voltage comes from the motion of the magnetic field near the coils of wire.

The generator shaft can be turned by any one of a number of energy sources. In a hydroelectric power plant, the shaft is turned by falling water from a natural waterfall or from a man-made dam. In a coal-fired or oil-fired power plant, heat from the burning coal or oil boils water into steam. The steam presses on a turbine, making it turn. It turns the generator shaft connected to the turbine. In a nuclear plant, heat from a nuclear reaction is used to boil water. This makes the steam that turns the turbine. In the solar plant described in Chapter 13, reflected sunlight heats a container of water, boiling it to produce steam. The steam is used to turn a turbine that is connected to the shaft of a generator. Wind-powered generators use the wind to turn propellers. This motion turns the shaft of the generator.

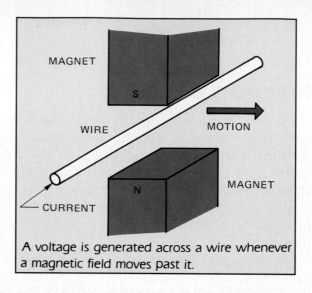

A voltage is generated across a wire whenever a magnetic field moves past it.

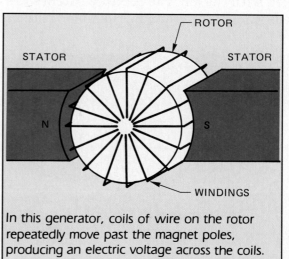

In this generator, coils of wire on the rotor repeatedly move past the magnet poles, producing an electric voltage across the coils.

These turbine generators are driven by steam from a nuclear reactor. (Courtesy of New York Power Authority)

gases rushing out the nozzle (the action) cause the jet to move forward (the reaction). Jet engines are used on airliners and fighter planes for two reasons. First, they can produce large amounts of power. Second, they need less maintenance than other kinds of engines.

Rocket engines work the same way as jet engines. However, rocket engines do not use the air around them to keep the fuel burning. Rocket engines carry their own oxygen supply. It is usually in the form of liquid oxygen. Rocket engines are used for rockets that are going high in the atmosphere where the air is thin, or into space where there is no air.

Nuclear Reactors

Nuclear fission reactions are described in Chapter 13. In such a reaction, huge amounts of energy are released when large atomic nuclei are split. In a reactor, this heat is used to boil water, making steam. The expanding steam is used to turn a turbine. On a ship, the turbine can drive the propeller to move the ship. Steam can also turn a turbine connected to a **generator** that changes rotary motion into electrical energy. In this way, the reactor can move the ship and supply electricity as well.

A generator changes rotary motion into electrical energy.

Nuclear power plants use heat from the fission reaction to boil water. The steam drives a turbine that is connected to a large electrical generator. The electricity generated is sent to users through an electrical power transmission system. The system consists of poles, wires, transformers, and other electrical parts. The system is the same as that used with non-nuclear (coal- or oil-fired) power plants.

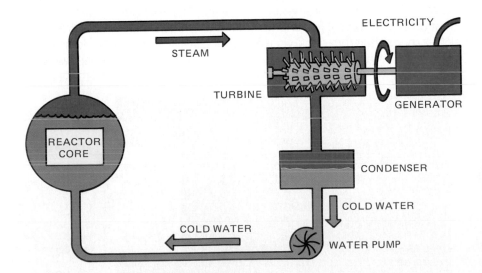

In a nuclear power plant, heat from the nuclear fission reaction boils water, making steam. The steam turns a turbine that is connected to a generator. The generator converts rotary mechanical motion to electrical energy.

Electric Motors

Electric motors are electromagnetic devices. They change electrical energy into rotary motion. The way they work is opposite to the way that generators work. Small motors are found in appliances, toys, and small machines. These are often called **fractional horsepower** motors. That's because they deliver less than one horsepower. Much larger motors are used to move subways, trains, and elevators.

Electric motors are easy to control. They respond right away to the need for power. They do not use energy when they are not working. However, they must either carry their power source with them (as in a battery), or they must be connected by wires to a power source.

An electric motor changes electrical energy into rotary motion.

TRANSMISSIONS

A transmission transmits (carries) force from one place to another or changes its direction. Transmissions are used to carry force and motion from the engine of a power system to the object to be moved (the load). Transmissions can be **mechanical**, **hydraulic** (using a fluid such as water), or **electrical**. They can also use some other means to transmit the force.

Mechanical Power Transmission

Some mechanical transmissions (sometimes called **mechanisms**) use very simple parts. Others combine simple parts into

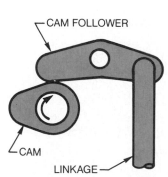
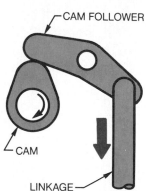
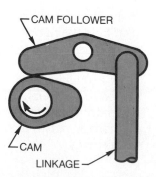

Simple parts with different physical shapes are used alone or in combination to transfer force in a transmission. A cam and cam follower convert rotary motion into reciprocal (up-and-down) motion. Gears change the direction of rotary motion from clockwise to counterclockwise, and make it faster or slower, depending on their sizes. (Photo courtesy of Prime Computers, Inc., Natick, MA, 1984 Annual Report)

GEARS

a complex device. In mechanical transmissions, parts with different shapes are used together to transmit the force. Some of these parts are gears, pulleys, cams, levers, and linkages.

Hydraulic Power Transmission

Hydraulic transmissions use water or other liquids to transmit force. Liquids do not compress (get smaller) under pressure. **Pressure** is the force on a liquid or object divided by the area over which it is applied. Because a liquid does not compress, the pressure is the same everywhere in it. Since the pressure is the same everywhere within a liquid, pushing a piston into a tube of liquid at one end will make the liquid push a second piston out at the other end of the tube. If pistons of different sizes are used at the two ends, the amount of force transmitted to the second piston will be more (or less) than the amount of force exerted by the first piston.

Hydraulic systems are used to transmit force from one place to another through tubing that carries the fluid. They are used in car brake systems to carry the force from your foot on the brake pedal to the brakes on the wheels. They are also used in robots to move their arms from one position to another.

Electrical Power Transmission

Electrical power is transmitted by wires that carry current from the place where it is generated to the places where it will be used. Motors and other electrical equipment can be used to change the electricity into force and motion.

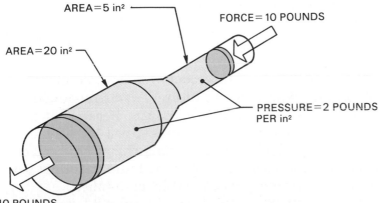

Pressure throughout the liquid is the same because the liquid will not compress. Pistons of different sizes can be used to obtain larger or smaller forces from this kind of transmission.

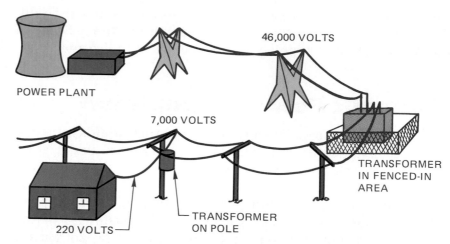

Power transformers at high voltage suffer fewer losses.
(Courtesy of New York Power Authority)

Transformers are used to change ac voltages in an electric power transmission system.

A pole-mounted transformer. Even the "low" voltage used in power transmission, and the power coming into homes, is enough to cause serious injury or death if someone touches it. You should never climb a power pole or go near power lines.
(Courtesy of Allegheny Ludlum Corporation)

Alternating current, or ac, is produced by generators at power plants. As the current is carried over wires from the plant to where it is used, some electrical energy is changed to heat by the resistance in the wires. Electricity changed to heat in this way is lost. It does not reach the user.

Wires carrying high-voltage electricity lose less to heat than low-voltage lines. Therefore, high voltage is sent on wires that carry electricity over long distances. **Transformers** are used to change the high voltage to lower voltage ("step-down") near the place where the electricity is used.

Power transmission lines from several power generating stations or power companies are often joined in a **grid**. In the grid, the high-voltage wires from one power station are joined to the wires from other power stations through a series of switches. A grid is useful when demand is so high that a station or company cannot meet electricity needs. The station or company can then tap into electricity from other stations or companies to supply needed power.

New discoveries in **superconductivity** hold great promise for power transmission in the future. A superconductor is a material that has no electrical resistance. Because of this, there is no loss to heat as electricity flows. Until 1986, superconductivity was only possible in materials that were cooled nearly to **absolute zero**. Absolute zero is the temperature at which molecules stop moving—about −459° Fahrenheit.

In 1986 and 1987, researchers in several laboratories around the world discovered new materials that were superconductors at well above absolute zero. With superconductors that work nearer air temperature, it becomes possible to build better transmission systems. In these systems, electricity is not lost as it flows through wires. Lines that do not lose power will mean less costly electricity.

CONTINUOUS VERSUS INTERMITTENT POWER SYSTEMS

Power systems get their energy from many different sources. An internal combustion engine can run on many different kinds of fuel. The shaft of an electric generator can be turned by falling water, the wind, or steam. It can be turned by energy that is a by-product of another system. For example, it can be turned by a bicycle wheel or by a turbine in the exhaust stream of a jet engine.

Some of these energy sources are continuous. That means that they are nearly always available. Others are intermittent. They are not always available. An internal combustion engine runs as long as fuel gets to it. A wind-driven generator, however, makes electricity only when the wind blows. A hydroelectric plant makes electricity only when there is enough water behind a dam to turn the turbines.

Intermittent power systems sometimes store energy. Then, when the usual energy is not available, the stored energy can

Superconducting wire, tap, and cable can carry electric current with no resistance. Researchers are now developing ways to allow superconductors to function at increasingly higher temperatures. (Courtesy of Intermagnetics General Corporation)

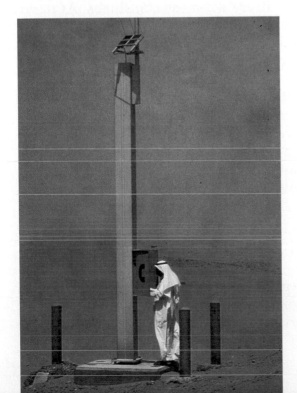

This desert telephone is being powered by solar cells. (Courtesy of Woodfin Camp and Associate/R. Azzi)

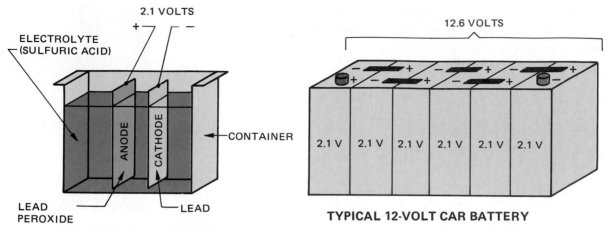

SIMPLE LEAD-ACID BATTERY CELL

TYPICAL 12-VOLT CAR BATTERY

A battery cell provides electric power released in the chemical reaction between the electrodes and the electrolyte. A battery is made by combining cells together.

be used. Sometimes, energy in these systems is stored during a period of light use. Then the stored energy can be used when more power is needed. For example, some hydroelectric plants use power produced at night, when demand is low, to pump water back up behind the dam. The next day, when more electricity is needed, the water is there to produce it.

Another way to store energy in a power system is in batteries. Radio relay stations in remote areas use solar cells for power. The solar cells charge a battery when the sun shines. At night, or during cloudy weather, the solar cells do not produce electricity. During this time, the equipment runs on power from the battery. When the sun shines again, the battery is recharged by the solar cells.

A battery is used to start a car. The battery is then recharged by a generator called an **alternator**. While the engine is running, most of the electric needs of the car are supplied by the alternator. When the engine is not running, or when the alternator cannot produce all the electric power that the car needs, the battery supplies power.

SUMMARY

Machines that use energy sources to provide power to perform work are called power systems. Power is the amount of work done during a given period of time. Power is measured in horsepower or watts.

Power systems generally have two major parts: an engine and a transmission. An engine is a machine that uses energy to create mechanical force and motion. A transmission, or drive, is a device that transfers force from one place to another or changes its direction. A transmission may also change the force by increasing, decreasing it, or dividing it.

Today's engines change the energy found in fuel to mechanical force and motion. Some different engine types are external and internal combustion engines, reaction engines, electric motors, and nuclear reactors.

In an external combustion engine, such as a steam engine, fuel burns in one chamber and water boils in another chamber. The steam from the boiling water expands, pushing a piston forward and back. The reciprocal motion of the piston is changed to continuous rotary motion by a flywheel.

In an internal combustion engine, the fuel is made to explode in a chamber, pushing a piston. The piston is connected to a crankshaft and flywheel, which produce rotary motion. In a gasoline engine, a spark plug is used to ignite the fuel. In a diesel engine, the air is compressed until it is hot enough to ignite the fuel. No spark plug is needed in a diesel engine.

Reaction engines produce motion based on Newton's third law of motion. Newton's third law states that for every action there is an equal and opposite reaction. The jet engine and rocket engine are reaction engines. A jet engine burns jet fuel mixed with air, making a rapidly expanding hot gas. The gas rushing out of the back of the engine pushes the jet forward. A rocket carries its own supply of oxygen to burn the fuel. Rockets are used at high altitudes where the air is thin or in space where there is no air.

In a nuclear reactor, the heat energy released in a nuclear fission reaction is used to boil water and make steam. The steam can then be used to turn a turbine that can move a ship or turn an electric generator.

(Courtesy of United States Department of Energy)

A generator is a machine that changes rotary motion into electrical energy. An electric motor is a machine that changes electrical energy into rotary motion.

Mechanical transmissions use simple parts such as gears, cams, levers, pulleys, and linkages connected together to transmit force from one place to another. Hydraulic transmissions use water or other liquids to transmit force.

Electrical power is transmitted over wires attached to poles or buried underground. To keep losses low, power is sent long distances at high voltage. Superconductivity holds great promise for reducing losses in electric tranmission. Using superconducting wires will lower power costs. Near the place where electricity is used, the voltage is reduced by devices called transformers. Even the "low" voltage entering a home is dangerous. You should never touch it in any way.

In some power systems, part of the power that is generated is stored for use when the energy source is unavailable. In other systems, part of the power is used to replenish the energy source that supplies it. Batteries are often used to store electric energy. Batteries change chemical energy into electrical energy.

REVIEW QUESTIONS

1. What is power? How is it different from work?
2. Name the two major parts of a power system. Describe what each part does.
3. List four different kinds of engines.
4. Describe the difference between an internal combustion engine and an external combustion engine. Give one example of each.
5. How is a gasoline engine different from a diesel engine?
6. Describe the steps by which a four-stroke engine turns the energy in fuel into the mechanical energy that moves an automobile.
7. State Newton's third law of motion. How is the third law related to reaction engines such as rocket and jet engines?
8. What is an electric motor? List four devices that contain an electric motor.
9. Tell how a nuclear power plant produces electricity.
10. Why is it necessary to send electric power at high voltage when it is sent over long distances?
11. Why would a superconductor that works at high temperatures be useful in an electric power transmission system?
12. Why is water sometimes pumped back up to the other side of a dam in a hydroelectric plant?
13. What is a battery? How does it work?

KEY WORDS

Absolute zero	Four-stroke cycle	Jet engine	Rocket engine
Alternating current	Fractional horsepower	Load	Rotor
Battery	Generator	Momentum	Stator
Diesel engine	Horsepower	Nuclear reactor	Superconductor
Electric motor	Hydraulic	Pneumatic	Transformer
Engine	Idler wheel	Poles	Transmission
External combustion engine	Internal combustion engine	Power	Two-stroke cycle
		Power system	Watt
		Pressure	
		Reaction engine	

SEE YOUR TEACHER FOR THE CROSSTECH PUZZLE

TROUBLESHOOTING

Setting the Stage

You've tried all of the deep pools in the river and have two good trout to bring home after an all-day excursion. Your fishing partner pulls twice on the starter, and off you go. Within a couple of minutes, however, the engine dies, then spurts back to life. It dies again, spurts, and finally stops altogether. What can be wrong with the engine?

Your Challenge

Engines do not run because of problems in one of three subsystems. Three subsystems have to be present for an internal combustion engine to operate: ignition, compression, and fuel.

1. You will be given three identical 0.049 glow-plug engines. Each engine will have a mechanical problem and will not run. Isolate the problem by identifying in which of the three subsystems the problem could exist.
2. Demonstrate how to check ignition, compression, and fuel on a two-cycle or four-cycle engine used for transportation or recreation.

Suggested Resources

3—0.049 glow-plug engines mounted on wooden test blocks

Small two- or four-cycle engine

Prime bottle for 0.049 engine (acrylic glue bottle)

Pump can for priming two- or four-cycle engine

Compression gauge

Spark checker or used spark plug

Gloves for starting and adjusting 0.049 engine

Safety glasses

Procedure

Glow-plug Engine

Here is how to check each subsystem. You then have to decide which subsystem or subsystems are faulty.

1. Ignition
   a. Look for the glow of the plug or listen for burning fuel with the cylinder open.
   b. Unscrew the glow plug and hook it to the battery. The plug element should have a dull red glow.
2. Compression
   a. Loosen the glow plug two turns.
   b. Spin the propeller.
   c. Now tighten the glow plug and spin the propeller. It should be harder to spin the propeller with the plug tight.
3. Fuel
   a. Place a small amount of fuel directly on the top of the piston. Spin the propeller and the engine should fire. If it does, richen the fuel/air mixture by turning the needle valve counterclockwise.

b. You may have too much fuel. To check for this, remove the glow plug and hook it to a battery. If fuel has to be burned off before the plug glows, too much fuel is present. Screw the needle valve clockwise for a leaner mixture. Another method is to blow into the cylinder when the cylinder is open. If the engine fires every time you do this, turn the needle valve clockwise (leaner).

Two- or Four-cycle Engine

Now put this knowledge to use on a two- or four-cycle engine used for transportation or recreational vehicles.

1. Ignition
Ignition is checked by grounding a plug to the engine block. (Make sure no fuel is present.) This plug has to have the electrode bent for a 1/4" gap for magneto ignition. Up to 7/16" gap is used on some electronic ignition systems. You may have to design and construct your own spark checker for these systems.
2. Compression
Place a compression gauge in the spark plug hole. A reading of 70–80 lbs. minimum should be in each cylinder. Readings in each cylinder should be similar.
3. Fuel
a. You can easily bypass the complete fuel system by using a metal pump can and dispensing a small amount of fuel directly into the air intake for the carburetor. If the engine runs for only a few seconds, you have a fuel problem.
b. Check for too much fuel by unscrewing the spark plug and examining the plug. If the plug is wet with fuel, there is too much fuel present or you may have problems with one of the other systems.

Technology Connections

1. By practicing on an engine, using the preceding suggestions, you will be able to attribute the engine problem to one of the three subsystems (fuel, compression, and ignition). These are the only systems that have to function to operate the engine for two minutes. Many other subsystems are present to maintain engine operation (for example, lubrication, cooling, transmission, electrical, charging).
2. Name and describe three non-fossil-fuel-burning power systems that could be used for transportation vehicles.

Science and Math Concepts

▶ For combustion to take place, three elements have to be present: fuel, air, and some form of ignition.
▶ Eighteen thousand volts are required to produce a spark 1/4" long in dry air at atmospheric pressure.
▶ Heat engines obtain their name from the basic principle on which they operate. They convert heat energy into usable power in the form of motion. Heat engines include all types of steam, gasoline, diesel, jet, and rocket engines.

MY HERO!

Setting the Stage

Location: aboard the crippled starcraft Delphi. Captain's log shows stardate 2011—emergency entry number 3.

As a result of gyroscopic failure, we have lost all electrical power aboard our ship. The power failure has caused a release of potentially explosive hydrogen gas into the ship's atmosphere.

To regain electrical power we must find a way to start the gyroscope spinning again without igniting the hydrogen gas. All available Delphi crew members have been given this most urgent problem to solve.

Your Challenge

Find a way to restart the gyroscope before a spark blows up the ship.

Procedure

1. Be sure to wear safety glasses and a lab coat.
2. Remove the cover from the film container.
3. Locate the center of the cover. Drill a small hole just large enough to push the end of the swivel through.
4. Hot glue the swivel in place on the inside. Take care to seal the hole completely. Make sure the swivel and top rotate freely.
5. Tie the piece of string to the free end of the swivel.
6. Cut the straw in half.
7. Drill two holes in the film container directly opposite each other and slightly smaller than the straw.
8. Curve the straw as close to a C shape as possible without kinking or closing off the tube.
9. Insert the curved straw about ¼" into the holes and hot glue in place. Again, take care to seal the hole completely.
10. Place about 1 teaspoon of baking powder in the container.
11. Hold the container in a deep sink, bucket, or tub.
12. Fill the rest of the container with warm water and immediately snap the cover tightly in place.
13. Hold the string a few inches above the swivel in one hand. Rapidly shake the container with the other hand and then let it hang free.
14. Be sure to keep the container in the sink or tub.
15. Remember . . . you may have saved the starship from disaster, but you still have to clean up the mess you made!

Suggested Resources

Safety glasses and lab apron
Plastic 35 mm film container
Small diameter plastic cocktail straw (the skinnier the better)
Small swivel
1 piece of string—15" long
Drill and small drill bits
Hot glue gun and glue stick
Baking *powder* (NOT baking SODA)
Cup of water
Teaspoon
A DEEP sink, bucket, fishtank, or washtub

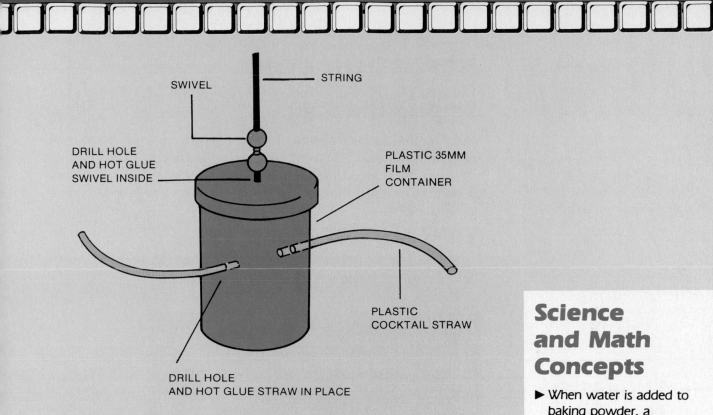

STRING

SWIVEL

DRILL HOLE
AND HOT GLUE
SWIVEL INSIDE

PLASTIC 35MM
FILM
CONTAINER

PLASTIC
COCKTAIL STRAW

DRILL HOLE
AND HOT GLUE STRAW IN PLACE

Technology Connections

1. The spinning cylinder you made is based on Hero's Engine, invented in the second century B.C. by Hero of Alexandria. The original engine used steam as the power source.
2. Where did your Hero's Engine get its power? What type of materials processing would this be considered?
3. Why did the cylinder continue to spin even after the fuel was used up?
4. If your engine was discharged in a weightless environment with no friction or air resistance, what would happen?
5. How is a jet plane similar to Hero's Engine?
6. People process materials by forming, separating, combining and conditioning. We used the separating and combining processes to make Hero's Engine. Can you explain where?
7. Glues and adhesives are used in combining processes. What process would nails and screws be used for? Scissors? Saws?

Science and Math Concepts

▶ When water is added to baking powder, a chemical reaction releases carbon dioxide gas (CO_2).
▶ Newton's third law of motion: When one object exerts a force on a second object, the second object exerts an equal and opposite force upon the first. (The cylinder and straws are one mass, and the exhaust gases are the other mass.)
▶ Remember Newton's first law of motion: If an object is at rest, it tends to stay at rest. If it is moving, it tends to keep on moving at the same speed and in the same direction. This is called *inertia.*
▶ Resistance to motion caused by one surface rubbing against another is called *friction.*

REPULSION COIL

Setting the Stage

All motors use a magnetic field to convert electrical energy into mechanical energy. Electrical inductance and electromagnetism are used by transformers to increase or decrease voltages. Someday, super-conducting magnets will be used to lift and propel high-speed trains.

Your Challenge

Build an electromagnetic repulsion coil that can lift an aluminum ring into the air using low-voltage alternating current (AC).

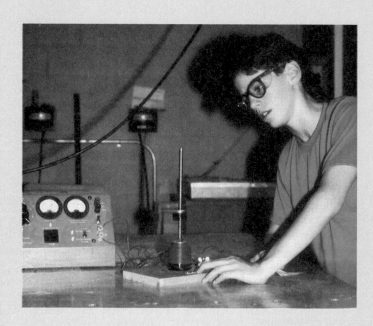

Suggested Resources

Safety glasses and lab aprons
Magnet wire (copper, enameled)—#22
Soft iron rod—⅜" diameter, 12" long
Aluminum washer—½" inside diameter
Fiber or plastic tube
Soft iron wire—#22
Bell wire—#20
3 soft iron washers—⅜"
Spring brass or momentary contact switch
Soldering iron and solder
Threading die (⅜"-16 NC)
2 soft iron nuts—⅜"-16 NC
Wood base—¾" thick
Rubber, plastic, or wood legs for the base—½" high
Black electrical tape
Round head wood screws—½" #4
Assorted machines, supplies, and tools as needed

Procedure

1. Be sure to wear safety glasses and a lab coat.
2. Cut a 6" × 9" wood base from ¾" stock. Sand and finish as desired. Install ½" high legs (rubber stick-ons work fine)
3. Drill a ⅜" hole in the center of the base.
4. Cut a 12" long ⅜" soft iron rod with a hacksaw. File both ends.
5. Thread 4½" of one end of the ⅜" rod with a ⅜"-16 NC die. (Use cutting oil and take your time.)
6. Cut 2¼" lengths of the soft iron wire.
7. Thread a ⅜"-16 nut all the way up on the ⅜" rod.
8. Cut a 2½" long piece from the fiber or plastic tube.
9. Slide a ⅜" washer over the threaded end of the rod.
10. Slide the fiber tube on next.

11. Fill the gap between the fiber tube and the rod with the 2¼"
    pieces of soft iron wire.
12. Slide the second ⅜" washer on next. (Careful . . . don't lose the
    wires!)
13. Insert the rod through the hole in the base and secure with a ⅜"
    washer and nut.
14. Wind at least 3 layers of #22 magnet wire over the fiber tube.
    (Be neat.)
15. Make and install the switch from the spring brass or use a
    commercial momentary contact switch (springs open automatically
    when you let go).
16. Hook up all the components with bell wire.
17. Place the ½" aluminum washer over the soft iron rod.
18. Apply 6 volts AC to the circuit.

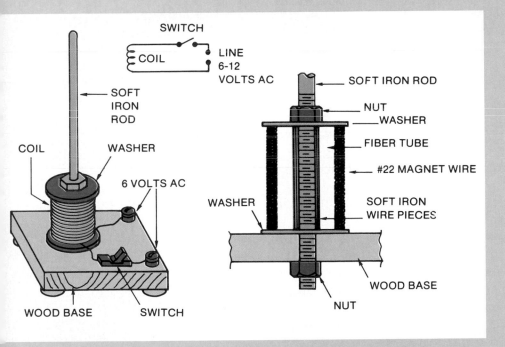

Technology Connections

1. Electronic circuits are made up of *components*. Each component
   has a specific function in the circuit. What is the function of the
   switch in the repulsion coil circuit? The coil?
2. Why is it important to use low voltage (6–12 volts AC) in this
   circuit? What will happen if too much voltage is applied?
3. Why can this device be used on *alternating current (AC)* only?
4. What is *induction*?

Science and Math Concepts

▶ When electricity flows
  through a wire, a
  magnetic field builds up
  around the wire. A *coil*
  of wire concentrates the
  magnetic field. A metallic
  object brought near the
  coil may have an electric
  current *induced* into it
  even without direct
  physical contact.
▶ When *alternating
  current* (AC) passes
  through a coil, the
  magnetic lines of force
  around the coil expand
  and collapse very
  quickly.
▶ A *transformer* uses two
  coils close to each other
  to increase or decrease
  AC voltages. The primary
  coil of a transformer
  induces an electric
  current into the
  secondary coil. A
  transformer will not
  work with *direct current
  (DC)*.

CHAPTER 15

TRANSPORTATION

MAJOR CONCEPTS

After reading this chapter, you will know that:

- A transportation system is used to move people or goods from one location to another.
- Modern transportation systems have helped to make countries interdependent.
- The availability of rapid, efficient transportation systems has changed the way we live.
- Transportation systems convert energy into motion.
- Steam was the first important source of mechanical power for transportation systems.
- Modern transportation systems often use internal combustion engines or electric motors.
- Intermodal transportation systems make optimum use of each type of transportation used in the system.
- Most transportation systems use vehicles to carry people or goods, but some systems do not use any vehicles.

Today's traveler can travel around the world in eighty hours with plenty of time left over to sightsee along the way. (Courtesy of British Airways)

EXPLORING OUR WORLD

Humans have needed transportation since they first walked the earth. Prehistoric people traveled far in search of food and raw materials, which they had to carry home.

As farming developed, people found ways to move food from fields to storage places. Sometimes a sled was used, pulled by an ox or other animal or by people. Around 3500 B.C., the wheel was invented in Sumeria, in the Middle East. The wheel made it possible to move larger loads.

Transportation also became a means of communication. People on horses or horse-drawn wagons carried messages to and from distant places.

The early Phoenecians and Scandinavians traveled by boat, exploring new lands and trading with other people. A great age of exploration began in the late 1400s. European sailors explored and mapped much of the world.

The steam engine came into use during the Industrial Revolution of the 1700s and 1800s. Steam-powered boats and trains moved quickly across great distances. In his novel *Around the World in Eighty Days*, Jules Verne described a journey around the world in the 1800s. Flying in the *Concorde* supersonic transport (SST), today's traveler can make the same trip in much less than eighty hours.

Today we can travel faster and farther than ever before. We are exploring our solar system, as well as the ocean depths. With new transportation technology, we are at the start of an exciting new age of exploration.

A transportation system is used to move people or goods from one location to another.

The first fast forms of transportation were used to communicate with people in faraway places. (Courtesy of The Museum of Modern Art/Film Stills Archive, W. 53rd Street, New York City)

New types of vehicles enable us to explore the harsh environments of space and the deep sea.
(Courtesy of NASA)   (Courtesy of Lockheed Corp.)

THE WORLD IS A GLOBAL VILLAGE

Modern transportation systems have helped to make countries interdependent.

Fast, cheap transportation has brought us closer to other countries. We can eat foods from other countries and buy goods made in other countries. We can sell our food and manufactured products to people in other countries. The economies of countries have come to depend on each other.

Transportation technology has made **tourism** possible. People are able to travel to distant places. Tourism promotes goodwill and understanding between people of different cultures and customs.

CREATING A NEW STYLE OF LIVING

In 1900, the average U.S. citizen traveled 400 miles a year. In 1986, the average U.S. driver traveled 12,000 miles each year. Once people lived close to their work. Now, many must **commute**, or travel on a regular basis, to get to work.

The availability of rapid, efficient transportation systems has changed the way we live.

Suburbs, or outlying areas around cities, have grown up. Many people commute to and from the suburbs each day. Some travel more than four hours a day, by train or car. Car pools, in which several people ride together and take turns driving, save money and wear-and-tear.

RESOURCES FOR TRANSPORTATION SYSTEMS

The way resources are used makes one kind of technological system different from another. This is true in the case of transportation systems.

Energy

Transportation systems convert energy into motion.

Early forms of transportation used wind, animal, water, and human power. Energy was changed to motion using devices such as sails and wheels.

Many of today's transportation systems are based on **vehicles**, containers that hold the people or goods being moved. Vehicles generally use stored energy. Automobiles, for example, use energy stored in chemical form such as gasoline. Subways and some trains use electricity. The part of the system that changes energy to motion is called the **engine** or motor.

Electric motors change electricity into rotary motion. The shaft of the motor is connected through gears or belts to the wheels of the vehicle. As the motor turns, the wheels turn and the vehicle moves. The gears or belts that connect the motor to the wheels are called the **transmission** or **drive** (sometimes called the drive train).

The advantages of electric motors are that they are small, easy to control, and don't pollute the area around the vehicle. A disadvantage is that getting electricity to the motor may be difficult. It must be supplied along the vehicle's path by wires or on a "third rail," or carried on the vehicle in the form of batteries. These batteries are heavy and must be recharged fairly often.

Gasoline is one of the most efficient ways to supply energy. It burns easily, producing a large amount of energy. It can be stored and moved in tanks. Because it burns easily, it must be used carefully. Gasoline engines are called **internal combustion engines** because the burning of the gasoline takes place within the engine.

Gasoline is made from oil that has been pumped from the ground. Diesel fuel, home heating oil, propane, and jet fuel are other oil-based fuels. Airplanes, trucks, and ships use oil-based fuels.

Many car manufacturers are now experimenting with cars powered by electricity. (Courtesy General Motors Corporation)

People

Transportation systems are used by people. They are also designed, built, and operated by people. Motormen drive trains and pilots fly jets. People handle the business of transportation, too. They sell the tickets, make the schedules, clean and maintain the vehicles, and buy supplies.

Many trains use electric power that comes from overhead wires. (Photo by Jeremy Plant)

Many kinds of vehicles must carry enough fuel with them to last the entire trip. (Courtesy of U.S. Navy)

Information

Designing and operating transportation systems requires information of many kinds. People who drive cars, fly planes, or sail ships need information to guide them. Information about location, course or route, speed, and vehicle operation is important for a safe and rapid trip. Many tools are used to provide such information. These include road signs, radar, two-way radios, and on-board computers.

Materials

Transportation systems use not only vehicles but sometimes roadways, as well. Tracks or canals are roadways. No roadways are used with airplanes or ships, but airports and seaports are needed for loading and unloading. The materials used for vehicles and roadways depend on the transportation system.

Airplanes must be made of strong, lightweight materials. Aluminum and titanium are often used. New **composite** (see Chapter 8) materials are also being used. Composites are fibers mixed with epoxies. They are stronger than metals. Cars and trucks are made of metal, usually steel. Other lightweight materials are used in cars and trucks to save on fuel. They include aluminum, plastics, fiberglass, and composites.

Materials such as concrete and asphalt are used to build roads. Roads must be strong enough to hold heavy weights, such as trailer trucks, without breaking. They must withstand heavy use and changes in temperature.

This advanced plane must use composites that are stronger than metal to withstand stresses during flight. (Courtesy of Grumman Corp.)

Tools and Machines

The tools and machines used in transportation systems are more than just the vehicles. They include support equipment such as automatic controllers and maintenance equipment. For example, test equipment is used to check systems on airplanes and automobiles.

Capital

A large amount of capital is needed for transportation systems. Building ports, roadways, and vehicles is costly. Maintenance is important, especially in systems that carry people, and it costs money, too.

Private companies most often pay for vehicles. Government or public agencies pay for roadways and ports, for two reasons.

Tools and machines include the support equipment for vehicles. (Courtesy of International Business Machines Corp.)

First, few companies can afford the huge costs of building a highway or an airport. Second, these facilities are shared by many. Roadways are built and maintained using money collected through taxes or tolls.

Time

In a transportation system, travel time depends on distance and technology. Time can be the few seconds it takes to move parts from one work station to the next on an assembly line. It can be the weeks it takes for a ship to cross the ocean. It can be the years required to travel from our planet to Neptune.

Mass transit systems move thousands of people on a regular basis. Time is important to the smooth operation of these systems. Vehicles must move on a set schedule. Schedules must be kept so that people traveling one route arrive on time to transfer to a train, a plane, or a bus on another route.

TYPES OF TRANSPORTATION SYSTEMS

Transportation systems are alike in some ways and different in others. Most use vehicles to carry people or goods. But some, such as conveyor belts or pipelines that carry oil, do not. Most systems are made up of subsystems. For example, an automo-

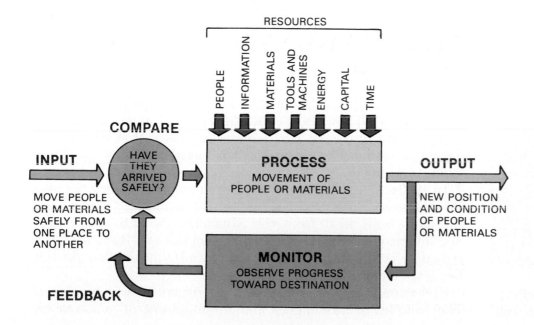

Like all other systems, transportation systems can be represented with system diagrams.

In the Malagasy Republic, people-powered push-pushes provide transportation. (Photo by Michael Hacker)

Many obstacles had to be overcome to build the railroad through the rugged west. (Courtesy of Oregon Historical Society)

Steam was the first important source of mechanical power for transportation systems.

A steam-powered logging engine. (Photo by Jeremy Plant)

bile has a steering subsystem and a suspension subsystem, among others.

Subsystems can be put together in different ways to form different transportation systems. A diesel engine can be put in a floating hull to make a boat, a marine transportation system. It can also be placed in a vehicle with wheels to make a truck, a land transportation system. One way to classify systems is by the environment in which they move (land, sea, air, space).

LAND TRANSPORTATION

The earliest form of land transportation, after walking, was riding on animals. Next, animals were used to drag heavy loads on sleds. The wheel made it possible to pull heavier loads more quickly. Some cultures today still use animals and people for most transportation needs.

Steam-Powered Vehicles

When the **steam engine** was invented, people tried to use it to move vehicles. In 1769, Nicolas-Joseph Cugnot built the first steam-engine-powered vehicle in France. It was a tractor that moved at about 2 miles an hour. Its weight and steering system made it hard to control. It crashed into a wall. Cugnot's tractor idea failed to catch on. But steam engines were found useful in powering boats and trains.

The first **railroad** to use steam engines was opened in England in 1830. The engine could pull the train at up to 30 miles an hour. Both people and cargo (freight) were carried. Railroads were started in the U.S. about the same time. They quickly came into widespread use.

After the Civil War, several inventions made railroads much safer. One was the air brake, invented by George Westinghouse. All the cars on the train could be stopped at the same time using the air brake. In 1893 a law was passed that required its use on all trains. The air brake is still used on trains, as well as trucks and buses.

In 1862, construction was started on a railroad track between the Missouri River and Sacramento, California. One railroad company built west from the Missouri, the other east from Sacramento. In 1869, they met in Promontory, Utah. The eastern and western parts of the country were joined. This aided in the settlement of the American West.

Steam engines were improved. Better track was developed. The comfort of passengers and maintenance of systems im-

Steam Engines

Steam engines are **external combustion engines**. Fuel, such as wood, coal, or oil, is burned in an open chamber. A boiler of water is heated, creating steam pressure, which is used to push a pis-ton. The piston's reciprocating (back-and forth) motion is changed to rotary motion, which is transferred to wheels. Steam locomotives must stop often to take on supplies of water and fuel.

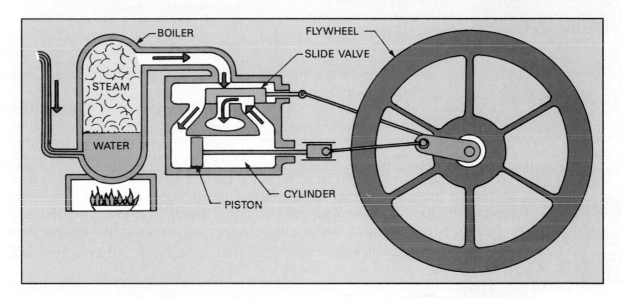

proved. By the late 1800s, trains could travel at speeds of 100 miles per hour. Special trains such as the Orient Express (London-Istanbul) let people travel in luxury.

Gasoline-Powered Vehicles

In 1876, the internal combustion engine was invented by Nickolas Otto of Germany. It was lightweight and could be used to power a carriage. Such a carriage could travel many miles on a small amount of gasoline. "Automobiles" quickly became popular. (See Chapter 14 for a description of how the internal combustion engine works.)

Because of its small size and greater fuel economy, this engine replaced steam engines in many vehicles. The Stanley Steamer was a steam-powered car that could go very fast. (One set a world's record of 122 miles per hour in 1906.) But it needed a fresh supply of water every fifty miles. It was soon replaced by

Cutaway view of
an automobile.
(Courtesy of Saab)

Henry Ford at the wheel of
his first car. (Courtesy of Ford
Motor Company)

A modern luxury car. (Courtesy of Ford Motor Company)

automobiles using internal combustion engines. By 1920, steamers were no longer being built.

The automobile was improved and improved again. Many companies were formed. They built many kinds of automobiles, from sporty "raceabouts" to family sedans. American families soon found it necessary to have an automobile. By the 1920s, millions had been sold. Since then, many companies have gone out of business. Automobiles built by some of them—the Pierce-Arrow, Duesenberg, Stutz, and Franklin—can now be seen only in museums. Only a few large companies build automobiles today. The automobile industry is America's largest industry.

Diesel-Powered Vehicles

A modern truck used to
deliver large amounts of
freight economically. (Courtesy
of Fruehauf)

The **diesel** engine also came into use during the early 1900s. A diesel engine is like a gasoline engine, except that it has no spark plugs. In a regular gasoline engine, spark plugs cause the fuel and air mixture to explode, providing power to the engine. In a diesel engine, this job is done by a piston that squeezes the mixture more tightly. When a gas is squeezed, or put under pressure, it gets hotter. With enough pressure, it will explode by itself.

Diesel engines are good for carrying heavy loads at a constant speed. They need less maintenance. A vehicle gets good mileage and lasts a long time. Diesel engines are used in cars, trucks, buses, locomotives, and construction machinery.

Modern diesel engines.
(Photo by Jeremy Plant)

The railroads quickly changed over from steam engines to diesel engines after World War II. Railroad companies liked the better mileage, cleaner burning, and lower maintenance of diesel engines. In 1949, the last steam locomotive built for regular service was delivered. A few hundred steam locomotives remain in the U.S. Most are only on display, but a few are used as excursion trains and tourist attractions.

This electric-powered subway runs both underground and above ground in San Francisco, California. (Courtesy of Bay Area Rapid Transit District)

The electric-powered Japanese "Bullet Train" provides passenger service at 130 miles per hour. (Courtesy of Dave Bartruff)

Electric Vehicles

Electricity was used to power trains and cars almost as early as steam engines were. An electric car was first run in 1839. It used batteries to store energy and electric motors to turn the wheels. Electric cars ran very well, but their batteries had to be recharged before they could go far. The same is true today, although batteries have improved. With further advances in battery technology, it is likely that electric cars will come into general use.

Vehicles powered by electricity from overhead lines or a third rail are in wide use. Electric buses or trolleys running on overhead lines were common in cities. Much of the nation's railroad track is electrified, especially in cities, where clean electric engines are preferred. Most city subways are powered by electricity.

Modern transportation systems often use internal combustion engines or electric motors.

WATER TRANSPORTATION

People have always traveled on streams, rivers, lakes, and oceans. Large cities are often found on natural harbors because water makes travel and trade easier. Different forms of energy have been used to move boats throughout history.

Use of Natural Resources

At first, human muscle powered boats. With poles, paddles, and oars, people moved small boats on trips close to shore. They soon learned how to use the wind to move their boats. The ancient Egyptians, Phoenecians, and Romans had ships with dozens of rowers as well as sails.

With sails, people could travel farther. They began to explore. They found new trade routes, and people to trade with. The ancient Phoenecians, on the Mediterranean, traded with people of Great Britain. The Romans traded with people in the Far East. Early Scandinavian explorers may have been the first

Sailing ships explored and traded with all parts of the world. (Courtesy of the U.S. Navy)

Europeans to visit North America. From the 1400s through the 1800s, Portuguese, Spanish, English, and French sailors explored widely. Their two- and three-masted sailing ships carried enough supplies for long trips. North and South America, Africa, and many Pacific islands were explored, mapped, and

What Makes a Boat Float?

Early boats were made of wood. Today, boats are made of many different materials, including steel, fiberglass, and cement. A solid piece of most of these materials would sink, but boats made of them float. Why?

A boat floats for a reason stated as Archimedes' Principle. That is, an object placed in water (or any fluid) is pushed upward by a force equal to the weight of the water displaced (pushed aside) by the object. The object has **buoyancy**. Buoyancy makes things feel lighter under water than they are in air.

For example, a 32-pound piece of metal in the form of an open box displaces a cubic foot of water. Water weighs 64 pounds per cubic foot. The water pushes up on the box with 64 pounds of force. The box pushes down with only 32 pounds, so it floats.

A solid metal block weighing 32 pounds takes up only ⅛ of a cubic foot. That's 8 pounds of water. The water pushes up with 8 pounds of force, and the block pushes down with 32 pounds. The block sinks.

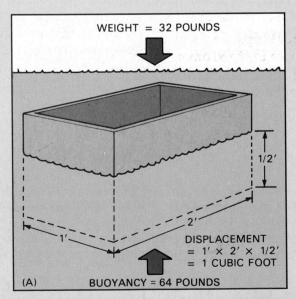

WEIGHT = 32 POUNDS

1/2′

2′

1′

DISPLACEMENT
= 1′ × 2′ × 1/2′
= 1 CUBIC FOOT

(A)   BUOYANCY = 64 POUNDS

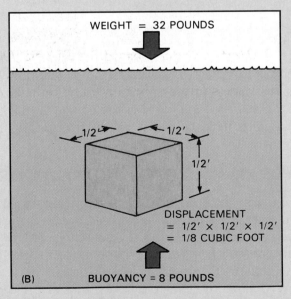

WEIGHT = 32 POUNDS

1/2′   1/2′

1/2′

DISPLACEMENT
= 1/2′ × 1/2′ × 1/2′
= 1/8 CUBIC FOOT

(B)   BUOYANCY = 8 POUNDS

Buoyancy equals the weight of the water that is displaced by an object.
(A) A box floats in water. (B) A solid piece of metal weighing the same as
the box sinks in water.

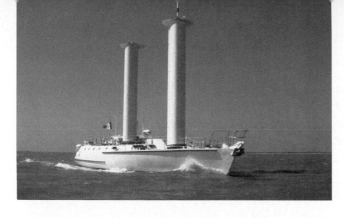

The use of wind power in a modern ship is demonstrated by the *Alcyone*, built by famed ocean researcher Jacques Cousteau. (Photo courtesy of The Cousteau Society, a member-supported environmental organization)

settled. Throughout this time, water travel was powered by natural resources (human, animal, and wind).

Steam-Powered Ships

In 1807, Robert Fulton built a ship powered by steam. The *Clermont* carried people and cargo between New York City and Albany, N.Y. It was the first steam-powered boat to be used successfully. The engine pushed a paddle wheel that pushed against the water, moving the boat.

More steamship designs followed. Some used paddle wheels on the sides, some on the back, and some used screw propellers. Some used sails, as well. They could sail when the wind was blowing, and stay underway when it died. Sails were used less and less as ocean-going ships grew much larger, carrying many passengers.

Modern Ships

Better hull design and engines made for faster ships. In 1952, the S.S. *United States* crossed the Atlantic Ocean in three days, ten hours, and forty minutes. But air travel, taking a matter of hours for the same trip, was even faster. Fewer passenger ships were built. Almost all of the great ocean liners have disappeared, but smaller cruise ships are still popular.

However, ships still carry most intercontinental freight. Tankers carry crude oil. Freighters carry everything from automo-

While other passenger ship travel has declined, cruise ships still remain popular, such as Cunard's flagship, *Queen Elizabeth 2.* (Courtesy of Cunard)

Large tankers like this one carry oil from the producing sites to user countries. (Courtesy of Exxon Corp.)

Nuclear-powered submarines can stay submerged for months at a time. (Courtesy of the U.S. Navy)

biles to bananas. Ships carry large, heavy cargoes more cheaply than airplanes. Because ships can carry such tremendous loads, extra care must be used to avoid spilling any of the load into the sea, where it might damage the environment.

Submersibles

Most ships travel over the water's surface. Some, however, also operate below the surface. They are called **submersibles** or **submarines**. They can operate either on or below the water's surface because they can change their weight without changing their buoyancy. Special tanks are filled with water, causing the ships to sink. Or the tanks can be filled with air, causing them to rise. These ships can float at any depth by changing the amount of air in the tanks.

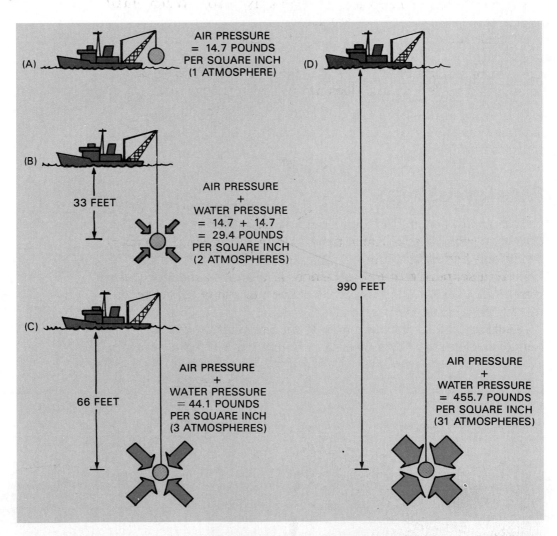

Pressure under water is a challenge to designers of underwater vehicles.

These underwater ships must withstand the huge pressures exerted by water at depth. We live at the bottom of an ocean of air. It has weight, and so it exerts pressure on us. Water is heavier than air, and exerts a much greater pressure. At a depth of 33 feet, water exerts 14.7 pounds of pressure per square inch. This is the same amount of pressure as the entire height of the atmosphere (more than 100,000 feet). At a depth of 66 feet, this pressure is doubled; at 99 feet, it is tripled. Spheres and cylinders are strong shapes for hollow containers. Most submersibles are made of one or both of these shapes.

Hydrofoils and Air Cushion Vehicles

Surface ships include hydrofoils and air cushion vehicles (ACVs). A boat with a fairly flat bottom rises up in the water as it goes faster. This idea is used in a hydrofoil. When small hydrofoils, or flat surfaces, are attached to a boat's bottom, the boat will ride on them once it goes fast enough. There is little water resistance, so hydrofoils can go very fast. ACVs use large fans to push air under the boat, lifting it on a cushion of air. The boat travels fast and does not roll with the waves.

INTERMODAL TRANSPORTATION

Goods moved over long distances often travel on several different kinds of transportation systems. Freight may be loaded into a special container at a factory. The container is a trailer-truck-size box that travels by truck or on a railroad flatcar. It goes to a seaport where it is loaded on a ship to another port. From there, it may be loaded on a train or moved by truck to its destination.

Such a system is called an **intermodal** transportation system. The ships used are called **container ships**. The carrying of tractor trailers by trains is called **piggyback**. In an intermodal system, freight does not have to be unloaded along the way.

Intermodal transportation systems make optimum use of each type of transportation used in the system.

The hull of a hydrofoil comes completely out of the water, reducing water resistance.
(Boeing photo)

Trucks are loaded piggyback onto a train.
(Courtesy of Santa Fe Railway)

There is less damage and loss. An intermodal system is so reliable that it is often used to supply parts for "just-in time" manufacturing. (See Chapter 9.)

AIR TRANSPORTATION

People have always dreamed of flying, but some of the earliest flyers were forced into it. Marco Polo was an Italian who traveled in China in the 1200s and later wrote about his adventures. He reported that sometimes Chinese sailors would tie a person to a kite and try to fly it. If the kite flew well, it meant a safe journey. If the kite crashed, it meant bad luck, and their ship remained in port for the rest of the year. Of course, it was also bad luck for the person tied to the kite!

Lighter-Than-Air (LTA) Vehicles

Flying really began in 1783 when two Frenchmen built a hot-air balloon that could carry people. Objects in water have buoyancy. Objects in air have **lift**, an upward force equal to the weight of the air displaced by the object. For an object to float in air, it must weigh less than the air that it has displaced. This occurs when a lightweight container is filled with a gas (hot

container ship is used in an intermodal transportation system. (Courtesy of Sea-Land Service, Inc.)

Balloons float because they are filled with a gas that is lighter than air. (Courtesy of Albuquerque Convention and Visitors Bureau)

The hydrogen gas in the *Hindenburg* caught fire and burned as the dirigible was docking in New Jersey after a trans-Atlantic crossing. (Courtesy of New York Daily News)

air, hydrogen, or helium) that is lighter than air (LTA). The two together weigh less than the air that they displace.

In the early 1900s, huge LTA ships called **dirigibles** carried passengers and cargo around the world. They had rigid metal frames and were filled with hydrogen gas. The largest was the *Hindenburg*. More than 800 feet long, it could carry 100 people. Hydrogen burns easily, and many large dirigibles exploded, among them the *Hindenburg*. Thirty-six of the ninety-seven people aboard were killed.

Today, LTA ships called **blimps** use helium gas. Helium is heavier than hydrogen, but it doesn't burn. Blimps are not rigid LTAs. They are used for advertising, for some kinds of cargo-lifting, and as platforms for cameras.

LTA vehicles use **passive lift**. They float in the air because of their volume and weight. **Active-lift** vehicles create lift by their movement through the air. They are said to be in **powered flight** because they must have power to fly.

Active-Lift Aircraft

The first powered flight was made by Orville Wright on December 17, 1903. Orville and his brother Wilbur had been experimenting with gliders (unpowered planes). They added a 12-horsepower engine driving two propellers to a glider to build the first airplane.

Early planes were made of wood and cloth. They had two or three wings to increase lift. As engines became more powerful, heavier, stronger materials were used. The number of wings was reduced to one. Passenger service started in the United States in 1914. The U.S. Post Office started delivering air mail in 1919.

World War II brought many advances in airplane design and manufacture. Airplanes were mass-produced. Airframe design and electronics were improved. A very important advance was the jet engine. Jet engines were used on military planes right after World War II. They were not used on passenger planes until 1952.

The first person to fly faster than the speed of sound was Chuck Yeager. He flew an X-1 experimental plane to more than Mach 1 (about 700 miles per hour) in 1947. **Mach 1** is the speed of sound. **Mach 2** is twice the speed of sound. When an airplane gets near the speed of sound, the air it pushes ahead of it forms a shock wave called the sound barrier. The shock wave makes the plane hard to handle. Once the plane goes faster than Mach 1, the plane is easier to control.

The first passenger jets were the British DeHavilland Comets. Many of them crashed. Their problems were caused by

Planes like this one carry hundreds of people over thousands of miles economically. (Courtesy of Boeing Aerospace Company)

metal parts that failed because of the stress put on the planes when they climbed and accelerated. But the Comet was redesigned as a much safer plane. The planes that came after it were built better, as well.

Since the Comet, many other passenger jets have been built. The jets of today have an excellent safety record for many rea-

How Planes Fly

Four forces act on an airplane. They are weight, lift, drag, and thrust. **Weight** is caused by gravity. It is the force pulling the plane toward the earth. **Drag** is the wind resistance. This tends to hold the plane back when it moves forward. **Lift** is the upward force that must be created to make the airplane fly. **Thrust** is the forward force produced by the engines that move the airplane.

Airplane engines move airplanes forward at speeds of 100 to over 1,000 miles per hour. The wing is shaped so that air rushing over it produces a higher pressure on its bottom side than on its top.

Bernoulli's Principle describes this effect. It says that as air flows over a surface, its pressure decreases in places where the air speed increases. The curve at the top of the wing makes the air rush over the top faster than under the bottom. Lower pressure is created on the top. The higher pressure on the bottom of the wing results in upward force on the wing, lifting it.

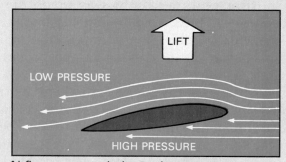

Airflow over an airplane wing.

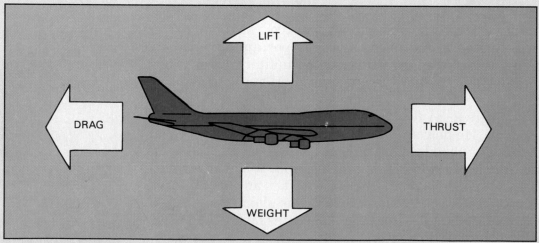

The four forces acting on an airplane.

sons. Jet engines require less maintenance than internal combustion engines. Their flight crews are extensively trained. Modern air traffic control systems keep planes apart in the sky.

Many different kinds of planes are used today. Small private planes carry two to six people over short distances. Airliners that can land and take off on short runways handle commuter traffic. **Jumbo jets** carry hundreds of people at a time over long

The Wright brothers' first flight could have taken place in the cargo compartment of this C-5A. (Courtesy of Lockheed Corporation)

Aircraft Engines

Many planes have used internal combustion engines that turn **propellers** to provide thrust. As airplane propellers turn, they cut into the air. They move the air from front to back. An airplane propeller can be used as a pusher, when mounted on the back of the wing. Or it can be used as a puller, mounted on the front of the wing. Most propeller-driven planes today use pullers.

The **jet** engine takes advantage of Newton's Third Law of Motion. Newton's third law states that **to every action there is an equal and opposite reaction**. For example, a balloon filled with air, suddenly let go, will fly around the room. The air rushing out of the balloon in one direction (the action) moves the balloon in the opposite direction (the reaction).

In a jet engine, a **compressor** forces air into a combustion chamber. There the air is mixed with a fine spray of fuel and burned. The burning mixture expands and rushes out. The force of the gases rushing out the back of the engine pushes the plane in the opposite direction, forward. The burning gases also turn a turbine as they leave the engine. The turbine turns the compressor and other devices such as electrical generators. In a **turbo-prop** engine, the turbine drives a propeller.

A jet engines uses oxygen in the air to burn the jet fuel. A **rocket** carries its own oxygen. It can fly where there is little or no oxygen, at high altitudes or in space. The rocket does not have a turbine, since there is no compressor.

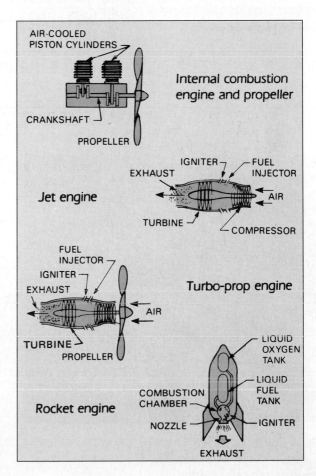

Rockets are used to attain the high speeds needed to achieve orbit. (Courtesy of Lockheed Corporation)

distances. The British and French **Concorde** carries passengers at twice the speed of sound. Military planes carry large cargoes and refuel in-flight. They can travel anywhere without having to land to refuel. Small jets that travel at more than Mach 2 protect our borders.

SPACE TRANSPORTATION

The world entered the space age in 1957, when the U.S.S.R. launched *Sputnik*. *Sputnik* was a satellite, circling the earth once every 90 minutes. Yuri Gagarin of the U.S.S.R. made the first manned flight in 1961. Two American astronauts followed him later that year. During the 1960s, both the U.S. and the U.S.S.R. made more space flights. In July 1969, Americans Neil Armstrong and Edwin Aldrin became the first people to set foot on the moon.

Space vehicles must carry oxygen to burn their fuel because space is airless. So far, all space vehicles have been launched using rocket engines. The engines have used both liquid and solid fuels. Ideas for other kinds of engines are being studied.

To reach orbit, a speed of more than 17,000 miles per hour must be reached. An additional thrust is needed to accelerate the vehicle to 25,000 miles per hour, the speed needed to escape earth orbit.

Great advances had to be made in many areas of technology during the *Apollo* moon-landing program. Many of

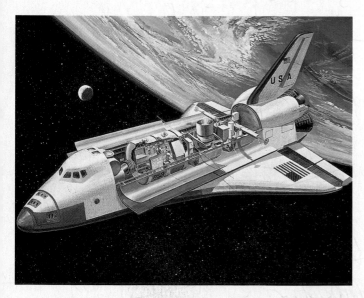

The space shuttle has a large cargo bay area to transport satellites and other equipment to and from orbit. (Courtesy of NASA)

The shuttle missions helped to improve technology for space walks for service and repair of satellites. (Courtesy of NASA)

Transportation Safety

Most transportation systems that carry people put safety first. New ways for making transportation safer are constantly being designed and tested.

Sometimes new safety measures come about because of terrible accidents. In 1912, the largest steamship in the world, the R.M.S. *Titanic*, hit an iceberg on her first voyage. She sank in the North Atlantic. Over half of the 2,207 aboard were killed. As a result, new rules were set regarding lifeboats, lifejackets, and radios. These rules have made travel by ship much safer.

Many safety features are designed into transportation systems. Most vehicles must meet safety standards before being sold or used. Features such as air bags and improved bumpers on cars provide safer vehicles but also increase the cost to manufacture them. Designers, law makers, and public interest groups are constantly discussing the tradeoffs between costs and improved safety.

Some of the most important safety measures depend on the people who use transportation systems. For example, it is estimated that 17,000 fewer people would die in traffic accidents each year if people used seat belts. Only about 14 percent of adults, however, do use seat belts. Always buckle up!

Planes are dropped from this test stand to test for crash worthiness. (Courtesy of NASA)

An airbag being tested in an automobile. (Courtesy of Ford Motor Company)

Always buckle up. (Courtesy of Ford Motor Company)

This plane has just been dropped from the test stand. (Courtesy of N^SA)

The space shuttle can travel in space, glide back to earth like a plane, and be used again for another trip. (Courtesy of NASA)

these advances had spin-offs that are now used in everyday life. They include the intensive care unit in hospitals, new fire-fighting equipment, and the integrated circuits used in many electric appliances.

Space travel poses many problems never faced before. In space, there is no air. Space travelers must carry their atmosphere with them. Once away from the earth's gravity, space travelers experience weightlessness. This is fun and exciting, but also presents problems such as how to take a shower or drink a liquid.

Space exploration brings up another very important problem. The great distances involved mean months and even years are needed for a journey. It took *Voyager*, an exploratory space vehicle, twelve years to travel from the earth to Neptune.

The space shuttle is the first reusable space vehicle. It is used as a space truck, carrying objects and people back and forth from the earth to low earth orbit. The shuttle uses three engines and two solid fuel rocket boosters to reach escape velocity. When it returns, it uses its wings to glide to a landing.

NONVEHICLE TRANSPORTATION SYSTEMS

Most transportation systems use vehicles to carry people or goods, but some systems do not use any vehicles.

Some transportation systems use vehicles to carry people or cargo. Vehicles can be trains, boats, planes, or space ships. But other transportation systems move materials and people without vehicles. These transportation systems include pipelines and conveyor belts.

Pipelines

Pipelines are used for moving crude oil or natural gas. They extend from the field where these resources are pumped to the

When completed, this pipeline will carry natural gas from the wells to a major city. (Courtesy of National Society of Professional Engineers)

Materials are automatically moved along an assembly line by a conveyor system. (Courtesy of Cincinnati Milacron, Inc.)

place where they are refined or loaded aboard trucks or ships. The Trans-Alaska pipeline moves crude oil from northern Alaska to tankers at Valdez, a port on Alaska's southern coast. The pipeline is heated and insulated. This keeps the oil liquid enough so pumps can move it even in cold weather. Great care must be taken when designing and maintaining pipelines so that they do not leak any oil or gas.

Conveyors

In most assembly lines, parts are moved from work station to work station by **conveyors**. Most cars are assembled this way. Large metal parts are cut, drilled, and machined at stations along conveyor belts.

Small objects can be moved along a guide path with their motion driven by vibrating the path. Coal and electronic parts are often moved this way.

PEOPLE MOVERS

Some transportation systems move people over short distances. These **people movers** include **escalators**, **elevators**, and **personal rapid transit systems (PRTs)**.

Freight elevators had been used for some time before 1852, when Elisha Otis invented a device to keep them from falling. Otis's invention, and other advances, helped to make high-rise buildings possible. Without elevators, cities would be more spread out. They would not have central clusters of skyscrapers.

Elevators move people up and down. PRTs move people

Escalators provide quick,
easy movement from one
level to another. (Courtesy of
Otis Elevator Company)

horizontally from one place to another. PRTs use small cars
that people stand in. They move along tracks from one part of
an airport to another or from one part of a city to another.
They are controlled automatically.

Elevators and PRTs use vehicles. Escalators and moving
sidewalks do not. They can move people a little more quickly
than walking or climbing stairs. They are often used where
people are likely to be carrying packages or luggage, such as in
department stores or airports.

SUMMARY

People have used transportation systems since ancient times.
They have moved themselves and goods, and they have explored
their world.

Transportation technology made it possible for people living
far apart to exchange goods and ideas. This exchange has made
countries economically dependent on each other. Transportation technology has changed our way of life by making travel
an important aspect of modern life.

Most transportation systems use vehicles to carry people or
cargo. An engine or motor changes energy to motion.

People are an important part of a transportation system.
They do many jobs in managing the system. Many transporta-
tion systems include roadways or ports built with public money.
Vehicles are often owned privately. Schedules are important in

transportation systems.

Transportation systems include land, sea, air, space, and nonvehicle transportation. These systems are alike in some ways and different in others. The way in which subsystems are connected is determined by use.

Early vehicles that were mechanically powered were powered by steam. Railroads changed the way people lived. American railroads opened the West to settlement.

Automobiles have become necessary to many Americans. Cars are usually powered by the internal combustion engine.

The first mechanically powered ships were steamships. Passenger travel by ship has decreased because planes are faster. But ships are still used to carry freight and for vacation cruises.

Intermodal transportation combines different forms of transportation. Freight is packed into containers, and the containers are moved by different means. They arrive without having been opened.

The first powered flight in 1903 began air transportation. Air transportation vehicles were first powered by internal combustion engines. Now they are also powered by jet engines, turbo-prop engines, and rocket engines. Jet engines and rocket engines enable planes and rockets to fly faster than the speed of sound.

Safety is important in transportation systems. Safety measures come about as a result of accidents or through careful design.

Space transportation systems must solve problems of great distance, weightlessness, and airlessness. Vehicles can orbit the earth if they can reach escape velocity—more than 17,000 miles per hour.

(Courtesy General Motors Corporation)

Some transportation systems do not use vehicles. They include pipelines and conveyors. They are used to carry oil from oilfields to ports and materials from station to station on assembly lines.

People movers carry people for short distances. Elevators and PRTs use vehicles. Escalators and moving sidewalks do not.

(Courtesy of Lockheed-California Company)

REVIEW QUESTIONS

1. Describe how transportation and communication systems have made countries interdependent.
2. In what way(s) have modern transportation systems affected the way your family lives?
3. Is an automobile a necessity or a luxury in your family? Why?
4. Why were steam engines replaced by internal combustion engines in cars?
5. Why were steam engines replaced by diesel and electric engines in trains?
6. What role did trains play in the settling of the American west?
7. Why are electric engines used on railroads that travel into major cities?
8. Describe why a boat made out of steel and cement can float.
9. Describe how intermodal transportation works and what its advantages are.
10. What shapes do submarines and submersibles use? Why?
11. Describe how a wing enables a plane to fly.
12. Give at least two reasons why jet engines have replaced internal combustion engines on commercial passenger planes.
13. How is a rocket different from a jet engine?
14. Why are rocket engines used for space vehicles?
15. Name two kinds of transportation systems that don't use vehicles. Describe how they work.
16. Name a human-powered vehicle that is widely used for sport or leisure traveling in this country, but that is used as basic transportation in other countries.

KEY WORDS

Buoyancy	Engine	Lift	Thrust
Commute	Intermodal	Piggyback	Transmission
Container ship	Internal	Pipeline	Turbo-prop
Conveyor	combustion	Propeller	Vehicle
Diesel	engine	Rocket	Weight
Drag	Jet	Steam engine	

SEE YOUR TEACHER FOR THE CROSSTECH PUZZLE

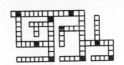

AIR FLIGHT

Setting the Stage

A lightweight spacecraft capable of traveling at speeds of over 4000 miles per hour is being developed. Once in orbit, this national aerospace plane would be capable of speeds in excess of 17,000 miles per hour. It would be like an airplane and a space shuttle; however, it would not have the cumbersome rocket boosters like the shuttle. Unlike an airplane, its capabilities would include travel in orbit over 300 miles above the earth and its atmosphere.

The space shuttle was designed to carry payloads of satellites, experimental equipment, and a space station into orbit. The aerospace plane is being developed as a more fuel efficient and faster means of air travel. Airplanes, the space shuttle, and the national aerospace plane all have led to the exploration and development of the new frontier—space.

Our pioneers in space, such as John Glenn, Robert Goddard, and Christa McAuliffe, once were students like you in school. They all contributed to some aspect of our bridging earth to outer space. You are the future astronauts, engineers, research scientists, and aircraft designers.

Your Challenge

Design and construct a model of an aircraft that could travel within or above the earth's atmosphere.

Suggested Resources

Styrofoam trays
Sketching paper
Carbon paper
Glue
Scissors
Utility or X-Acto® knife
Weight (dime or penny)

(Courtesy of NASA)

Procedure

1. After receiving proper instruction on lab safety and studying available literature on aircraft, sketch five designs for an aircraft.
2. Choose one of these and draw the parts of the aircraft to be used as the pattern.
3. Place the carbon paper onto the styrofoam tray. Place your sketch on top of the carbon paper. Trace the pattern onto the styrofoam.
4. Cut all parts and slots of the aircraft. Score areas requiring bending.
5. Assemble the aircraft. Attach weight as needed for flight.
6. With permission from the instructor, fly the aircraft.

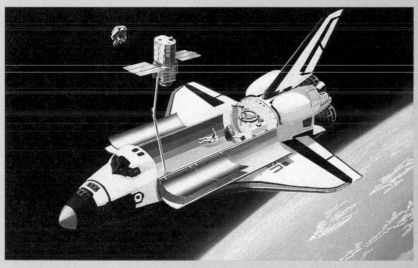

(Artist's concept by Robert W. Womack for NASA)

Technology Connections

1. What are vehicles that travel above the land and water surfaces of the earth called?
2. What is a vehicle with rocket boosters capable of traveling above the earth's atmosphere carrying large payloads called?
3. Describe what the projected national aerospace plane will be like.
4. Explain the difference among the following aircraft: airplane, space shuttle, national aerospace plane.

YOU'RE ON THE RIGHT TRACK!

Setting the Stage

Traffic jams have become more and more of a problem. Therefore, you've been asked to design a public transit system that can replace the automobile.

Your Challenge

Design and build a monorail car that can ride above a 1" wide flat rail track. The car must have a motor and be battery powered. If your teacher approves, teams of 2–3 students may work together to make one vehicle.

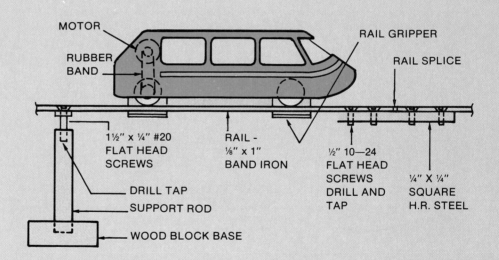

MOTOR
RUBBER BAND
RAIL GRIPPER
RAIL SPLICE
1½" x ¼" #20 FLAT HEAD SCREWS
DRILL TAP
SUPPORT ROD
WOOD BLOCK BASE
RAIL - ⅛" x 1" BAND IRON
½" 10—24 FLAT HEAD SCREWS DRILL AND TAP
¼" X ¼" SQUARE H.R. STEEL

Suggested Resources

Safety glasses and lab aprons
9 volt DC electric motor with pulley
9 volt alkaline battery
9 volt battery snaps
9 volt battery holder
SPST miniature switch (optional)
Soldering pencils and solder
Band iron—⅛" X 1"
Hot rolled steel rods—½" diameter
Flat head machine screws with hex nuts—1½" X 1¼" #20
10–24 flat head machine screws—½" long
Assorted materials such as metal, wood, plastics, cardboard, fasteners, etc.
Assorted shop tools and machinery

Procedure

NOTE—If you have not been told how to use any tool or machine that you need to use in this activity, check with your teacher BEFORE going any further.

The amount of material needed for the track depends on its length. Plan accordingly.

1. Be sure to wear safety glasses and a lab coat.
2. The track can be designed and built by the entire class. It should be made from ⅛" X 1" band iron and supported by ½" diameter, 12" long steel rods. Support rods should be spaced approximately 36" apart.

3. The track can be made any length desired by joining the rail on the bottom with ¼" × ¼" square stock drilled and tapped with a 10–24 NC tap. Use ½", 10–24 flat head machine screws for this assembly.

4. Drill and tap one end of the ½" diameter support rods with a ¼" × 20 NC tap.

5. Cut blocks of wood 1½" × 6" × 9". Drill a ½" hole halfway through the center of a larger side of these base blocks. The untapped ends of the ½" support rods are inserted into these holes.

6. Assemble the track using screws and nuts. Be careful not to bend or kink the rail.

7. The first step in constructing the monorail car is to design the *drive wheel and undercarriage*. The electric motor comes with a pulley attached. You must determine how the motor will be mounted and how it will turn the drive wheel/axle. (Rubber bands are helpful. So are wing nuts for fast assembly/disassembly.)

8. Also, plan the mechanism that will keep the vehicle from falling off the track (small L-shaped pieces usually work fine.)

9. Make sketches and plans of your monorail car *before* beginning construction.

10. Consider the *weight* and *traction* of the monorail car during the design stages. If your monorail weighs too much, or if there is too much friction in the drive system, it will not run properly. Use washers and lubrication when possible.

11. The body of your monorail should be added last. It can be made from mat board, cardboard, etc. and painted as desired.

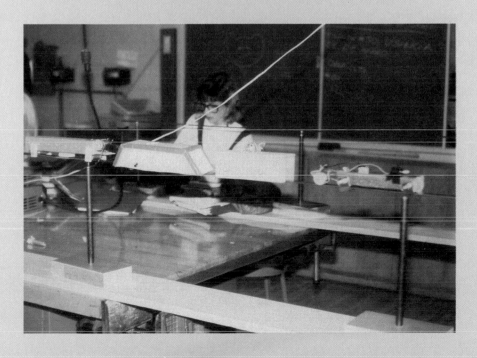

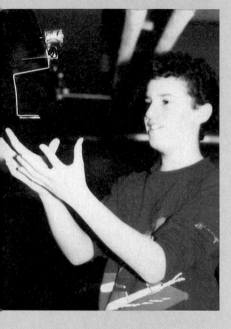

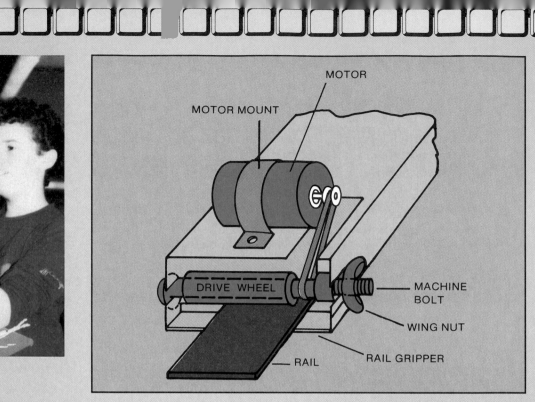

MOTOR

MOTOR MOUNT

DRIVE WHEEL

MACHINE BOLT

WING NUT

RAIL GRIPPER

RAIL

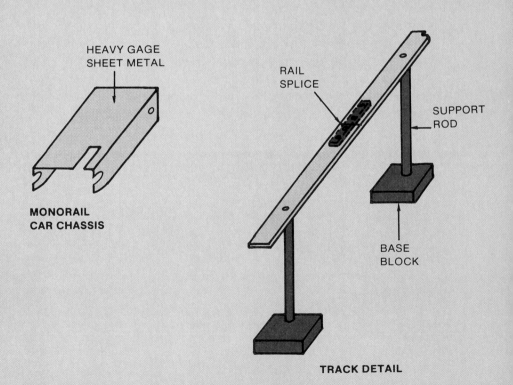

HEAVY GAGE
SHEET METAL

**MONORAIL
CAR CHASSIS**

RAIL
SPLICE

SUPPORT
ROD

BASE
BLOCK

TRACK DETAIL

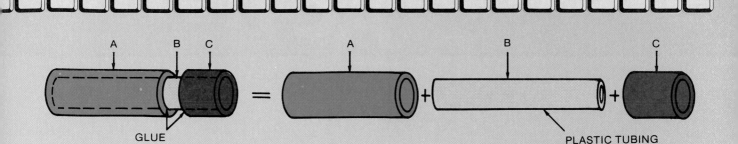

A B C = A + B + C

GLUE

PLASTIC TUBING

DRIVE WHEEL DETAIL

Technology Connections

1. Existing technological systems act together to produce new, more powerful technologies. What technologies did you use to make your monorail car?
2. High-speed monorail systems could replace the fairly slow rail system used today. What undesirable outcomes could result?
3. *Magnetic levitation (maglev)* can be used to lift a train off its track. Why does this allow the train to go faster?
4. The transportation systems of the future will make more and more use of computers for design and control. These systems will be much faster, safer, and more efficient than present ones. Super-conductors will mean even greater advances.

Science and Math Concepts

▶ *Magnetic levitation* uses the principle that similar magnetic poles repel each other.
▶ *Friction* is a force that opposes the motion of a body.
▶ An electric motor converts *electrical energy* from the battery into *mechanical energy.*
▶ *Superconductors* conduct electricity with little or no loss due to resistance.

Equipment and Supplies

NOTE: The following equipment and supplies list contains just some of the materials your group may use to build your vehicle. Except for the chassis, you may use whatever is available, provided it is safe. Do not limit yourself only to the materials suggested here.

Chassis
Plywood — ¼" thick
2" × 4" scraps
Glue
Wood screws

Wheels
Hardwood — ¾" × 2¼"
Purchased rubber wheels

Body
Wood
Fiberglass supplies
Vacuum forming sheets
Paper and wire

Miscellaneous
Balsa wood
Band iron
Sheet metal
Acrylic
Miscellaneous bolts
  and nuts
Screws
Pop rivets and riveter
Copper tubing
Clay
Brass welding rod
Plaster
Springs
Swivels and pulleys

SCRAMBLER

Objectives

When you have finished this activity, you should be able to :
- Identify the subsystems of a land transportation vehicle.
- Explain the role of management in an engineering project.

Concepts and Information

In your reading you have learned that there are many types of energy converters. Though some of these may be more efficient as a power source for transportation, none have proven as reliable and as easy to operate as the internal combustion engine. Because of this, it is still used to power the majority of transportation systems.

The internal combustion engine is referred to as a heat engine. It is so called this because as it burns fuel it produces hot gases. These hot gases expand and are converted into mechanical power. In most internal combustion engines, the fuel is ignited by a spark plug, but in this activity you will use an engine called a glow plug engine. Its name is derived from the glowing hot "plug" it uses to ignite the fuel. The glow plug is initially heated with a battery connected to it. Once the engine is operating, the burning gases from the combustion cycle continuously heat the glow plug.

SECTION ACTIVITIES

Activity

The internal combustion engine is only one of several subsystems in a vehicle. Steering, lighting, suspension, brakes, and heating are examples of other subsystems in a transportation vehicle. As a group, your task is to form a design team which will design and construct a vehicle powered by a .049 two-cycle engine. This vehicle will contain steering and suspension, guidance, body, and chassis/engine mount subsystems. The body may be tested in a wind tunnel before final construction. A management team will oversee the design and construction of the vehicle. The vehicle will then be raced on a 12' radius track in competition with vehicles made by the other technology classes. A well-designed vehicle will achieve speeds of 35 mph or more.

Procedure

1. Your instructor will divide each group into the following four teams.
    1. **Management Team**
    2. **Steering and Suspension Subsystem Team**
    3. **Chassis and Engine Mount Subsystem Team**
    4. **Body Subsystem Team**
2. Read the following descriptions of each team's responsibilities so that you have a clear understanding of each team's responsibilities:
   Management team — Your team will be responsible for overseeing the design and construction of the vehicle. You will coordinate the activities of the other three teams and monitor their progress. For effective monitoring, you may want to assign a consultant/manager to each of the other three teams. You must be able to foresee and prevent any interference one subsystem may have with another subsystem. To do this, you must continuously take careful measurements to create a master drawing of the vehicle.

   You will also be the track manager. You are responsible for making sure the guidance subsystem is constructed and assembled. The guidance subsystem must guide the glow plug vehicle in a circular path 24 feet in diameter. This must be done by using a tether which will connect the vehicle to a central pivot. You will also assign the track personnel.

   Above all, you must be aware of all safety rules and help the teacher enforce them among the other teams.

Equipment and Supplies

Power System
.049 COX Black Widow glow plug engine
Glow plug fuel
1.5-volt glow plug power supply

Safety Equipment for Operating the Engine and Vehicle
Safety glasses
Leather gloves (2 pairs)
Large soft cloths for stopping the engine
Nylon utility line (165 lb. test) for Tether block — 12' long
Fishing swivel
Blacktop or concrete running surface — 30' in diameter

Steering and Suspension Subsystem Team — Your team will have the following major responsibilities. First, you will design a steering system for the front axle and wheels. Second, a stationary mounting system for the rear wheels of the vehicle must be designed. Third, you must design a method for attaching the tether line to, and detaching the tether line from, the chassis of the vehicle. Be sure to inform the body subsystem team how you will do this since it may affect their design.

Your team is also responsible for designing and constructing a suspension system for the glow plug vehicle. The smoother the travel of the vehicle, the faster it will go. Therefore, the suspension system you design must be able to absorb the shocks caused by any bumps or dips in the track.

Chassis and Engine Mount Subsystem Team — Your team will be responsible for constructing the chassis and engine mount. Refer to the chassis drawing for specific guidance as to how to build the chassis.

Body Subsystem Team — Your team is responsible for designing and constructing a body for the glow plug vehicle. One of the most important factors in determining the speed of a car is drag. **Drag** is the friction caused by the air as it flows over the body of a vehicle. You need to design the body so that it is smooth and sleek, and you may want to make clay prototypes to test in a wind tunnel. Be sure to engineer a method of attaching the body to, and detaching the body from, the chassis of the vehicle. You may paint or decorate the body of the vehicle in an attractive way.

3. Discuss with the rest of your class the design limitations listed below. You may want to add to these.

   a. **Chassis** — To construct the chassis, follow the design outlined in the chassis drawing. The chassis may be drilled and/or cut, but not in such a way as to alter its outside dimensions.

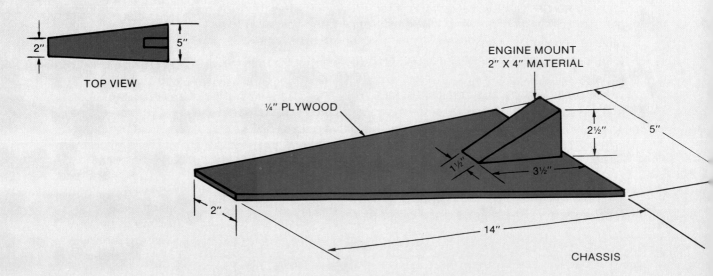

TOP VIEW

2"

5"

ENGINE MOUNT
2" X 4" MATERIAL

¼" PLYWOOD

2½"

5"

1½"

3½"

2"

14"

CHASSIS

b. **Power Plant** — .049 COX Black Widow glow plug engine. Must be mounted so that the propeller maintains one inch minimum ground clearance. Also, the engine should be mounted at a 5° angle. This will help the vehicle steer to the outside of the circle until centrifugal force takes over.

c. **Wheels** — Wood (turned on a machine lathe), rubber, or hard plastic (purchased).

d. **Body** — Material such as:
   - Fiberglass, drape-form molded over clay, paper-mache, or plastic. Use paraffin wax for a release agent.
   - Vacuum-formed plastic
   - Newspaper soaked in wallpaper paste applied to a frame of wood and/or wire
   - Carve the body out of balsa wood

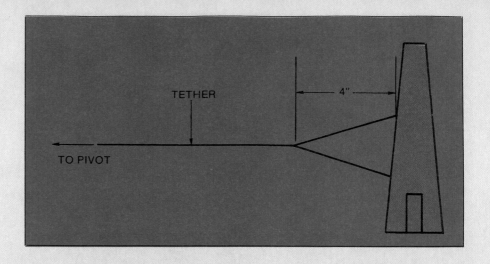

TETHER

4"

TO PIVOT

   e. **Tether** — Must end in a "V" shape four inches in length, so as to attach to the vehicle chassis in two places. (See tether drawing.)

   f. **Central Pivot** — Must allow the tether to turn freely without wrapping. The height of the tether where it attaches to the pivot must be no more than 8 inches.

4. After all teams have completed their design work, construct the vehicle. Take it outside to test and race it.

5. Once outside, test the steering subsystem. To do this, hold a piece of chalk at one end of the tether line. Draw a half circle on the pavement by keeping the tether line taut. Push the car to see if it will track the chalkline. Make any necessary steering adjustments.

6. Test run the car. For safety, reverse the propeller for any test run. This will reduce the maximum speed the vehicle will travel. The following personnel are needed for the test run: head starter and fuel adjuster; holder of car; safety inspector (each person should wear safety glasses and leather gloves).

7. Race the car. The following personnel are needed for the race: head starter and fuel adjuster; person who holds and releases the car; safety inspector; three track supervisors (each carries a large cloth to stop cars not tracking properly); timer track recorder; spectator supervisor.

Review Questions

1. Use the following formula to calculate how fast your vehicle traveled.

   Circumference of a circle = $2\pi r$ (r = radius of a circle; π = 3.14)

   Velocity = $\dfrac{\text{Distance traveled in feet}}{\text{Time (in seconds)}}$

2. How do local speedways compensate for centrifugal force that is developed on ¼-mile and ½-mile oval tracks.

3. Change the weight of your vehicle and time it again. How much does weight affect the speed?

4. Test the speed of the vehicle with the body removed. Does the speed change? (Remember, you are also reducing the weight of the vehicle when you remove the body.)

5. Tape a white piece of paper to the wall. Start the glow plug engine and let it run with the exhaust aimed at the paper. What is the result? Why does this happen?

CAREERS IN ENERGY, POWER, AND TRANSPORTATION

OCCUPATION	FORMAL EDUCATION OR TRAINING	SKILLS NEEDED	EMPLOYMENT OPPORTUNITIES
AIRCRAFT PILOT—Transports passengers, cargo, and mail. Some pilots dust crops, spread seed, test aircraft, and take photographs.	A commercial pilot's license issued by the Federal Aviation Administration (FAA) requires at least 250 hours of flight experience. Flying can be learned in military or civilian flying schools.	An understanding of flight theory and the ability to interpret data provided by instruments.	Above average. The growth in cargo and passenger traffic will create a need for more pilots, and more flight instructors.
PETROLEUM ENGINEER— Explores and drills for oil and gas. Determines the most efficient methods to recover oil and gas from petroleum deposits.	Four-year college engineering degree. Courses in energy technology, mathematics, physics, chemistry, mechanical drawing, and computers are useful.	Excellent mathematical and computer skills. Good background in chemistry.	Average. Oil and gas are becoming harder to find. More people will be needed to explore new sources, like the oceans and the polar regions.
TRUCKDRIVER—Transports goods from producer to consumer. Long-distance truckdrivers spend most of their time behind the wheel. Local truckdrivers spend much time loading and unloading.	In most states, a chauffeur's license is required. Employers prefer applicants with a good driving record. New drivers often start on small panel trucks and advance to larger trucks.	Ability to drive large vehicles in crowded areas and in highway traffic; knowledge of federal, state, and local regulations. Ability to inspect trucks and freight.	Average. However, this occupation is among the largest. The number of job openings each year will be very high.
VEHICLE MECHANIC—Repairs and maintains motor vehicles and construction equipment. Types of mechanics include aircraft, automotive and motorcycle, diesel, farm equipment, and heavy equipment.	Mechanics training is provided by the military, by private trade schools, or public vocational schools. Aircraft mechanics must be licensed by the FAA. Auto mechanics still can learn the trade by working with experienced mechanics, but formal training is becoming more important due to the complexity of new cars.	Knowledge of electronics and engine technology; knowledge of mechanical, hydraulic, pneumatic, and electrical systems. Good manual dexterity.	Above average. Rising incomes and a growing population will stimulate the demand for airline transportation. Expansion of the driving population, and more complex automotive systems will require more skilled mechanics.

Data from *Occupational Outlook Handbook, 1986-87*, U.S. Department of Labor.

SECTION

5

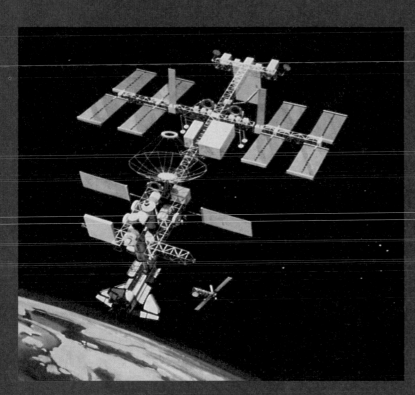

(Courtesy of NASA)

CONCLUSION: LOOKING INTO THE FUTURE

CHAPTER 16

IMPACTS FOR TODAY AND TOMORROW

MAJOR CONCEPTS

After reading this chapter, you will know that:

- Outputs of a technological system can be desired, undesired, expected, or unexpected.
- People determine whether technology is good or bad by the way they use it.
- Technology produces many positive outputs and solves many problems. Sometimes, however, negative outputs create new problems.
- Technology must be fitted to human needs.
- Technology must be adapted to the environment.
- Existing technological systems will act together to produce new, more powerful technologies.
- Using futuring techniques, people can anticipate the consequences of a new technology.

INTRODUCTION

Long ago, travel across the United States took weeks or even months. The pony express was the quickest way of delivering mail. People had to make many products by hand. Today, we can buy the goods we need, goods produced by manufacturing technology. Jets take us across the country in hours. Technology makes it possible to move information at nearly the speed of light.

There is another side to technology. In December 1984, poison gas leaked from a chemical plant in Bhopal, India. More than 2,000 people were killed. In January 1986, the space shuttle *Challenger* exploded seconds after launch. All seven astronauts were killed. In April 1986, an accident occurred at a nuclear power plant in Chernobyl, in the Soviet Union. People died from the radiation given off in the accident.

Some people say that we have lost control over our technology. They say that technology results in tragedies like the explosion of the *Challenger*. They say we should stop building nuclear power plants because of the dangers of radiation. They blame technology for pollution, noise, and crowded cities and highways.

Is technology good or evil? Would we want to go back to the days when we had simpler technology—and could we, if we wanted to? What effects will technology have on our world in the future? These questions are the subject of this chapter.

The Challenger crew included (clockwise from top left) Ellison S. Onizuka, Sharon Christa McAuliffe, Gregory Jarvis, Judith Resnick, Ronald McNair, Francis R. Scobee, and Michael J. Smith. (Courtesy of NASA)

IMPACTS OF TECHNOLOGY

In Chapter 3 we learned that there are four possible outputs from any technological system. It is the unexpected and undesirable output that is of greatest concern to us. If we cannot plan for an event, we may not be able to deal with it.

The accident at Chernobyl was one such event. It took the Soviets several days to evacuate the people who lived near the plant. Moreover, all the harmful effects of the accident will not be known for a long time, since radiation can cause cancer deaths years later.

Still, technology is neither good nor evil. It can be used for good, or it can hurt us. How we control it determines whether it is useful or harmful. For example, the U.S. Nuclear Regulatory Commission (NRC) sets standards for nuclear power plants. A plant must have a 9-inch-thick steel shell and a 3-foot-thick concrete building around the nuclear core. The

Outputs of a technological system can be desired, undesired, expected, or unexpected.

People determine whether technology is good or bad by the way they use it.

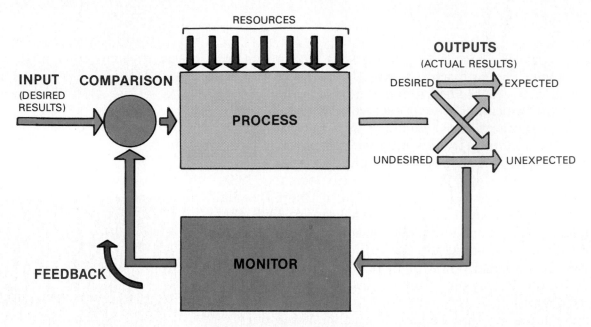

Technological systems create four kinds of outputs.

Technology produces many positive outputs and solves many problems. Sometimes, however, negative outputs create new problems.

Chernobyl reactor was built without such protection. Of course, an accident is possible even in NRC-approved plants in the U.S. But control of technology lowers the risks.

Today, **pollution** is a worldwide issue. Millions of automobiles and trucks give off dangerous gases. These gases pollute our air. Some factories dump their wastes into rivers and oceans. These wastes have polluted our water supply.

This automated control room in a nuclear power plant is watched over by human workers. (Courtesy of Rochester Gas & Electric Co.)

Technology itself is not harmful. Rather, it is the way we use technology that causes problems. And, just as technology can cause problems, it can solve them. For example, pollution control devices on cars and scrubbers on factory smokestacks are reducing pollution.

Should We Go Back to Nature?

If we went back to a simpler life, would problems like pollution disappear? No. Pollution has been a problem since people first began to live in cities. The rivers around Rome were so full of wastes that people were forbidden to bathe there. Before the automobile, one hundred years ago, 150,000 horses in New York City produced over 500,000 tons of manure a year.

We face other problems. Our environment is noisy. People who live near airports hear jets taking off and landing day and night. Subways roar. Road traffic makes constant noise. Factory workers listen to the pounding of machinery all day long. Even loud music may damage our hearing.

In earlier days, there were other noise problems. Factories were even more noisy than they are today, when we have laws that protect workers. Trains rumbled through cities, shaking the buildings as they passed. That's only the beginning. Medical care was crude. People lived in unsanitary conditions and in unsafe buildings.

The fact is, we depend on technology. Our lives and our routines are built around it. We could not go back to a life without automobiles, flush toilets, telephones, and modern medical care. Technology is here to stay. But it is up to us to use it well. We can pass laws that protect us and our environment. We can control technology.

Sanitation man sweeping manure in New York City. (Courtesy of the Museum of the City of New York)

Matching Technology to the Individual

Products can be designed to make our lives more comfortable. The field of **ergonomics**, or **human factors engineering**, uses technology to meet the physical needs of people. Chairs fit the shape of the back. Drinking glasses are easy to hold. Tables and desks are the right height. Auto seats make driving more comfortable.

Computer keyboards are a good example of ergonomic design. One company tried out different designs on hundreds of secretaries. The secretaries typed on the keyboards and provided

Technology must be fitted to human needs.

feedback on how comfortable they were. The shape of the keys, the pressure needed, and the way they sprang back were things that determined how "user friendly" the keyboard was.

Making products safe is another way ergonomics helps. The blades of kitchen machines such as food processors must be guarded for safety. Automobiles are designed for people's safety.

Special needs can be met. People with disabilities can choose from many new products. Bicycles, cars, and skis have been designed for people who do not have the use of their legs.

Handbikes
and Sunbursts

Bicycling can help people learn good balance and it is also an excellent form of exercise. Some people, however, are unable to pedal a bike. To meet their needs, an arm-powered bike has been designed at the Veterans Administration Rehabilitation Research and Development Center in Palo Alto, California.

The Handbike, as it is called, comes in adult, child, and racing versions. The bike combines the best ideas from bicycles, people-powered vehicles, and sport wheelchairs.

The Sunburst Tandem is a spin-off of the Handbike. The front rider pedals with arms or legs or both. The back rider steers. The Handbike and Sunburst show how technology can help the physically challenged to enjoy activities that would otherwise not be possible.

Macy Tackitt on her Handbike. Macy was partly paralyzed as a result of an auto accident. (Courtesy of VA Rehabilitation R & D Center, Palo Alto, California)

Designer Douglas Schwandt, a biomedical engineer, and friend Dianna Gubber riding the Sunburst. (Courtesy of VA Rehabilitation R & D Center, Palo Alto, California)

Matching Technology to the Environment

Technology has been damaging the environment for thousands of years. Forests were cut down for fuel in the 1600s. Garbage was burned in open fires. Human wastes were poured into rivers. However, all this occurred on a small scale. Today, technology could harm the environment on a worldwide scale.

We burn over 700 million tons of coal each year to provide energy, producing pollutants like **sulfur dioxide**. In the United States, nearly 170 million vehicles burn about 125 billion gallons of fuel each year, adding huge amounts of pollutants to the air.

Chemicals given off by automobiles and industrial plants can rise into the atmosphere and return to the earth as acid rain. **Acid rain** has killed forests in some parts of the United States, Canada, and Scandinavia. It has killed lake fish. In New York State, fish have been completely killed off in about 200 lakes. The same thing may happen in hundreds more.

Over the last thirty years, new chemicals have come into use in farming. They control pests and disease. But they may remain in the soil and air. They can get into the food we eat and the water we drink.

Some factories make chemicals that can harm people. Many companies try to limit this harm by doing **technology assessment studies**. Laboratory animals are exposed to the chemicals. The results help determine the effect chemicals will have on people. Such studies can save lives. In Niagara Falls, New York, chemicals dumped by local industries caused illness and death. About 800 families living in an area called Love Canal had to leave their homes.

Our **environment** must be treated with care. We must use resources wisely and look for alternatives for scarce resources. We must develop technologies that do not cause environmental harm. For example, solar energy can provide for our energy needs without harming the environment.

Technology must be adapted to the environment.

Today, federal laws like the Clean Air Act ban industries from polluting the environment. (Courtesy of Carnegie Library of Pittsburgh—Pittsburgh Photographic Library)

SEEING INTO THE FUTURE OF TECHNOLOGY

How will technology affect the way we live in the future?

In recent years, it has brought about enormous changes. Twenty-five years ago there were no video games, home computers, or industrial robots. Artificial hearts had not been used.

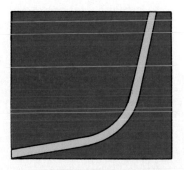

Technology is growing at an exponential (ever-increasing) rate.

We didn't have genetic engineering. Only in the last decade have we had space shuttles, test-tube babies, and fully automated factories.

Artificial Intelligence

Artificial intelligence is an important new field in computer science. It is made up of many different kinds of research and applications. Some of the most important areas of artificial intelligence include voice recognition and robotics. What all these areas have in common is that in one way or another they try to get computers to think and behave like humans. This is the origins of the name, Artificial Intelligence.

Voice recognition allows a computer to recognize words when people talk to it. The computer analyzes the sound waves (vibrations in the air) when a person talks. The computer must be trained to recognize a person's voice. This is because every person speaks somewhat differently.

Voice recognition technology will change how people live and work. Spoken commands will control word processors

An experimental voice recognition system. Some voice recognition systems have a vocabulary of 20,000 words. That is about 38% of the average person's vocabulary. (Courtesy of Kurzweil Applied Intelligence, Inc.)

in the office and machines in factories. Even home appliances will be controlled with spoken commands!

Robotics is the area of artificial intelligence that designs and builds robots. Several different types of problems need to be solved when designing a robot. Mechanical problems might include designing the robot's arm so that it can move strongly in all directions. Sensing problems include designing the robot so that it can pick up fragile objects without breaking them. The robot must be programmed to "think," so that it can develop a plan for doing a job. One of the great benefits of robotics is that robots have been developed to do work that is very dangerous for humans.

Various research is part of robotics. It is an effort to create robots that can see. Seeing is more than receiving visual images; it is also being able to recognize objects and interpret the visual images. When you look around, recognizing desks or chairs is easy! For a robot it is very difficult. Another problem that is very easy for you, but hard for a robot is finding a path from one place to another. Knowing how to find to avoid bumping into objects must be programmed into the robot.

There has been much success in these various areas of artificial intelligence, but more research and development needs to be done.

Technology is growing at an ever-increasing rate. Think about the changes that have happened in the last twenty-five years. What might happen in the next twenty-five? Let's look ahead and see what technological systems of the future might be like.

COMMUNICATION IN THE FUTURE

In the future, we will be able to "talk" to machines. Already, computers can speak like humans. The technology that makes this possible is called **speech synthesis**.

You may already know about synthesized music. This is music made by electrical devices rather than by acoustic instruments. Telephone companies use speech synthesis. When you call directory assistance to ask for someone's number, a human operator switches you to a computerized device. The device gives you the number, using a computer-generated voice.

Soon **voice recognition** technology will be in widespread use. Computers will be able to respond to human voice commands. The telephone operator may no longer be needed. These systems may be used in typing. You will be able to speak to a typewriter, and it will print whatever you say. The disabled may be helped by this technology. Computers, robots, and wheelchairs will be controlled by voice. A machine for the blind that can read the words of a printed page aloud has already been developed.

This typewriter can recognize 1,000 spoken words.
(Courtesy of Kurzweil Applied Intelligence, Inc.)

Communication at Home

Homes will have robots with whom it will be possible to communicate. People can order their household pet robots to fetch a glass of water or shine their shoes. Robots will help with housework, watch children, and aid the elderly and disabled. Robots will be made so they seem more like people.

We will be able to communicate with appliances. We will tell lights to turn on and television sets to turn off. Our telephones will talk to us. When we come home, a telephone will tell us who called, at what time, and give us the message. Telephones will become even more portable. We will be able to carry one in a pocket and talk anywhere or anytime we wish. They will also become more powerful. We will be able to see the person we are talking to in 3-D.

Digital Audio Tape

A new technology, **digital audio tape (DAT)**, may be as revolutionary to tape recording as the compact disc was to the phonograph record. DAT combines magnetic recording with digital technology.

In DAT, music that is to be recorded is first converted to digital data. The digital data is similar to computer data. It is stored on the tape. When it is to be played back, the data is read from the tape and converted back into music by the DAT player.

DAT recorders and players produce music very clearly. There is no noise present in DAT recorders and players. Because the information is stored as digital data it will not deteriorate with time. This means the tape will be useful longer. DAT is far superior to standard audio tape technology.

WABOT II, The Keyboard-Playing Robot

Robots of the future will not only be factory workers but will provide personal services for people. Service robots will look and act more like people.

WABOT II is an intelligent robot musician. It can talk. It can read sheet music and play an electric organ, using both hands and legs. The robot was constructed by a research group at a Japanese university.

The fingers of both hands play keyboards. The feet work the bass keyboards and the pedals. A video camera picks up the musical score. WABOT II can accompany a singer, playing in tune with the singer's pitch.

(Courtesy of Ichiro Kato)

Cameras will be video machines that use video disks, or cassettes no larger than an audio cassette. We will view our pictures on a home TV screen or hook up a printer to print them on paper.

Television sets will be bigger and better. With a new technology called HDTV (high-definition television), pictures will be clearer. On today's TV screens, the picture is made up of 525 fine horizontal lines called **scanning lines**. HDTV will have 1,125 scanning lines. and provide more detailed pictures.

Communication at Work

Satellites are used today to send telephone conversations, sporting events, and military information around the world. A technology called **video conferencing** is helping people to communicate by TV.

Meetings between people in different places are possible by way of a TV screen. An electronic blackboard allows people to draw diagrams and send them instantly to a screen in another country, or even in space.

We may someday be able to put a microchip in the brain, and connect people up to computer data bases. In the distant future, we may be able to record our thought patterns for future generations. Some people fear that this technology will be used to monitor a worker's job performance. Employers might be able to control the thoughts and feelings of workers by sending signals to the microchip.

Would this ever happen? Some unions, such as the Newspaper Guild, the United Auto Workers, and the Communication Workers of America, have asked for antimonitoring clauses in their contracts with employers.

Only uses of technology that enhance the quality of life should be encouraged. Computers, for example, have made telephone operators more productive. However, the operators report that they are now expected to answer more calls per minute than ever before. This has made their jobs more stressful.

Communication and the Consumer

Computers are being connected to telephone lines, changing the way people shop. You may use your computer to search through lists of merchandise, order, and pay without leaving home. This method of communicating will become more common in the future. You will be able to pay bills and move money from a checking account to savings. You will be able to reserve a flight and buy airline tickets. You will be able to use video

Videoconferencing is becoming more and more common. (Courtesy of Concept Communications, Inc., Dallas, TX)

Personal computers can communicate with mainframe computers over telephone lines. (Courtesy of AT&T, Bell Laboratories)

This woman is using a computerized mirror to "try on" a new outfit. (Courtesy of L.S. Ayres)

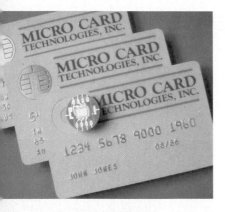

One of the new "smart cards." (Courtesy of Motorola, Inc.)

disk images to choose a vacation place, a hotel, and the sights you want to see.

You'll use the same technology to choose a new hairstyle or a new outfit. Your hair stylist will combine your image with that of a new hairstyle on a computer screen. In the same way, you'll be able to see yourself wearing new clothes in a computerized mirror.

Computers and credit cards could turn our country into a cashless society. Credit cards will have miniature computers in them. You'll be able to use them to buy anything you need.

These **smart cards** have an integrated circuit memory chip within them. The chip keeps track of the consumer's bank balance. After a card is used, the chip's memory stores the new balance. Smart cards will be used to pay for telephone calls and pay TV. They will store information about you, such as your blood type, drug allergies, and medical insurance information.

MANUFACTURING IN THE FUTURE

Robots will do more and more manufacturing jobs. More of our factories will operate almost without people. Today, robots do simple jobs such as welding and painting parts, and moving them from one place to another. Putting products together most often requires people, because this requires human skills. Future robots will be smarter. They will be able to see and feel and learn. They will be able to put products together as well as make parts. Many people will lose factory jobs. Those jobs that remain will go to people in countries where labor is cheap. Those whose jobs have been taken by robots will have to be retrained to learn new jobs.

A hundred years ago, factory workers in textile plants worked 75 hours a week. Today, the average worker puts in 42 hours a week. Fifty years from now, some people forecast, the work week will be only 20 hours. There will be "parents' hours" jobs, from 9:00 A.M. to 3:00 P.M. There will be jobs with "students' hours," from 3:00 to 6:00 P.M. What will people do with all this leisure time? Will the extra time parents can spend with their children result in happier, stronger families?

Manufacturing in Space

Some products can be manufactured in space more easily than they can be on earth. Low gravity is one reason.

Gravity pulls the molecules of materials down, making it difficult to separate and purify materials. Suppose you wanted to take certain cells out of a group of living cells so you could find a cure for a disease. On earth, because of gravity, only a tiny number of the cells could be removed at a time.

There is almost no gravity in space. Materials "float." They can be given an electric charge and pulled apart by an electric field. The pure materials can be collected. In space, it is possible to purify 700 times as much of certain materials as on earth.

Making some kinds of electronic chips requires a very pure form of a material called gallium arsenide. Right now, large numbers of these chips cannot be used because the material is not pure. In space, very pure crystals of gallium arsenide can be grown.

Optical glass, used in microscope lenses, must be pure. To make this kind of glass on earth, sand and limestone must be heated to about 3100°F. At these high temperatures, the glass is corrosive. It will corrode its container, so little bits of the container get mixed with the glass. The glass is no longer pure.

In space, glass can be melted without containers. The molten glass is contained by sound waves. The glass produced in this way is pure.

This symbolic photograph shows a group of pure, needle-shaped urea crystals. The crystals were grown aboard the orbiter "Discovery" in a gravity-free environment. (Courtesy of NASA)

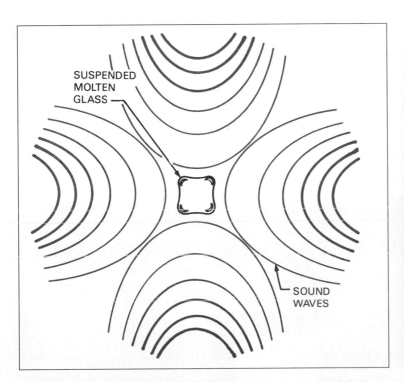

Acoustic waves (sound) hold molten glass during gravity-free processing in space.

SUSPENDED MOLTEN GLASS

SOUND WAVES

Model of a space factory.
(Courtesy of NASA)

It costs a great deal today to make products in space. We make cost-benefit trade-offs. We choose whether to make very pure optical glass in space at high cost or less pure glass on the earth at lower cost.

The first Industrial Space Facility (ISF) will be launched by a space shuttle in the 1990s. It will serve as a platform to make pure optical glass and develop new kinds of alloys. It will also be used to grow pure crystals for use in electronic devices.

As more low-gravity processing is done, space factories will be started. They will use minerals available on the moon and nearby planets. They will use solar energy for power. Although people will be able to visit these factories, they will operate automatically. The moon's soil is rich in minerals like aluminum, silicon, and titanium. A factory on the moon could use these materials to build other factories.

CONSTRUCTION IN THE FUTURE

Space construction will become a big business. Space stations will orbit the earth, serving as bases for people who come into space to work on satellites and space factories. Space stations will grow larger as more workers are needed in space. Eventually, they will become cities. People will live in space for months or years at a time.

A futuristic space station. (Courtesy of Boeing Aerospace Company)

The community of Arcosanti, located in the Arizona desert. (Courtesy of Ivan Pintar)

A city of the future, complete with parking for your personal hovercraft. (Courtesy of General Electric Company)

One design for a space city is a cylinder that spins slowly on its axis. Spinning would create an artificial gravity. People would live on the inside surface of the cylinder. A person could look up and see people and structures upside down on the opposite side of the cylinder.

On earth, more homes will be factory built and moved to a site to be put together. Today it takes five people two days to frame a wood-frame house. A factory-built house can be put up by two people in two days.

As energy costs go on rising, communities of energy efficient homes will be built. One such community is Arcosanti, in the Arizona desert. Arcosanti is a town of 5,000 people that contains high-rise apartment buildings and covers a small area of land.

Arcosanti has homes, businesses, and offices. There are spaces for parks, recreation, performances, and small meetings. The apartment buildings surround a shopping mall. From their apartments, people can look inside at the shops or outside toward the wilderness. In the community there are no roads or cars. People walk instead. Greenhouses allow residents to grow their own food year round. Garbage is used for energy. Water is recycled and purified. The architect, Paolo Soleri, said, "The need to plan for tomorrow is a part of all life."

Built-in computers will control many systems in buildings in the future. **Smart houses** will have bathrooms in which you can choose a shower, spring rain, or warm breeze. Bedrooms will have voice-activated radio and TV systems. Houses of the future will be built so people can live and work at home.

Office buildings will be "**intelligent buildings**," wired with data communications lines. Each will have a central computer tying all the offices together. People will be able to communicate between offices using desktop terminals. Energy use will be computerized, as will security. Each building will have a word-processing center and a long-distance data communication system.

TRANSPORTATION IN THE FUTURE

In 1889 Nellie Bly traveled around the world by coach, ship, train, and camel. It took 72 days to do so. In 1977 a Boeing 747 made the trip in 54 hours. Today it takes 3½ hours to travel from New York City to Paris on the Concorde, an aircraft that can fly at speeds of over 1,400 miles an hour. How fast will we travel in the future?

The lighter-than-air Magnus.
(Courtesy of Magnus Aerospace Corp.)

A transatmospheric aircraft.
(Courtesy of Lockheed—California Company)

Air Transportation

New ways of moving people and goods will meet the needs of the future. One new vehicle is the LTA (lighter-than-air) airship. This airship will take off and land vertically and will be able to carry very heavy loads.

The Magnus LTA will be able to move over 50 tons, more than the largest helicopters, and do it more cheaply. It will be made of a 200-foot nylon sphere filled with helium. The cabin will carry two engines, which will provide power for takeoff. The ship will travel at a maximum speed of 70 miles per hour and will be able to travel 500 miles before landing.

Engines will also make the sphere spin. When a sphere spins in air, forces cause it to rise. This is known as the *Magnus effect*. It was discovered in 1853 by a German physicist named H. G. Magnus. The Magnus effect causes a spinning baseball to rise as it nears the plate.

Soon a transatmospheric aircraft will be built for military use. It will travel through the atmosphere, then move into low earth orbit. The aircraft will blast off like a rocket but travel like an airplane. In less than two hours, it will come down on the other side of the world.

Space Transportation

Future travel will take people far from earth. Already travel agencies are selling tickets for rides on the space shuttle. The tickets cost $50,000. A lottery was held in 1991 for rides aboard a Soviet space vehicle.

Someday tourists will vacation in space. They will visit space colonies, the moon, and nearby planets. Small vehicles will carry people in space to and from space stations. It is not known when it will take place.

Ground Transportation

On the ground, vehicles will be faster and more energy efficient. Railroads will make use of **magnetic levitation**. Maglev trains, as they are called, will use strong magnets to repel the train from its track. This will make the train float just above the track, providing a fast, smooth ride.

A maglev train. (Courtesy of General Motors Corporation)

Automobiles of the future will be sleeker, safer, and more energy efficient. Their streamlined shapes will save on gas. More automobile systems will be computer controlled. Cars will talk to drivers. A computer will tell us that the lights are on or ask who we are before the door can be unlocked. The driver's voice print will be on record in the car's computer and will have to match the speaker's voice before the door will open.

New electronic systems will be added. A sonar system will warn of objects behind the car as the car backs up. A four-wheel steering system will let the driver turn all four wheels toward the curb to make parking easier. Doze alerts on the steering wheel will sound an alarm if the driver gets sleepy and relaxes his or her grip on the wheel. Windshield wipers will start automatically as soon as rain falls on the windshield. A navigating system will show the car's location on a video screen map. It will also give the best way to get to the driver's destination.

This satellite navigational system is combined with a laser disk map that indicates the car's position. (Courtesy of Chrysler Motors)

Cars will use new energy sources. Electric cars will become popular. They will run on large banks of batteries that will last for several hundred miles. The driver will pull into a service station when the batteries run down to exchange them for a new set.

Cars will travel on "autopilot." Future superhighways will work with computers in cars, sending signals to keep the car on the road until the right exit is reached. The driver will then take over for travel on local roads.

Personal rapid transport vehicles (**PRTs**) will become popular. PRTs are automated vehicles that travel on tracks or guideways. They can be built either above or below the ground. Using PRTs, people will be able to avoid heavy highway traffic.

The Moller 400 is a flying car that carries four people, can be parked in a normal garage, takes off vertically, and flies at speeds of up to 400 miles per hour. (Photo courtesy Moller International)

A PRT system. (Courtesy of West Virginia University)

BIOTECHNICAL SYSTEMS IN THE FUTURE

New drugs and treatments will cure or prevent many diseases, such as cancer and heart disease. We may even learn what causes the aging process. We could then slow the progress of aging or even stop it. Already, scientists have had success in keeping older rats from aging. Their hearts and lungs are as strong as those of young rats.

As we have been able to clone plants and some lower animals, we might begin to clone people. We could put the nucleus of a person's cell into an egg cell and let it grow. In this way, it would be possible to have a hundred or even a thousand people who were exactly alike. It may also be possible to engineer humans to live in hostile environments. For example, a fish-like gill could be put in a person to allow breathing under water.

Ethics

Ethics are the standards of right and wrong that people use to govern their behavior. The ethics of bioengineering will probably cause as much debate in the future as it does now. Should scientists grow human embryos to experiment on? Should we produce hundreds or even thousands of clones of a certain kind of person? Should we change people so they can live under the sea or in polluted or unsafe environments?

Who should make decisions about bioengineering? Should we leave it to scientists? To religious leaders? Should decisions be made by governments? Or by the United Nations? Could we reach worldwide agreement?

Food Production

How about a nice bowl of newspaper for breakfast? Or a plateful of maple leaves for lunch? It may not sound very good, but foods of the future may be taken from such sources. Chemists are learning how to break down materials into their basic

From the control panel on a desert farm, people will harvest crops with robotic harvestors. (Courtesy of General Electric Company)

Salt-tolerant plants, called halophytes, will be grown with seawater. (Courtesy of Environmental Research Laboratory, University of Arizona)

elements, such as carbon, hydrogen, and oxygen. They could combine these elements to make nutrients. The nutrients would then be made into artificial foods, just as healthful and maybe even as tasty as those we eat today.

Many of us would probably want an old-fashioned hamburger, but artificial foods could prevent starvation in some parts of the world. Feeding people in developing nations is becoming a problem. We could use technology to grow crops in the desert, irrigating them with salt water from the sea. These plants, called **halophytes**, would first be used to feed animals and as a source of plant oils. Later, they could be used to make foods.

Within 35 years, the earth will have a population of 8 billion people. We will need to find new ways to feed all of these people. Farmers will use **growth hormones** to produce larger, less fatty animals. Cows will produce more milk. Chickens might be developed that have no wings or feathers, making more meat with less chicken feed. Vegetables and fruit will be improved, too. For example, beet genes could be transferred to tomatoes to give tomatoes tougher skins and make them easier to ship. We may even be able to implant genes from cows into fish and raise sea steaks!

An artist's idea of an algae farm. (Courtesy of Solar Energy Research Institute)

ENERGY IN THE FUTURE

As nations become more technological, more energy will be needed. Fossil fuels will run out. Renewable energy sources

481

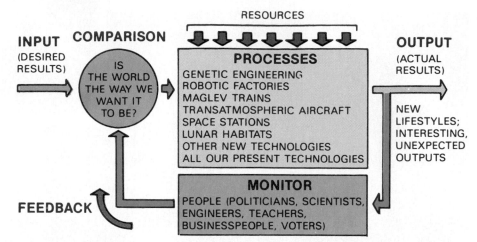

This system diagram shows how future technologies will affect our lives.

will fill most of our energy needs. Space-based power stations will send microwave energy to the earth.

Green algae plants may provide energy. Algae contain large amounts of oils and fats. These oils and fats are easily separated from the algae and can be changed into fuels. One acre of water or ground covered with algae can produce as much as 100 barrels of oil a year, which could be used to make gasoline.

One new energy source may be **nuclear fusion**. In fusion, atoms join together, giving off energy. But fusion reactions need huge amounts of energy to start. Researchers are trying to find ways to get at least as much energy from the reaction as is needed to start it. This balance is called **break-even**. Once the reaction makes more energy than is needed to start it, the excess energy can be used to generate electricity. Some researchers predict that fusion reactors will be built by the year 2020. Fusion is better than fission because it produces clean energy. There is little or no nuclear waste or radiation.

FUTURING— FORECASTING NEW TECHNOLOGIES

Existing technological systems will act together to produce new, more powerful technologies.

The newest technologies are the most complex. Many different technological systems work together. Space shuttles, satellites, robotic factories, and maglev trains, for example, require the newest in transportation, communication, manufacturing, and construction systems. This **confluence** (flowing together) of systems will mean that new technologies will not be separate and distinct. Many systems will be combined to produce new technologies.

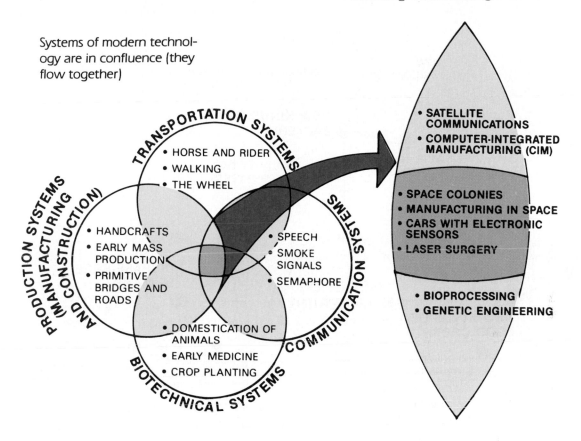

Systems of modern technology are in confluence (they flow together)

Modern biotechnology is an example of the confluence of systems. Genetic engineering is really a manufacturing process. New kinds of organisms are produced. When doing genetic engineering, technologists and scientists make use of construction, manufacturing, and communication technologies. They construct structures (like fermentation vats) to house processing operations. They use manufactured tools and instruments. They use communication and information technology when they do computer modeling.

Futuring Techniques

Futurists think about how technology will change our future. They can do this in at least four different ways.

One way to forecast the future is to use a futures wheel. A **futures wheel** is a diagram with one "big idea" at the center of a circle. The central idea leads to other ideas. Each of these ideas, in turn, has its own likely future outcomes.

Another way to forecast the future is a **cross-impact analysis**. Here, we look at many different future possibilities. We see what might happen when they are combined.

Using futuring techniques, people can anticipate the consequences of a new technology.

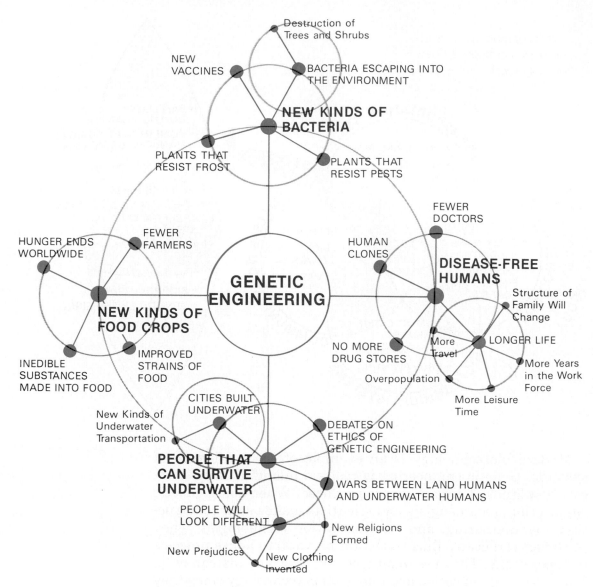

A futures wheel helps us determine possible outcomes of a new idea or technology. In this case, possible outcomes of genetic engineering are forecast.

A third way to forecast the future is through **Delphi surveys**. In a Delphi survey, experts list ten kinds of changes they expect in the future. All their ideas are put on a list that is sent to all of them. Each arranges the ideas in an order from most likely to happen to least likely to happen. A new list is made up of their lists. The new list is sent around and the experts rank the ideas again. The final list is their forecast of the future.

A **trend analysis** forecasts the future by looking at the past. For example, the cost of computers has dropped at an increasing rate over the last ten years. Forecasters might sug-

	GENETICALLY ENGINEERED HUMANS	CITIES ON THE MOON	LIFE ON OTHER PLANETS	CITIES UNDER THE SEA
AIR POLLUTION	• Humans will be able to breathe sulphur dioxide	• Moon societies will safeguard against the kind of pollution that occurred on earth	• People will vacation on nonpolluted planets	• Polluted air will be used as fuel by sea cities
RISING ENERGY COSTS	• Humans will be able to survive on fewer calories	• Energy will be beamed to earth from a moon base	• Energy sources will be exported from other planets to earth	• There will be new uses of sea water to provide energy
OVERPOPULATION	• Child-bearing will be forbidden • Only genetically engineered humans needed for specific purposes will be authorized • People will debate whether we should alter human life	• Societies will move to the moon	• Marriages will occur between earthlings and space beings • Attempts to transfer populations to other planets will meet with resistance; interspace wars will result	• People will work in new industries like mining sea beds
LONGER LIFE SPANS	• People will be altered several times during their lifetimes as conditions change on earth	• People will commute to "summer homes" on the moon • New travel agencies will specialize in moon-earth travel	• People will spend more time traveling to distant planets	• People will live part of their lives on land and part in sea cities to learn more about all forms of life

A cross-impact analysis.

gest that the price will continue to drop in this way. Computer prices in the year 2000 might be so low that they could be used everywhere and anywhere. On the other hand, just because things happened one way in the past does not mean that this trend will continue. Trend analysis does not always work.

SUMMARY

Some impacts of technology are helpful and some are harmful. It depends on how technology is used. Planning can limit the undesired outputs of technology.

We depend on technology. It would not be easy to go back to a simpler life-style. Technology must be fitted to the needs of people, and it must protect and work with the environment.

Technological change will continue to increase exponentially. Computers, telephones, satellites, and television will work together to provide new ways to communicate. Voice recogni-

(Courtesy of General Electric Company)

tion technology will allow us to speak to our typewriters. We will hold videoconferences with people in distant lands. Shopping, working, and studying will depend on the computer.

In developed nations such as the United States, robots will be used in more and more manufacturing jobs. Only in less developed nations will a large part of the work force work on factory production lines. Robots will do more for us, on the job and at home. Factories will be built in space. New materials will come from the sea, the moon, and other planets.

Space stations will orbit the earth. They will send energy back, and serve as stopping places for people on the way to the moon or the planets.

Construction technology on the earth will be more energy efficient. New housing developments will take up less space, preserve the wilderness, and use less energy. We will live in "smart houses" and work in "intelligent buildings" in which computers control many of the systems.

Future transportation will be faster and use less energy. Maglev trains will "float" on their rails, giving a fast, smooth ride. Space vehicles will carry us around space stations and space colonies. On the earth, personal vehicle systems such as PRTs will move us around cities.

Biotechnical systems will do important jobs for us. They will help us cure and prevent disease, extend our lifespans, and feed billions of people.

By early in the twenty-first century, we will use nuclear fusion to produce electricity. It will be a safe, cheap, and clean energy source.

Futuring techniques like futures wheels, cross-impact analysis, Delphi surveys, and trend analysis can help us forecast the changes technology will bring.

CONCLUSION

One thing is certain. Technology will continue to grow at an ever-increasing rate. Because of this, people must be ready to plan and direct it.

Life in the future will depend on how well we control technology. The quality of life on our planet should be our main concern. We must think in terms of the human race and less in terms of individual countries or groups. We must work together to ensure our own survival and that of the living things with which we share our planet.

Technology is not magic. As you learn more about science and mathematics, you will see that we can and must control technology, for our own good and for the good of future generations.

REVIEW QUESTIONS

1. What four possible combinations of outputs can result from technological systems?
2. Do you believe that technology is good, evil, or neutral? Explain why.
3. How can people control the development of a technology they feel may be harmful?
4. Give two examples showing that pollution is not just a recent problem.
5. Give an example of a technology that is poorly matched to the human user.
6. Give an example of a problem technology has caused and a solution technology has provided.
7. Explain how technology can make life easier for a disabled person.
8. Draw a design for a futuristic communication system that would allow you to communicate with a class of students in Europe.
9. What would be two good products to manufacture in space? Why?
10. How will future travel differ from present-day travel?
11. Would a personal rapid transit (PRT) system be useful in your town or city? Explain why or why not.
12. What kinds of moral questions will arise if people are able to engineer human life?
13. Give an example of how a modern or future technology will require inputs from several existing technological systems. (**Hint:** Think of how biotechnical, communication, construction, manufacturing, and transportation systems act together to produce new technologies, such as manufacturing in space.
14. Draw a futures wheel. At the center, place a skin cream that brings back youth. Predict the possible outcomes.

KEY WORDS

Acid rain	Futuring	Magnetic levita-	Pollution
Confluence	Growth hormone	tion (Maglev)	Smart houses
Environment	Halophyte	Manufacturing in	Speech synthesis
Ergonomics	Impact	space	Sulfur dioxide
Fusion	Intelligent	Personal rapid	Videoconference
Futures wheel	buildings	transit (PRT)	Voice recognition

SEE YOUR TEACHER FOR THE CROSSTECH PUZZLE

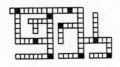

487

DUST OR BUST!

Setting the Stage

When you were sent from Earth to work on the desert planet Nala, you were told about the dust. But you hadn't thought it would be as bad as this. Without the air conditioning, you could choke to death in a matter of days.

Suddenly the air conditioning and emergency backup system fail. You have only a short time to find a way to remove the dust being carried in by the air ducts. You try filter paper and cloth, but the dust is so fine it goes right through.

Your Challenge

Find a way to remove the dust particles before your classroom becomes a death trap.

Procedure

CAUTION: As we are dealing with a high-voltage static electricity charge, the chances of getting a shock are high. Normally this is not dangerous, but those with health problems should not try this activity.

1. Be sure to wear safety glasses and a lab coat.
2. Cut the Plexiglas tube to length (24–26" long).
3. Drill two ⅜" holes in the wall of the tube 3–4" from the ends.
4. Cut the brass rod 3" longer than the Plexiglas tube.
5. Push the one-hole stoppers firmly into both ends of the tube.
6. Insert the brass rod through the stopper holes so that the extra length is all at one end.
7. Use hot glue to fasten the brass rod at the FLUSH end.
8. Using the copper wire, wrap a coil around the length of the tube. Tape both ends of the coil in place leaving 4–5' of extra wire at one end.
9. Fasten the rubber bulb or plastic squeeze bottle to one of the holes drilled in the Plexiglas.
10. Fasten the loose end of the copper wire to the base of the Van de Graaff generator.
11. Using the rubber bulb or plastic squeeze bottle, suck in some smoke or chalk dust (the more, the better).

Suggested Resources

Safety glasses and lab apron

Clear Plexiglas tubing (24–26" long, approximately 1½" diameter)

2 large one-hole rubber stoppers that fit tightly into the ends of the Plexiglas tubing

Brass rod (at least 3" longer than the Plexiglas tubing)—⅛" diameter

Copper wire (single strand, light gauge, 15–20')

Chalk dust (or other source of smoke or dust)

Electrical tape

Van de Graaff generator

Large rubber squeeze bulb or plastic squeeze bottle

Wire cutters

Drill and drill bits

Hot glue gun and glue stick

12. Turn on the Van de Graaff generator.
13. Slowly bring the protruding end of the brass rod near the top of the generator.
14. Be sure to keep your eyes on the dust or smoke to see what happens.

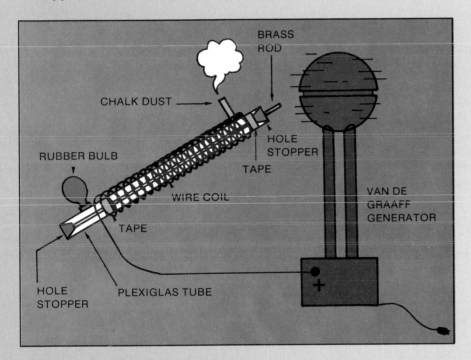

BRASS ROD

CHALK DUST

HOLE STOPPER

TAPE

RUBBER BULB

WIRE COIL

VAN DE GRAAFF GENERATOR

TAPE

HOLE STOPPER

PLEXIGLAS TUBE

Technology Connections

1. The device you have made is called an *electrostatic precipitator.* It filters tiny particles from the air by using static electricity.
2. What happened to the dust or smoke particles inside the tube when the brass rod was brought near the Van de Graaff generator? Why?
3. Would the electrostatic precipitator remove toxic (poisonous) *gases* from the air?
4. Many industries send smoke and other particles into the air as a result of production. Often they can add an electrostatic precipitator to their system to help filter out these pollutants. What industries do you think would make the most use of this device?
5. A good solution often requires a compromise. What is the trade-off (advantages *and* disadvantages) of adding an electrostatic precipitator to a power plant?

Science and Math Concepts

▶ Opposite electrical charges (+ and −) attract each other. Similar electrical charges (+ and +) or (− and −) repel each other.
▶ Plexiglas and rubber are *insulators.* Insulators are poor conductors of electricity.
▶ Metals such as copper and brass are good *conductors* of electricity.
▶ A negative (−) charge results from an excess of electrons. A positive (+) charge results from too few electrons.

SATEL-LOON

Setting the Stage

The storm has been building steadily. The waves are becoming gigantic. There seems to be no way to save the boat from the rocks. Hurriedly, you throw your gear into waterproof containers and toss them into the sea. At the signal, you and your fellow travelers jump into the water and make your way as best you can to shore.

By the light of day you spot some of the gear thrown up on shore. Luck is with you, and you find your Emergency Position Indicating Radio Beacons (EPIRBs). The emergency signal you send will be picked up by satellites as they pass overhead. At least you now have hope of being rescued.

Your Challenge

Simulate satellite communication by using a small transmitter to send a signal up to a satel-loon. The satel-loon will be capable of repeating the signal on another band or frequency and re-transmitting the signal back to another location on the ground.

Procedure

1. Enclose a small AM-FM radio and a 100 mw CB transceiver in a container with approximately 8" between the two units. This will be the repeater.
2. Place cushioning foam inside the container to protect the electronic gear from an accidental crash.
3. Use an FM transmitter and send a signal to the repeater. Tune the transmitter and receiver until you hear a clear signal.
4. Lock the CB located in the satel-loon in the transmit position. Use another CB about 30 feet away to receive the re-transmitted signal from the repeater.
5. Check all units for clarity.
6. Pick a clear day with no wind if you are using helium-filled balloons to fly the satel-loon. Choose a day with a steady wind if you are using a parafoil kite. Use anchor stakes for each system and 165 lb. test line.
7. After checking all units on the ground, send the satel-loon aloft.
8. Transmit a message using your satel-loon.
9. Invite the local newspaper to cover this activity. You are simulating the latest technology in communications.

Suggested Resources

AM or FM transmitter—100 mw
2 CB transceivers
AM-FM radio
Helium-filled balloons or parafoil kite
165 lb. test nylon line
Anchor stake
Cushioning foam

490

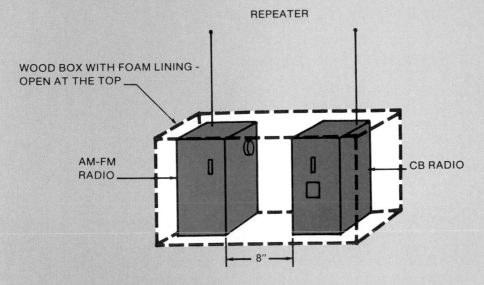

REPEATER

WOOD BOX WITH FOAM LINING - OPEN AT THE TOP

AM-FM RADIO

CB RADIO

8"

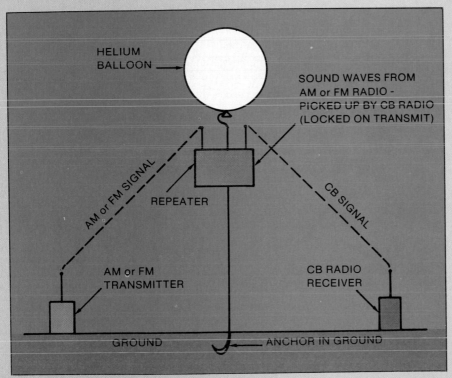

HELIUM BALLOON

SOUND WAVES FROM AM or FM RADIO - PICKED UP BY CB RADIO (LOCKED ON TRANSMIT)

AM or FM SIGNAL

CB SIGNAL

REPEATER

AM or FM TRANSMITTER

CB RADIO RECEIVER

GROUND

ANCHOR IN GROUND

Technology Connections

1. Who uses EPIRBs? Who else will receive the EPIRB's signals?
2. Compare the transmission of EPIRB signals via satellite with satellite communication using telephones or TVs.
3. What type of programs are transmitted via satellite?
4. What is videoconferencing? How are satellites used in videoconferencing?

Science and Math Concepts

▶ Radio signals travel at the speed of light.

MAPPING THE FUTURE

Setting the Stage

Futurists are people who study and forecast the future. They try to suggest things that might happen so people can plan for the future. One of the techniques used to study the future is called modeling. Futurists often use graphic or physical models to describe the relationships between their ideas so they can be more easily understood. One of the simplest models is called a futures wheel.

Your Challenge

Working in teams, develop a futures wheel that illustrates the effects a new technology might have on society in the future.

Procedure

1. Select one of the following emerging technologies for your futures wheel: plastic automobiles, electric automobiles, computer aided design, picture telephones, teleconferencing, robotics, computer integrated manufacturing, personal robots, super trains, lighter-than-air vehicles, wind generators, smart houses, industrial space facilities, and video conferencing.
2. Write the name of the topic on an 8 ½" × 11" sheet of paper. Post the name of your topic in the center of your bulletin board.
3. Identify the immediate consequences (effects) of using the new technology. For example, widespread use of solar energy might conserve fossil fuels, create new architectural styles, and lower home heating costs. Try to identify both positive and negative consequences.
4. Write the consequences on 3" × 5" cards. Post the cards around the central topic. Use string to create lines between the central topic and its immediate consequences.
5. Identify a second generation of consequences for each immediate consequence. For example, conserving fossil fuels might reduce air pollution, eliminate jobs, and cause fossil fuel prices to rise.
6. Write the secondary consequences on 3" × 5" cards. Post them around their immediate consequences. Using string, connect each immediate consequence to its secondary consequence. (Note: Can you use different-colored markers, different-shaped cards, or some other method to make the difference between the immediate and secondary consequences clear?)
7. Identify a third generation of consequences. For example, eliminating jobs might increase unemployment as well as create a need for retraining programs.

Suggested Resources

Composition board (sheathing)—½" × 4' × 4'
3" × 5" cards
String
Straight pins, staples, or thumb tacks
Magic markers

492

8. Write your third generation consequences on 3" × 5" cards. Post them near their secondary consequences. Using string, connect the secondary consequences to the next generation of consequences.
9. Share your futures wheel with the class. Assign each member of your team a section of the futures wheel that they can describe to the class.

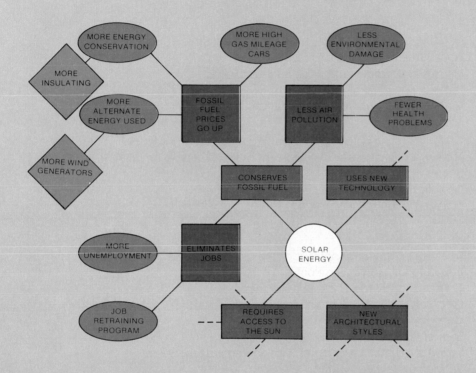

Technology Connections

1. *Futurists* are people who think about what might happen in the future. Are you a futurist?
2. Futures wheels help people discover and describe what might happen in the future. Could a futures wheel help you plan your future? What would you put in the center of your futures wheel?
3. Ever since humankind invented the wheel, technology has played an important role in the way we live and work. However, technological advancements are being made more rapidly than ever before. Will people continue to allow technology to shape the way they live and work in the future? Or, do you think people will reject technology and try to live simpler lives?

Science and Math Concepts

▶ Cause-and-effect relationships are events that result in changes. Cause is often a human activity and effect is the change caused by the activity.
▶ Modeling describes the relationships among a collection of ideas in a graphic, physical, or other form so it can be more easily understood.

TECHNOLOGICAL TIMELINE

STONE AGE

1,000,000 B.C.	Fire and the development of early stone tools
17,000 B.C.	Domestication of animals
12,000 B.C.	Early oil lamps that burned fish and animal oil
10,000 B.C.	Yeast for leavening bread

AGRICULTURAL ERA

8000 B.C.	Agriculture in the Fertile Crescent
6500 B.C.	Houses built from mud-bricks; dugout canoes
6000 B.C.	Pottery
3500 B.C.	Writing (cuneiform and hieroglyphics)

BRONZE AGE

3000 B.C.	Tools made from metal; development of the wheel; wine made from pressed grapes
1900 B.C.	Plowing with animals
1500 B.C.	Grinding of grain; glassmaking

IRON AGE

1200 B.C.	Smelting of iron; development of the Greek alphabet
700 B.C.	Irrigation and sewage in Rome
221 B.C.	Construction of the Great Wall of China
144 B.C.	First high-level aqueduct in Rome; use of cement
100 B.C.	Water wheels
410 A.D.	Sack of Rome by Visigoths
500 A.D.	Sailing ships that could travel with and against the wind
550 A.D.	Babylonian Talmud written
650 A.D.	Writing of the Koran
750 A.D.	Arabs learn papermaking from Chinese prisoners
765 A.D.	School of medicine founded in Baghdad
1024 A.D.	Chinese use first paper currency
1200 A.D.	Windmills
1281 A.D.	Chinese use gunpowder in war against Mongols
1400-1600 A.D.	Age of exploration and discovery; Balboa, Cabot, Columbus, de Gama, de Leon, Hudson, Magellan
1450 A.D.	Gutenberg invents movable type
1560 A.D.	Water-pumping machine
1600 A.D.	Magnetism discovered by William Gilbert
1610 A.D.	Galileo's telescope
1619 A.D.	First slaves brought to North America by British
1628 A.D.	Circulation of the blood discovered by William Harvey
1700 A.D.	Newton's Laws
1712 A.D.	Newcomen's steam engine
1721 A.D.	Bach completes Brandenburg concertos
1724 A.D.	Farenheit thermometer invented
1752 A.D.	Benjamin Franklin proves lightning is electricity

INDUSTRIAL ERA

1760-1840 A.D.	Industrial Revolution in Britain
1769 A.D.	James Watt's steam engine
1770 A.D.	Hargreaves's spinning jenny patented
1776 A.D.	U.S. Declaration of Independence
1780 A.D.	The lathe
1784 A.D.	Wrought-iron process by Henry Cort
1785 A.D.	Cartwright's loom
1789 A.D.	French Revolution
1789 A.D.	LaVoisier's theory of chemical combustion published
1793 A.D.	Eli Whitney's cotton gin
1798 A.D.	Eli Whitney's factory mass-produces firearms
1804 A.D.	Jacquard's loom
1807 A.D.	Britain abolishes the slave trade; Robert Fulton's steamboat
1808 A.D.	Slave trade ends in the United States
1811 A.D.	Luddites smash knitting machines in Britain
1812 A.D.	Napoleon invades Russia
1816 A.D.	Regular transatlantic sailing service begins between New York and Liverpool, England
1822 A.D.	First textile mill in United States, in Massachusetts
1829 A.D.	The steam locomotive
1835 A.D.	Bessemer process for making steel
1839 A.D.	Photography invented
1843 A.D.	Morse begins telegraph line between Baltimore, Md. and Washington, D.C.
1861-1865 A.D.	Civil War in the United States
1863 A.D.	Emancipation Proclamation
1864 A.D.	George Washington Carver born; he discovered over 300 uses for the peanut. He also founded the Tuskegee Institute
1876 A.D.	Alexander Graham Bell invents the telephone
1885 A.D.	Carl Benz, in Germany; first successful gasoline-driven motorcar
1887 A.D.	Daimler's internal combustion engine automobile
1888 A.D.	First Kodak hand-held camera
1893 A.D.	Diesel engine invented by Dr. Rudolf Diesel
1900 A.D.	EverReady flashlight invented; paper clip patented; incubator patented by Granville T. Woods
1901 A.D.	Marconi sends first transatlantic radio signals; spinal anesthesia developed in France
1902 A.D.	Rayon patented
1903 A.D.	Wright brothers' airplane
1905 A.D.	Albert Einstein proposes his theory of relativity
1906 A.D.	Freeze-drying invented in France; hot dog gets its name from a cartoon of a dachshund in a bun
1908 A.D.	Model T Ford built by mass production
1909 A.D.	Beginning of the age of plastics; Bakelite patented
1910 A.D.	Cellophane invented
1911 A.D.	Rutherford proposes his theory of atomic structure
1912 A.D.	Sinking of the Titanic—1,513 people die; first heart attack diagnosed in a living patient
1914 A.D.	Panama Canal opens; bacteria used to treat sewage; outbreak of World War I
1915 A.D.	SONAR invented

1918 A.D.	Red, green, and yellow traffic lights in New York
1919 A.D.	First transatlantic flight—Newfoundland to Ireland
1920 A.D.	First U.S. commercial broadcasting station—KDKA from Pittsburgh goes on the air
1921 A.D.	Hybrid corn greatly improves crop yields; Band-Aids invented; first lie detector; first cultured pearls
1923 A.D.	Automatic traffic light patented by Garrett A. Morgan
1924 A.D.	First round-the-world flight; Kleenex tissues
1925 A.D.	First successful experiments with hydroponics
1926 A.D.	First television demonstration; pop-up toaster
1927 A.D.	The theory of negative feedback developed
1928 A.D.	Penicillin invented by Alexander Fleming; Rice Krispies marketed by Kellogg cereal company; Scotch Tape produced by 3M company
1929 A.D.	Electroencephalograph (EEG); foam rubber
1930 A.D.	Packaged frozen foods go on sale in Massachusetts
1931 A.D.	First regular TV broadcasts (station W6XAO in California); Empire State Building in New York City
1934 A.D.	The electron microscope
1935 A.D.	Radar developed; Nylon patented; B-17 bomber produced by Boeing
1936 A.D.	Vitamin pills; Polaroid sunglasses
1938 A.D.	The ball-point pen is patented
1939 A.D.	Outbreak of World War II; DDT produced; first jet aircraft flies in Germany; Pan Am begins first regular commercial transatlantic flights
1940 A.D.	Freeze-drying used to preserve foods in United States
1942 A.D.	LORAN developed; first color snapshots
1944 A.D.	First automatic digital computer, the Mark I; DNA isolated at the Rockefeller Institute
1945 A.D.	Atom bomb used on Hiroshima and Nagasaki; ENIAC computer built using 18,000 vacuum tubes
1946 A.D.	Timex watches
1947 A.D.	Microwave oven; first Honda motorcycle; development of the transistor at Bell Laboratories
1948 A.D.	Polaroid camera; LP records; Teflon
1950 A.D.	Power steering; start of regular color TV broadcasts; first credit card (Diner's Club)
1952 A.D.	Salk polio vaccine; first sex-change operation—Christine Jorgensen; Sony pocket transistor radio; 3-D movies
1953 A.D.	First successful open heart surgery; supersonic jet aircraft built by Pratt and Whitney; Dacron developed in Britain; breeder reactor in Idaho; double helix model for structure of DNA proposed
1954 A.D.	Nuclear-powered submarine "Nautilus"; numerical control machining; photocell developed
1955 A.D.	Velcro fasteners patented; birth-control pills; nuclear-powered electricity generation; fiber optics; domestic freezers; multitrack recording
1956 A.D.	FORTRAN computer language; hydrogen bomb exploded; first videotape recorder; first desktop computer (Burroughs E-101)

SPACE AGE

1957 A.D.	Sputnik; Sabin oral polio vaccine; high-speed dental drill; mercury batteries

INFORMATION AGE

1958 A.D.   First integrated circuit made by Texas Instruments; bifocal contact lenses; first U.S. satellite

1959 A.D.   Pilkington float glass process perfected; Sony produces first transistorized TV; Russia sends unmanned spacecraft to the moon (Luna 2); Xerox copier

1960 A.D.   Lasers; light-emitting diodes (LEDs); weather satellites; felt-tip pens

1962 A.D.   TV signals sent across the Atlantic via satellite; world's first industrial robot produced by Unimation Corporation; Tang orange juice

1963 A.D.   John F. Kennedy assassinated; cassette tapes; Instamatic cameras; the tranquilizer Valium produced; Artificial heart used during surgery

1964 A.D.   China tests nuclear bomb; IBM word processors; photochromic eyeglasses that change in response to the amount of sunlight

1965 A.D.   First space walk; Super 8 cameras; reports link cigarette smoking to cancer

1966 A.D.   Flashcubes; electronic fuel injection; Russians make successful soft landing on the moon (Luna 9)

1967 A.D.   Christiaan Barnard performs first heart transplant; energy-absorbing bumpers; Frisbees

1969 A.D.   American manned moon landing; first Concorde SST flight

1970 A.D.   Russians land moon robot (Lunokhod); floppy disks; jumbo jets

1971 A.D.   Microprocessor developed by Intel; Mariner 9 orbits Mars

1972 A.D.   CAT scan; photography from satellites (Landsat); videodiscs

1973 A.D.   Genetic engineering; Skylab orbiting space station launched; supermarket optical price scanning; Selectric self-correcting typewriter; push-through tabs on cans

1974 A.D.   Toronto Communications Tower (tallest building in the world) opens

1975 A.D.   Liquid crystal displays; video games; disposable razors; cloning of a rabbit; Americans and Russians dock in space

1976 A.D.   Birth of the Apple computer; electronic cameras

1977 A.D.   Space shuttle; trans-Alaska pipeline system completed; neutron bomb developed

1978 A.D.   First test-tube baby born; programmable washing machines; computerized chess; auto-focus cameras

1979 A.D.   Skylab, the orbiting space station, falls back to earth

1980 A.D.   Solar-powered aircraft

1981 A.D.   Silicon 32-bit chip; nuclear magnetic resonance (NMR) scanner, first launch of a reusable space vehicle (the space shuttle *Columbia*)

1982 A.D.   Artificial heart

1983 A.D.   Biopol (biodegradable plastic); carbon-fiber aircraft wing; 512K dynamic access memory chip

1984 A.D.   Compact disk player; genetically engineered blood-clotting factor; megabit computer chip

1985 A.D.   CD-ROM (compact-disk read-only memory); image digitizer; soft bifocal contact lens

1986 A.D.   Uranus moons' photographs; DNA fingerprinting; diminished ozone shield

1987 A.D.   High-temperature superconductivity confirmed

1988 A.D.   Patented animal life

1990 A.D.   NASA's Hubble Space Telescope deployed by space shuttle Discovery

TECHNOLOGY EDUCATION STUDENT ASSOCIATIONS

Arvid Van Dyke

INTRODUCTION

Technology education student associations help you work with others in your technology class, your school, and your community. The technology student organization is the group in your school that uses technology in a variety of interesting activities, projects, and contests.

Think of the other groups in your school. Some, called "clubs," serve a special interest or offer after-school activities. Associations such as the Student Council serve all students in the school. The technology education student association, now called the Technology Student Association (TSA), serves all students taking Technology Education or Industrial Technology in their school.

Technology education student associations should meet the standards for technology education that have been established by an international association of teachers. These standards are helpful in making student associations serve the needs of students who must be technologically literate to live and work in our technological world.

Technology education student associations involve communication, construction, manufacturing, and transportation activities. Opportunities for creative thinking, problem solving, and decision making are also provided. Learning how technology works can be greatly enhanced by the student association's activities.

LEARNING TO BE LEADERS

Every group or organization has a set of leaders, called officers. Most officers are elected by group members. In a corporation, for example, a board of directors may appoint (or employ) a president to run the company. Vice presidents, treasurers, and other managers or leaders are the top people who make things happen in the organization.

Every student should serve at some time as an officer in the student association. You can volunteer to be a candidate or be nominated by someone else. Experience as an elected officer will improve your ability to lead and to work with others. Leadership skill is especially valuable when you are attending college or working. Employers look for people who are willing to learn and are able to get along well with others.

ASSOCIATIONS START IN CLASS

Many teachers recognize the benefit of student associations and involve all of their students in the associations. The students learn to lead and to use technology to make learning activities more significant. The officers and committees of an in-class student organization can help lead and manage activities during the class period. Each class may then want to take part in the school's technology student association activities.

Student organizations help build leadership and public speaking abilities. (Courtesy of Kramer Photos, Jerry Kramer, Box 87, 118 S. Main, Melvern, KS 66510)

THE SCHOOL ORGANIZATION OR CHAPTER

Most student groups in your school are organized to allow students to work together in activities related to a subject they take. A student association for technology education plans activities that relate to technology. By working together, the group accomplishes more than each member could accomplish individually.

The association forms committees to allow more of its members to lead activities. Each committee plans and leads at least one activity relating to the school's technology education classes. The activity adds to students' understanding of technology and its impact on our world.

The student association in your school **affiliates** (joins together) with the state association so that all school chapters throughout your state are stronger and can share information. In the same way, your state office affiliates with all other state offices to form a strong national association. The national association offers many services to its member states, schools, and students.

ADVANTAGES TO STUDENTS AND THEIR SCHOOL

The technology education student association can help you continue your exploration in the field of technology. You can learn about career options and opportunities. By working in groups, you learn leadership skills and work cooperatively with other students and adults. Your school technology education program becomes better known because the student association attains recognition through the success of its members. You prepare for contests, follow the Achievement Programs, and travel to conferences in your state. Attending a national conference is an honor and a very educational experience.

LEARNING ABOUT TECHNOLOGY WITH THE TECHNOLOGY STUDENT ASSOCIATION

Your class and chapter officers can select several activities that will help students learn more about technology. Each activity allows students an opportunity to make technology work. Begin a brainstorming session, and find activities that are closely related to the technology area you are currently studying. Try to use technology in your student association activities.

CONTESTS TO MOTIVATE AND TEACH

Contests start in the classroom or laboratory, like many other activities of the technology education student association. The contest or project can be one of your class assignments. For example, all students might be required to make a safety poster during the laboratory safety unit of instruction. All posters are then graded by the teacher before a student committee judges the posters for in-class awards. The top posters are entered (registered) in the TSA Safety Poster Contest for recognition at the state or national conferences.

Competitive events motivate students to learn and to use technology for problem solving. Contests should offer a challenge to students' minds, hands, and attitudes. Some types of contest test a student's understanding of technology and its impact. Other TSA contests recognize leadership skills. Still others allow students to use communication skills in speaking or writing about technology and its significance.

Working on technology activities is an important
part of your student organization membership.
(Courtesy of Kramer Photos, Jerry Kramer, Box 87, 118 S. Main,
Melvern, KS 66510)

GLOSSARY

Absolute Zero The temperature at which all molecular motion stops, approximately $-459°$ F or $-273°$ C.

Acid Rain Rain containing chemicals given off by automobiles and factories, often hundreds of miles away, that damages trees and other plants.

Active Solar The use of solar energy to perform a specific task, such as heating water or generating electricity.

Actual Results The outputs of the system.

Agriculture The production of plants and animals and the processing of them into food, clothing, and other products.

Alternating Current Current that changes direction in a circuit at a rate determined by its frequency.

Alternative The choice of one thing from out of two or more possibilities.

Ampere The unit in which electrical current is measured. An ampere is the amount of current that flows when one volt pushes electrons through one ohm of resistance.

Amplifier A device that makes a small mechanical force or electrical voltage larger.

Analog In electronics, a smoothly varying voltage or current that can be set to any desired value; as oposed to digital, which can be set only to a limited number of values (e.g., 1s and 0s in binary form).

Arch A curved structure used as a support over an open space.

Architect A person who designs buildings.

ASCII American Standard Code for Information Interchange. A digital code in which seven binary bits represent letters, numbers, and punctuation.

Asphalt A tarlike substance used to pave roads and produce roof shingles.

Assembly Line A manufacturing method in which each worker or machine does only a small part of the whole job, and the products being built move from worker to worker or machine to machine.

Automation The process of controlling machines automatically.

Bandwidth The measure of the ability of a communications channel to carry information. The larger (wider) the bandwidth, the more information the channel can carry.

Battery A device that stores energy chemically and converts it to electricity.

Biomass Vegetable and animal waste matter used for energy generation.

Biotechnology The use of living organisms to make commercial products; includes antibody production, bioprocessing, and genetic engineering.

Bit The smallest unit of digital information; a "1" or "0" in digital coding.

Bottom Plate A single 2×4 used to construct the bottom of a wall section.

Brainstorming A method of coming up with alternative solutions in which group members suggest ideas and no one criticizes them.

Broadcast The sending of a message to many receivers at the same time.

British Thermal Unit The amount of energy needed to raise the temperature of one pound of water one degree Fahrenheit.

Brittle A material that breaks more easily than it bends.

Bronze Age The period (3000 B.C. to 1200 B.C.) in which people discovered how to combine metals to make alloys. The most common alloy was bronze, made from copper and tin.

Building Permit   Permission received from a local authority to begin construction.

Buoyancy   The upward force on an object in a liquid.

Business Plan   A written plan that states the goals and objectives of a business, the strategy and methods to be used to achieve them, and the financial requirements of the business.

Byte   A group of bits, usually eight, that is used to represent information in digital form.

CAD   *Computer-Aided Design:* The use of a computer to assist in the process of designing a part, circuit, building, etc. *Computer-Aided Drafting:* The use of a computer to assist in the process of creating, storing, retrieving, modifying, and plotting of a technical drawing.

CAD/CAM   A technology that links computer-aided design with computer-aided manufacturing. Design information is communicated directly to the machine tool by computers.

CAM   Computer-Aided Manufacturing. The use of computers to control a manufacturing process.

Capital   One of the seven resources used in technological systems. Capital is the money or other form of wealth used to provide the machines, materials, and other resources needed in the system.

Cash Flow Analysis   A projection of how much money will have to be spent each week or month of operation and how much income is expected in the same period.

Casting   Forming a product by pouring a liquid material into a mold, letting it harden into a solid, and removing it from the mold.

Cement   A construction material made of limestone and clay.

Ceramics   Materials that are made from clay or similar inorganic materials.

Certificate of Occupancy   Issued by a municipality to the owner of a building after the building is completed and meets all building codes. It authorizes the owner to use the building.

Channel   The path that information takes from the transmitter to the receiver.

CIM   Computer-Integrated Manufacturing. The use of computers to control both the business and production aspects of a manufacturing facility.

Circuit   A group of components connected to perform a function.

Circuit Breaker   an electromagnetic device that acts like a fuse and interrupts an electrical circuit when too much current flows (as when a short circuit occurs).

Closed-Loop System   A system that uses feedback to affect the process, based on a comparison of the system's output(s) to its command input(s).

Coal   A hard substance that comes from decayed plant and animal matter under great pressure for millions of years. It is burned to obtain energy.

Coating   A combining process used to beautify or protect the surface of a material.

Code   A set of signals or symbols that has some specific meaning to both the sender of the message and the receiver of the message.

Combining   The joining of two or more materials in one of several ways, including fastening, coating, and making composites.

Communication   Successfully sending a message or idea from one person, animal, or machine (the origin) to a second person, animal, or machine (the destination).

Communication System   A system designed to communicate a message from sender to receiver. Like all systems, it includes an input, process, and output. Often, feedback is included.

Compact Disk A thin round disk on which information is stored digitally in the form of pits that reflect or absorb light from a laser.

Comparator The part of a closed-loop system that compares the output (actual results) to the command input (desired results).

Component A part that performs a specific function.

Composite A synthetic material made of other materials.

Compression A force that squeezes a material.

Concrete A construction material made of stone, sand, water, and cement.

Conditioning Changing the internal properties of a material.

Conductor A material whose atoms easily give up their outer electrons, letting an electrical current flow easily through it.

Confluence The flowing together of systems and technologies.

Conservation of Energy This principle states that energy can neither be created nor destroyed; it can only be changed from one form into another.

Construction The building of a structure on a site.

Container Ship A ship that carries freight prepacked in containers that are carried to and from the ship on railroad flat cars and trucks.

Contract A formal agreement between any two people. In construction, the agreement that describes in detail what will be built, when and how it will be paid for, and who assumes risks if something goes wrong.

Control An adjustment of the process which makes actual results conform more closely to the desired results.

Conveyor A transport system used to carry parts from workstation to workstation on an assembly line.

Coordination In construction, the cooperation between two or more groups of people to avoid interference when installing different systems in a single building.

Current The flow of electrons through a material.

Custom-Made Products that are specifically produced to meet an individual's specified needs.

Daisy Wheel Printer A daisy wheel printer uses a print head shaped like a daisy. It prints with letter quality. A daisy wheel is made from plastic and includes an entire set of characters (numbers, letters, and punctuation).

Data Raw facts and figures. Data may be processed into information. (See Information.)

Data Communication Communication between computers or from a computer to a terminal, printer, or other peripheral device.

Design Brief A simple statement that spells out the proposed solution to a problem. The design brief should include the design criteria and the constraints.

Design Elements Graphic designs like lines or bars that improve the appearance of a printed page.

Design Folder A place where a record of all the ideas and drawings that lead toward a solution can be kept.

Desired Results A system's command input; a statement of the expected output(s) of a system.

Desktop Publishing The linkup of a personal computer, special software, a mouse, and a high-quality laser printer to compose entire pages of text and pictures.

Diesel A type of internal combustion engine that does not use spark plugs.

Digital In electronics, the use of a limited number of values of voltage or current to represent information (e.g., 1s and 0s in a binary system).

Distributed Computing   The use of two or more computers connected by data communications to perform information processing.

Dot Matrix Printer   A computer printer that uses a group of pins, arranged in a rectangular format called a matrix, to press into a ribbon and print characters on paper.

Downlink   The portion of a satellite communication link from the satellite to the ground station(s).

Drag   The wind resistance that holds a plane back when it is moving forward.

Drilling   A separating process that cuts holes in materials.

Ductile   A material that bends more easily than it breaks is called ductile.

Educate   To provide instruction or training. One of the reasons communication systems are used.

Elastic   A ductile material that bends and then returns to its original shape is called elastic.

Electric Motor   A device that converts electric energy into rotary motion.

Electromagnetic Wave   The flow of energy through space at the speed of light in the form of a wave made up of electric and magnetic fields.

Electron   The negatively charged part of an atom that orbits the nucleus. The movement of electrons from one atom to another creates an electric current.

Electronic Communication   Those methods of communication where the channel uses electrical energy.

Energy   One of the seven resources used by technological systems. Energy is the capacity for doing work. It takes many forms (thermal, electrical, mechanical, etc.) and comes from many sources (solar, muscle, chemical, nuclear, etc.)

Energy Converter   A device that changes one form of energy into another.

Engine   A device that converts energy into motion and force.

Engineer   A person with an engineering degree and/or a state license who designs buildings, roads, electronic circuits, airplanes, computers, and other technological systems.

Entertain   To amuse or hold the attention of someone. One of the reasons communication systems are used.

Entrepreneur   A person who forms and runs a business that is often based on new ideas and/or inventions.

Environment   The land areas, atmosphere, and bodies of water that surround us on planet earth, and which must be protected from pollutants and treated with caring and respect.

EPA (Environmental Protection Agency)   A federal agency that enforces regulations designed to protect the environment.

Ergonomics   Fitting technology to human needs.

Estimator   A person who prepares an estimate of the cost of a construction job.

Exponential   Increasing or decreasing at a changing rate (as oposed to *linear*, increasing or decreasing at a constant rate).

External Combustion Engine   An engine in which fuel is burned (combustion takes place) in a chamber external to the chamber where motion is produced.

Extruding   A method of forming parts in which a softened material is squeezed through an opening, giving the part the shape of the opening.

Fastening   The process of attaching one part to another.

Feedback   The use of information about the output(s) of a system to modify the process.

Feedback Control   A method by which systems are controlled. Outputs are monitored and compared to desired results. Adjustments are made to the process.

Fermentation A process in which living organisms digest starch and sugar, producing by-products like alcohol and carbon dioxide gas.

Ferrous Metals Metals made from more than 50 percent iron.

Fiber Optic The passing of light through a flexible fiberglass or plastic light guide.

Finite Having limits.

Fission The splitting of an atomic nucleus into two smaller nuclei, neutrons, and energy.

Flexible Manufacturing A manufacturing process in which the tools and machines can be easily reprogrammed to produce different parts, making it economically feasible to make small quantities of any given part.

Floor Joists The long boards that support the floor in a house.

Footing The base of the foundation; generally made from concrete.

Forging Heating a metal part and hammering it into shape.

Forming Changing a material's shape without cutting it.

Forms In construction, molds that give concrete its shape while it is hardening.

Fossil Fuel A fuel formed from the partially decomposed remains of plants and animals buried in the earth over extremely long periods of time. Examples of fossil fuels include coal, oil, and natural gas.

Foundation In construction, the portion of a structure that supports its weight; the substructure. The foundation includes the footing and the foundation wall.

Foundation Wall The part of the foundation above the footing.

Framing The process of constructing the skeleton of the house.

Frequency The number of times an electromagnetic wave changes polarities in a specified period of time, usually cycles per second (hertz).

Frost Line The depth to which the ground freezes in a particular location.

Fusion The combining of two atomic nuclei into a single nucleus plus a large amount of energy.

Futures Wheel A graphic method of forecasting the future. It is used to forecast second- and third-order impacts that result from a technology.

Futuring Projecting possible future outcomes of a given system or situation and analyzing the effects of each.

Gantt Chart A type of bar chart used to plan and track a job's schedule.

Gas *Natural gas:* A mixture of methane and other gasses that can be obtained from the earth and burned to provide energy. *Gasoline:* A liquid, obtained by refining crude oil, that is used as a fuel in internal combustion engines.

Gasahol A fuel used in internal combustion engines made from combining gasoline with alcohol.

Gasification The process of deriving methane gas from biomass or coal.

General Contractor A person or company who accepts the total and complete responsibility for building a construction project.

Generator A device that converts rotary motion into electric energy.

Geothermal An energy source derived from the heat of the earth.

Girder A strong horizontal structural support made from wood or steel.

Gluing A method of fastening materials using glue, which creates chemical bonds between itself and the materials being glued.

Goal In problem solving, the desired result of the proposed solution.

Graphic Communication Those methods of communication where the channel carries images or printed words.

Gravure Printing Printing from a recessed surface; intaglio printing.

Grinding The process in which small amounts of a material are removed by rubbing it with an abrasive.

Growth Hormone A hormone injected into animals or plants to stimulate greater growth.

Halophyte A plant that can grow using salt water irrigation.

Hardness The ability of a material to resist being dented or scratched.

Header A wooden support used on top of windows and doors to distribute the load from above to the studs.

Heat Treating A conditioning process in which a material's internal properties are changed through the use of heat.

Horsepower A measure of power equal to 550 foot-pounds per second, 746 watts, or 33,000 foot-pounds per minute.

Hydraulic Activated by fluid pressure.

Hydroelectricity Electricity produced by turbines driven by falling water.

I/O (Input/Output) The exchange of information from people to computers through input and output devices such as keyboards and printers.

Impact The effect a technology has on people, society, the economy, or the environment.

Implementation In problem solving, trying out the proposed solution.

Inclined Plane A surface placed at an angle to a flat surface. It is used to enable a small force to lift a heavy object from one level to another.

Industrial Era The period during which many mechanical devices and machines were invented and became central to the manufacturing process. The Industrial Era began in Great Britain about 1750. It began in the United States in about 1800.

Industrial Materials The intermediate step between primary raw materials and finished products. Primary raw materials are made into industrial materials, which are made into end products.

Industrial Revolution A period of inventive activity, beginning around 1750 in Britain. During this time machines mechanized what had previously been manual work. The Industrial Revolution was responsible for many social changes, as well as changes in the way things were manufactured.

Inform To impart knowledge of facts or circumstances. One of the reasons communication systems are used.

Information One of the seven resources used by technological systems. Data is raw facts and figures; information is data that has been processed (recorded, classified, calculated, stored and/or retrieved). Knowledge is gained when different kinds of information are compared and conclusions are drawn.

Information Era The present-day period, in which many inventions are based upon electronics and the computer.

Input The command entered into a system; the desired results of the system.

Insight A process of conceiving possible solutions to a problem in which solutions leap into the mind of the problem solver.

Insulation Material that does not conduct heat or electricity very well.

Insulator A material whose atoms hold their outer electrons tightly, resisting the flow of electrical current through it.

Integrated Circuit A complete electronic circuit built on a single piece of semiconductor material. Integrated circuits contain from dozens to over 500,000 transistors and other circuit components. They can perform extremely complex functions.

Intelligent Building A building with advanced communications capabilities built in to be shared by different tenants.

Interchangeable Parts that are manufactured to be precisely alike so that they can be substituted for each other.

Intermodal A transportation system that uses more than one type (mode) of transportation (e.g., ships, railroads, trucks).

Internal Combustion Engine An engine that burns its fuel within a totally enclosed chamber.

Iron Age The Period during which people learned to extract iron from iron ore and to make tools with it. In the Middle East, this happened around 1200 B.C.

Isometric A drawing within an isometric axis. This axis includes a framework of three lines; one is vertical, the other two are drawn at angles of 30 degrees to the horizontal.

Jet An aircraft that uses a jet engine. A jet engine is one that provides thrust from the burning of fuel and air, and the rapid expansion of the burning gases.

Just in Time Manufacturing A manufacturing process in which the raw materials and other required parts arrive at the factory just before they are needed in the assembly process.

Kinetic Energy The energy of an object due to its motion.

Laser Light Amplification by Stimulated Emission of Radiation. A laser is a source of very pure (single color) light that is focused into a very narrow beam.

Laser Printer A laser printer uses a laser beam to expose a photosensitive drum. It can be used to print letter quality text and graphics very rapidly.

Lift The upward force on an object in the air, resulting from its weight and volume (passive lift) or its shape and movement through the air (active lift).

Load An object upon which work is done, causing it to move.

Local Area Network (LAN) Combination of a small number of personal computers which share data and peripheral devices.

Macadam A road surface made from asphalt.

Machines With tools, one of the seven resources used in technological systems. Machines change the amount, speed, or direction of a force.

Machine Communication Communication between people and machines (such as the use of a joystick or a mouse with a computer); or between two or more machines (such as when computers control manufacturing machinery).

Magnetic Levitation (Maglev) Use of superconducting magnets to repel railroad trains from their track, thereby reducing friction and increasing speed.

Manufactured Housing Housing that is built in modules in a factory, transported to the construction site, and placed on a foundation, where the utilities are installed.

Manufacturing The building of products in a workshop or factory.

Mason A craftsperson who is skilled in the art of working with concrete.

Mass Media Communication systems such as magazines, newspapers, radio, and television, that are used to reach large numbers of people.

Mass Production The manufacture of many goods of the same type at one time, frequently involving interchangeable parts and the use of an assembly line.

Materials One of the seven resources used in technological systems. The physical substances (e.g., wood, iron, oil, water, sand) that are used in a process.

Memory The place in a computer system where data are stored. Internal memory includes random access memory (RAM) and read only memory (ROM). External memory includes tapes, floppy disks, hard disks, and optical disks.

Modeling The testing of a problem solution or a system itself. Modeling includes using small physical replicas of the solution (scale models) and intangible representations of the solution (mathematical models, computer models, etc.).

Modem (MODulator-DEModulator) A device used to send data signals over analog communication channels (such as telephone circuits).

Momentum The tendency of an object in motion to stay in motion or an object at rest to stay at rest.

Monitor To observe the output of a system.

Mortar A mushy cementlike substance that hardens and acts like glue to hold concrete blocks together.

Mortgage A loan that is secured by a home, building, or other large physical asset.

National Electrical Code A set of standards developed by the National Fire Protection Association which establishes safe methods of installing electrical wiring and equipment.

Negative A reversed image on photographic film, used for printing pictures.

Network Information transmitters and two or more receivers connected by channels. A data network connects computers and/or computer devices. A voice network connects telephones. A video network connects television cameras and receivers.

Noise An imperfection in a communication channel or equipment. Noise makes the message more likely to be misunderstood.

Nuclear Energy Energy derived from the splitting (fission) or combining (fusion) of atoms.

Nuclear Reactor An engine or power plant that harnesses the energy released in a controlled atomic reaction in which atoms are split (fission) or combined (fusion).

Numerical Control The control of manufacturing machines by punched tape.

Oblique A pictorial drawing where one surface is seen straight-on.

Office Automation The use of computers and communications in an office setting to increase productivity.

Offset Printing A printing process in which the image to be printed is photographically placed on a metal plate, transferred to a cylinder covered by a rubber blanket, and then transferred (offset) to paper.

Oil Any of a number of liquids that can be burned to obtain energy, or that can be used as lubricants. Oils come from animals, vegetables, and minerals. Petroleum oil is found under the ground and may be refined to kerosene, jet fuel, and gasoline.

Open-Loop System A system that does not use information about the output(s) to affect the process.

Operating System Computer software that allows the user or other programs to access a computer's memories (disk, tape, semiconductor, etc.), printers, and other attached devices.

Optical Having to do with light or sight.

Optimization In problem solving, the process of making an alternative work as well as it can.

Orthographic A way or drawing an object using several straight-on views. Usually, the top, front, and side views are drawn.

OSHA (Occupational Safety and Health Administration) A U.S. government agency responsible for making sure that health and safety laws are followed in factories and on construction sites.

Output The actual result obtained from a system.

Parabolic Reflector A curved reflector that focuses light, heat, or radio waves to a single point, called the focal point.

Passive Solar Taking the heating effects of the sun into account when designing walls, doors, and window placement in buildings.

People   One of the seven resources in a technological system. People design systems, operate them, and benefit from them.

Permits   Written permission given by various government agencies for construction work to proceed. Permits are often issued by zoning boards, planning boards, fire departments, building departments, and other agencies.

Perspective   A method of drawing that makes things look realistic. Parts of an object or scene that are further away appear smaller.

Persuade   To convince someone to do something. One of the reasons communication systems are used.

Pert Chart   A flow chart used to plan and track tasks within a project.

Phototypesetter   A machine that uses a photographic process to convert computer output to high-quality printed text.

Pictorial   Pictorial drawings show an object in three dimensions. Three common types of pictorial drawings are isometric, oblique, and perspective.

Piggyback   The use of railroad flat cars to carry truck trailers.

Pitch   The amount a roof slopes. It is equal to the number of inches the roof rises vertically for each foot of horizontal span.

Plasticity   The property of a material that allows it to bend and stay bent.

Plumb   The condition that exists when a structural element is perfectly vertical.

Plumbing   The systems in a structure that have to do with carrying water and waste materials.

Pneumatic   Activated by air pressure.

Pollution   Outputs of technology that affect the environment negatively.

Polymers   Materials, like plastics, which are made from long chains of molecules. (*Poly* means many, *Meros* means parts in Greek).

Potential Energy   The energy stored in an object due to its position, shape, or other feature.

Power   The amount of work done in a given period of time; the time rate of doing work.

Prefabricate   In construction, to build a building or a portion of it at a location other than the construction site.

Pressing   A forming process where a plunger forces material into a mold.

Pressure   The amount of force exerted on an object's surface, divided by the area over which it is exerted.

Printed Circuit Board   A thin board made of insulating materials with copper conducting paths plated in patterns on the board. Electric components are mounted to the board, forming complete circuits.

Problem Solving   A multistep process used to reach a solution in response to a human need or want. It includes defining the problem; specifying desired results; gathering information; developing alternative ideas; selecting the best solution, implementing the solution; and evaluating the results and making necessary changes.

Process   The part of a system that combines resources to produce an output in response to a command input.

Processor   In computers, the part that controls the flow, storage, and manipulation of data.

Production   The system people use to make products. Products can be made in a factory or workshop (manufacturing) or on site (construction).

Productizing   The process of improving a prototype, changing it into a finished product.

Profit   In a business, the amount of money left after subtracting expenses from income.

Program   A list of instructions that directs a computer's activities.

Project Manager A person or company whose job it is to oversee contracts, scheduling, material deliveries, and overall progress on a construction job.

Properties of Materials The characteristics of materials (such as hardness and plasticity) that make them suitable or not suitable for certain applications.

Prototype A model of a final product or structure that is built to help evaluate the soundness of a design and to discover unanticipated problems.

Quad One quadrillion British Thermal Units of energy. (1,000,000,000,000,000)

Quality Control The act of testing for faults in a product and correcting their causes.

Radiation High-energy particles given off by the fuel and waste products of a nuclear plant. Radiation can injure or kill people, animals, and plants.

Rafters The sloping elements that make up a framed roof.

RAM Random Access Memory. The largest portion of a computer's main memory, in which the program is stored while it is being worked on, and in which at least some of the data and results are temporarily stored.

Raw Materials Those extracted from the earth and processed into basic industrial materials or finished products.

Reaction Engine An engine that produces forward thrust from expanding hot gas rushing out the rear-facing nozzle. Reaction engines operate on the principle of Newton's third law of motion.

Receiver The part of a communication system that accepts the message from the channel and presents it to the destination.

Recycle To reuse all or portions of a substance.

Relief Printing Printing from a raised surface; letterpress printing.

Research A process carried out to discover information. Basic research involves investigating a subject to find out facts. Market research involves surveying people about their attitudes toward a product and surveying the process and capabilities of competing products.

Resistance The opposition to electrical current flow.

Resources The things needed to get a job done. In a technological system, seven types of resources are processed to produce outputs. The seven types of resources are: people, information, materials, tools and machines, energy, capital, and time.

Robot A multifunction, reprogrammable machine capable of movement.

Rocket Engine An engine that provides thrust from the rapid expansion of burning fuel and oxygen, which it must carry with it.

Sawing Sawing involves separating material with a blade that has teeth.

Science The study and description of natural phenomena.

Screen Printing A printing process in which ink is pressed onto the paper or object to be imprinted through holes in a master stencil (the screen).

Semiconductor A material that is neither a good conductor nor a good insulator. Transistors, diodes, integrated circuits, and some other electronic components are made of semiconductor material.

Separating A category of processes that divides or puts apart materials. Separating processes include shearing, sawing, drilling, grinding, shaping, turning, filtering, and chemical and magnetic separation.

Shaping Processes used to change the shape or contour of materials.

Shareholder A person who has purchased a part ownership in a company by buying some of its stock.

Shear A pair of forces that act on an object in opposite directions along the same line or plane, as the two blades on a pair of scissors.

Shearing Using shears to separate materials.

Sheathing The outer layer of material (often plywood, particleboard, or foamboard) that covers and protects the walls and the roof.

Sill Plate A wooden board that is installed on top of the foundation before the joists are attached.

Smart House A home with computer control of many routine functions.

Smelting The process of making iron from iron ore.

Solar Coming from the sun.

Solar Cell A device that converts light energy into electrical energy.

Soldering A method of joining two wires together by melting a metal called solder onto them.

Specification Detailed statement of requirements. In problem solving, a goal is a broad or general statement of requirements, and a specification is a detailed and specific statement of requirements.

Speech Synthesis The simulation of speech by a computer or electronic circuit.

Steam Engine An engine that delivers power generated from the expansion of steam created by boiling water.

Steel A hard, strong alloy of iron and carbon, widely used in construction.

Stone Age The period during which people used stones to make tools and weapons. In the Middle East, this was before 3000 B.C.

Structure Something built or constructed on a construction site. Structures can include buildings, bridges, dams, tunnels, roads, airports, canals, harbors, pipelines, and towers.

Studs The vertical members that make up a wall section.

Subcontractor A person or company whose job it is to build a part of a construction project.

Subfloor The rough flooring, usually plywood or particleboard, that is nailed to the floor joists before finish flooring is applied.

Subroutine A routine (sequence of actions) that is a part of a larger routine. A subroutine may be examined separately from the larger routine.

Subsystem A small system that, together with other subsystems, makes up a larger system.

Supercomputer A computer vastly superior in size and speed to the mainframe computers in use at any given time. Because of the rapid progress in computer technology, supercomputer performance of yesterday is commonplace today.

Superconductor A material whose electrical resistance suddenly drops to nearly zero at a certain low temperature.

Superstructure In construction, that part of the structure above the foundation; it is usually the part of the structure that is visible above the ground.

Surveyor A person who shows construction workers exactly where a structure should be placed.

Synthetic Human-made; not occurring in nature.

System A means of achieving a desired result through the processing of resources in response to a command input. A system may be open-loop (no feedback) or closed-loop (using feedback).

Technical Drawing Drawing using instruments and tools to accurately communicate information about the size and shape of objects.

Technologically Literate Able to understand the fundamental concepts of technology, and to make informed choices of which technology to use and the likely impacts of using it.

Technology The use of accumulated knowledge to process resources to satisfy human needs and wants.

Telecommute Working at home using computers, terminals, and data communications rather than physically traveling to work.

Teleconference A meeting conducted by people located at different sites, using communications to link them together. The attendees can use voice only (telephone conference call), voice with still pictures, or full motion pictures and voice (videoconference).

Tension A force that stretches an object.

Thermal Having to do with heat or the transfer of heat.

Thermoplastic Plastic material that softens when heated.

Thermoset Plastic Plastic material that will char and burn when heated. It does not soften.

Thrust The force developed to move an airplane forward through the air.

Time One of the seven resources used in technological systems. In modern systems, time ranges from less than one billionth of a second to human lifetimes.

Tools With machines, one of the seven resources used in technological systems. Tools extend the natural capabilities of people, and they are used to process or maintain other resources in systems.

Top Plate A double layer of 2 × 4s used to construct the top of a wall section.

Torsion A force that twists an object.

Toughness The ability of a material to absorb shocks without breaking.

Trade-off An exchange of the benefits in one solution for the disadvantages in another solution.

Transformer A device used in alternating current electric power systems to increase (step-up) or decrease (step-down) voltage.

Transistor A three terminal electronic component made of semiconductor material that enables the control of a large amount of current with a small amount of control current.

Transmission A system that transfers (carries) force from one place to another, or changes its direction.

Transmitter The part of a communication system that accepts the message from the originator and places it on the channel.

Trial and Error A method of solving problems in which many solutions are tried until one is found to be acceptable.

Truss A carefully engineered, large prefabricated wooden triangle used as a section of a roof.

Turbo-Prop An aircraft engine in which rapidly expanding hot gases turn a turbine that is connected to a propeller.

Turning A separating process where the material, not the cutting tool, moves. A lathe is an example of a turning tool.

Union A labor organization representing a group of workers that bargains with employers to set wages and work practices for its members.

Uplink The part of a satellite communication system from a ground station to the satellite.

Vapor Barrier A layer of plastic, paper, or foil that covers insulation. It prevents warm moist air inside the house from condensing on cooler studs, thereby preventing rot.

Vehicle A container for transporting people, animals, or goods. Vehicles can operate on fixed routes (elevators, railroad trains, monorails, trolley cars), or random routes (bicycles, cars, trucks, airplanes, rockets).

Venture Capitalist   A person or company who invests money in a new or growing business in exchange for part ownership in the business.

Videoconference   A meeting between people at different locations which uses television signals and communication links to transmit voice and pictures from each meeting location to the other.

Voice Recognition   The technology of using human voice as an input to a computer or machine.

Voltage   The force necessary to move electrons from one atom to another in a material.

Watt   A measure of power equal to one kilogram-meter per second. One watt also equals one ampere × one volt.

Wavelength   The distance covered by one cycle of an electromagnetic or other wave.

Weight   In aeronautics, the downward force on a plane, opposing lift.

Wind Load   The effect of wind as it blows against a structure.

Word Processor   A machine that combines typing and computer technologies to help an operator create, store, retrieve, modify, and print text.

Work   The product of a force needed to move an object and the distance that it is moved in the direction of the force. If a force is applied against an object, but the object does not move, then no work is done.

Zoning   The act of reserving areas of a community for specific uses. Some areas may be zoned for residential use (homes) and factories would not be permitted, while others would be zoned for industrial or factory use.

ADDITIONAL ACTIVITIES

(Courtesy of Corning Glass Works)

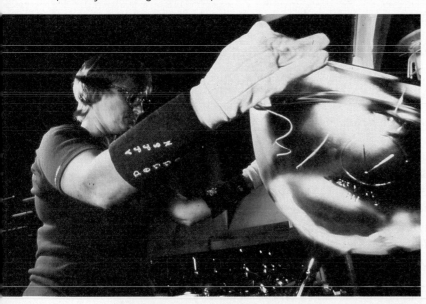

HURRICANE ALLEY

Setting the Stage

Hurricane racing does not use motor cars, motorcycles, rockets or antigravity engines for power. It uses wind. Windmobiles, of all shapes and designs, mounted with high-density woven metallic fiber sails, are the only vehicles permitted on the track. A windmobile hitting the smallest bump on the track at such high speeds would probably be destroyed.

Your Challenge

Design and construct a wind-powered vehicle that will roll the longest distance when propelled by the exhaust of a heavy duty shop vacuum. You may only use the supplies listed below.

Suggested Resources

Safety glasses and lab apron
Three pieces of cherry or other hardwood—
1/4" × 1/4" × 36"
Four plastic wheels
One 9" piece of 1/8" diameter steel axle rod
One 12" x 12" piece of mirrored mylar for the sail
One soda straw—for the axle bearing
Hot glue gun and glue sticks
Model cement
Drill press, jig saw and/or band saw, belt sander, table saw, miter box, hack saw, files, and other miscellaneous hand tools and machines
Assorted fasteners
Graphite lubricant
Heavy duty shop vacuum

Procedure

1. Be sure to wear safety glasses when working with tools and machinery.
2. Design your wind-powered vehicle on graph paper. Draw a number of sketches before you settle on one particular design.
3. Try to develop as many alternative design solutions as you can. As your supplies are limited, you may have to make some compromises.
4. Do not use any tools or equipment until your teacher has shown you the safe and proper operating procedures. SAFETY FIRST!
5. Carefully cut the pieces of hardwood to size. Use a very fine-toothed saw.
6. Drill 3/16" diameter axle holes where necessary.
7. Assemble the vehicle using hot glue. Be careful . . . hot glue is HOT!
8. Use the straw as an axle bearing. This will cut down on *friction*.
9. As hot glue doesn't stick very well to the mylar sail material, model cement can be used as an alternative. Let the cement dry thoroughly.
10. Give your vehicle a test run. Evaluate the results and make any necessary design changes.

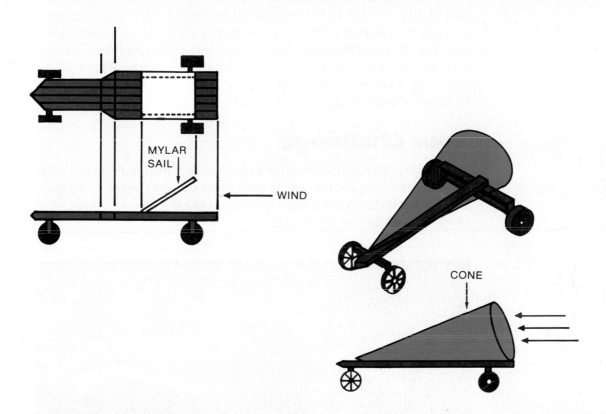

MYLAR SAIL

WIND

CONE

Technology Connections

1. Can you draw a systems diagram that reflects the problem-solving approach used with the wind-powered vehicle? Label the input, process, output, monitor, feedback, and comparison steps in the diagram.
2. The design, selection, and construction of the wind-powered vehicle fall into the *process* step of the systems diagram. What method is used to monitor the *output* results?
3. What do we mean by *feedback* in the problem-solving system? How is this used to optimize the performance of the wind-powered vehicle?
4. What is brainstorming? What is trial and error?
5. Why will the same vehicle go a greater distance if the wheels turn more freely?
6. Why does the wind-powered vehicle continue to roll after the 'wind' is removed?

Science and Math Concepts

▶ *Friction* is a force opposing the motion of a body.
▶ *Inertia* is the property of matter that resists a change in motion. An object at rest tends to stay at rest, and an object in motion tends to stay in motion unless acted upon by an outside force.

517

POLE POSITION

Setting the Stage

The Formula I Race takes place in a few days. You are one of the top drivers and are due at the course in one hour for the last qualifying session. At the end of the day yesterday, your car suffered engine damage. The head mechanic called last night to say it won't be ready in time for the race. Two friends have offered their extra cars for you to use. They have the same engines, but look very different. In order to have a chance to win, you must select the best car.

Your Challenge

Design and build the body for a race car. Test the results in the wind tunnel. Then compare the results with other students' results. The body design that disturbs the smoke the least will have the least amount of drag and will be the fastest car.

Procedure

1. Experiment with the drag form factors of various shapes you may wish to use for your car body design. First, shape clay into a teardrop approximately 1¼" diameter × 3½" long. Test this shape in the wind tunnel by lighting a piece of firecracker punk or stick incense to create smoke. Do the same test on other clay shapes such as spheres, cubes, and rectangles. Use shapes of different sizes. (Note: Do not change the air flow in the tunnel when you are doing comparison testing.)

2. Now do a test to determine the best angle of transition between two different shapes. Form the clay test shapes on a small ⅛" piece of acrylic. The closer the smoke trail is to the surface of the clay, the better the drag form factor. If the smoke curls behind the clay, this displays wind turbulence and increased drag.

3. Choose the type of car body and the scale you would like to use.

4. Sketch the front, side, and top views of the vehicle.

Suggested Resources

Modeling clay
Ceramic clay
Plaster of paris
Paper mache
Basswood
Wind tunnel
Architect's scale
Drafting equipment

5. Using the data from your wind tunnel tests, modify your drawing to decrease the drag.
6. Using modeling materials, form a scale model of the design you have chosen.
7. Test your model in the wind tunnel at various wind speeds. (Note: All models should be tested at the same wind speed before adjusting the air pressure for another wind speed.)

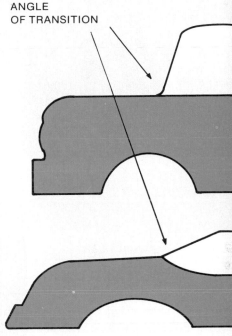

ANGLE OF TRANSITION

Technology Connections

1. Research the car companies that publish their drag form factors. Which have the best drag factors?
2. What is the purpose of each part of the wind tunnel?
3. Compare the volumes of the model cars, using a water displacement method. Does volume affect drag? How does this affect surface area?
4. Why are wings used on Formula I cars?
5. Sand an airfoil shape used for airplane wings. Test this shape in the wind tunnel. Can you determine from the smoke pattern why lift is created with this shape?
6. What other factors influence what cars we purchase?
7. Why do car companies use these same modeling techniques and similar wind tunnel tests?
8. What else could you use to simulate tests and mechanical operations?

Science and Math Concepts

▶ The amount of pressure drag and friction drag depends on the shape of the body.
▶ Turbulence—large fluctuations in speed and the mixing of the different layers of air.
▶ Laminar—different layers of air flow smoothly over each other.
▶ The product of the aerodynamic drag coefficient (C_D) and the frontal area of the object (A) is commonly referred to as the drag form factor $(C_D A)$ of the object.

GLASSMAKING

Setting the Stage

Materials are an important resource for technology. Materials are often processed to be made more useful. Sand, for example, can be processed into glass. The glass can then be made into useful objects by means of forming processes.

Your Challenge

Mix (batch) materials and produce a small glass object.

Suggested Resources

Enameling kiln
Porcelain crucibles
Aluminum or graphite molds
Glassmaking chemicals
Scales
Mortar and pestle
Storage containers
Polariscope
Drilling and boring tools

Safety Considerations

1. Be very careful as the materials are at extremely high temperatures.
2. Wear eye protection at all times.
3. Wear insulating gloves.
4. Avoid taking crucibles in and out of the kiln. Rapid changes in temperature can cause cracking.
5. If a crucible develops cracks, discontinue using it immediately, and call the instructor to assist you.
6. Hot glass looks just like cold glass. Never leave newly formed pieces out in the open where an unsuspecting individual could touch them.
7. Always use tongs to handle hot crucibles. Never reach into the kiln with your hands to insert or remove a crucible, even while wearing insulated gloves.

8. Finished objects must be properly annealed, or they are liable to explode. Test for stress using polariscope.

9. For borosilicate glass: It should be noted that chlorine gas will be liberated during the melt. This gas is poisonous. However, in the quantities used here, this gas should not be dangerous. Therefore, measurement of the NaCl component should be strictly monitored. Any fumes should be vented. It is possible to produce the glass without adding NaCl if desired.

Procedure

1. Review the safety considerations.
2. Carefully weigh and mix the ingredients for the glass. This is called **batching.** Various metals can be introduced to the batch to provide color. (See batch ingredients table.)
3. With the kiln off, practice the procedure for melting and casting the glass. This will contribute to safe operation when you are actually doing the procedure.
4. **Calcine** the batch in a crucible by heating it to a temperature lower than its melting temperature. The batch will bubble vigorously as the gases escape. Calcining occurs at approximately 400°C (750°F).
5. Once all the gases have been liberated during calcining, the temperature of the batch may be increased. This melts the remaining chemicals. Melting temperature is approximately 815°C (1500°F).

MODIFIED BOROSILICATE GLASS BATCH INGREDIENTS*

Material	Oxide	# Grams in 200 gm Batch
Georgia Feldspar ($K_2O + Al_2O_3 + SiO_2 +$ $Na_2O + CaO$)	SiO_2 Al_2O_3 K_2O Na_2O CaO	88.4
Sodium Tetraborate ($Na_2B_4O_7$)	B_2O_3 Na_2O	65
Sodium Chloride (NaCl)	Cl Na_2O	2.0
Sodium Carbonate (Na_2CO_3)	Na_2O	44.6
TOTAL		200 grams

For blue color, add 1% by weight of black copper oxide (2 grams) to batch. For green color, add 0.32% chromium oxide (0.65 grams) and 0.1% black copper oxide (0.2 grams).

*This glass was developed by Elton Harris, Corning Glass Works Experimental Melting Division.

6. When all the batch material is completely melted, **fine** the glass by heating it to a temperature slightly above the melting temperature. The high temperature materials in the batch need time to dissolve completely. Also, any remaining gas bubbles need to escape. Fining occurs slightly above the melting temperature and is necessary to achieve clear, uniform, bubble-free glass.

7. Form the glass. To form a coaster, use a **press mold** machined from a piece of 1/2" aluminum plate in two halves. You can also try a **dump mold** made by milling or drilling shapes into the top of an aluminum block. Using a pair of tongs and insulating gloves, remove the crucible containing the molten glass from the kiln. Pour the glass into the mold and then dump it once it's solidified.

8. The glass must be placed immediately into an annealing oven in order to relieve stress and avoid shattering. While you were forming the glass, the rapid cooling put stress on the material. Annealing relieves that stress. To anneal the glass, heat it at an intermediate temperature for half an hour, and then permit it to cool slowly. Annealing temperature is 464°C (870°F).

9. You can do rotational casting by machining an aluminum or graphite cylinder measuring two inches in outside diameter and four inches in length. Use a boring tool to machine the inside into the desired shape. Machine a shaft onto the mold. Pour the molten glass into the mold, cap the top, and spin with an electric drill or vertically mounted motor at 1,750 RPM. Centrifugal force conforms the glass to the inside shape.

10. Inspect the glass visually to determine if the stress has been relieved. To do this, construct a polariscope by placing two polarizing filters (or sheets of polarizing film) at 90° to each other, separated by a space into which the glass sample is inserted (see drawing). Inspect the sample by looking through the polariscope toward an incandescent light source. If you see bands of color or streaks of black, the glass is unsafe and may shatter. It needs to be annealed again.

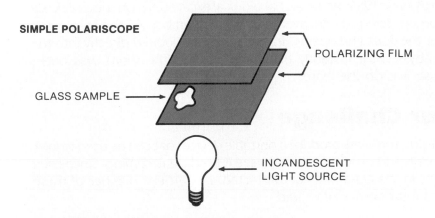

SIMPLE POLARISCOPE

POLARIZING FILM

GLASS SAMPLE

INCANDESCENT
LIGHT SOURCE

Technology Connections

1. Bring in samples of glass. Identify the origin of the samples and what processing method was used.
2. Research and describe how window glass is produced. Contrast window glass with some glass produced for special purposes, such as Corning's Steuben glass.
3. Place the operations you used in this activity in categories of forming, separating, combining, and conditioning.
4. Processing materials involves changing their form to make them more useful to people.

(Courtesy of Corning Glass Works)

Science and Math Concepts

▶ Changes occur in the molecular structure of ceramic materials when they are fired in a kiln. The material melts and fuses together. This forms a new molecular structure. The process cannot be reversed.
▶ Glass is a supercooled liquid. Antique window glass is thicker on the bottom of the pane than on the top because the glass molecules have slowly moved down the pane.

THE MEDUSA SYNDROME

Setting the Stage

Medusa was a Greek goddess who was so ugly that anyone who looked upon her for even a second instantly turned to stone. As everyone knows, Medusa was a myth, a fantasy of some ancient story teller. But was she?

In the year 1999, at the archaeological excavations on the Greek Isle of Gorgon, scientists discovered a sealed chamber. As they broke the seal of the door and opened it, everyone who looked directly into the dark abyss went instantly blind. Within days the word was out—Medusa was on the loose.

Your Challenge

Design and mass produce a portable device that can be used to look over walls and around corners to see if Medusa is coming. Since each student in the class must be protected, a sufficient number of these devices must be manufactured.

Suggested Resources

Safety glass and lab apron
1 piece of 1 1/2" diameter rigid plastic pipe—18" to 24" per student
1 plastic 35 mm film cartridge—(1 per student)
Mirrored plexiglass 2 1/2" x 3 1/2"—two per student
Bench rules—12" and 36"
Combination square
Fine point felt-tip pen
Miter boxes
Drill press
Belt and/or disk sander
1 3/8" diameter hole saw
1 1/4" diameter hole saw
Hammer
Center punch
Jig saws and/or band saws
Files
Hot glue guns and glue sticks
Assorted jigs and fixtures (determined and constructed by the teacher)

Procedure

Note: The assembly line stations, quality control devices, jigs and fixtures, exact specifications, etc., can be determined and constructed by the entire class.

1. Be sure to wear safety glasses and a lab coat.
2. All students must make sketches and plans of the periscope device before beginning the mass production manufacturing and assembly line process.
3. Computer-aided drafting (CAD) is recommended after an initial sketch is made.
4. If you have not been instructed in the proper and safe use of any tool or machine that you need to use with this activity, check with your teacher BEFORE going any further.
5. Using a miter box, carefully cut 45 degree angles on both ends of the 1 1/2" diameter pipe. These angles must parallel and 'lean' in the same direction. The pipes should be 18-24" long after cutting.
6. Cut or sand off the bottom of the 35 mm film cartridge. (This is the eyepiece!)
7. Using the drill press and the 1 3/8" hole saw, drill a hole opposite the 45 degree angle cut on the 1 1/2" pipe. (DO THIS ONLY ON ONE END!)
8. Repeat step 7 using the 1 1/4" drill on the other end of the pipe. (For the eyepiece!)
9. Using the files, sander, sandpaper, etc., remove any rough edges from the holes and pieces of pipe.

10. On the mirrored plexiglass, use the felt-tipped pen to duplicate the elliptical shape of the 45 degree angles cut on the end of the 1 1/2" pipe. (Make a template or pattern!)
11. Use the band or jigsaw to cut out the ellipses of the mirrored plexiglass. STAY OUTSIDE THE LINES!
12. Use the belt or disc sander to bring the mirrors to their final shape.
13. Use the hot glue gun to fasten the film cartidge eyepiece tube in place on the inside.
14. Temporarily hold or tape the mirrors in place. Look through the eyepiece to make sure the periscope is working properly. Make any needed adjustments.
15. Use the hot glue gun to fasten the mirrors in place. (Shiny side in!). Remember—Hot glue is HOT!

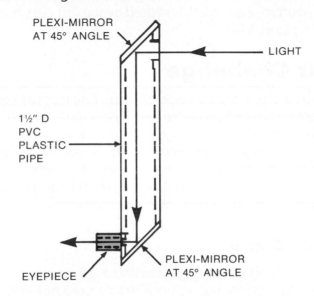

PLEXI-MIRROR
AT 45° ANGLE

LIGHT

1½" D
PVC
PLASTIC
PIPE

EYEPIECE

PLEXI-MIRROR
AT 45° ANGLE

Technology Connections

1. How does *mass production* and the factory system help bring prices down?
2. What is an *assembly line?* What is a *conveyor belt?*
3. Why are *interchangeable parts* important to an assembly line?
4. What happens if you look through the periscope eyepiece with a small telescope?
5. What happens if you look through two periscopes at the same time? (One for each eye, of course!) Now you know how a newt views the world!

Science and Math Concepts

▶ Plane mirrors obey the *Law of Reflection*—The angle of reflection equals the angle of incidence. A ball bouncing on a flat surface also obeys the Law of Reflection.
▶ When light strikes a smooth surface, the light is reflected in an even pattern.
▶ Lenses *refract* (or bend) light. This is because light travels at different speeds through different substances.

SPACE COMMUNITY

Setting the Stage

The President's announcement at the press conference sent a shockwave throughout the room. "Ladies and gentlemen of the press . . . the scientists at the Advanced Systems Lab have received and delivered to me this evening a message from an extraterrestrial life source.

The extraterrestrials have requested an urgent meeting with representatives of our entire planet. This meeting will be held on the fourth planet in our solar system—the planet Mars. Our rocket scientists have assured me that we have the ability to reach that planet safely. The only problem that remains is to design and construct a structure that can be transported, assembled, and used by the first permanent settlers of the 'red' planet Mars."

Your Challenge

Design and construct a model of a structure that will be transported, assembled, and used by the first permanent settlers on the planet Mars. Your structure must provide systems to support human life, including a pressurized oxygen environment with temperature control; a place to grow food, perhaps hydroponically; a source for water; and recreational facilities. If desired, groups of students may combine their structures to develop a small Martian community.

Suggested Resources

Safety glasses and lab apron
Balloons—various shapes and sizes (Don't use the cheap, thin kind!)
Pariscraft—A gauze material coated with plaster of paris
Large bucket or bowl of water
Masking tape
Tempera paints—assorted colors
Paint brushes—assorted sizes
1/2" sheet of plywood
Modeling clay
Cardboard paper towel rolls
Wood, plastic, and metal supplies as needed
Assorted tools and machinery as needed
Hot glue, model cement, assorted fasteners

Procedure

1. Be sure to wear safety glasses and a lab coat.
2. Keeping in mind that balloons will be used as forms, sketch some possible designs for the Martian structure. Don't forget the air-locks, passageways, windows, supports, etc.
3. Inflate the appropriate shape balloons. Attach multiple balloon structures together with masking tape. Paper towel rolls can be used, if desired, as passageways.
4. Cut short strips of the Pariscraft material with a scissors.
5. Dip the strips into a bucket of water and carefully coat the entire balloon structure with two to three layers of Pariscraft. Carefully rub the Pariscraft to smooth out any wrinkles. Make sure there are no loose ends.
6. If possible, hang the structure to dry overnight.
7. Make any minor design changes at this time. Pariscraft can be lightly sanded to smooth surface areas. Be careful you don't sand completely through the shell.
8. Paint the completed structure as desired. Windows can be drilled and cut into the structure. Clear acetate can be used for glass. Use your imagination!

9. Construct modules within your structure to simulate earth-like conditions.
10. Using a plywood base, determine the location of your structure. Construct a support 'foundation' using pieces of wood and/or plastic.
11. Use hot glue to fasten the structure and foundation in place.
12. Go to the library and find a picture of the Martian surface. (NASA has published photographs of the Viking Lander.)
13. Your Martian landscape can be developed using clay, Pariscraft, sandpaper (for texture), paints, assorted scraps, etc. Again, use your imagination.

Technology Connections

1. Construction sites must be chosen to fit in with the needs of people and the environment.
2. How does the design of your structure meet the demands of the hostile Martian environment?
3. What special life-support systems would probably be needed on Mars? (i.e. temperature, oxygen, water, food, etc.)
4. Do you think the balloon-type construction technique used in this activity could be used on a full-scale structure? Why shouldn't plaster be used for exterior walls on Earth?

Science and Math Concepts

▶ Plaster is made from a rock called *gypsum*. Gypsum is the mineral *calcium sulfate* ($CaSO_4 \cdot 2H_2O$).
▶ When gypsum is heated, it loses part of its water and becomes plaster of paris (($CaSO_4)_2 \cdot H_2O$).
▶ When water is added to plaster of paris, the plaster hardens back into gypsum.

CYCLOID CURVE

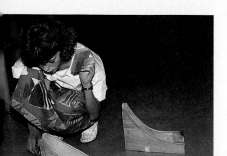

Setting the Stage

The name and type of a new roller coaster for the amusement park has already been determined. The next stage is to design the best curves, turns, and elevations for a thrilling ride. The project on the drawing board is a curve that will allow the person to ride down an incline, gaining the greatest speed in order to be propelled up the next incline. This will take some modeling and trial runs to find the best curve.

Your Challenge

Design and construct a ramp that will allow an object to move down an incline and obtain the greatest speed. The ramp will be exactly 12" high and will end at the floor. Any length ramp may be used. The ramp that propels the object across the finish line first and is constructed using the best structural engineering techniques and craftsmanship wins!

Procedure

1. A common cycloid curve is developed when the path of a fixed point on the circumference of a circle is recorded as the circle is rolled along a straight line. To develop a cycloid curve, cut out a cardboard circle 12" in diameter. Tape a pencil perpendicular to the circle. Make sure the lead is flush with the outside edge of the circle. Holding the pencil and circle against a large piece of paper taped to the wall, trace the curve that develps as you roll the circle along a straight line. Turn this tracing upside down and you will have the profile or side view of the cycloid curve ramp.
2. Experiment with designs for the sides of the ramp. To do this, place popsicle sticks on your tracing in positions that will give the ramp structure its greatest strength. Try several different popsicle-stick configurations before deciding on your final design for the sides of the ramp.
3. Trace the final design for the sides. (Note: Allow in your drawing for the thickness of any support structures that will underlay the ramp. The final ramp surface must match perfectly the cycloid curve that you developed.)
4. Place wax paper over your drawing. Glue popsicle sticks together according to your design. (The popsicle sticks and glue will release easily from the wax paper.)
5. Lift the wax paper, along with the first side, off the drawing. Place a new sheet of wax paper on the drawing and construct the second side.

Suggested Resources

White glue
Popsicle sticks
Drafting equipment
Oak tag
Illustration board
Steel ball bearing or Hot
　Wheels® car
Tape

6. Fasten the two constructed sides together with glue and popsicle sticks. Install the ramp surface and side walls to hold objects in place as they roll down the ramp.
7. Conduct your contest for the fastest ramp. Remember, craftsmanship counts, too!

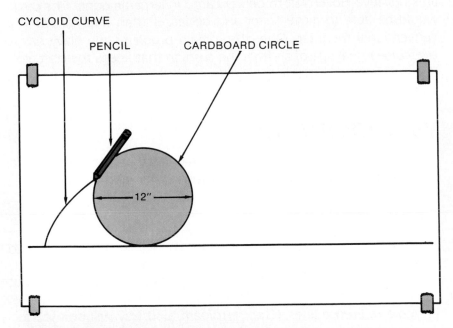

CYCLOID CURVE

PENCIL   CARDBOARD CIRCLE

12"

Technology Connections

1. Make several different types of ramps by cutting the profile curve out of ¾" thick wood. Using a shaper bit, your teacher will cut a groove in the ramp for a marble. Compare the performance of these samples with the performance of the cycloid curve by rolling marbles down the ramps and trying to hit a target approximately 4 feet away.
2. Could you hook a timing device to the computer and record the marble's speed or time?
3. Based on your research of structures, determine the materials that would be used to construct an amusement ride.
4. List other structures that would utilize the same construction techniques as the cycloid amusement ride.
5. Sketch the shape of the foundation that would be used for a roller coaster amusement ride.

Science and Math Concepts

▶ In about 1696, Jacques Bernoulli discovered that a cycloid curve is the curve along which a particle can move under gravity from a high point to a lower point in the shortest possible time.
▶ As a roller coaster and its occupants descend, their gravitational potential energy changes to kinetic energy.

HOVERCRAFT

Setting the Stage

Your engineering firm has been asked to assist the Navy in designing an innovative Hovercraft to deliver cargo in large amounts. The cargo would be able to move faster and be larger than that carried in a conventional freighter. One of the main problems the Navy has to overcome is leakage of air from the cushion that keeps the craft aloft. If your firm is successful in solving these challenges, the next step may be to replace many ships with fast transoceanic vessels.

Your Challenge

Design, find, and assemble the materials necessary to build a model Hovercraft that will be capable of traveling over land or water.

Procedure

1. Bring pictures of Hovercraft into class. You will use these pictures to help determine the location of the major parts.
2. On one of the styrofoam food trays, draw a center line in both directions, dividing it into four parts. You may want to add a few more reference lines. (One styrofoam food tray will be used for a second try.)
3. Cut a hole for the hair dryer motor one-third of the distance in from one side and on the center line. Tape the hair dryer motor and fan blades in place.
4. Use the top half of a styrofoam cup to house the fan, and fasten it to the body of the Hovercraft with glue or tape so no air will escape to the sides when the motor is running. (Adding this seal directs the air flow toward the underside of the Hovercraft.)
5. Tape a plastic-wrap skirt approximately 1" wide around the edge of the container.
6. Using tape, temporarily mount the battery case near the center of the container. (In the photograph, the battery case has been permanently affixed to the underside of the Hovercraft.)
7. Mount a small propeller on the AFX® or Sizzlers® engine shaft.
8. Design a supporting system to hold the AFX® or Sizzlers® engine and the propeller. Tape this subsystem near the rear of the container.
9. Add a styrofoam or balsa wood rudder for steering.
10. Add a switch and wire the motors to the batteries.
11. Now you must become a true designer, making adjustments just as professionals do, to make your Hovercraft fly.

Suggested Resources

Two styrofoam food trays, or a similarly shaped styrofoam substitute

Hair dryer fan and motor (3 to 6 volt, DC)

AFX®, Sizzlers®, or similar motor from a model car

Glue and tape

Cardboard

Plastic wrap

Styrofoam cups

Tape

Batteries (AA)

Balsa wood

Plastic battery case

Small propeller from a hobby store

12. Following are a few of the options you may want to try in order to properly balance and operate the Hovercraft:
   - Keep sketches of the location of the subsystems and how the Hovercraft functions. You may have to refer back to your data to improve the design.
   - Reposition some of the subsystems if the Hovercraft is unbalanced.
   - Change the size of the batteries. (Use AA batteries first.)
   - Change the number of batteries used.
   - Change the skirt thickness.
   - Use a different motor in the hair dryer fan.
   - Use a motor for solar cells for the drive system. Be careful when you test the Hovercraft as its speed and inability to stop against a wall will surprise you.
   - When all your subsystems are properly balanced and the motors are operating properly, carefully remount them permanently in a new container.

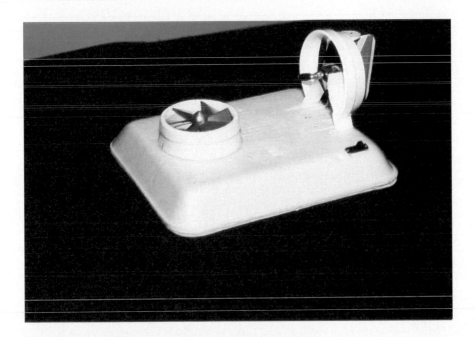

Technology Connections

1. How closely does your Hovercraft resemble full-size ones?
2. Hovercraft usually have one motor. How do they move ahead? How do they control direction? Can Hovercraft climb inclines? Why or why not?
3. Air-cushion vehicles (ACVs) or Hovercraft are used to cross the English Channel. Research this area and fill in a resource chart with information relating to Hovercraft. (Ideas can be found in this chapter.)

Science and Math Concepts

▶ The ACV operates on a long-known principle: the resistance of air to compression. Fans blow downward through the hull and establish a cushion of air between the ACV and the water.

▶ There is a direct ratio between the dimensions of the hull and the power needed to lift the ACV. If the beam and length are doubled, the power must be doubled to maintain the same height. When the beam and length are doubled, however, the load-carrying area is quadrupled. Therefore, the larger the craft, the more efficiently power is used.

INDEX